Praise for *Becoming Madison*

"*Becoming Madison* is superb. The history is lively and engaging. But Michael Signer's greatest contribution is to turn a biography of Madison into a manual on leadership that is as relevant and valuable today as it was 200 years ago."

—Anne-Marie Slaughter, Director of Policy Planning, U.S. State Department, 2009–2011 and President and CEO, New America Foundation

"For centuries James Madison has been overshadowed by the more striking and charismatic members of America's founding generation. And Madison's youth has been even less well known than his maturity. Michael Signer goes far toward filling this historical gap with an engaging, insightful account of how the unassuming young Madison became the hero of the Constitution."

—H. W. Brands, University of Texas at Austin, author of *Andrew Jackson, His Life and Times* and *The Man Who Saved the Union: Ulysses Grant in War and Peace*

"James Madison would be called a 'flip-flopper' in today's political climate. Thank God he changed his mind and concluded that adding a Bill of Rights to the Constitution was not just good politics but necessary policy. This is just one of the wonderful aspects of James Madison's life that Michael Signer captures so well in this important biography. Our nation owes huge debts to Madison, and today's civic leaders owe a huge debt to Signer for reminding us why."

—United States Senator Tim Kaine

"This engagingly written, carefully researched book is the fullest account we have of the development of Madison's thought and statesmanship through the promotion and drafting of the Constitution to the greatest triumph of his life, the ratification of the Virginia Convention of 1788. Signer shows how there, in face-to-face debate with Patrick Henry, Madison proved what John Marshall termed Madison's unmatched ability to *convince* could overcome Henry's supreme power to persuade. This capacity characterized Madison's style and career in a way that allowed him to become the master philosopher and practitioner of Lincoln's Union 'conceived in liberty and dedicated to the proposition that all . . . are created equal.' Signer also shows brilliantly how Madison's studies at Princeton under John Witherspoon began an influential and revealing partnership in public spirited citizenship for good government. Altogether the book brings us closer to understanding how Madison became able to be, all things considered, the father of the Constitution."

—Ralph Ketcham, Maxwell Professor Emeritus of Citizenship and Public Affairs, Syracuse University, author of *James Madison: A Biography*

"One of the great contributions of Michael Signer's *Becoming Madison* is the relevance of Madison's role in the epochal debates surrounding the birth of our nation to the issues we face today, especially Madison's commitment to attacking ideas rather than individuals. (Would that we now had *more* such advocates.) Signer helps us better understand how Madison's towering intellect and unquenchable passion for the principled tenets necessary to create a lasting republic forged his character, and how he related to the other, better known, giants of his time, particularly to Patrick Henry. The way Signer captures the palpable tension, vitriol, and passion in Madison's war of words and ideas with Henry is masterful. The reader can't help but wonder, if it hadn't been for the tenacity of Madison, would we have truly become the UNITED States of America?"

—Charles S. Robb, former Virginia Governor and United States Senator

"Michael Signer's *Becoming Madison* offers a gripping portrait of the emergence and development of the leadership of one of our country's great architects. We are wonderfully reminded of the power of a single person's passion, humility, and statesmanship in shaping a nation's destiny."

**—Michael Useem, Professor of Management and Director
of the Center for Leadership and Change at the
Wharton School, University of Pennsylvania**

"In this highly readable and often insightful treatment, Signer colors in the portrait, finding the essential Madison in the young man…. A perfect introduction to a deeply private and immensely important man."

—Kirkus

Becoming

MADISON

◆

THE EXTRAORDINARY ORIGINS *of the* LEAST LIKELY FOUNDING FATHER

MICHAEL SIGNER

PublicAffairs
New York

PublicAffairs books are available at special discounts for bulk purchases in the U.S. by corporations, institutions, and other organizations. For more information, please contact the Special Markets Department at the Perseus Books Group, 2300 Chestnut Street, Suite 200, Philadelphia, PA 19103, call (800) 810-4145, ext. 5000, or e-mail special.markets@perseusbooks.com.

Book design by Jack Lenzo

Library of Congress Cataloging-in-Publication Data
Signer, Michael.
  Becoming Madison : the extraordinary origins of the least likely founding father / Michael Signer. -- First edition.
     pages cm
  Includes bibliographical references and index.
  ISBN 978-1-61039-295-2 (hardcover : alk. paper) -- ISBN 978-1-61039-296-9 (ebook)
1. Madison, James, 1751-1836. 2. Presidents--United States--Biography. 3. United States--Politics and government--1783-1809. I. Title.
  E342.S544 2015
  973.5'1092--dc23
  [B]
                          2014038885

First Edition

10 9 8 7 6 5 4 3 2 1

For Emily
and Jacoby and William

Contents

PART III

Time Line of Events

in the Life of James Madison, 1751–1789

Year	Events
1751	On March 15, James Madison is born at the home of his maternal grandmother at Port Conway in King George County, Virginia.
1762	Madison attends Donald Robertson's school in King and Queen County, Virginia.
1765	The Stamp Act is announced. On May 29, Patrick Henry delivers his "If this be treason, make the most of it" speech.
1767	Madison returns home to Orange County and begins studies under the Reverend Thomas Martin.
1769	In August, Madison leaves Orange to attend the College of New Jersey in Princeton, where John Witherspoon has recently become the new president.
1771	On September 29, Madison receives his baccalaureate degree (though he is not present for the ceremony). He stays in Princeton through the winter and spring for additional studies with John Witherspoon.
1772	In April, Madison leaves Princeton to return to Orange County.
1773	Late in the year, Baptists are imprisoned in Culpeper, leading Madison to "squabble and scold abuse and ridicule" the policy. On December 16, the Boston Tea Party is held.
1774	Madison is elected to the Orange County Committee on Public Safety, with his father as chairman. In September, the first Continental Congress meets in Philadelphia.
1775	On March 23, Patrick Henry delivers his "Give me liberty or give me death" speech. In May, the second Continental Congress meets in Philadelphia. Also in May, Madison attempts to join Henry's mission to retake gunpowder from Lord Dunmore and meets Henry along the way. Madison collapses from an anxiety attack in drills with the Orange

County militia. In November, Great Britain's governor of Virginia, Lord Dunmore, announces martial law in Virginia. Madison begins researching the issue of religious freedom.

1776 On July 4, the Declaration of Independence is signed. On July 30, British soldiers burn an effigy of John Witherspoon. From May to December, Madison serves as a delegate from Orange County to the Virginia Convention, where he succeeds in replacing the "toleration" of religion in the new constitution with the freedom of conscience. Madison then joins the General Assembly as a delegate.

1777 In his re-election bid for the House of Delegates, Madison opposes the practice of providing spirits to voters. On April 24, Madison is defeated. On November 15, the General Assembly elects him to serve as a councilor to Governor Patrick Henry. George Washington's army spends the winter in Valley Forge

1778 On February 6, the US and France sign the French Alliance. Madison advises Governor Henry to take assertive roles to resolve the military's supply problems.

1779 Thomas Jefferson is elected governor of Virginia. On December 14, Madison is elected to the Continental Congress in Philadelphia. He chooses to spend the winter in Montpelier studying inflation.

1780 In March, Madison arrives in Philadelphia and lambasts the "defect of adequate statesmen." On June 3, Thomas Jefferson's term as governor of Virginia expires. On June 14, Madison is re-elected to Congress.

1781 In January, Madison proposes a 5 percent tariff that states will pay to the federal government. Madison then drafts an amendment to the Articles of Confederation to arm the federal government with coercive power. In October, Washington leads his troops in a siege of the British at Yorktown.

1782 In May, the Virginia General Assembly passes a resolution instructing delegates to continue the war with "Vigour and Effect." In Philadelphia, Madison experiences extreme financial difficulties. On November 30, the US and Great Britain sign preliminary Articles of Peace.

1783 On January 28, Madison delivers a major speech on the impost, or forced contribution, which is reprinted and distributed nationally. Jefferson moves to Madison's boardinghouse, and the two begin work on the congressional library. Madison meets and becomes engaged to Kitty Floyd. In Virginia, Henry attacks the impost, which the Virginia legislature rejects on June 11. Under attack by mutinying soldiers, Congress flees Philadelphia for Princeton. In August, Kitty Floyd breaks off the engagement by mail. On September 3, the US and Great Britain sign the Treaty of Paris. Madison returns to Orange that winter.

1784   Henry encourages Madison to return to politics. In May, Madison rejoins the Virginia House of Delegates. In September, he travels with Lafayette from Baltimore to Albany. He retakes his seat in Richmond in November, where he challenges Patrick Henry's religious assessment bill.

1785   Madison asks Jefferson to send books on the history of confederacies from Paris. In June, Madison writes his "Memorial and Remonstrance Against Religious Assessments." In the autumn legislative session, Henry's assessment bill is defeated. Madison also launches an effort to reform the Code of Virginia.

1786   Madison authors "Notes on Modern and Ancient Confederacies." He embarks on a failed real estate venture with James Monroe. On August 29, Shays' Rebellion occurs. In September, Madison attends the failed commercial convention in Annapolis. In November, he opposes paper money in Richmond, in a speech that is reprinted and distributed nationally.

1787   Madison arrives in New York in February and begins work on "Vices of the Political System of the United States" and the framework for the Virginia Plan. In May, he travels to Philadelphia for the Constitutional Convention, which signs the Constitution on September 17. He returns to New York for Congress's passage of the Constitution, where he remains to author the Federalist Papers, along with Alexander Hamilton and John Jay.

1788   Madison delays returning to Virginia and completes his share of the Federalist Papers. In March he returns to Orange to campaign for a seat to Virginia's ratifying convention. In June he attends the convention, defeating Patrick Henry and the anti-Federalists. In the fall, he returns to New York for the last meeting of the Continental Congress. Delayed in his return home by illness, Madison is defeated for the US Senate by Patrick Henry.

1789   Madison defeats James Monroe and is elected to the US House of Representatives. In June, Madison introduces the Bill of Rights to the Constitution in Congress.

From nature, from habit, it may be even from the imperfect state of health to which [Madison] was reduced at the outset of his career, his was the most passionless course of education and elevation. He never addressed a passion or required a prejudice: but relying on reason alone for every conviction, he effected his purpose without any appeal to prejudices.

—*National Portrait Gallery of Distinguished Americans*, 1836

The truth is . . . that through the whole frame of nature, and the whole system of human life, that which promises most, performs the least. The flowers of finest colour seldom have the sweetest fragrance. The trees of quickest growth, or fairest form, are seldom of the greatest value or duration. Deep waters move with the least noise. Men who think most are seldom talkative. And, I think it holds as much in war as in any thing, that every boaster is a coward.

—**John Witherspoon, "The Dominion of Providence over the Passions of Man"**

Sweet are the uses of adversity,
Which like the toad, ugly and venomous,
Wears yet a precious jewel in his head.

—**William Shakespeare,** *As You Like It*

Introduction

I F YOU WANT TO SEARCH FOR THE GRAVE OF JAMES MADISON—WHICH NOT many people do—you will most likely begin on Virginia's Route 15, which occasional small signs cheerily label "the Constitution Highway." Like many rural roads in central Virginia, Route 15 unfolds drowsily, a strip of asphalt rolling through a sparsely populated plain. Even though medium-height deciduous trees stand like lush sentinels along the road, there is a dusty, arid feel to the highway, even in winter, an effect that is enhanced by the relative quiet and slight disrepair of the streetscape. Entering the hamlet of Orange, at the intersection with Route 20, you will find Orange Tire & Recap, next to the boarded-up Jean's Cafe, which itself sits to the left of Advance Auto Parts.

On your way to Montpelier, the brick mansion where Madison spent most of his life and on whose estate he's now buried, you'll understandably be tempted to stop by the James Madison Museum. But entering the modest brick street front, flanked by unassuming faux capitals, you're also forgiven for taking a startled step back. For, if you were expecting a polished memorial to our fourth president, you will behold, instead, a ramshackle assemblage of bizarrely heterogeneous items. Identified by yellowing cardboard tags with typed labels, there are dresses and petticoats from the early nineteenth century, as well as an exhibit by a modern artist named Earl Worick, who specializes in "bringing out the art in nature," as well as a cavernous room filled with dusty, rusty antique farm equipment and, strangely, a 1924 Ford Model A (all intended to "honor James Madison, the 'Father of Agriculture,' according to Thomas Jefferson"). If you ask the kindly proprietor, she will show you the handful of original manuscripts, including the will of Madison's murdered grandfather Ambrose. But that's about it.

Leaving, you'll eventually make your way to Montpelier, which feels a little like a horse farm. That's unsurprising, because it *was* one for most of the twentieth century, owned by the DuPont family and used as a headquarters for the steeplechase course that loops just near the house's main entrance. You'll drive past the racing lanes, then go a short distance up a quiet lane to Montpelier itself. You'll enter a scrubbed, spare, largely bare two-floor house that's been meticulously restored from its DuPont-era excesses to its bare bones. That has mostly been an exercise in subtraction rather than addition. While the staff is gradually adding artifacts and speculative dioramas to try to put Madison's personality in the house, the major impetus is archaeological, which is because most of the funds directed toward James Madison have been focused on archaeology—uncovering the bones and pottery shards, the burial ground of the enslaved people, the kitchen leavings up in the densely wooded hills.[1]

Walking outside in search of his grave, you'll wander to a small turf surrounded by a short square wall of bricks. This is still the Madison family cemetery today. When you push open the small wrought-iron gate and walk up to a large obelisk, you will see a carved inscription that reads, simply,

MADISON
Born March 16th, 1751
Died June 28th, 1836

The engraving does not include Madison's first name, or even any description of him or his life. It's as if the memorialists either thought he was above modifiers, iconic in his own right, or that there was really nothing else to say other than his last name.

The gravestone itself has a depressing and decidedly noniconic history. For the two decades after Madison's death, any visitor seeking to visit the Father of the Constitution's burial site had to tramp through private property to the unmarked grave. That was because after he died in 1836, his widow, Dolley, was forced to sell Montpelier, a deeply troubled farm. Madison's graveyard, in the family plot, also entered into private hands. In 1857, a group of Orange County gentlemen agreed the situation was shameful; at the very least, Madison deserved a *gravestone*. So they retained a stonemason to build an obelisk-type monument similar, in many respects, to the very famous one Thomas Jefferson had requested for himself before he died. When delivered, the piece was far more ostentatious than Jefferson's. It was twenty-five feet

IMAGE I.I. JAMES MADISON'S GRAVESTONE. COURTESY OF THE
MONTPELIER FOUNDATION, JAMES MADISON'S MONTPELIER.

tall, made of seven pieces of granite quarried from the James River, together
weighing thirty-two thousand pounds.[2]

Beneath a hanging canopy of autumn leaves, the monument was trans-
ported to Montpelier. The workmen positioned the obelisk into place and
began digging the foundation for the stone, but quickly realized the monument
was so massive they would need to dig the hole below Madison's coffin itself.
As they shoveled around the coffin, they noticed that the boards had rotted,
and the lid was out of place. In the process of resetting the coffin lid, they
beheld the remains of James Madison—bones and teeth and shreds of cloth.[3]

A more or less random group of strangers peering at the marooned remains
was a perfect symbol for the peculiar legacy just beginning for Madison. At the
cemetery, the obelisk still towers over dozens of minor family gravestones, softened and rendered illegible by time. During the 1990s, vandals attacked several
of the gravestones, toppling Dolley's over, which then broke in three places.[4]
Although her monument was repaired, there's a stark and lonely feeling in the
cemetery. In several visits, I have never seen another visitor present.

For a striking contrast with Madison's final resting place, you just have to head about an hour southwest from Montpelier to Monticello. You'll quickly notice how much the roads change. You're no longer on the dusty, forgotten throughways of Orange County; now, you're close to prosperous Charlottesville and the well-maintained Interstate 64, then manicured Route 20, which goes by apple orchards and wealthy plots before putting you on a winding, gentle road that leads up to the great mansion that, in the words of a recent study, "stands atop his mountain like the Platonic ideal of a house."[5]

Walking up to Monticello, you'll traverse gardens as lovely and manicured as those of any palace in Europe. Entering the house, you'll meander through a lovingly maintained museum, stocked with original artifacts and Jefferson's inventions, staffed by docents so passionate about the cause of expanding Jefferson's legacy they might as well be members of a religion. About 500,000 people visit each year. Monticello is on the face of the American nickel.

And when you walk up to Jefferson's famously modest gravestone at Monticello, surrounded by the murmurings of hundreds of avid visitors in what is effectively a secular national temple, you'll see the strange collision between the overt modesty of the grave and the outsize memorialization occurring just around it. Jefferson laid out specific instructions for a "plain die or cube" "without any mouldings" but surmounted by a six-foot obelisk. The monument was to be "coarse stone" so that "no one might be tempted hereafter to destroy it for the value of the materials." And it was to mention only three things:

Thomas Jefferson
Author of the Declaration of American Independence
of the Statute of Virginia for religious freedom
Father of the University of Virginia

These items, Jefferson explained, were the "testimonials that I have lived" and the things "I wish most to be remembered."[6]

And we haven't even gotten to Jefferson's memorial—the gleaming, oval, white marble edifice that sits on the Tidal Basin in Washington, DC, like a Greek temple. Inside the circle, a bronze Jefferson stands, cloaked, one foot gently but confidently placed ahead of the other, overseeing his creation. Quotes from Jefferson's life and writings emblazon the interior walls. Cherry trees gifted to the United States by Japan are planted in the Tidal Basin that spreads out from the memorial, magically draping the entire site, every spring, with a perfumed corona of pink, red, and magenta blossoms. The National Park Service recorded over 2 million visitors to Jefferson's Memorial in 2012—and no wonder. Who can stay away?[7]

There is no similar memorial to James Madison. There *is* the Madison Building, a stark, modern library with flat, stylized columns and many thousands of square feet of plate glass that sits, placidly, in Washington, DC. The Library of Congress's *third* building, it opened on May 28, 1980, to scarce fanfare, rationalized on the slender reed of Madison's own attempt to build a national library in 1783. The building includes three depictions of Madison himself. The first is a statue off the entrance hall to the immediate left of Madison as a young man in his thirties, holding in his right hand a volume of the *Encyclopédie méthodique*, published in Paris between 1782 and 1832. Two quotations by Madison float above the door, and eight other quotations decorate the walls, along with two bronze medallions of Madison.

Note that there are two other buildings in the Library of Congress. One is named the John Adams Building. And the other one—the main one— is, of course, named the Thomas Jefferson Building. Only Madison's has the word *memorial* in the title, because his building *is* the United States of America's only formal memorial to him.[8]

I T'S TEMPTING TO BLAME OURSELVES FOR THE PALTRY STATE OF THE MEMORI-alization of Madison—to think that if only we were better, we would honor his constitutional wizardry, his brilliance in conventions, and his conceptual insights about checks and balances, as much as the romance and glamor of Jefferson's blazing pursuit of our freedoms.

But perhaps Madison himself was at fault. For he was very different from the other men who dominated American history during the nation's crucial early years.

Alexander Hamilton, for instance, at the age of thirteen and just off the boat in New York, wrote a friend that his ambition was so "prevalent" that "I contemn the groveling and condition of a clerk or the like, to which my fortune, etc. condemns me, and would willingly risk my life, though not my character, to exalt my station."[9] Years later, seeking to break into America's aristocracy, he wrote his friend John Laurens that he needed a wife who would be "sensible (a little learning will do), well bred, chaste, and tender." As important, she would need to bring a "fortune, the larger stock of that the better," for "money is an essential ingredient to happiness in this world."[10] He succeeded in precisely these aims, marrying Elizabeth Schuyler the next year.

As a youth about fifteen years old, George Washington bridled a notoriously vicious horse and after a long and violent struggle, killed the stallion—blood flowing from the beast's nostrils.[11] In 1774, a Colonel Muse, while drunk, wrote Washington to attack the latter's efforts to secure bounty lands for his soldiers. Washington responded to the "stupidity and sottishness" of the letter, as if challenged to a duel, his pugnacious physicality bristling through the letter. "All my concern," he wrote Muse, "is that I ever engaged myself in behalf of so ungrateful and dirty a fellow as you are."[12] As president, when he learned of the defeat of a company by Indians, Washington burst into "bitter lamentations," strode around the room so agitated he could not speak, and then, when his "wrath became terrible," in a "paroxysm of anguish," he began hitting himself on the forehead with his fists "with fearful force," swearing, "Oh God, oh God."[13] This is the same man who, after his first fight on the frontier, wrote to his brother John, "I have heard the bullets whistle and, believe me, there is something charming in the sound."[14]

At the age of twenty, John Adams called his vanity his "cardinal vice and cardinal folly," and recognized, "I am in continual danger, when in company, of being led into an *ignis fatuus* chase by it." He also saw that the love of fame could lead to "weaknesses and fopperies" and, thus, to "defeat itself."[15] In 1783, when Adams was serving as minister to France, Madison told Jefferson that Adams's letters were "not remarkable for any thing" except for their "display of his vanity, his prejudice against the French Court & his venom against Doct. Franklin."[16] In January 1787, after seven months of serving with Adams in France, Jefferson wrote Madison to condemn both Adams's "vanity" and his "blindness to it." He wrote, "He is vain irritable and a bad calculator" of men's motives. But still, Jefferson noted that anyone "will love" Adams who gets to know him. "He would be," he predicted, "as he was, a great man in Congress."[17]

As profoundly different as they were, these passionate men shared one trait: At a profound historical moment, they jostled to be larger than life, to transcend ordinary politics and to enter, along with their new nation, the pantheon of history.

Madison is illuminated by contrast. He lacked Hamilton's mercurial drives and personal calculation. He did not share Washington's physical forcefulness or sublimated violence. The self-love of Adams was a mystery to him. Jefferson's flights of fancy and grand projects (whether Monticello or the University of Virginia) were alien to him. While he contained the same multitudes as any human being—particularly anyone extraordinary—he was so absorbed in affairs of state that he simply neglected to develop an outsize character for the history books.

And so it is perfectly fitting that the young statesman who designed our Constitution subsumed himself so completely in its development and ratification that his fame actually *suffered*—even though he mattered more than any other individual in the making of the Constitution.

That outcome is especially perverse because of the contrast between how Madison talked about himself and what he *actually did*.

In 1784, when he was thirty-three, Madison, back from a three-year term in Congress, was a delegate in Virginia's General Assembly. He weighed about a hundred pounds, and he stood between five foot four and five foot six inches tall. He was kinetically anxious, almost feverish, and people seemed either to like or dislike him instantly. A fellow congressman wrote Madison that "there never was a crisis, threatening an event more unfavorable to the happiness of the United States, than the present."[18] An apocalyptic mood descended on Virginia—a frenzy, even, where ordinarily rational men became convinced that everyday affairs were all conspiring to destroy the very country itself. It did not help that the economy was in a free fall, and that the state's government could barely even fund its daily operations.

He knew people pray in such moments; he was no exception. But he began to worry as the panic whipsawed in a menacing turn. Just eight years earlier, at the beginning of the Revolution, Virginia had what was thought to be a healthy religious establishment, numbering ninety-one clergymen and 164 churches and chapels. But while Great Britain had dragged the war on and on, a staggering decline had taken place. Now, only twenty-eight ministers were preaching around the state.[19]

Madison learned that Virginia's former governor, Patrick Henry, saw a ripe political issue in the collapse of Virginia's churches. Henry was perhaps

the most astute and opportunistic politician in the country. In the years leading up to the Revolution, he led a raid on the British governor of Virginia's
stolen stores of gunpowder. He later declared, to instant fame, "Give me liberty or give me death!" in St. John's Church in Richmond. In Henry's first
term as governor, in 1777, Madison eagerly joined his administration in the
prestigious post of governor's councilor. Yet in the years since the Revolution,
much had changed. The British forces were brutal and predatory. The colonies were unable to join together and govern themselves. The jewel of the
Revolution seemed to be turning into charcoal before his very eyes.

For Madison, nothing personified that disheartening transformation
more than Henry himself. In the spring of 1784, he grimly watched from
the floor of the General Assembly as Henry rose and proposed to force every
taxpayer to dedicate a portion of his taxes to a Christian organization. (It
was little consolation that Henry said that if a citizen refused to name such
an organization, the state would put the funds to a government-run school
instead.)

In the months that followed, Madison worked over the problem in his
mind. From the Holy Roman Empire to the recent repression of Baptists in
Virginia, he thought government had always been unable to provide impartial justice when supporting one sect—even Christianity, writ large—over
another. More broadly, he wondered, a country with aspirations to join the
pantheon of nations on a political theory of modern liberalism could not take
such an obvious step backward. Yet the matter would require delicate political
tactics, for the very danger of the proposal lay in its popularity.

Madison began devising a counterattack. He employed what I will call
his "Method," which was an interlocking set of nine tactics:

> *Find passion in your conscience. Focus on the idea, not the man.*
> *Develop multiple and independent lines of attack. Embrace impatience.*
> *Establish a competitive advantage through preparation. Conquer bad*
> *ideas by dividing them. Master your opponent as you master yourself.*
> *Push the state to the highest version of itself. Govern the passions.*

He began taking notes on the back of an envelope for an assault on
Henry's bill. The true question, he wrote, was not whether religion was

necessary. It was whether religious establishments were necessary for religion. The answer to that, he scribbled, was simple—"no."

In November, Henry stood to speak in favor of his bill. He painted an antediluvian picture of the decline in American morals. He argued with passion that nations fell when religion decayed. Madison noted the reverberant power of Henry's words among the gathered men, remarking years later on the distinct eloquence of the speech.[20]

Madison then rose on the floor of the General Assembly. The building itself felt impermanent and makeshift. The cornerstone for a new capitol building nearby was scheduled to be laid in two months; the delegates knew they were on their way out of the aging and musty structure.

Small as he was, Madison appeared fit and muscular, if young for his age. He did not seem anxious, exactly—more tensile, as if he had captured and retained the energy of anxiety, like a coiled spring. Several of the men in the room knew of Madison's pattern of succumbing to what he called his "bilious" or "epileptic" fits at moments just like these, and they must have watched with particular alertness for signs that he might quail and flee.

Reading from the scribbled outline, he assailed Henry's assessment for being unnecessary and contradictory to liberty. Henry had blamed the downfall of states on the decline of religion. But Madison charged that states had fallen precisely where church and state were mixed. He challenged Henry's assumption that moral decay was caused by the collapse in religious institutions; "war and bad laws" were instead at fault.

He concluded with what he called his "panegyric" on Christianity—an emotional endorsement of the power of faith. Henry's assessment would actually "dishonor Christianity," he claimed, by putting the state between man and God.

During this onslaught, many of the other delegates watched him uneasily. The topic was raw, particularly for those from Virginia's more religious and conservative regions, where they had been raised to worship the Bible as the word of God and their ministers as the elders in their communities. Religion, to them, was an institution, a structure as necessary to society as the foundations were to their homes.

Yet many also held deep misgivings about Henry's policy. To prevent a church from collapsing was one thing. To introduce a *tax* for that purpose was quite another. The idea felt illiberal and suffocating, at odds with the spirit of the new country they were trying to build.

But instead of leading the assembly to separate church and state entirely, Madison only succeeded in provoking them to consider supporting *additional* religions. A heated debate broke out among the delegates about the fact that only Christian organizations would receive the funds. They sent Henry's bill to a committee of the whole, where the majority voted to change the word "Christian" to "religious." But then the opportunistic and political sitting governor, Benjamin Harrison, with "pathetic zeal," according to Madison, recruited a majority back to "Christian."[21]

Even though Madison had, in the words of a colleague, "display'd great Learning & Ingenuity, with all the power of a close reasoner," he could not overcome Patrick Henry's power in the assembly.[22] In December, Henry's bill passed its first reading (three were required for passage) by 47 to 32 votes. Henry seized the momentum and rammed through another measure to provide state incorporation to all Christian societies who applied. That bill passed 62 to 23.

Madison wanted to take Henry out of the arena entirely, and so he supported a motion to reelect Henry as governor. Henry accepted without fully thinking through the consequences. But now, for procedural reasons, he would be barred from voting for his own bill. Smiling, Madison informed his friend James Monroe that Henry's elevation had "much disheartened" the supporters of the assessment.[23]

That was just the beginning. In the next days, before Christmas, Madison completed his battle plan to crush the assessment once and for all. First, he needed a delay and he got it. On Christmas Eve, the assembly agreed to postpone the final vote until well into the next year, a pause that gave Madison almost a full year to grind away at the bill.[24]

Christmas passed. The more Madison stewed on the bill, the more he hated it. He acidly told Thomas Jefferson the proposal was "obnoxious" for its "dishonorable principle" and "dangerous tendency."[25] But he predicted that its fate was, as best, "very uncertain"—meaning it could very well pass.

In mid-January, after the winter legislative session concluded, he took to the rutted, frozen red clay road that led from Williamsburg to Orange County, the site of Montpelier, where he still lived, unmarried, with his parents. What he heard in the coming weeks alarmed him—citizens, especially Episcopals and Presbyterians, were joining Henry's lament for the collapse of religion in what he described as a "noise thro' the Country." But public opinion was also churning, reflecting the same restlessness that had given rise to the bill in the first place. By early spring, he noted that the zeal of some of the supporters had begun to cool.[26]

Meanwhile, he worked. He composed a plan of attack to obliterate Henry's "obnoxious" proposal—to burn up the weed, chop up its roots, and forever prevent its ability to spread. His outline on that envelope would be key.

In June, Madison completed an essay, which became known as his "Memorial and Remonstrance Against Religious Assessments." Centuries after his death, it echoes as perhaps *the* defining declaration of the principle of the freedom of religion. His essay reveals the pure power of ideas in politics, handed from person to person like a talisman, like a scripture.

Madison delivered fifteen separate assaults against Henry's assessment. His strategy was reminiscent of George Washington's famous encirclement of Lord Cornwallis three years earlier at Yorktown—a stranglehold from all sides.

He launched with the most fundamental issue of all. Religion, Madison declared, belonged to the realm of conscience, not government. Men, considering only the evidence "contemplated by their own minds," could not be forced to follow the dictates of other men. Religion therefore was, and must always be, unreachable by politics, by the state, and indeed by any instruments of human power. He explained that was precisely what Jefferson had meant by his already famous term "unalienable" in the Declaration of Independence. The state *cannot actually support* religion, because religion's strength depends on men's mind, their reason, and their conscience alone.

Henry, for all of the protestations against a strong central government he would later pronounce on behalf of the anti-Federalists, saw problems through the prism of government. Religion was under siege; the state must defend it. But with this first attack, Madison had succeeded in yanking the prism away and revealing a brilliant and very different new world. Not only was Henry's basic position implausible; it *could not succeed.*

He then thrust fourteen more arguments into the flank of Henry's wounded bill.

He declared that the assessment violated the principle of equality by treating the religious class differently from others.

He lambasted the "arrogant pretension" that the civil magistrate, represented by the legislature and tax authority, could be a "competent judge" of religious truth.

He demanded, of fifteen centuries of the legal establishment of Christianity, "What have been its fruits?" Sarcastically, he observed that state involvement in religion had generated only pride and indolence in the clergy; ignorance and servility among the laity; and, in both, superstition, bigotry, and persecution.

Madison then effortlessly moved to a new front. A bankrupt farmer named Daniel Shays had recently led a violent uprising of debtors in Massachusetts, which had sparked widespread anxiety among the landed gentry who were well represented among the delegates in the room. Madison ominously suggested that Henry's assessment could lead to public unrest. What "mischiefs may not be dreaded," he asked, if the "enemy to the public quiet" were "armed with the force of law?"

Then, Madison swiftly shifted from disaster to idealism. Henry's bill, he declared, was simply "adverse" to the "diffusion of the light of Christianity." He meant that enlightenment was actually available to Virginians; they could *support* religion by *opposing* Henry's bill. Henry, obsessed with taxation and government involvement, was in effect standing in the way of faith.

He concluded on hope rather than fear. The freedom of religion, he said, was a "gift of nature." If Henry's bill passed, the legislature might just as easily "swallow up" the executive and judiciary branches, as well as all the individual freedoms. If, on the other hand, Virginians met their duty to God, to the "Supreme Lawgiver of the Universe," they could "establish more firmly the liberties, the prosperity and the happiness of the Commonwealth."[27]

For an uncommitted Virginian handed one of the proliferating copies of the essay, Madison's Remonstrance had a dazzling effect. It was as if by so thoroughly ribboning Henry's bill, he had allowed sunlight to stream through it. Henry was powerless to stop the Remonstrance, whose contagious force began growing.

But a strange obstacle quickly appeared. Madison's friends wanted to reprint his essay as a pamphlet for mass distribution, but he amazed them by announcing that its authorship must be kept secret. They did the best they could to respect his frustrating and eccentric request. After printing copies in Alexandria, George Mason sent them to friends and neighbors with a cover letter requesting anonymity for the author. He explained that he was "a particular Freind, whose Name I am not at Liberty to mention."[28] Madison himself mailed a friend a copy, while demanding that "my name not be associated with it."[29]

Despite—or perhaps because of—the Remonstrance's alluring anonymity, the civil movement against the assessment quickened.

Initially, thirteen separate petitions supporting the Remonstrance sprouted up around the Commonwealth, gathering 1,552 combined signatures. A friend from Orange County told Madison he had convinced 150 of "our most respectable freeholders" to sign a petition—in a single day.[30] Twenty-nine other petitions went even further than Madison's, asserting that Henry's proposed act contradicted the "Spirit of the Gospel," and attracted another 5,000 signatures. In the end, over 10,000 Virginians signed some sort of an anti-Assessment petition.[31]

In November 1785, a little over a year after Henry had first introduced a real threat to religious liberty in the new nation, the Virginia delegates, gathered in Assembly—with Governor Henry watching, powerless, sent Henry's bill to a legislative "pigeonhole" where it was left to die—killed by James Madison. Meanwhile, Madison had developed the template for the principle he would embed in the Bill of Rights five years later: "Congress shall make no law respecting the establishment of religion, or prohibiting the free exercise thereof."

T HE MAN WHO COULD MAKE SUCH AN IMPACT THROUGH A SINGLE essay—through paper rather than performance—has been profoundly misunderstood. Madison *seemed* to be less attractive, seductive, amusing, engaging, and passionate than the other Founding Fathers. This—along with his own stubborn refusal to pursue fame—might explain his decrepit legacy. But consider an additional hypothesis: that Madison was not actually as uninteresting as he often *appeared* to be. Instead, his unstinting self-control was a mask, or a shell, for his sensitivity. The fact is that he was painfully self-conscious, frequently consumed by anxiety, and often, in his public life, more focused on getting by than on performing for his peers, let alone history.

His friends recognized this all along. Staying for months at a time at a well-regarded boardinghouse in Philadelphia, Madison formed a trusting friendship with Eliza House Trist, the daughter of the owner. The two maintained an intimate correspondence for many years later. Madison often wrote her, with empathy, about her family, her health, and her life in general, and was devastated when her husband died, soliciting help for her from friends.

Trist gladly returned these favors. When Madison left Philadelphia after his first term in Congress, Jefferson felt he could easily be elected governor of Virginia, if he wanted the post. Jefferson mentioned that fact to Trist in a letter. She responded with a note containing a profound insight. Madison, she wrote, deserved "everything that can be done for him." But she thought it would be "rather too great a sacrifice" to make him governor. That was because her friend had a "soul replete with gentleness, humanity and every social virtue." And she was, she said, "certain" that in the process of a political campaign, "some wretch or other" would "write against him." "Mr. Madison," she wrote, was "too amiable in his disposition to bear up against a torrent of abuse," she concluded. "It will hurt his feelings and injure his health, take my word."[32]

Trist's tender concern for her friend reveals as much about his basic nature as about his bond with friends and allies, which helped him survive and thrive in what was, for him, an unnatural arena. Eliza House Trist wanted Madison to stay as far as possible *away* from politics. That he ultimately decided to plunge into a realm so perilous for his well-being suggests the high stakes he saw in the enterprise. He was willing to build the government the country needed, even if he might jeopardize himself in the process.

Perversely, through history's increasingly dusty lens, Madison's mask has become more famous than the man underneath. Our general impression remains as severe as the title of a 1994 book: *If Men Were Angels: James Madison and the Heartless Empire of Reason.* Most Americans, if they know anything about him at all, see him as calculating, intellectual, politically astute, dry, and remote. This pattern has lasted for a long time. In 1941, in his one-page preface to his authoritative four-volume history of Madison's life, the historian Irving Brant wrote, "Among all the men who shaped the present government of the United States of America, the one who did the most is known the least."

But to his contemporaries, Madison was never dry or remote or calculating. In June 1824, when Madison was seventy-three years old, an itinerant bookseller named Samuel Whitcomb met with him. He wrote that "instead of being a cool reserved austere man," Madison was "very sociable, rather jocose, quite sprightly, and active"; yet he also had "a quizzical, careless, almost waggish bluntness of looks and expression which is not at all prepossessing."[33] Yes,

Madison was cold to strangers—as well as to history. But to those he invited in, his friends and allies and coadventurers, he was warm and full of life, seductive, hilarious, and even entrancing. The stunning story of his victories is simply incomprehensible without the passion, charisma, energy, humor, and fierceness of Madison the actual man.

A FTER THE RATIFICATION OF THE CONSTITUTION, MADISON SPENT another four decades in public life—as a US representative of Virginia in Congress, as secretary of state to President Thomas Jefferson, and as president, for two terms. As an outgoing president, he was quite popular, despite his unsure conduct of the War of 1812, and he was also succeeded by James Monroe, a member of his own party, which usually means that the outgoing president did his job pretty well.[34] Despite his morbid hypochondria, Madison outlived his father, who died at the age of seventy-seven. He outlived George Washington. He outlived Thomas Jefferson and John Adams, who both died on July 4, 1826. He lived so long that he was alive well into the presidency of Andrew Jackson.

Yet he achieved his summit in his earlier years, as a young man. Irving Brant was always troubled by the elusiveness of Madison's younger self. "What of the James Madison who helped to carry on the War of the American Revolution and at the age of thirty-six earned the title of Father of the Constitution?" Brant asked. That young man, he said, "is known only through a backward projection of his later self, and therefore is not known at all." Brant concluded, "When a man rises to greatness in youth, it is with his youth that we should first concern ourselves."[35]

At long last, this book attempts to answer Brant's call. Madison's story, and the broader ideas he fought so hard and well for, can help democracy at a moment of unique crisis. Franklin Delano Roosevelt said the only thing we had to fear was fear itself. Today, we have to fear cynicism about leadership itself. Our era teems with a series of unenviable superlatives. The 113th Congress was the least effective in history. It was also the most unpopular in recorded history.[36] In their best-selling *It's Even Worse Than It Looks*, the political scientists Thomas Mann and Norman Ornstein argued that a culture of hostage-taking in the Republican Party was largely to blame, coupled with systematic trends in campaign finance and fund-raising, and the disappearance of friendships between senators and representatives.[37] The authors recount then-House minority leader Newt Gingrich's decision, in 1994, to run against incumbent Democrats by pursuing "relentlessly the charge that Congress was corrupt and needed to be blown up to change things." Gingrich developed a tactical memo instructing candidates to use certain words when talking about the Democratic enemy: "betray, bizarre, decay, anti-flag, anti-family, pathetic, lie, cheat, radical, sick, and traitors."[38] Today, a similar nihilism has appeared in many of the actions of legislators and activists associating themselves with the "Tea Party" movement. And there are striking parallels between the threats posed by Patrick Henry and certain of the anti-Federalists in young Madison's time and the "Tea Party" forces in American politics today.*

The general dissatisfaction with our political leaders has migrated into many other branches of leadership. After departing as secretary of defense to President Barack Obama, Robert Gates described members of Congress en masse as "uncivil, incompetent at fulfilling their basic constitutional responsibilities (such as timely appropriations), micromanagerial, parochial, hypocritical, egotistical, thin-skinned and prone to put self (and re-election) before country."[39]

Amid such scorched earth, it has become disconcertingly difficult to cite leaders we would readily describe as "statesmen." In dozens of conversations with current and former members of Congress, journalists, academics, and political activists while researching this book, I watched as people struggled to cite an example of a statesman. This was not a problem even a generation ago, as Ira Shapiro points out in *The Last Great Senate*, where figures, including Daniel Patrick Moynihan, Frank Church, Margaret Chase Smith, Hubert Humphrey, Jacob Javitz, Gaylord Nelson, Scoop Jackson, Ted

---

* As the historian Jackson Turner Main has noted, the anti-Federalists were a large tent of many thousands of political actors, with a wide range of motivations and political philosophies. Some were motivated by a good-faith concern for the common good. Among those general interests were a worry about the proper balance of power between federal and state governments, on the assumption that "to vest total power in a national government was unnecessary and dangerous (128)." Others wanted to protect private rights and liberties "from encroachments from above (158)." Still others focused on the proper functioning and powers of the Constitution's branches of government. Jackson Turner Main, *The Anti-Federalists: Critics of the Constitution, 1781–1788* (Chapel Hill: University of North Carolina Press, 1961), 128, 158. Yet many anti-Federalists also pursued private or special interests, whether commercial, parochial, or personal.

Kennedy, George McGovern, William Proxmire, and Robert Byrd, all sought to elevate the United States through the US Senate. Bipartisanship was common, as were long campaigns on difficult legislative issues where the legislator would develop personal expertise, as were serious deliberative sessions where lawmakers would personally take charge of negotiating the fine details of a generational issue. For all of these, a consensus on the need for statesmanship was the sine qua non.

If there were more statesmen in America, *and* more citizens who looked up to them and bolstered them, then our country—like Madison's—could advance beyond the sclerosis and mutual hatreds that have paralyzed us. Those problems particularly afflict one institution in particular—the US Senate—which was designed precisely as a home for statesmen, yet has become infected by the same virus that has invaded our other institutions. For we desperately need venues where serious men and women contest each other in depth on the country's critical issues, where they assemble coalitions, battle valiantly, and accept defeat, when it comes.

The story of Madison's leadership is relevant not just for politics, but can be applied in business, in nonprofit management and social entrepreneurship, in education, in social media campaigns, and in virtually every arena where leadership matters. Any group facing a seeming total failure to rise to a challenge would do well to study Madison's approach of a sustained campaign to destroy bad ideas and raise up good ones, through conviction, preparation, and self-governance.

Statesmanship is an old-fashioned solution for a very new world. Leadership has fallen somewhat out of fashion in political science. In a social media age where we think more readily of networks and of community organizing as principles for power, leaders seem antiquated, much less statesmen. As the leadership scholar Warren Bennis has written, "A decade from now, the terms *leader* and *follower* will seem as dated as bell bottoms and Nehru jackets. . . . What does leadership mean in a world in which anonymous bloggers can choose presidents and bring down regimes?"[40]

But if young Madison's story proves anything, it is that leadership—and statesmanship—are as essential to a healthy democracy as constitutionalism. Indeed, both are required—from the bottom up, engaged citizens; and from the top down, statesmen who challenge and lead.

Madison's model of statesmanship appears in his method, which he employed in the Remonstrance as well as eight other instances by the time he was thirty-seven years old: addressing the nation's inflation crisis in 1780, upon first arriving in Congress; battling for the federal impost (which I call the "forced contribution") in 1783, which led to his first nationally famous speech; pushing through a sweeping set of reforms to Virginia's legal code in 1785; confronting Patrick Henry's proposed tax for religion in 1785, which became his Memorial and Remonstrance; attacking paper money in another speech that became nationally famous in 1786; introducing the Virginia Plan in the Constitutional Convention in 1787; defeating the rival New Jersey Plan at the convention; campaigning on the Constitution through the Federalist Papers in 1787 and 1788; and his personal command, in 1788, of the Federalists' strategy at Virginia's ratifying convention against Patrick Henry.

Throughout, it becomes clear that Madison belonged to that rare breed of quietly attractive historical figures: the reluctant pugilist. He did not *want* to fight; he took no joy in confrontation. Indeed, conflicts often led to anxiety attacks so debilitating he mistook them for epilepsy. But he saw the fights as necessary events in the larger purpose of the life he set out for himself at a young age: to push the American state to achieve its potential, no matter what obstacles the country and small-minded men might throw in his way.

In all of these ways, Madison set out to become a statesman. Today, we often use this word to refer to a public official who represents a country in international affairs. Yet the word meant something very different to Madison when he wrote to Jefferson, soon after arriving in Philadelphia to first serve in Congress, that the country was afflicted by a "defect of adequate statesmen." Madison did not mean either a dignified international diplomat or an elder above the fray. Instead, his statesmen were political leaders who made it their business, their raison d'être, to lead the state to become the highest, the best, and the most noble version of itself.

He set out, in the months and years to follow, to become such a statesman himself. His quest culminated in June of 1788, the year following the passage of the Constitution in Philadelphia. That summer, Madison again traveled to Richmond, again with the goal of battling Patrick Henry and the anti-Federalists. For Madison, the arena was a crowded, bustling amphitheater called the New Academy, packed with hundreds of onlookers—and the stakes were dramatically higher. Nine states were required to ratify the Constitution, and Virginia was the last. For months, Henry and his anti-Federalists had been raising "mad freaks," in Jefferson's words. They were threatening that the new Constitution would ruin Virginia's proud independence, destroy the commercial interests of the wealthy delegates voting on it, and undermine the very future of the country herself.

In that room, Madison needed to fight not only Patrick Henry but himself. Standing in the theater, he watched as Henry slashed away at him and his Federalist allies with barely hidden contempt, mocking their "illumined ideas, which the well-born are so happily possessed of." As for Madison's vaunted idea that statesmanship could rescue Virginia, Henry mocked the "microscopic eyes of modern statesmen" for seeing an "abundance of defects in old systems." In contrast, Henry thundered, "I tremble for my country!"[41]

That afternoon, Madison experienced an anxiety attack that left him quaking and on the verge of collapse. He fled the hall for his boardinghouse, where he lay, racked not only by his churning stomach, but by the shame of abandoning the fight. As he lay in his room on that June day in Richmond, the question facing the quailing young man was whether he could overcome the rebellion of his body and the storm Henry was whipping up in the New Academy. The fate of the nation hung in the balance. Madison's lifelong battle with these attacks contains the secret not only to his political victories, but to his political philosophy. His problem was not that he felt too little, but that, like the raw young country he loved, he felt too much.

NOT MUCH HAS CHANGED IN TWO CENTURIES. OPPONENTS ARE STILL wily and opportunistic. Issues become emotions and slip from our grasp. Reason falls prey to rhetoric. The attractive and the charismatic dance among the colorless and the shy. Yet despite all these hostile factors, young James Madison succeeded in leading his country to adopt a philosophy of governance that would in turn become an essential crossbar in the nation's new architecture of constitutional democracy. That crossbar—and Madisonian control must be understood that way, as a hidden structural element so intimately bound up with the building itself that it would collapse without it—is familiar to many who have sought to understand Madison. In his cele-brated 1989 book *The Last of the Fathers*, for instance, historian Drew McCoy argued that Madison "sought and achieved the banishment of selfish, disrup-tive passion from his temperament for his own and his country's good."[42]

Together, Madison's ideal of self-governance (for the statesman as well as the state) helps solve one of the great puzzles of Revolutionary America: how this one man, already such an unlikely candidate for leadership, and provably so ignored by history, had such an outsize impact on the country. The secret lies in the double helix of Madison's statesmanship: his ideas and his char-acter, spiraling around each other. As Madison found his way from a child to a young man, he developed a personality that addressed the failings of his nation. As he puzzled out the problems crushing the nation, he wove those lessons into his character. And so as he became more forceful, his character and his ideas entwined and thrust forward, like Dylan Thomas's green fuse of nature.[43] In the process, he at last became the statesman he thought America needed.

Two millennia ago, Plato tackled the problem of the passions in his famous dialogue "Phaedrus," by imagining these urges as massive steeds, one good, one bad. One horse, he wrote—the "follower of true glory"—was white, with a "lofty neck" and dark eyes. The other horse—the "mate of insolence and pride"—was dark, with gray eyes and a blood red complexion. When the passions take control, he said, the dark steed suddenly starts away, clench-ing the bit in his teeth and galloping from the charioteer—the person who stands, in his metaphor, for each of us. Plato described how we can only con-trol the dark steed by yanking at his bit so violently that it wrenches from his mouth, coating his tongue and jaws with blood, and then forcing the horse to the ground and whipping him. Only then, Plato wrote, will the passions be tamed and humbled.[44]

When the passions rule, Plato wrote, that "power of misrule" should be called "excess." But when "opinion by the help of reason leads us to the best," he wrote, this "conquering" would happen through "temperance."[45] In other words, the violence of breaking the dark steed can be avoided—by training him never to bolt, through moderation, reason, and discipline.

For the most part, Madison tamed his own unruly self, just as his Con-stitution, for the most part, tamed the furies summoned by Patrick Henry. Of course, the most difficult times occurred when the steed broke away, as it did on that June day when Madison collapsed in the New Academy. The question then was whether he, and the young country he loved, could rise to the occasion and break the defiant steed.

And if we get that story right, then Route 15 might become a little less lonely, and Madison's graveyard a little more crowded.

With that, let us explore how that young man became James Madison.

Part I

1 "Our Passions Are Like Torrents"

————————◆————————

THE TWELVE-YEAR-OLD BOY LOOKED WATCHFULLY OUT ON THE ROLLING blue mountains that seemed to float along the horizon. Informed by his father that he would soon be sent seventy miles away to attend a boarding school run by a mysterious Scotsman, the boy had been flooded with strong emotions. He had large dark eyes, delicate cheekbones, a strong nose, a pointed chin, thin lips, and feathery hair that would begin thinning soon enough. He was introverted, preferring to watch as others spoke, to digest information rather than spew it out. He tended to hover at the edges of rooms, as if seeking an escape. He was intensely sensitive, responding like a tuning fork to the slightest disturbance. Yet his seemingly brittle exterior masked a warm and humorous inner self that quickly became apparent to his friends.

It had already been an unsettling year. His father had recently moved the family, including the boy's tough, independent grandmother Frances (a matriarch who owned and ran the majority of the family's plantation) from a rough outpost they called Mount Pleasant to this large brick home. The wildness of the land was haunted by chaos and death. Iroquois, Shawnee, Oneida, and Cherokee lurked in the lands to the west, stories of violent clashes with Virginian settlers filling the boy's head with vivid tableaux of blood and scalps.[1] In Orange County, slave rebellions arose and were crushed with brutal executions. Before the boy's birth, his grandfather Ambrose had been believed poisoned by his slaves and died.

His father's intent, it was clear, was to create a fresh seat for a family empire. The library where the boy was sitting was one of the house's largest rooms, with three large, lovely windows looking out west on the Shenandoah Mountains. Such a large space for books and thought was unusual in a planter's house, but his father seemed to have designed Montpelier with his precocious son in mind. Yet if one thing was paramount, it was that his father wanted his eldest son to avoid vainglory.

Not many letters from Madison's father, James Madison Sr., exist. But one long letter he wrote to a cousin he hadn't seen in years helps explain how he tried to raise his son. The letter was written in 1793, when James Madison Jr. was forty-two years old. After sharing many pages of details about his family, the senior Madison apologized for going on at such length, reprimanding himself for indulgence. "However ostentatious it may appear," he wrote to his cousin, "it is to you only that I have indulged a vein of vanity, which is a vice I have always despised." He concluded with a telling sentence that "I shall now only add that my very dear Wife, and daughter Fanny, with myself, who are the whole of my White family when my son James is absent," sent their love, affection, and best wishes to his cousin and his family.[2]

Those sentences were telling, in three key respects. First, Madison's father "always despised" vanity and raised his son, in turn, to take great pains to avoid even any *impression of* vanity. Second, even though his son was, at the time, a former congressman recognized as the father of the Constitution, he barely mentioned him—save to state that his family was not "whole" while James was gone. That suggests strong, but suppressed, emotion, another characteristic his son would later share.

Third, his father referred to his "White family," suggesting that, without the modified "White," he thought he had another sort of family at Montpelier as well, one that included the enslaved men and women he owned, including Sawney, the enslaved man his son James first met when he was a baby. Sawney was fourteen at the time and probably belonged to the group of about a dozen slaves that Nelly brought into the marriage. Madison Jr. became so comfortable with Sawney over the years that in 1769, when he was eighteen, Sawney accompanied him on the journey to attend college at Princeton, New Jersey. Sawney was thirty-two at the time.

Sawney's role in the "family" defied category. Madison always referred to Sawney in letters familiarly, as a fellow man. By 1782, when Madison was thirty-one, his father would make Sawney one of the plantation overseers in charge of one of the land's four quarters. Sawney harvested tobacco himself and sold it to James Madison Sr., listed in plantation records as "Sawney's . . . own crop." In the mid-1780s, Madison's father enabled Sawney to purchase

IMAGE 1.1. JAMES MADISON, SR., BY CHARLES PEALE POLK.
COURTESY OF BELLE GROVE.

special "English" shoes of the sort worn by white men. He also gave him an actual overseer's house to live in, rather than a typical slave's cabin.[3]

Two ideas took root in young Madison's mind. Despite Virginia law holding to the contrary, the enslaved men and women around him were, in fact, human beings. And he would need to transcend the vulgarity of Virginia's master-slave relationship in his own way.

That second aim would unfold over his long life. His longtime manservant, Paul Jennings, would later accompany him to the White House and outlive him. Jennings published a memoir in 1865, the year the Civil War ended, in which he wrote, "Mr. Madison, I think, was one of the best men that ever lived. I never saw him in a passion, and never knew him to strike a slave, although he had over one hundred; neither would he allow an overseer to do it." Jennings quoted Madison as saying, "I never allow a negro to excel me in politeness."[4]

That self-control in an arena too often given instead to outbursts and brutal violence began in Madison's youth. Madison Jr. was almost certainly aware of the fate of Ambrose Madison, his father's father. Ambrose was an imperious, hard man who was likely an equally hard master of his slaves. His roughhouse ways were legendary in Orange County. As a new arrival, he immediately filed lawsuits against other men for trespassing on the property, including one alleging damages of 600 pounds of tobacco.[5]

In 1729, a merchant named Daniel Lamport plaintively wrote, "I am sorry to find you complain of the cost of the Goods I sent you, 'tis a complaint I am not used to, & Sorry it should fall on you . . . " Two years later, Lamport, clearly worn down by Ambrose, resignedly wrote, "[I] have Ship'd the Goods you ordered and hope [they] will please," but ended with a jab: "I don't expect that you'll like the Cotton, you order the Cheapest."[6] Ambrose likely applied this abrasive and tight-fisted approach to all of his legal property, including human beings.

In 1732—nineteen years before Madison Jr. was born—Ambrose Madison died after a lingering summertime illness of several months. Soon after he died, two men and a woman, named respectively Turk, Pompey, and Dido, were arrested and charged with his murder.

Ambrose had owned Dido and Turk, while Pompey belonged to a neighbor. In a trial that lasted less than a day, all three were tried and convicted for "Suspition of Poysoning" and "conspiring the death" of Ambrose. The court ruled that Dido and Turk were guilty but "not in such a degree as to be punished by death," and sentenced each to twenty-nine lashes on the back. Pompey, however, was sentenced to death, and hanged the next morning on a freshly built gallows, for which the court paid a builder one hundred pounds of tobacco.[7]

A possible explanation for the different sentences, and for the court's wording, is that the court was forced to acknowledge the predicament of Ambrose's own slaves, given Ambrose's acknowledged brutality. In any event, Ambrose was grasping and acquisitive and ruthless—all qualities that his grandson James would repudiate, two generations later, with every fiber of his being.

S ITTING IN THE LIBRARY, THE BOY MUST HAVE KNOWN HIS PARENTS worried about him. They worried about their intellectual son's eventual

ability to make a living for himself, and about whether the physically fragile child (who often had stomach-aches and complained frequently about
his health) would even survive to adulthood in a time when many teenagers
did not. But he also knew that James and Nelly Madison believed he had a
unique intellect and a curious drive and that, if nothing else, his sheer potential demanded an investment. The trip about to take place, he understood,
was as much for them as it was for him. He had much to live up to.

He rested his feet on the floor, contemplating the future. Many decades
later, he would say, of the man he was about to meet, "All that I have been in
life I owe largely to that man."[8]

M ADISON'S PARTY CLATTERED ALONG THE LONG ROAD TO THE SCHOOL.
Approaching, he saw a broad expanse of land, well over a hundred
acres, gently sloping down to the banks of the Mattaponi River, which teemed
with catfish, crapple, and glittering spring runs of shad. Eastern Virginia was
busier, more crowded, and more cosmopolitan than agrarian Orange County.
Meeting his schoolmates for the first time, Madison gathered that they knew
the big cities well—Richmond, even Philadelphia. As they chattered about
their fathers' resentment of Great Britain's increasingly heavy hand over its colony, he heard the same tones of anger and frustration his father voiced at home.

In the boisterous den, Madison was greeted by a teacher of warmth and
evident dedication to the boys. Donald Robertson had an independence of
thought and courageous spirit that immediately set him apart from the stuffy
men so common in Virginia's merchant circles. Madison and the other boys
noted, with sympathetic affection, a mournful note in their fierce instructor. In his short autobiography written as an old man, in which he described
Robertson as a man of "extensive learning" and a "distinguished Teacher,"
Madison would include the peculiar detail that the unmarried Robertson was
"himself a boarder in the neighborhood."[9]

Gradually, the boys probably learned the sad story behind Robertson's
notable solitude. He had studied Greek, Latin, mathematics, algebra, geom-
etry, philosophy, and theology at the University of Edinburgh; married a
woman named Henrietta; and become a minister. When Prince Charles of
Britain (also known as "Bonnie Prince Charlie") invaded Scotland, Robertson

had supported the Scottish troops, but his father had joined Charlie . . . and died in the spectacularly bloody Battle of Culloden. Scotland's economy was horrible, and Robertson eventually decided to leave for America to seek more profitable employment through teaching. He planned to bring his wife and their children soon after he arrived, but she died shortly after he left Scotland for America, leaving him marooned in a strange land.[10]

In America, Robertson took a dramatic turn away from his early road as a licensed Christian preacher. In a private autobiography that was never published, Madison delved into more personal and scandalous recollections. He recalled that the man he met was now "probably of the Celtic Religion," which he carefully noted "would have been obnoxious" for Robertson to "avow publickly." In other words, the boys had learned that their teacher was not an Anglican (the establishment Christian religion in Virginia); he was not even a *Christian* but a heathen, perhaps even a secret pagan, a polytheist worshiping Celtic gods and demigods. Madison intensely admired him regardless. Robertson was the first of many examples of a man Madison defended despite, or perhaps because of, his defiance of the mainstream faith. Six decades later, Madison was quick to defend his teacher's reputation from any charges of impiety. Robertson was "exemplary in his morals," the old man warmly remembered, "fond of his pupils," had a "warm temper," and was "just & liberal in his conduct towards them."[11] As Robertson stood before the boys, Madison glanced down at the pages of his commonplace book. Parents and relatives gave these expensive, sewn volumes to boys for taking notes in class. Madison received his when he was eight years old, but waited four years to start filling it, as if he was treasuring its raw potential.

Robertson called Madison "Jamie," an adulteration of his parents' nickname of "Jemmy."[12] During his time with Robertson, Madison purchased both Latin and Greek books. In Latin, he read Virgil, Horace, Justinian, Cornelius Nepos, Caesar, Tacitus, Lucretius, Eutropius, and Phaedrus. In Greek, he read Plato as well as Plutarch, Herodotus, and Thucydides.[13]

But he did not fill his commonplace book with lessons from any of these august figures. What seemed to resonate most with the teenager were instead the personal essays that Robertson assigned. In the first pages of the book, Madison scribbled aphorisms from the memoirs of John Francis Paul de Gondi (Cardinal de Retz), a seventeenth-century French archbishop who, in the words of the preface to the book, had been "violent and inconstant in his intrigues of love as well as those of politics" and "so indiscreet as to boast of his successful amours with certain ladies whom he ought not to have named." With this attitude, Gondi became a sworn enemy of the reigning cardinal, who imprisoned him. He escaped and fled to Rome. His tormentor then pursued him through a dizzying hopscotch journey that spanned Switzerland, Strasbourg, Frankfurt, Cologne, and, finally, Holland.[14] After the cardinal died, Gondi reconciled with the pope and lived out his days in Paris, a subject of fascination for many in both Europe and America.

This tempestuous, hunted man has been largely forgotten today. But the nonconformist Robertson used astonishingly frank memoirs to free the minds of his young charges. It was a true exercise of the *liberal* arts, and young Madison avidly took notes, reframing Gondi's ideas in his own words.

The first sentence he wrote in his commonplace book was, "Nothing is more Subject to Delusion than Piety." Other glimmers of the wisdom to come:

"Irresolute minds waver most when they are upon the point of Action."

"A Grave Air hides many defects."

"One is oftner deceiv'd by mistrusting People than by confiding in them."

"There is a wonderful Sympathy between some minds. Like Unisones, they are moved alike, and move one another."

"There is a Critical Minute in every thing, & the master-piece of Good Conduct is to perceive it and take hold of it."

"In great affairs the Head signifies nothing without the heart."

And, finally, "All the World is, & will be for ever decieved in things which flatter their passions."[15]

The teenager was eerily assembling the rudiments of the philosophy he would bring to the nation's new Constitution as a grown man.

On another day, Robertson stood in front of the boys to discuss the French essayist Michel de Montaigne. It was another all-too-human, fallible text by a man painfully aware of his limitations.

Quill in hand, the boy reframed Montaigne's ideas in his own words:

"People who are too tender of their Reputation, & too deeply piqued by Slander, are too conscious to themselves of some inward Infirmity."

"A Reputation grounded on true Virtue is like the Sun that may be clouded, but not extinguished."

Madison then coined a metaphor that would perfectly capture the approach he would take as he grew older and began shaping and leading his rising nation: "Our passions are like Torrents which may be diverted, but not obstructed."[16]

Instead of cowering before the rushing force of our hopes and anxieties, or vainly trying to suppress them, he meant, we must channel them instead.

In Robertson's warm schoolroom, above the flowing Mattaponi River, young Madison was gathering the full mental power that he would need to master his heart's torrents. It might take years, but he could build a future in which he would be in control—if he knew himself above all else.

W HEN THEY WERE NOT IN CLASS AND EVEN WHEN THEY WERE IN IT, Madison and his friends whispered about politics. At home for visits and vacations, they noted the tide of rage sweeping across Virginia. Then, in 1765, when he turned fourteen, the British Parliament passed the Stamp Act. The American colonies could now use only paper with embossed seals produced in London and sailed across the ocean. This unwonted tax by their faraway masters infuriated anyone who wanted to write out a legal document on a plain sheet of paper made in America—or anyone, like Madison, scribbling away in his schoolboy's commonplace book.

2 The Good Doctor

◆───

ROM DONALD ROBERTSON, MADISON'S FATHER GATHERED THAT HIS SON'S
preternatural intellect indeed presented extraordinary potential. Madison returned home when he was sixteen. His father invested some of the plantation's profits in arranging for his son to receive precollege instruction from the Reverend Thomas Martin, a personal friend.

Martin had graduated from the increasingly prestigious College of New Jersey run by free-thinking Presbyterians rather than the stuffy Anglicans who dominated almost every institution in Virginia. He was kind, studious, trustworthy, and earnest—an immediately reassuring presence in Madison's anxious life, someone Madison could, and would, grow to look up to.

At seventeen, the time to attend college was quickly approaching. The question was where. The standard choice was the College of William and Mary, which had been established by King William III and Queen Mary II in 1693 with a charter envisioning a "perpetual College of Divinity, Philosophy, Languages, and other good Arts and Sciences." George Washington studied there, as did Thomas Jefferson. The school, located in the established and wealthy Tidewater region, was prestigious and the natural choice for a planting family like the Madisons.

But Madison's fiercely self-reliant father saw it differently. He didn't care for the conventional wisdom that James *must* go to William and Mary, for the school was controlled by Anglicans. Virginia's Anglicans were intimately bound up with the colonial government and loyalists to the Church of England. Their moralism, theocratic tendency, and addiction to political power had been wearing on him for years.

James Madison Sr. knew a civil war was brewing within the college that mirrored tensions within Virginia as a whole. The majority of the college's faculty were English-born graduates of Oxford University. Intrinsically conservative, they were wedded to British customs and history and skeptical of trends toward modern literature and modern science, as well as mistrusted modern philosophies centered on individual freedom and justice. They tendentiously argued that the college's curriculum must follow the rigid classical outlines that had guided generations of British students.[1] James Madison wanted none of this for his precious son.

Madison's parents also considered the nagging issue of their nervous son's health. Orange County was considered "mountainous," even though the hills outside were gentle at best. It took days to travel to Williamsburg, through climates so different they felt to the Madisons like different nations. William and Mary, within the reach of the Atlantic Ocean, was low and humid. It teemed with unfamiliar vegetation, mosquitoes—and unseen diseases. His mother feared the thought of sending her frail son there for years.

All the while, Thomas Martin was glowingly describing his alma mater. The College of New Jersey, located in Princeton, had earned a reputation for teaching integrity, moral probity, and intellectual quality to a small segment of the northern states' leading men. He told Madison's father exciting tales about John Witherspoon, the college's renowned new president. Witherspoon was a reformer, a defiant Scottish Presbyterian skeptic, with a famous habit of deliciously skewering the sanctimonious and the tyrannical alike, particularly among the Anglicans. And that appealed even more to James Madison Sr.

Before dogma could poison his promising young son's mind, the father acted. James Madison Jr. would go to the College of New Jersey.

I N THE SUMMER OF 1769, THE FOUR-MEMBER BAND—MADISON, JONATHAN Martin, his brother Alexander, and Madison's personal slave, Sawney— loaded their horses with food, light and heavy clothes, water, and books for James's months-long stay in Princeton, New Jersey. The journey north would take almost two weeks. They traipsed through the Virginia woods, then crossed the Acquia, Quantico, and Occoquan Rivers on ferries. They passed through the quaint town of Alexandria. Throughout, Jonathan Martin told Madison stories from his time as a student in Princeton. Together, they speculated about Witherspoon. They clopped along the banks of the Potomac River for several miles, then boarded another ferry over to George Town.

They followed a leafy trail along Rock Creek and proceeded on to Annapolis. After two days, they reached the broad Susquehanna River, which spread around them like the sea itself. Ferrying across, they stepped onto the marshy sands of Delaware. After another day, they reached Pennsylvania, and then made their way to Philadelphia.

Madison had never seen anything like the city. He only knew the small hamlets and homey towns of Virginia. The twenty-five-thousand-strong metropolis was bracing. The group stayed at the London Coffee House, which was operated by the Bradford family, and he learned that their son William had already left for Princeton.[2]

They covered the forty-mile road from Philadelphia to Princeton in one day, the horses walking steadily on the dirt path along the Delaware River. As the afternoon shadows lengthened, the four entered Trenton. Twelve miles later, with darkness fallen, they finally came to the peaceful town of Princeton in the humid summer night.[3] Tired from the long trip, an excited James looked around at the small town where his new life would begin, and beheld the massive building that would provide home, mayhem, and Lyceum—sometimes all at once.

W HEN MADISON ENTERED NASSAU HALL FOR THE FIRST TIME, HE beheld the largest stone structure in the colonies, built to house a student body as large as 150. The building was little over a decade old and settling nicely into its bones. The college's ambitious founders had aimed for permanence. They chose locally quarried sandstone over brick as building material, giving the walls, which were over two feet thick, a weighty, slablike quality. The hall was three stories tall, with an elegant cupola perched on the center of its roof. Exploring inside, he walked through recitation rooms and a prayer room on the first floor; a library on the second; and a refectory, kitchen, storeroom, and more student rooms in the basement. His feet stepped lightly on hallways paved with brick to protect the building from fire and to retain warmth from the wood-burning fireplaces.[4]

Madison moved into a room with two other students, hardwood floors underfoot, cool plaster walls around. Everything happened in this building, which was a village unto itself. And the village had a chief.

A FTER HEARING SO MUCH ABOUT WITHERSPOON'S WIT, INTELLIGENCE, and fearlessness from his father, Jonathan Martin, and nearly everyone else, Madison was prepared to be intimidated. He wasn't disappointed. Ashbel Green, a student of Witherspoon's who went on to become a minister and later the college's eighth president, later recounted that effect of Witherspoon's. "He had more of the quality called *presence*—a quality powerfully felt, but not to be described," Green wrote, "than any other individual with whom the writer has ever had intercourse, Washington alone excepted."[5]

Witherspoon seemed transcendent, somehow, his thoughts sweeping up into a higher plane. In the months and years to come, Madison began to learn more about the man and his extraordinary journey.

Witherspoon was a fighter and a moralist, a man of courage and principle. For him, defiance—in politics and philosophy—was as natural and necessary as oxygen. He was born on a cold Scottish February day in 1723 to a minister's daughter. His father was also a minister. Like James Madison decades later, Witherspoon would become the eldest brother of six brothers and sisters. His mother, in Witherspoon's description, was pious, a serious woman passionately driven by faith. His father made the church not only his profession but his life, serving as the minister of his local parish for almost forty years. But he was ambitious as well, with a political bug that expressed itself within the domestic empire of the Presbyterian Church. He preached before and was a commissioner to the Presbytery's General Assembly, and in 1744, was appointed to the high post of royal chaplain.[6]

No surprise that when Witherspoon was just four years old, his father handed him a Bible and taught him to read it out loud.[7] At thirteen, he arrived at the University of Edinburgh to begin full-time study. At university, Witherspoon's peers immediately noticed that he lacked social graces. The Reverend Alexander Carlyle, his instructor, described him as having a "disagreeable temper" and an "awkward manner." But still—he was also "a good scholar, far advanced for his age." He was "very sensible." And—he was "shrewd."[8] Witherspoon, in other words, was not well adjusted, but his drive could power him through any awkwardness.

He was impatient to make more of his education than his fellow students would. Although many of them left without doing any independent scholarly work—indeed, some left without graduating at all—when he was seventeen, he requested permission to present a graduation thesis before his professors and fellow students. The bulky young man stood in the university's common hall and read a twelve-page thesis titled "Philosophical Disputation: Concerning the Immortality of the Mind."[9] Afterward, he bent his large head to receive the hood; he had entered the learned profession, achieving his mother's and father's dreams. Edinburgh's gothic spires surrounded him, reaching for the sky. He stayed on at Edinburgh to study divinity for three more years. In 1743, he passed the examinations that would license him to preach. He worked for his own father for a year and a half more, and then was installed as minister of Beith Parish. He was just twenty-two.[10]

His friends saw in him a special potential—a forcefulness that seemed to warp the space around him. He was a big man who projected both solidity and acuity, like a sharpened ax. But his wicked sense of humor was another weapon entirely, lashing out quickly and without warning, like a whip.

As a young cleric, he stood tall, with piercing blue eyes and a sardonic, phlegmatic manner. He had a quick temper and did not suffer fools easily. For him, as for Donald Robertson, there was no bigger fool than Bonnie Prince Charlie. That Charlie aspired to a new monarchy was bad enough. But the prince was also undermining an enlightened intellectual and cultural wave spreading across the country like a brightening dawn. Witherspoon felt Charlie would yank Scotland back into the gnarled grip of medievalism. The combative young man gradually narrowed his options. He could see no choice other than to fight the arrogant prince himself. He made the astonishing decision to scrape together *his own* militia to repel the invasion.

He hectored students, colleagues, and friends. He raised a small company. Surrounded by his band, he strode out from Edinburgh in search of a fight. But after days of looking, they never found a battle. Only reluctantly did the cleric-warrior disband his little force.[11]

The next year, he learned about a looming battle at Falkirk, where Prince Charlie himself would confront thousands of Scottish troops. Witherspoon again put together a company of his parishioners. Leading the troops, he marched them toward Glasgow, where they heard that the king's troops would be victorious; they were ordered to turn back. But Witherspoon refused, and marched on to the battle. The battle was bloody, and the king did not win.

The prince, glamorously outfitted in a tricorne, drove five thousand of his scruffy Highlander troops toward seven thousand government men. When they clashed, his troops killed or wounded some 350 of the enemy. The prince saw only fifty dead and seventy wounded.[12] Witherspoon, along with five of his volunteers, was seized as a prisoner of war.

Doune, a squat, symmetrical castle, had served as a royal second home in the fifteenth and sixteenth centuries. But in 1746 it was requisitioned as a torture chamber. Witherspoon was thrown into a room in the highest part of the castle, along with two men who had been captured as spies. In the neighboring room were another eight prisoners.

Their British captors brutally tortured Witherspoon and the other men.

Witherspoon's men came up with the idea of escaping their situation by stringing their blankets together into a rope that would drop seventy feet to the ground.[13] Witherspoon agreed to join them. The men grabbed their blankets and knotted them together into a long, unsteady rope. They drew lots for the order of descent, with Witherspoon drawing second to last. Four men successfully climbed down to the ground. When a fifth—one of the heaviest of the group—went down the rope, it broke just as he touched the ground. When the next man descended, the rope broke again and he fell a distance to the ground, badly injuring himself. Witherspoon and one other man were left in the castle. They hauled up the rope and attempted to rebuild it. The other man, who had drawn the longer straw, then climbed down. When he reached the part of the rope that had been repaired, it was so thick that he lost his grip and fell a long distance to the earth. He was so badly injured that he soon died.

Witherspoon, looking down, realized he was trapped. He remained in the castle, the only prisoner in the room.[14] While there is no record of the torture that followed, his captors must have avenged themselves on the lone man with redoubled fury.

Witherspoon was twenty-four years old when he was released. His experience caused him a severe nervous shock. For three years afterward, even when he was preaching, he would be overcome by a sudden and overwhelming feeling that he would die. Those experiences were understandably terrifying. He credited his father with helping to ease him out of crisis. But for the rest of his life, his nerves were easily disturbed. In the words of a friend, he always had to "keep the strictest check on himself."[15] That was, perhaps, one basis for the sympathy John Witherspoon felt for the young and vulnerable James Madison.

After his release, in friendlier arenas, Witherspoon won election as a commissioner to the Kirk, the Scottish General Assembly. He married the strong-minded Elizabeth Montgomery, who would bear him ten children, but not without considerable heartbreak; only five survived to adulthood.* For the decade from 1758 to 1768, he served as a minister of the Laigh Kirk in Paisley, but he never intended to be just an ordinary clergyman—not with the Enlightenment just sweeping the United Kingdom.

WHAT BECAME KNOWN AS THE SCOTTISH ENLIGHTENMENT TOOK ROOT in Edinburgh, Scotland's capital, where the law courts met, the General Assembly convened, and the university community thrived.[16] The movement's leaders were impatient with dogmas clotted with centuries of aged ideas. They strove for realism and common sense and reveled in the simple power of experience. They disliked theorists trumpeting about historical trajectories and the gravitational pull of abstract (and often religious) ideals. They aimed instead for ideas grounded in how people lived and what their physical senses told them about the world. Like many other Enlightenment leaders, Witherspoon developed a dislike for metaphysics and, in later years, usually only used the word with distaste.[17]

As a working cleric, Witherspoon joined the Popular Party of the Church of Scotland, which was in the midst of a clash with the so-called Moderate Party. The conflict was as much cultural as theological.[18] The Moderates saw themselves as refined and worldly, the Populars as pious and humble. The Moderates approved of public dancing and the theater. The Populars thought them vulgar and degrading. The Moderates lampooned the Populars as aloof "Highflyers." The Populars called the Moderates debaucherous equivocators.[19]

The hostility led to vicious internecine battles on church policy. For instance, under the system known as lay patronage, wealthy landowners

---

* After Witherspoon and his family moved to America, his oldest son, James, joined the rebel forces and was killed at the Battle of Germantown. Varnum Lansing Collins, Introduction, in Lectures on Moral Philosophy by John Witherspoon (Princeton, NJ: Princeton University Press, 1912), xvii.

appointed ministers, as opposed to the congregation's democratically choosing its leader. Witherspoon led the Populars in supporting the democratic position.[20] A leading Moderate attacked Witherspoon as "close, and suspicious, and jealous, and always aspiring of a superiority that he was not able to maintain."[21] Witherspoon, in turn, began to assail the Moderates in public.

In 1753, he delivered a lecture, titled "Ecclesiastical Characteristics," with a gibing subtitle: "The Arcana of Church Policy, being an humble attempt to open up the mystery of moderation." Witherspoon assumed the first-person voice of a buffoonish Moderate. "I believe that the universe is a huge machine," he announced sardonically, "consisting of an infinite number of *links* and chains, each in a progressive motion towards the zenith of perfection, and meridian of glory." He derided the Moderates' fatuous assumption that the universe was designed around their own concepts of right and wrong. He believed that there was "no ill in the universe," nor even "virtue absolutely considered." Worse, "those things vulgarly called *sins*" were nothing of the sort; there were instead "foils to set off the beauty of Nature, or patches to adorn her face."[22] In this Alice in Wonderland moral universe, he proclaimed that "even the devils themselves" would be happy, while Judas Iscariot would become "a glorified saint."[23]

The passions were the villains in Witherspoon's public morality play. In an essay that was enthusiastically distributed across Scotland, he warned against the sins of excess and intemperance. Scots needed to guard against "idle fancies" and "romantic suppositions of happiness." He charged them to "set bounds to" and "endeavor to moderate" their passions, instead of voluntarily and unnecessarily exciting them. Persons of "furious and ungoverned tempers," he said, would not be successful, respected, or even useful.[24] He wanted Scots to sublimate their appetites into conviction, in turn translated into purpose—and then power.

That elegantly balanced philosophy became, for Witherspoon, a constant call. A decade later, in 1764, writing from a long stay in London, he introduced a book of his works with a bracing claim. The "immediate and most powerful cause of degeneracy," he declared, was a corruption of principle. *All* moral actions, he would write, must arise from principle.[25]

With that political philosophy firmly in place, Witherspoon openly pursued, like many Enlightenment thinkers (including the economist Adam

Smith, the philosopher David Hume, and the Reverend Thomas Reid), the course of a self-made public intellectual. He came to see his clerical job not as a calling, but as a platform. He could lead not only Scotland, but man, to resist darker seductions and to pursue a horizon illuminated by principle.

His growing fame spread across the Atlantic with the ships bound for America. Leaders in the New World were looking for just such a clarion voice. They began to take note of the Scottish cleric growing famous for his sardonic sense of certainty.

I N 1766, THE COLLEGE OF NEW JERSEY'S TRUSTEES ANNOUNCED A SEARCH for a new president who would give the college "breadth and flexibility, virility and permanence." In November 1766, William Peartree Smith, the board's acting president, sent a letter to Witherspoon, asking him to become the new president of the school informally known as Princeton. Smith's letter was only the beginning of a serious campaign. A delegation sailed for Scotland the next year to appeal to Witherspoon in person. Other preeminent citizens, including Richard Stockton and Dr. Benjamin Rush, sent letters pleading Princeton's case.[26]

Although he seemed interested—very interested—they were unsure whether Witherspoon would ever say yes. His wife, Elizabeth, clearly opposed the prospect, fearing the effects of the transatlantic journey on their children. But she finally acceded to her husband's ambition, and he sent word that he would accept Princeton's offer.

The small Princeton community (consisting of only three professors) had been waiting in limbo for a new leader. One reverend wrote that after the town received the word that Elizabeth "like another Sarah was willing to follow her husband," Witherspoon's name "dwelt upon every tongue." For weeks, Princeton "resounded with nothing but the name of Witherspoon."[27]

After a twelve-week-long voyage, Witherspoon, Elizabeth, and their five exhausted children arrived on Sunday, August 7, 1768. Ann was the oldest; James was a college student; John was eleven; Frances was nine; and David, his father's pet, was eight.[28] They entered a pastoral town surrounded by rolling farmland, oriented around the foundational building of Nassau Hall. The family settled in a small house nearby reserved for the president.

Witherspoon set to interviewing his new colleagues. He was dismayed to find the school polluted with metaphysics. Jonathan Edwards, the third president of the college who had a short-lived tenure in 1758 (he died after two months of smallpox), had been a proud idealist. The idealists believed the universe consisted of minds and ideas, refusing to consider that matter could exist independent of the mind. Their approach led them into unsettling dogmatic fervor; Edwards Sr., in particular, was a "New Light" revivalist, stoking contagious religious celebrations. Witherspoon discovered that Edwards's influence had shaped the entire school. The three tutors—Edwards's son Jonathan; Samuel Johnson, who had tutored President Edwards at Yale; and Bishop Edward Berkeley—were all metaphysicians.

Witherspoon began a purge. By the end of 1769, his first full year, he fired all three tutors, replacing them with tutors more to his liking.[29]

W ITHERSPOON STROVE TO EDUCATE HIS STUDENTS FOR A LIFE NOT just of scholarship, or business, but of impact on the world around them. In a recruitment letter he later sent to potential students, he claimed higher education was necessary for those who "do not wish to live for themselves alone, but would apply their talents to the service of the Public and the good of mankind." Education, he declared, was required for "the benefit of society in offices of power or trust."[30]

Madison was doubtless aware of the great changes at the college he had just entered. But for the time being, he was more focused on the day-to-day challenges of his brand-new world. He took to heart Princeton's formal mission, as enlightened as the president the trustees had bravely chosen: to liberate young minds, to "cherish a spirit of liberty, and free enquiry," and to encourage their right of private judgment, without an "air of infallibility" or demanding an "implicit assent" from their professors.[31]

In August, just after arriving, young Madison revealed his intense impatience. He told Witherspoon he wanted to finish the three years at Princeton in only two years, and he wanted to begin by bypassing the normal freshman curriculum by taking early exams, enabling him to skip the first year. Witherspoon found the request by his slender, shy student surprising but appealing and granted it. The exams required proficiency in Horace, Cicero's *Orations*, the Old Testament in Greek, Lucian's *Dialogues*, and Xenophon's *Cyropaedia*. The rigor he learned from Robertson and Martin bore fruit, and Madison passed the exams.

Madison then approached another student—the studious, earnest Joseph Ross—with his plan. The young men agreed to work together to cram their three years of college into two. With approval from Witherspoon, they began to spend over ten hours a day together studying. The first signs of Madison's intensity, his ability to disappear into a plan or campaign, appeared. Sixty years later, Madison recounted the marathon with almost masochistic satisfaction. His "indiscreet experiment of the minimum of sleep & the maximum of application" was a test, he recalled, of "which the constitution would bear." He slept, he said, for several weeks at a time less than five hours a night. The result was "very infirm health," which he admitted was caused by his "doubled labour."[32]

Why did Madison so urgently need to race through college? He seemed to revel in the bravado of the accomplishment, in the act of bending a rigid curriculum to his will. The damage to his health, he recalled in his old age, came from the "extraordinary exertion made to justify the indulgence granted by the Faculty and to insure the attainment of his object." The old man—intent, as always, to snuff out the slightest flares of his father's hated vanity—emphasized that his was not "any extraordinary achievement." Other students, he asserted, could have done the same with "little more than ordinary exertion."[33]

But he was obviously protesting too much. He was deeply proud of his achievement—as was Witherspoon.

Witherspoon took note of the anxious, intense teenager's tenacity in the classroom. He liked Madison's perspicacity, which was leavened by a dry and sometimes wicked sense of humor. For Madison's part, the men in his life had prepared him to see Witherspoon fondly. His father, too, was a contrarian. Robertson had relished fights against monarchy and hypocrisy. But what was most congenial to him was the older man's impatience with any effort falling short of excellence. With war with Great Britain almost certainly ahead, the desire, the *need*, for action drew the young man and the cleric even closer.

But life at Princeton was not, thank goodness, all seriousness and revolution.

MADISON DISCOVERED THE JOYS OF MALE CAMARADERIE. THE BOYS quickly fell into an imposed routine. A bell first sounded at five o'clock in the morning, rousing the reluctant students. At six, another bell rang, sending them to morning prayers with Witherspoon, who would explore a single Biblical passage at length. After prayers, they studied for an hour—hungry—before eating breakfast at nine a.m. They then studied for three more hours. They scarfed down dinner at one p.m., then enjoyed two hours reserved for recreation, conversation, sports. From three to five p.m., they studied and practiced rhetoric and recitation. At five o'clock, the bell sounded again for evening prayers. Supper was served at seven, and by nine p.m. they were required to be in their rooms.[34]

It was a busy day, meant to end quietly, but with three boys to a room, Madison likely found plenty of time for both extra study and mischief. The college allowed students a dish of tea in their apartments, provided it be "done after evening prayer [and] not interfere with hours of study."[35] The caffeine fomented fervent conversations by candlelight. The mayhem that erupted at night caught shy Madison up like a leaf in a storm. The young men invented ribald names and theatrical characters for one another. They took turns aping their roles, hiding in the dark entryways of Nassau Hall to leap out at and shove one another. They knocked on doors in the small town and then ran off, cackling. They soaked feathers with grease from the cook's heavy supper and strewed them in front of the entryways, pratfalling their friends. Now and then, they stole a plump hen or turkey and let it loose indoors for entertainment. They manufactured packages of gunpowder and exploded them in the rooms of the more timorous boys. In the winter, they poured water into the infernal bell to freeze its constant ringing to their studies.[36]

It was an adolescent maelstrom, with few women anywhere. Wives and daughters in town found themselves the objects of the students' constant fascination. Madison and the other students crowded into each other's already small bedrooms in Nassau Hall late at night, gathering around telescopes to ogle women in town.

His friends *liked* Madison, and cheerfully called him his childhood nickname, Jemmy. They approved of his sincerity, his enthusiasm for ideas, his loyalty, and his defenseless, contagious hilarity. They also liked how much he plainly cared for them—he listened, empathized, and understood. His small head somehow held an ocean of insight into human nature. And even though they knew he was smarter than most of them, they also liked that his sensitivity checked any tendency toward arrogance (he would shrink at a single harsh word, had no desire for public speaking, and exhibited no ability whatsoever to strut). And they loved to poke him about his discomfort about the most crucial topic for them—females.

Madison began making close friends. He was particularly fond of kind, inquisitive William Bradford, who had an oval face, with large eyes, curved eyebrows, a dimpled chin, and a perpetual slight smile. The pair would spend hours on end talking. He also liked the sardonic, irreverent Philip Freneau, with his a mop of messy hair, unruly demeanor, and passion for poetry—a wonderfully colorful character who always seemed to be performing on stage.

Sometimes, Madison found relief from his own intensity by himself. He would frequently take to the woods outside Nassau Hall, accompanied by a slave, to chop wood. He would set up logs, steady them, and swing down his ax, sweating profusely as chips flew around him.[37] The hard exercise stretched his muscles and took him out of his head entirely.

There was an existing social group playfully called the Plain Dealing Society, whose enemy was the Well Meaning Society (later the Clio Society). Out of the first group, Madison, Bradford, and Freneau helped found a debating club they called the Whig Society.[38] The two cliques mirrored the students' home cultures and regions. Southerners and Pennsylvanians dominated among the Whigs, while New Englanders joined the Clios. Madison and the others met in private to brainstorm their strategy for the two societies' beloved "paper wars."

In these contests, they would exchange and then read out verses to outwit the other team. The goal was to be as cutting, outrageous, and intelligent as possible, and to win the favor of the crowd.

Madison, charged with penning lyrics, hatched a new persona: the irrepressible joker. His vulgar scenes were explosively funny. One imagined the other team as "Clio," a seductive and "ever grateful muse." When Clio "sprinkled my head with healing dews," Madison crowed, she "then took me to her private room." We can imagine him or his chosen actor reading out the following lines in an increasingly high falsetto: "And straight an Eunuch out I come," he cried, "my voice to render more melodious, a recompence for sufferings odious!" Clio, under the guise of a temptress, had castrated Whig, which the boys naturally found hilarious.

But Madison could slash with that rapier wit as well. He gained a fearsome reputation for taking subtle—and not so subtle—jabs at peers who had offended him. When a rascally student named Moses Allen was widely rumored to have visited a prostitute, Madison turned on him with a combination of satire and venom. Calling out Allen as a "lecherous rascal," Madison predicted, in rhyming couplets, that he would find a place "just suited to his mind," where he could "whore and pimp and drink and swear," nor "more the garb of Christians wear."

While the verses were read in a spirit of hilarity, they had a cutting edge. Thrown out into that libertine wilderness, Madison said, Allen would "free Nassau from such a pest." He was, cried Madison, "a dunce a fool an ass at best!"[39]

Poor Allen. For his sexual experience, Madison would cast him out not only from Princeton (Nassau) but from Christendom. Madison's Puritanical intolerance in matters of the flesh seemed to know no bounds. He was, after all, almost certainly a virgin. Something about Allen's freedom and recklessness seemed to make the ambitious, driven young man uncomfortable and, perhaps, envious. And so it should come as no surprise that he began taking a special interest in the ancient passions.

3 A *Nexus Imperii*

———————————————◆———————————————

MADISON HAD HEARD THAT ONE FAMOUS LECTURE OF WITHERSPOON'S focused on the passions. When that day arrived, he sat down in the classroom with anticipation. Witherspoon's wife would destroy her husband's own copies of his lectures just before his death,[1] but they would live on through his students, who laboriously recorded nearly every word of the lectures in thick books, which were then bound into leather volumes, passed within families, handed down to descendants and libraries like holy texts. Thaddeus Dod (who would later get into trouble with the passions himself, after impregnating a young woman not his wife) meticulously recorded this lecture.

The teacher stood and sternly stared at the boys. The passions, he declared, were "very numerous, and may be greatly diversified." Every single thing that was the object of desire, he explained, could grow by "accident or indulgence" into a passion. Every one of those passions, he explained, belonged under love or hatred. Passions of love included admiration, desire, and delight, and passions of hatred envy, malice, rage, and revenge. Simple emotions—he gave the examples of hope, fear, joy, and sorrow—were frequently *called* passions, but this was a mistake. They were instead just states of mind, their object "probable or improbable, possessed or lost." The passions, in other words, were like Plato's steeds—physical beings stampeding toward a goal.

Most significantly, Witherspoon explained the other "great and real" distinction between the passions. They were either selfish or benevolent. A selfish passion stemmed from an interest in gratification, whereas a benevolent one came from the happiness of others. And they were either public or private. Public passions included the love of fame, power, and pleasure, while private passions were family affections, friendship, and patriotism. The benevolent, public passions were the noblest ones. And for those, Witherspoon advised his students—Madison listening closely—many brave souls had been willing to sacrifice everything, even their lives.[2]

Madison worked late into the night in his room, bending to take notes from John Locke's "Signs of Ideas." The English philosopher's argument was that our external behavior is related to our mind, and Madison was fascinated by the difference between exterior and interior. Translating into his own words, he wrote that the external signs or marks of ideas included indications of joy, such as smiling, laughing, and others. Indications of sorrow, on the other hand, were dejection, weeping, wailing, paleness, trembling, and blushing.[3] An "Acute Man," he wrote, should be able to penetrate "far into the most secret sentiments and affections of others."

He knew he rarely displayed such "natural signs" himself—except for the appalling attacks that came during his most anxious moments. He was, he knew, more sensitive than most of his friends. The full range of passions—from love to hatred, from public to private—seemed to have a tenfold impact on him. He had always assumed that this made him weak, vulnerable. But now he considered a different proposition altogether. Distilling Locke's thoughts, he scribbled that politicians and "other cunning Men of Business" could, by "great and refin'd dissimulation," confound, and even stifle, the "natural Indications of their inmost thoughts."[4] He put down his quill. Hiding his feelings, he realized, could be a source of strength, not just weakness.

In the ninth of sixteen lectures Witherspoon delivered on morals, he brought the students to the great center: conscience. Conscience, he told the boys, was real, and "much founded in the moral principle." Those who neglected their conscience risked great personal harm—leading not only to misery, but to shame. Self-government demanded that men keep their thoughts, desires, and affections in due moderation.[5] Madison took notes hungrily, the teacher's fierce injunction burning into his mind—into his conscience.

The greater issue, as always, was England. To exert monetary pressure on the kingdom, a wide-ranging group of merchants had agreed no longer to import spirits from England. But a smaller group of New

York merchants had recently buckled to the economic pressure and decided to break the embargo. They then sent a letter encouraging Philadelphia merchants to break the agreement. Word of the letter had quickly spread, and with it, fury at the New York merchants' perfidy.

A group of students donned black gowns and began a solemn procession toward the front lawn of Nassau Hall. Other young men pulled on a rope that led up to the bell atop Nassau Hall. The bell's pealing and the ominous costumes combined to create a haunting effect that hinted at the violence to come.

Once the protesters had gathered in front of Nassau Hall, one student brandished with disgust the merchants' offending letter. A man dressed as a hangman appeared, whom the students theatrically handed the letter, the crowd jeering. The hangman then loudly read a statement declaring the "Promoters of such a daring Breach of Faith" would be "blasted in the Eyes of every Lover of Liberty" and their "Names handed down to Posterity" as "Betrayers of their Country."[6] He set the letter on fire, riveted the crowd as it burnt to ash.

Afterward, back in his room, Madison excitedly described the incident in a letter to his father. The New York merchants were guilty, he said, of "base conduct." The scene at Nassau Hall was awesome, with the students "appearing in their black Gowns & the bell Tolling."[7]

Madison and all the boys were keenly aware that war with Great Britain was looming. Witherspoon, resentful of abusive British rule, openly stoked the flame, urging his students to view the British as occupiers. He took advantage of a college president's unique weapons. Honorary degrees were only usually conferred on renowned clergy at Princeton, but in his first full year at the college, Witherspoon instead made them an instrument of dissent, granting degrees to John Dickinson, Joseph Galloway, and John Hancock—all renowned for defying England.[8]

For the Princeton president, ethics and statecraft had never been separate. In the classroom, his students could not separate the man from his teachings, and young Madison took from Witherspoon not just a set of ideas, but a way of being political in a world where decisions mattered, where a new nation was discovering what it wanted, and did not want, to be. But he was disturbed by one problem: in an uncertain time, how could pernicious ideas be defeated? For that, he paid close attention to his story of history's most famous gadfly.

I N CLASS, MADISON LEARNED ABOUT SOCRATES'S MURDER BY THE GREEK masses he savagely satirized. The philosopher was charged and convicted of worshipping false idols and corrupting the youth who followed him around like the Pied Piper. Madison began using a single word—"Method" (which he carefully capitalized)—to understand why Socrates failed. The teenager captured the Socratic Method—its strengths and weaknesses—as confidently and economically as a philosophy professor. Socrates would "introduce some Topick suitable to his Design," he said, but refrain from declaring his own opinion. He would then start "wheeling the Stream of the Discourse Slyly to his Purpose," only then stunning his opponent "into sudden conviction of an absurdity."

As impressive as Socrates's intellectual sleights of hand were, Madison didn't like them. The problem, he explained, was that the Method was "very captitious and insidious." Even though Socrates would "surprize" his opponent—having "no suspicion of an attack"—that tactic was infuriating, to the point of violence. To "interrogate others in this manner," Madison wrote," is not well taken," and "probably help'd to kindle & blow up that hatred against Socrates, which put a violent Period to his Life."⁹ In other words, the way in which Socrates debated his opponents was so frustrating that they decided they would rather have him dead than so relentlessly expose their faults. When they falsely convicted him of charges of corrupting the youth of Athens and worshipping false gods, they were really venting their fury at his Method.

But young Madison had an alternative in mind. One should "not so much to confute" an opponent's argument, he wrote. Instead, it was far better to "show the superiour advantage" and the "Honour and Justice of your own opinion."¹⁰ Instead of revealing your opponent as a fool, you should instead concentrate on the intensity of your own convictions, the integrity of your own conscience, and the soundness of your own arguments compared with the flaws in your opponents'. What Madison wanted to avoid was the arrogant *authority* on which the Socratic Method depended, which so often ended in trickery. Socrates's Method could not work without elevating the teacher and humiliating the student. A new Method, Madison realized—one that both parties threw on the same field, demanding an open contest between them—could change history.

The brash young scholar was schooling Socrates himself. What he had learned would become, as the boy became a man, the basis of his own very non-Socratic Method.

The great question then was what would inspire his budding young conscience—what Madison would use a new Method *for*. And for that, Witherspoon had an answer as well.

W ITHERSPOON TURNED TO THE TOPIC OF HISTORY. MADISON WATCHED closely as the teacher stood before the students and announced that the study of history was "honorable" and "at present in high repute," and "useful" and "delightful." Yet it was also the bloodiest topic imaginable. He wanted them to understand what they were dealing with.

What they must understand, Witherspoon emphasized, was that men had clawed their way into history from the state of nature. In that primal condition, before society and before government, Witherspoon said, men had

IMAGE 3.1. *JOHN WITHERSPOON*, BY CHARLES WILLSON PEALE, AFTER CHARLES WILLSON PEALE, 1783–1784. COURTESY OF INDEPENDENCE NATIONAL PARK.

fought like beasts for everything they wanted: their food, females, a cave, or a spring. They could use no other weapons, he said, but those furnished by nature—their arms, teeth, fists, and feet. Fury, he stated, was their only guide. In the state of nature, he said, men would "endeavor to destroy, torture, exterminate, and even devour one another."

Devour one another. Without government, Witherspoon believed, men would rip each other apart with their bare hands. They would consume each other's flesh. His portrait of mankind, which could just as easily have appeared in a ghoulish painting by Brueghel or Goya, was bloodier and more brutal even than Thomas Hobbes's "poore, nasty, brutish, and short" state of nature. Hobbes had been writing after the massacres of the English Civil War, where he had witnessed men reduced to their bestial selves. But Witherspoon had experienced Doune Castle. All alone, as the solitary target of his torturers, he had evidently concluded that man, without restraint, was even worse.

He was briefly overcome and abruptly interrupted himself. "Let us," he announced, "leave their horrible state."* Madison and the others were left to contemplate man himself in a harsh new light. Man could only escape his brutal nature through government. But each form of government had damning weaknesses—and democracy was no exception at all.

WITHERSPOON LED HIS STUDENTS THROUGH THE BRAMBLES OF history. Of the three forms of government, Witherspoon said, he sympathized the most with monarchy, which had plain advantages in "unity, secrecy, and expedition."[11] Monarchy's weakness lay not in its principle, but in the difficulty of finding men with the ability to command other men as capably and simply as an army: "No man can be found," he declared, who had "either skill sufficient, or if he had, could give attention to the whole departments of a great empire."[12] And he said that a hereditary monarchy could provide no security whatsoever for either wisdom or goodness.[13]

More than anything else, every nation needed wisdom in its deliberations, and that, he said, should give aristocracy an advantage over all the

---

* Abel Johnson, "Lectures on History" by the Reverend John Witherspoon, president of New Jersey College, 1784, John Witherspoon Collection, Box 1, Folder 40, Princeton Library, 1–43.

other forms. In an aristocracy, the "persons of first rank" would be able to discover the public interest. But aristocracy also had a fatal flaw: the inherent fractiousness of elites, who have "little, or no prospect of fidelity or union." On the contrary, aristocracies, he said, lead to the "most violent and implacable factions."[14]

Witherspoon collected his thoughts; his students waited, quills poised. Democracy, Witherspoon said finally, was superior to both of the others for fidelity, because the multitude were collectively "true in intention to the interest of the public, because it is their own." But there was a dark side to this collective truth. Democracy, he continued, had "very little advantage for wisdom, or union" and "none at all for secrecy, and expedition." And there was a broader vulnerability as well: demagogues and other "ambitious persons." In the ancient Greek, a demagogue was a "leader of the people." A demagogue, by insinuating himself into the people's graces, could create a separate power center within democracy, ultimately destroying and overturning the system. Perversely, the demagogue launched that cycle through the people themselves, so "very apt to trust a man who serves them well, with such power as that he is able to make them serve him."[15]

However, democracy also could draw brilliance from its leaders. "Democracy is the nurse of eloquence," Witherspoon went on, because when the multitude had power, "persuasion is the only way to govern them."[16]

Witherspoon was building up to his Holy Grail—an alchemical answer to the conflict between the three pure forms. No one of the three, he told them, could exist on its own. Every good government must be "complex," so that "the one principle may check the other." Madison took notes furiously. "They must be so balanced," the professor said, so that when "every one draws to his own interest or inclination," there would be an "over poise upon the whole."[17]

In other words, it was not as simple as planting the three forms separately. They must be interwoven like a rope's fibers, so that when one element demanded attention, it would pull on the others.

This, Witherspoon declared, was a "nexus imperii."

Some students frowned at the unfamiliar Latin phrase, but Madison must have understood it immediately. Nexus came from the verb necto, which means "to tie, bind, or weave something together." In the modern sense, imperio means "power." The "binding of power" is what Witherspoon meant by his phrase.[18] "Something to make one of them necessary to the other," Witherspoon explained. Otherwise, they would "not only draw different ways," but would "often separate altogether from each other."

That would not do. The way to prevent the strands separating—the rope from fraying—was by splitting the "great essential rights of rulers" among the different branches of government. The readiest example, he said, was Great Britain, where one branch had the power of making war and peace, but the British Parliament had the levying and distribution of money. That power over money, he concluded, was a sufficient restraint on all.[19]

Another harsh secret Witherspoon disclosed to his students about democracy: liberty was not necessary to the virtue a democracy would supposedly produce, because virtue was "perhaps equally possible" in *every* form of government. Furthermore, he rejected the idea that liberty would produce happiness in democracies, because they actually had more "impatience and discontent" than any other form.

Liberty's only true advantage, Witherspoon declared, was in what it could do for humanity itself. In the grand sum of things, liberty could "put in motion all the human power" by promoting industry, and thus happiness. In that cool assessment, liberty was desirable not for moral or metaphysical reasons, but because it produces "every latent quality" and because it improves the human mind. Liberty, he told them, was the "nurse of riches, literature and heroism."[20]

It was a reasoned assessment of an aspiration that could inflame men to topple governments. And Madison found it profoundly attractive. But liberty itself was not so carefully contained; on the contrary, he watched as the storms of an unsettled time surged through Princeton's bucolic campus.

During Madison's last year at Princeton, Witherspoon watched with dismay as a mysterious explosion of religious sentiment took over the school. In 1772, students began chattering excitedly about the power of the Christian faith to transform the nation. What became known as the great Princeton "revival" incensed its president, who deemed the viral event "not true and rational religion, but fanaticism."[21] His own religiosity—like the one Madison would take away from Princeton like a compass—charted a careful course through the shoals of excess, grandiosity, and arrogance. Witherspoon was interested in probity, not popularity. Lecturing divinity students at Princeton about the revival, he said that, whatever one's calling or profession, "the salvation of our souls is the one thing needful."[22]

Madison was growing to appreciate freedom in an entirely new way. Sometime in his final year of college, it is possible that Madison had his own run-in with the passions, with a mysterious "pretty Philadelphian."* The relationship was serious enough for Madison to commission an ivory locket by the well-regarded artist Charles Willson Peale, into which Madison sealed a lock of his own hair.

But his father would not make things so easy.

IN WHAT WAS SUPPOSED TO BE HIS FINAL YEAR AT PRINCETON, MADISON opened a letter from his father to find a disturbing request. James Madison Sr. wanted him to find a friend willing to come down to Orange County to tutor his sisters and brothers. But the letter contained no information about the salary his father would pay or the duration he would expect. With a sinking feeling, Madison realized that the tutor might end up being him.

In the days ahead, he haplessly took his parent's vague demand to one friend, then another, but they wanted, of course, to know the compensation first. In late July, Madison frantically wrote his father that he had spoken to several members of the senior class about serving as his tutor, but that none would commit unless they "knew what you would allow them." He complained that they could not "remain in suspense" until after he had returned

---

* For many years, it was assumed that an ivory miniature of Madison painted by Charles Willson Peale was given to Kitty Floyd, whom he would meet in 1783 and become briefly engaged to. But consider that in his portrait, Madison looks much younger than thirty-two years old. He looks twenty-one—the age he would have been in college. Also, the miniature he received from Kitty—long assumed to be one of a pair the couple exchanged that year—was dramatically different from another made of her that same year. The one of Madison was also made to hold hair, whereas Kitty's was not. Most important, in a paper discovered with Madison's miniature, a descendant of Madison's sister Nelly Hite wrote, "While President Madison was attending Princeton College, aged 20–1, family tradition says, his heart was captured by a pretty Philadelphian, who accepted his offer of heart and hand. . . . Alas! The fair one proved false and returned the locket. It was an unpleasant reminder of his disappointment, so he sent it to his sister Nelly who [later] gave it to her only daughter Nelly." Virginia Moore, *The Madisons* (New York: McGraw-Hill, 1979), 36.

IMAGE 3.2. JAMES MADISON AT PRINCETON, BY CHARLES WILLSON PEALE.
COURTESY OF THE LIBRARY OF CONGRESS.

from his next trip back home to Virginia with the answer. He pleaded with his father, by the middle of September at the latest, to tell him the "most you would be willing to give," in which case, "I think there would be a greater probability of my engaging one for you."[23]

But his father never provided the figure, effectively trapping his son in the web of a proposal that was really a requirement. Madison, of course, failed to find a replacement. And so he realized he would have to come home and do the job himself. Agonized, on October 9, Madison wrote for permission to stay the winter. He vainly attempted to manipulate Madison Sr. through his weak spot—money. After telling him of his "past & future expences," he said he had reached a "bare competency" with his father's funds, which he would "not ascribe to extravagance." Yes, he could come home in the spring, but that would require the purchase of a horse and expenses for the journey, which, he said, "I am apprehensive will amount to more than I can reserve out of my present Stock." He asked his father for "a few Half-Jos" in exchange (a Johannes—"Jo" for short—was a valuable gold Portuguese coin commonly used in America). Otherwise, he reiterated his decision to stay in Princeton for the winter ("I need say nothing more in this place, my sentiments being still the same."[24])

In one version of the autobiography he wrote six decades later (transcribed by an anonymous author who emphasized "These facts are authentic. They are cop[ied] from his own pen."), Madison rationalized that he stayed because "intense study had left him too weak to make the journey home."[25] But he stayed because he wanted to.

His graduation date was scheduled for the last Wednesday of September 1771. Among the twelve graduating students, he was the only one who was not there. He felt too agitated and nauseated to appear in public. Irving Brant argued that though other historians have speculated Madison was simply ill at the graduation, he was instead likely suffering from "his physical debility due to overstudy" combined with "his diffidence about public speaking."[26] In other words, the problem, as ever, was anxiety.

Having wrestled his respite for the winter and spring from his father, he studied the most advanced liberal arts available—Hebrew, theology, moral philosophy, and history with Witherspoon—effectively becoming Princeton's first graduate student. He contemplated a future in the clergy, Witherspoon's great example beckoning yet more urgently.

Through the winter, he clung to the place—the late-night conversations; the private lessons with Witherspoon; the close, woodsmoke-scented warmth of Nassau Hall. But when April came, he sadly reconciled himself to the long return home.

MADISON STEPPED UP ONTO HIS HORSE IN PRINCETON. HE GAZED AT THE cobblestone underfoot, the rocks on a winding road that would inevitably route him back to his father's house. While his life should have been commencing, he was instead a man without a profession. With the ferment of New York and Philadelphia so tantalizingly close, and with war in the air, he feared the journey back to the parochial countryside of Orange. He began the long trip home with a sense of dread, a familiar anxiety closing in on him.

4 The High Tract of Public Life

ITOOK THE MEN ABOUT TWO DAYS TO REACH WILLIAM BRADFORD'S HOUSE in Philadelphia. The friends welcomed and embraced each other, Madison's spirits immediately lifting. Over meals at the Bradfords' London Coffee Shop, they regaled Bradford's family with stories about Princeton, gossiping about their classmates—the ones getting married, the ones indecently occupied, the ones who would be famous, who were dying or already dead.

After the visit ended, Madison took back to the road. *Plock plock plock* went the horses' hoofs, syncopating a depressing journey back in time. The journey took another week before he arrived back on the plantation. Approaching the mansion's porch, his parents welcomed him, his siblings scrambled around him. The eldest brother, returned! In the days to come, aunts, uncles, cousins stopped by for cider, for dinner, to talk and inquire, to hear what he'd learned, to ask him, over and over, what he was going to *do*. Would he be a lawyer? A planter?

But for Madison, the arc of his young life was flattening, the momentum disappearing. He was going to stay there, at home, in the dead-end occupation of a tutor—a *tutor!*

"IHAVE UNDERTAKEN TO INSTRUCT MY BROTHERS AND SISTERS IN SOME OF the first rudiments of literature," Madison informed Bradford in a tone of frustration, "but it does not take up so much of my time." Why was he so bothered that he wasn't busy? He was burning up with excess energy. It was like running full speed into a stone fence. "[I] shall always have leisure to recieve and answer your letters which are very grateful to me I assure you," he told Bradford, "and for reading any performances you may be kind enough to send me whether of Mr. Freneau or any body else."[1]

IMAGE 4.1. PORTRAIT OF WILLIAM BRADFORD, BY WILLIAM E. WINNER.
COURTESY OF THE NATIONAL GALLERY OF ART.

He *did* have extra time, but he spent it on the stifling role of full-time
eldest brother. Madison was twenty-one when he returned home. His brothers
Francis, Ambrose, Willey, and Reuben were nineteen, seventeen, ten, and
one. His sisters Nelly, Sarah, and Elizabeth were twelve, eight, and four. He
began tutoring Nelly, Willey, and Sarah in literature, grammar, mathematics,
Latin, Greek, and French. Every morning, he sat down in the house with the
trio and worked through lesson plans, dividing each day and each week carefully into segments.

His mother, almost always in sight, was fiercely glad to have her eldest
back in the home. Throughout her long life, Nelly was both doting and over-
wrought. She was, first of all, kind; in an interview with a longtime docent
from Montpelier, I heard a long-repeated story that Nelly always kept a candy
jar nearby for the children who would visit and that she darned socks for children with their names.[2] William Cabell Rives, who knew Madison personally

IMAGE 4.2. *NELLY MADISON*, BY CHARLES PEALE POLK. COURTESY OF BELLE GROVE.

and wrote the first authoritative biography of him in 1859, described his devoted tenderness toward his mother and how Madison "ever recurring with anxious thoughtfulness, in the midst of his most important preoccupations" attended to her "delicate health."[3] When she was a young bride, Madison Sr.'s envious cousin Joseph Chew complained that his cousin James was so completely absorbed by his "young, agreeable wife." A "few hours," he complained, "is due to your friend," but, he admitted, a wife like Nelly could "certainly make moments slide away pleasantly."[4]

While sweet-natured, Nelly was also high-strung and hypersensitive. To have her first baby, she traveled to be with her mother in Port Royal, a town that still sits, quiet and small, about sixty miles from Montpelier; Madison was born in Port Royal. In one of many draft autobiographies he took up and then discarded as an adult, Madison recalled that in his "earliest years" he was taught the "ordinary elements" in a school in Port Royal, while "living at his house with his grandmother."[5]

Why did his parents send their first child away? Perhaps it had something to do with the wildness of life on the frontier at Mount Pleasant. And what were the effects on a young boy of living away from his mother and father, with his maternal grandmother, for long stretches of time? Even as a teenager, Madison had become strikingly independent. But he also exhibited painful sensitivity to slights and threats to his health. Perhaps he took away a sense of specialness and vulnerability—and reserve—through his removal from the family seat.

He also saw a powerful hypochondria in his mother. Like her son, she seemed almost constantly to be ill. The specter of her sickness cast a pall over the house and was echoed in Madison's later continuing melodrama about his health.

Yet a Frenchman visiting Montpelier in 1816 revealed what might be an (if not *the*) origin of Nelly's constant illnesses. The visitor recorded that Nelly, then eighty-six, was a "very active women" who "enjoys perfect health" and "busies herself with the different occupations of her sex, as in the flower of her youth." He had learned, he said, that Nelly had been "delicate and a semi-invalid" until she turned seventy, where her health had suddenly improved.[6] Madison's father also died when Nelly was about seventy. It seems unlikely that Nelly's bursting into life exactly when her husband passed from life was a coincidence.

But she always stayed close to her first son. When Madison retired to Montpelier with his wife, Dolley, after serving two terms as president in 1817, long after his father had died in 1801, Nelly was still there. In his retirement, Rives wrote, Madison was "personally watching over and nursing her old age with such pious care that her life was protracted to within a few years of the term of his own."[7] James and Dolley would take care of Nelly until she died in 1829, at the age of ninety-eight.

I N THE HOUSE, SURROUNDED BY HIS MOTHER, HIS FATHER, AND HIS SIBLINGS, the hours plodded by. Madison mournfully looked outside at the placid landscape. It did not change. It *never* changed. His father checked in now and then on the school for siblings, before heading out to survey the slaves and measure the crops; his mother oversaw the preparation of meals, asking her children gentle but probing questions to assess their progress.

As bogged down as he felt, Madison always took good care of his brothers and sisters. As chief of a band of siblings, he displayed warmth and authority among them. But his relations with his siblings also featured a ruminative and insecure side. That doubling—of confidence and sensitivity, warmth and neediness—is common to eldest brothers.[8] Madison was particularly anxious about his wandering, wayward, but loveable younger brother Willey. When he had returned home from college and Willey began college at William and Mary, their cousin, the Reverend James Madison, was the president of the college. William and Mary was in the midst of a radical restructuring; the Board of Visitors had just decided to remove the grammar school and two schools of divinity, in the process of deemphasizing religion and the humanities at the expense of a new, more technocratic focus on the hard sciences.

Madison felt keenly the risks for Willey and believed his brother's malleable nature required the deep sort of humanistic learning he himself had received to shore up his wandering tendency. Madison wrote his father in exasperation that he was "much at a loss how to dispose of Willey." "I can not think it would be expedient in the present state of things to send him out of the State," he fretted, but at William and Mary, there was "nothing new to be taught but the higher & rarer branches of Science." Madison urged his father to install Willey instead in private schools or academies, but he said he must be very particular; Willey's sensitive character required it. Madison recommended to his father that Willey be sent home, where he would study English, geography, and arithmetic until he was mature enough to return to William and Mary.[9]

In April 1781, when Madison had entered his second year as a congressman in Philadelphia, he again chose to advise his father on Willey. He was "well pleased," he wrote, that Willey had turned to thinking seriously about studying the law, but he worried that his preparatory studies had not been "sufficiently ripened for the purpose." He went on to suggest that Willey "place himself in a situation for alternately persuing both" his studies *and* the law, as well as move near a respectable court where he could learn the rules of law practice. Madison fixedly concluded, "It is of great importance that no time be lost." Madison, a failed student of law, probably had no business advising anyone on success as a practicing lawyer. But he shouldered Willey's burdens as if they were his own.

That pattern continued in later years. In 1787, after the Constitutional Convention, Willey ventured a plan to enter politics. Madison was in New

York at the time, trying to push the document through Congress, yet still found time to write his brother Ambrose, about Willey's plan, "I am at a loss what to say." Politics did not, Madison said impatiently, "call for much personal sacrifice" (which was what the indulgent Willey needed above all). Nor did he think Willey would earn "the honor, the profit or the pleasure of the undertaking." Further, Willey should "not make an attempt without a tolerable certainty of success." What he really wanted his brother to do was to take more time for the "only durable as well as honorable plan": to "establish a character that merits" winning office.

The most succor the eldest brother would grudgingly offer his impetuous younger brother for his political ambition was this: "I would not be understood to discountenance the measure."[10]

M ERE MONTHS AFTER HE HAD RETURNED HOME, MADISON OPENED A letter from William Bradford to find a terrible shock. Bradford began with the tender address, "My dear Jemmy" and regaled Madison with the story of his recent graduation from Princeton. Bradford was suffering the bittersweet sensation of leaving a warm and beloved place for an uncertain future. "I leave Nassau Hall with the same regret," he told Madison, "that a fond son would feel who parts with an indulgent mother to tempt the dangers of the sea." He informed Madison he was disappointed that the latter hadn't traveled north for the commencement. "I had some expectations of seeing you & Ross there," he wrote, referring to Joe Ross, who also had left Princeton.

"But alas!" Bradford wrote. "You have doubtless heard of Poor Joe's death."

Madison's stomach must have dropped. Bradford closed with kindness, as if he knew the news of his study partner's early death would wound Madison. "When you write be particular," he urged, for nothing that "concerns my dear Jemmy" could be "indifferent to one who esteems it his happiness."[11]

Madison painfully realized that life was short, indeed.

5 "The Annals of Heaven"

———————————◆———————————

JOE ROSS'S DEATH INTENSIFIED MADISON'S DISQUIET ABOUT HIS PRESENT AND future. Notwithstanding, he quickly adopted the role of mentor to Bradford, who was struggling with his own future. "Strong desires and great Hopes instigate us to arduous enterprises, fortitude, and perseverance," he responded to his friend. "Nevertheless a watchful eye must be kept on ourselves, lest while we are building ideal monuments of Renown and Bliss here, we neglect to have our names enrolled in the Annals of Heaven." Bradford took Madison's advice and studied law. He would later become attorney general of Pennsylvania.

As for Madison, at twenty-two, the itch for immortal achievements had taken root in his character. The more he struggled against that desire, the more he was entangled in it. The aches returned to his stomach. He felt trapped and suffocated in the house and could not fathom what he would do with his life, how he would make his mark.

There was a strong belief at the time in the curative, almost baptismal effect of mineral spring waters. Years later, Madison's mother, experiencing what her husband called a "most troublesome and weakening disorder," would consult with eminent physicians and take a wide variety of medicine for four long years—to no effect. Then, after she bathed in and drank the water of a sulfurous mineral spring for several weeks, Madison's father breathlessly described his "inexpressible satisfaction and pleasure" that she had overcome her "deplorable state." Through the "salutary virtue of the water," he proudly exclaimed, his wife had been restored—and was even "fatter than she ever was before."[1]

Now, Madison decided to escape Montpelier for the hot springs of the Alleghany Highlands.[2] James and Nelly agreed to fund a restorative trip west for their complaining, nervous son. Loaded with several weeks of supplies and his parents' blessings, Madison and Sawney took to the road.

The two men followed the trail away from Montpelier. The horses jounced and jostled on the red-orange clay road as the house receded in the background, shimmering slightly in the humid July air. Horseflies buzzed around Madison's ears, magenta sprays of redbud decorating the dark walls of forest.

At once, he must have felt lighter, less encumbered. The 120-mile trip took about four days. Finally, the pair arrived. The pool rested like a small blue-green jewel in the vast Shenandoah Valley. A few thousand feet away, the gentle hills soared up and away, blanketed with deciduous trees and pines. There was almost no sound, save for the falling waters. A sulfurous odor—at once grating and strangely pleasant—suffused the air. A broad circular pool, some twenty feet in diameter, sat placidly, while an overflow channel steadily splashed into a stream.

The pool was about six feet deep, and so Madison, upon slipping into the water, was either quickly underwater or clinging to the stony side. The water, heated by natural springs, always stayed slightly warm, like breath itself. Madison, looking into the glassy surface, saw himself—his thin nose, his small eyes, his shock of thinning hair, his pale skin. He looked through his face to the pool's depths, to the bottom, filled with thousands of pebbles and smooth rocks, painted with a blue-green surface of algae.

With the combination of the water's warmth, the devilish scent, the blue-green depths, and the gentle lapping as his fellows entered and left the pool, Madison quieted, the unease in his stomach and nerves settling. No surprise that he would go often to the pools and encourage his friends to do the same. In late October 1779, when Bradford was ailing, Madison would write to encourage him to travel to Virginia to enjoy the "beneficial affects" for his health that "I flatter myself" had helped Madison so much.[3]

The waters were balm for Madison's choked ambitions, the physical effects of his anxiety. They become another instance of his personal system of checks and balances.

WHEN HE RETURNED, ORANGE COUNTY SEEMED EVEN MORE STAID, especially in contrast to the ferment of Princeton and the bonhomie of Philadelphia. Day by day in that autumn of 1772, Madison began to feel trapped. As autumn descended coolly on the Blue Ridge, he told Bradford to prevent the "impertinent fops that abound in every City" from diverting him from "your business and philosophical amusements." Those "fops," Madison believed, would pursue Bradford because of his "indignation at their follies" and because he—with his habitual discretion and good taste—would keep them at a "becoming distance."[4] As for his part, Madison told his friend, he was "luckily out of the way at such troubles," but he imagined they were virtually swarming Bradford, "for they breed in Towns and populous places, as naturally as flies do in the Shambles."[5]

He would not admit, even to himself, his plain envy of the sirens Bradford had to avoid. Although Madison protested that he was above such degraded seductions, he would have traded his father's pristine home for such "shambles" in an instant. He hated his remove from the flow of ideas and the clash of events. "You are the only valuable friend I have settled in so public a place," he told Bradford, and so "must rely on you for an account of all literary transactions in your part of the world."[6]

He badly missed the friendship of school, the ease of conversation and the bonding around ideas in the close quarters of Nassau Hall. For the rest of his life, he would seek to re-create that intensity of friendship around ideas wherever he could, whether with Thomas Jefferson, Alexander Hamilton, George Washington, or James Monroe.

After a long winter, the air began to warm, bringing along Madison's nostalgia for a life of ideas. In April 1773, he yearningly asked Bradford to write to him "when you feel as you used to do when we were under the same Roof and you found it a recreation and release from Business and Books to come and chat an hour or two with me." In the country, he complained, he was "too remote from the Post" even to have the luxury of immediately expressing himself through a letter.[7]

He felt stuck and frantic. But he spent another three seasons at home— summer, fall, winter—until, finally, he had had enough.

In the freezing month of January 1774, he sent an agonized letter from his effective prison to his friend.

"I WANT AGAIN TO BREATHE YOUR FREE AIR," HE CRIED TO BRADFORD. HIS anxiety, intensified at Montpelier, gave free rein to his hypochondria. He conflated Philadelphia's cosmopolitan culture with health-giving properties. "I expect it will mend my Constitution," he declared, and "confirm my principles." Immersion in a fresh city—brimming with new ideas and new people—would, like the pools, make him well. He had, he complained, "nothing to brag of as to the State and Liberty of my Country."[8]

He told Bradford he was lucky to be "dwelling in a Land where those inestimable privileges are fully enjoyed" and where people had "long felt the good effects of their religious as well as Civil Liberty." The difference was cultural; outsiders, as well as new ideas, were welcomed in Philadelphia: "Foreigners have been encouraged to settle amg. you." Diversity, pluralism, and progressivism followed. "Industry and Virtue" stoked by "mutual emulation and mutual Inspection," the "Commerce and Arts" flourishing. The cause was the "continual exertions of Genius," which were always accompanied by Philadelphians' "love of Fame and Knowledge."

Virginia's closed thinking was dramatically different. In his Commonwealth, he lamented, "religious bondage shackles and debilitates the mind" for every "noble enterprize" and every "expanded prospect."[9]

He asked his friend for a reprieve. Bradford happily agreed to host Madison on a visit to Philadelphia. Madison excitedly packed his bags for the trip. In the beginning of May, he traveled to stay with Bradford for a few days, before and after a trip to Albany whose purpose is unknown.[10]

Stirring Philadelphia lit a lamp in Madison's mind. When he returned to Orange County, he was afire for a life of true principle. It seemed a perfect time for his awakening, coinciding with the pitiless harassment in Virginia of a defenseless religious minority. The question was what Madison would do about it.

I N THE SPRING OF 1774, CELL DOORS SHUT ON FIVE MEN IN CULPEPER, A deeply conservative county about twenty miles north of Montpelier. The prisoners were Baptists who had been traveling throughout central Virginia, distributing tracts proclaiming their faith. They were proclaiming their direct connection to God (circumventing clergy) and their skepticism about the Anglican Church's sweeping power in government. After they arrived in Culpeper, the sheriff jailed them for the crime of preaching without a required license. But their real offense was challenging the Anglicans.

Through heavy recruitment and a dizzying service style marked by their ministers' "holy whine" and wild gesticulations, Baptists had been spreading through Virginia like wildfire; in 1771, there had been fourteen churches throughout the Piedmont; in 1772, thirty-four; and by 1774, fifty-four. By 1776, the year of the Revolution, there would be seventy-four Baptist churches in Virginia.[11] In almost every respect, this contagious growth undermined both the Anglicans' theology and their practice. The Baptists regularly elevated unlearned leaders to ministers, finding a natural congregant base among the poor and the illiterate, which the Anglicans saw instead as the blasphemous seduction of the ignorant.[12] Like Witherspoon's Moderates in Scotland, they infuriated their established opponents. They seemed ungovernable, a tribe of passionate separatists who refused to ask permission to pray in public, to assemble, to protest.

In the General Assembly, "incredible and extravagant stories" were circulated about the Baptists, describing the "monstrous effects" of their "Enthusiasm." The outrage of the paranoid attacks lay in their very baseness—their appeal to the lowest common denominator. The audacity was precisely what made the Baptists so weak. The Baptists were "so greedily swallowed by their Enemies," Madison darkly observed, that they "lost footing by it." Their oppressors were "too much devoted" to the Anglican establishment even to "hear of the Toleration of Dissentients."[13]

Madison saw in the Baptists conscience that deserved protection from the state rather than oppression. The Baptists, after all, weren't pursuing state power or tax revenue. They were promoting their faith in baptism, their practice of plunging adherents into the cool waters of Virginia's rivers and lakes to cleanse their sins. But they were now crying out for food through the cold bars of their jail. Their captors threw them only dry crusts of rye bread to eat. One tormentor even stood on a stool and urinated through the bars into their cell.[14]

The inhumane treatment became notorious throughout Virginia. In Orange, young Madison was enraged. As an older man, Madison recollected that he was under "very early and strong impressions in favour of Liberty both Civil and Religious." His conscience, he said, led him to spare "no exertion to save" the Baptists from imprisonment.[15] At the time, he proudly told Bradford that he "squabbled and scolded abused and ridiculed" the shameful action with everyone he could.[16] He later recalled that the "interposition" was "a mere duty prescribed by conscience."[17] He had absorbed Witherspoon's teachings entirely; he simply had no choice in the matter.

Everywhere he went and with anyone he thought could make a difference, he remonstrated on behalf of the imprisoned men. Their crime, he wrote Bradford, was simply publishing "religious sentiments" that were actually "very orthodox."[18] Bradford sympathetically responded, "I am sorry to hear that Persecution has got so much footing among you." But he couldn't resist a jab at his friend's bumpkin land. "The description you give of your Country," he informed Madison, "makes me more in love with mine."[19] Persecution, he declared, was a "weed that grows not in our happy soil." He could not even recall a single person being imprisoned for his religious beliefs, "however heritical or unepiscopal they might be."[20]

In late March, Madison proudly reported to Bradford that a contingent of Virginians was attempting to rescue the Baptists. With the General Assembly scheduled to meet on May 1, defenders of the imprisoned men began circulating petitions in central Virginia and the Shenandoah Valley. Meanwhile, a clutch of Presbyterians were planning a direct intervention with the Culpeper authorities. Madison was at once enthusiastic and skeptical, admitting to Bradford that he was "very doubtful of their succeeding in the Attempt."[21]

Frighteningly, with the arrival of hot Virginia months, he watched the persecution begin to spread beyond the Baptists. When James Herdman, a Scottish parson, refused to observe the Sunday fast required by the Anglicans, more Culpeper politicians sent a delegation to demand he comply. "When called on," Madison wrote admiringly, he "pleaded Conscience." Inspired, Madison wrote that Herdman was "alledging that it was his duty to pay no regard to any such appointments made by unconstitutional authority." Drily, he observed that the politicians seemed to "have their Consciences too." They ordered the sheriff to seal the doors of Herdman's church and stop his salary.

For young Madison, the affair echoed Witherspoon's battles between conscience and power, minority and majority. He described for Bradford the notorious case of John Wingate, a reverend who had angered the local Anglicans so intensely that they publicly considered tarring and feathering him. At the last minute, Wingate recanted. Madison was not impressed. Once Wingate noticed that he would be protected "not so much in the law as the favor of the people," he satirically observed, he became "very supple & obsequious."[22]

He was disgusted by the fact that, all around him, conscience always seemed to play David to power's Goliath. He blamed culture. The Virginia gentry's sentiments were "vastly different," he told Bradford, from "what you have been used to." Virginia, with its profound cultural connections to the

English landed class and Anglican religion, differed radically from Pennsylvania's immigrant culture. Philadelphians had a "liberal catholic and equitable way of thinking as to the rights of Conscience" that was "little known," he remarked angrily, among the "Zealous adherents of our Hierarchy."[23]

For Madison, diversity led to challenge, challenge to truth—and truth to wisdom. Witherspoon's beacon was shining above the storm. The twenty-three-year-old, fresh off his birthday, began formulating his vision of a future free of tyranny.

ON CHRISTMAS DAY 1773, AS MADISON SETTLED INTO HIS SECOND LONG winter at home, tutoring, Bradford clipped a story from a Philadelphia newspaper about the stunning "tea party" in Boston. He folded the article and inserted it in an envelope he addressed to Madison, along with a letter relishing the "Destruction of the Tea at Boston."[24] Madison read Bradford's words with a combination of jealousy and atavistic pride. He was thrilled the British were being repulsed in the north, but he badly wanted his more desultory Commonwealth to do the same.

As he pondered whether such a revolution could happen in Virginia, he gradually came to a crucial insight. He picked up his quill. If the Church of England remained the established religion in the colonies, Madison argued, then "slavery and Subjection" would be "gradually insinuated among us." Such "Ecclesiastical Establishments," he excitedly explained, "tend to great ignorance and Corruption," which only lead to "mischievous Projects." The destruction of a state monopoly on religion could leave behind not spiritual anarchy or nihilism, but instead an archipelago of principled beliefs. "I verily believe," he wrote, that the "frequent Assaults" on America would "in the end prove of real advantage."[25]

This picture, in turn, led Madison to a fresh new thought about the power of federalism—of a nation comprised of vigorous and competing states. Two centuries later, Justice Louis Brandeis would enthusiastically describe the states as "laboratories of democracy."[26] Witherspoon had lectured at Princeton that "every good form of government" must be "complex, so that the one principle may check the other." Madison realized now that if a single religion were allowed to entrench itself through state government, it would colonize the minds of all the citizens. The differences between Virginia and Pennsylvania, as seen in the tea party, *were* the country's strength. Through its own squabbling elements—its own Bradfords and Madisons—the young nation would learn to embrace the checks and balances inherent in human belief itself.[27]

In the coming months, Madison continued to devour the news. As he stewed on the oppression of the British, he became not only a war hawk, but a distinctly impatient one. "Would it not be advisable as soon as possible to begin our defence & to let its continuance or cessation depend on the success of a petition presented to his majesty," he wrote Bradford. Delay only "emboldens our adversaries and improves their schemes," he wrote. Meanwhile, waiting would degrade the "ardor of the Americans inspired with recent Injuries" while giving an opportunity to "our secret enemies to disseminate discord & disunion."[28]

Public opinion, he felt, needed to be galvanized—and quickly.

Meanwhile, Bradford conscientiously apprised Madison of the strange tensions building at Princeton, where people were suddenly having apocalyptic visions. In August 1774, he wrote Madison, "Indeed my friend the world wears a strange aspect at the present day; to use Shakespeare's expression 'the times seem to be out of joint.'" It was not just the Indians, or the British, or the turmoil in Europe—it was everything together, a combination that created the disorienting sensation that the end of the days were afoot. "Something at hand," Bradford believed, would "greatly augment the history of the world." People everywhere were calculating the "commencement of the Millenium in the present Century."

It seemed, Bradford wrote, as if they were all heading toward the "consummation of all things." Indeed, when the "plot thickens," everyone expected the "conclusion of the drama."[29]

But Bradford wasn't waiting for the apocalypse. He wanted Congress to begin "effectually warding off the attacks of Slavery and fixing the boundaries of Liberties." He believed the nation most needed the confirmation and the grant of "certain rights" necessary to liberty. But he was pessimistic; the delegates in Philadelphia, he thought, lacked unanimity. Several of them, he observed, were even "inimical to the Liberties of America."[30]

Madison responded with a rare admonishment. While he greatly admired the "wisdom of the advice & the elegance and cogency" of instructions that had been given to Philadelphia's delegates, mere words would not be enough against the British. He questioned Bradford's proposal of "deferring all endeavors" until America received concessions from England. Instead, he declared, Americans should take the offensive—immediately. The impatient young man told Bradford it would be "advisable as soon as possible to begin our defence." Only then should a petition be delivered to the king.[31]

Madison was agitating to attack *now*. Pennsylvania had recently elected two well-known doves to Congress; that, he told Bradford, augured only "difficulties and divisions" ahead. But even worse, he said, were the "selfish Quakers in your House," who, in their maddening denial of any right of government to use violence, would "frustrate the generous designs & manly efforts of the real friends to American Freedom."[32]

James Rivington—the publisher of the influential *Gazetteer*—especially enraged Madison. Rivington was a dignified, gentlemanly figure who had emigrated from London in 1760. He had initially stayed neutral in the brewing conflict. But as revolutionary sentiment grew, Rivington began advocating for the British, and the front page of his paper proudly announced his title as "Printer to the King's Most Excellent Majesty." In 1774, with tensions growing, Rivington said the Whig *New-York Journal* was "abhorrent to all good men" and a "pest to society."[33]

Madison saw a rat. "I wish most heartily we had Rivington & his ministerial Gazetteers for 24 hours in this place," he railed to Bradford. "Execrable as their designs are, they would meet with adequate punishment." While he usually described his home state as a sort of backwater, in this respect— Virginia's harshness to the disloyal—he was proud. "How different is the Spirit of Virginia from that of N York?," he asked Bradford, rhetorically. "A fellow was lately tarred & feathered for treating one [of] our county committees with disrespect; in NY. they insult the whole Colony and Continent with impunity!"[34]

But then death came to Madison's own door.

P EOPLE AT MONTPELIER BEGAN FALLING ILL. THEIR BODIES WERE RACKED by waves of diarrhea and bloody stools. They were constantly vomiting. Dysentery is transmitted through dirty water infected with fecal matter, but nobody knew that. What they knew was that it often killed, slowly and relentlessly.

Everyone walked around with palpable dread. Madison's sister Elizabeth and brother Reuben were under eight years old. In May 1775, both children fell ill. Their little bodies heaved with diarrhea and burned with fever. On May 17, Elizabeth died. Reuben followed three weeks later, on June 5.

Madison's mother, Nelly, had already endured both a miscarriage and an infant death. Now, she was in agony; his father, more stoic, was still clearly shaken. Madison suffered quietly and intensely. He was also terrified that he himself might die. Two weeks later, he wrote Bradford a clipped letter, employing formal, ancient English as a wall against fear. "Since I wrote last a Dysentry hath made an Irruption in my father's family," he wrote. "It has carried off a little sister about seven & a brother about four years of age." Madison briskly composed himself and moved onto the secondary victims—"It is still among us but principally among the blacks," adding, "I have escaped hitherto" and "it is now out of the house I live in, I hope the danger is over." But reassurance was difficult for the disease was "pretty incident to this Country" and he feared that it would "range more generally this year than common."[35]

Bradford was less equable in his response, responding with warmth and empathy. "I am grieved to hear the dysentery prevails so much with you," he wrote, "& for the loss you have sustained." And he suggested a solution for his friend: escape. "If the disorder should not abate," he urged, "I would recommend a Journey this way to you: & if you can find nothing to amuse you here you may prosecute your journey to Cambridge."[36]

Madison could at least save himself. But he did not move in time. The dreaded disease returned. Two weeks later, he wrote Bradford that the dysentery was "again in our family & is now among the slaves." He felt he was living on borrowed time. "I have hitherto Escaped," he said, "and hope it has no commission to attack me." There was a small hope, however, in that the new wave seemed "less severe than it was at first."[37]

Madison was amazed he had escaped death's grasp. He agonized even more intensively about what he should do with his life. He decided to try his hand at the law. It would be a descent into hell for his restless, passionate mind.

H E DIFFIDENTLY INFORMED BRADFORD, "I INTEND MYSELF TO READ LAW occasionally and have procured books for that purpose so that you need not fear offending me by Allusions to that science."[38] He was taking his own medicine. When Bradford had pressed him for advice on his career, Madison had advised that the law was the "most eligeble" for Bradford's "endowments" and had confidently explained that the law was "a sort of General Lover that wooes all the Muses and Graces," unlike commerce or physics, which required "less Learning & smaller understanding." He had expansively praised Bradford's "adherence to probity and Truth in the Character of a Lawyer," but had advised that dissimulating clients would often "occasion doubt and ignorance."[39]

It was one thing to give such smooth advice; it was another altogether to take it. One became a lawyer by learning case after case, principle after principle, usually studying in solitude. Madison sat down with a new commonplace book of forty sewn pages to study the *Reports*, a book of cases and rules by a noted lawyer named William Salkeld that covered English common law from 1689 to 1712.[40] The common law Salkeld covered was a disordered mess. Over centuries, English judges had decided countless disputes by examining other judges' previous decisions, all the while trying to guess what other judges might follow in the future.

He closed the door in the library upstairs and set Salkeld's tome before him. The low blue mountains spread out enticingly, miles away, like all the horizons he would never reach. In the library, Madison picked his way through dozens of cases, but he found his interest dwindling, his pen wandering into doodles. For a disinterested mind, gathering wisdom from the common law was like picking vegetables in an overgrown summer garden, stalked by buzzing mosquitoes. He yawned. He tried to fit in his studies before and after the tutoring sessions with Willey, Nelly, and Sarah but easily became distracted, and it showed in his notes.

His commonplace book cruelly tracked his declining progress. When beginning the book, he diligently employed wide-ruled margins, carefully including significant blank space under each case name. He wrote carefully, in neat and unrushed script. But as the weeks and months wore on, his well-laid plans slipped. His handwriting became small and hurried. He began carelessly squishing in notes to fit on a single page.

He half-heartedly designed a system to copy Salkeld's cases and topics in alphabetical order, but the notes revealed his diminishing focus. Section A took up twelve pages, for instance. Sections B, C, D, and E each used four or five pages. But when he reached F, Madison's boredom swamped him, and he could only manage a single page. When he got to G, on page 32, the game was up; he accidentally wrote everything upside-down.

He also skipped certain important areas of the law entirely—Law, Common and Civil, for instance, as well as most of the W's: Wager of Law, Warranty, Weights and Measures, Wills and Testaments, Witnesses, and Words. The only W he included was a case under Writ.[41]

His boredom emerged in his summary of one property case called *Ashby v. White*, where the court rejected a voter's complaint that his vote for Parliament had not been counted. Salkeld included a dissent by a judge eloquently standing up for a property-owner's right to a remedy through law. The state, the judge argued, should respond to what was a moral injury. Such a ringing case about voter participation should have captured Madison's imagination. But instead he wrote, "Case by voter for refusing to receive his vote in election for members of parliament. [Judges] adjudged the action not maintainable." Stultified as he was, he totally ignored the dissenting judge's reasoning and, by extension, the principle in the case.[42]

Sometimes he even lost his temper, such as in his caustic response to learning that Bradford was readily progressing in his studies. He was happy, he said, that his friend would "converse with the Edwards and Henry's & Charles &c&c who have swayed the British Scepter." But he sardonically warned that they would be "dirty and unprofitable Companions," unless Bradford would "fall more in love with Liberty" by beholding such "detestable pictures of Tyranny and Cruelty." Jealousy lurked in his words like a cancer.

He did laugh at himself, from time to time, grimly mocking his inability to master the law: "I was afraid you would not easily have loosened your Affections from the Belles Lettres," he wrote Bradford. He paid his friend a sideways compliment. A "Delicate Taste and warm imagination like yours," he said, "must find it hard to give up such refined & exquisite enjoyments for the coarse and dry study of the Law." All his sentiment repressed by Salkeld's oppressive logic came rushing out. Madison groped for language that could wing him away from his problem: "It is like leaving a pleasant flourishing field for a barren desert," he waxed. "Perhaps I should not say barren either because the Law does bear fruit but it is a sour fruit that must be gathered and pressed and distilled before it can bring pleasure or profit."[43]

He bemusedly read over what he had written. He admitted that he had made a "very awkward Comparison." He was right; who would distill a "sour fruit" for pleasure? But he had "gone too far to quit," he wrote wryly, "before I perceived that it was too much entangled in my brain to run it through." In closing, he told Bradford, "You must forgive it."[44]

In September 1774, his father tried to resolve his unemployed son's clear professional predicament by giving him two hundred acres of land near Montpelier.[45] But it must have been clear to all that if Madison had little interest in being a lawyer, he had even less in being a farmer or lord of a plantation.

So what would he do?

THE YOUNG MAN FELT HE WAS ATROPHYING. NOT ONLY HAD BEING PULLED in as his siblings' tutor enmired him as thoroughly as quicksand, it seemed increasingly likely he would be a lifelong bachelor. Stuck in his father's house, he doubted he would ever meet a wife in Orange County, and tried to deflect that worry through harsh asides about the excesses of others. When John Witherspoon visited Philadelphia, Bradford learned from him that Thaddeus Dod—who had transcribed Witherspoon's lectures on the passions and, after graduation, entered theological studies—had gotten a young woman pregnant. He friends, Bradford reported, had forced the "Old fellow's head in the noose" and made Dod marry her. Bradford laughed that this was putting the "Cart before the horse."[46]

Madison responded acidly that the "World needs to be peopled"—but not with "bastards as my old friend Dod." Sarcastically (but with a hint of envy), he wrote, "Who could have thought the old monk had been so letcherous," and further observed that Dod's mistake might have stemmed from his own religious repression. "I hope his Religion," Madison snapped, "like that of some enthusiasts, was not of such a nature as to fan the amorous fire."[47] Dod had clearly failed to channel his own passions; as for Madison, he was about to realize his own best bet would be a "political career," with the example, again, coming from Witherspoon.

THE CONGREGATION, RUSTLING AND BUZZING, LOOKED UP AT THE BEARISH form in the pulpit. It was May 17, 1775, in Princeton, a month after the battles of Lexinton and Concord, and Witherspoon was about to deliver his first public sermon on revolutionary politics. "You are all my witnesses," he proclaimed to the crowd, "that this is the first time of my introducing any political subject into the pulpit." He was, he said, "declaring my opinion, without any hesitation."

Witherspoon began with deceptive simplicity. His purpose, he said, was to explore the meaning of Psalm 76.10: "Surely the wrath of man shall praise thee, and the remainder of wrath shalt thou restrain." He explained that all the "disorderly passions of men" were, in the end, to the "praise of God."[48] He regarded his listeners. Even the infuriating circumstances of the colonies—the "plague of war," the "ambition of mistaken princes," the "cunning and cruelty of oppressive and corrupt ministers," the "inhumanity of brutal soldiers"—all of these, he proclaimed, "however dreadful," would "finally promote the glory of God."

God would therefore aid the coming revolution, and "while the storm continues, his mercy and kindness shall appear in prescribing bounds to their rage and fury."[49]

As they sharpened their bayonets, he instructed those assembled, they must keep one item paramount: humility. "Ostentation and confidence," he said sternly, were an "outrage upon providence." Arrogance was contagious, and when it "infuses itself into the spirit of a people," became a "sure forerunner of destruction." Witherspoon recounted for his flock the story of David and the Philistine. The Philistine taunted David, threatening that he would tear off his flesh and feed it to the fowls of the air and to the beasts of the field. But David, unruffled, offered a "just and modest" reply: "Thou comest to me with a sword, and with a spear, and with a shield: but I come unto thee in the name of the Lord of Hosts, the God of the Armies of Israel whom thou hast defied."[50]

It was through that purity of his purpose, Witherspoon explained, that David prevailed. *All* forms of self-aggrandizement, bloviation, and puffery were not only bad spiritual practice—they undermined war and statesmanship. Such "profane ostentation" appeared in the braggart names given to ships of war—he cited with derision the "Thunderer," the "Dread-nought," the "Terrible," the "Fire-brand," the "Infernal." When navies gave their ships such names, he declared, it was "not likely to obtain the blessing of the God of Heaven."[51]

At last, he openly proclaimed himself a revolutionary. Rebellion, he declared, was the "cause of justice, of liberty, and of human nature."[52] The confederacy of the colonies had "not been the effect of pride, resentment, or sedition"; rather, of a "deep and general conviction" in civil and religious liberty. All of this was driven by faith, by the "knowledge of God and his truths" which naturally surface with "some degree of liberty and political justice." "There is not a single instance in history," he declared, "in which civil liberty was lost and religious liberty preserved entire." If his congregation loved God, in other words, they must expel the British.

He pled for his adoptive countrymen to abandon the chauvinism that had divided rich from poor and north from south. Merchants and landholders must not separate into parties. Everyone must guard against "local provincial pride and jealousy." By the "contempt of the courage, character, manners, or even language, of particular places," he declared, they would do a "greater injury to the common cause." The common good, above all else, should drive them.[53]

He closed with a ringing injunction about the dangers of incivility. "Every good man," he announced, must take a deep concern in "national character and manners" and the cause of "promoting public virtue, and bearing down impiety and vice." Why the urgency of that seemingly minor concern about vanity, when the country was fast approaching war? "Nothing is more certain," he said, than that a "general profligacy and corruption of manners" would make America "ripe for destruction." Even though government could "hold the rotten materials together for some time," after a certain point, he darkly predicted, even the "best constitution" would be ineffectual, and "slavery must ensue."[54]

He thus imparted an almost physical sense of urgency to this fusion of humility, principle, passion, and military might.

But he had one more thing to say.

"Certain classes of men," Witherspoon added, were "under peculiar obligations, to the discharge of this duty." These classes, he explained, were the magistrates, ministers, parents, heads of families, commanding military officers, and "those whom age has rendered venerable." These natural leaders within society all had a special duty to elevate the country—to stand for not only political independence, but independence of conscience.[55]

Over the next three years, this sermon would be printed and sent not only around the thirteen states, but across the Atlantic to England and Scotland. In the late summer of 1775, copies begin circulating around Virginia.

Madison read a copy and recognized a bracing new political philosophy that married faith, rebellion, and statesmanship—and supplied him with a cause.

B ACK IN VIRGINIA, YOUNG MADISON REALIZED THAT WITHERSPOON'S closing injunction to America's "certain classes" described the role he was envisioning for himself. The profession he ultimately chose—the states-man—was a new role for a new country. Decades later, scribbling away in his autobiography, Madison summarized his movement into government—a radi-cal departure from the law, planting, or the merchant's life—in a simple, new phrase. He would soon be, he recalled, "initiated into the political career."[56] *Politics*—with its intrigues and designs, its ambitions and pitfalls, and, above all, its capacity to help the young country become what she was meant to be—*that* is what began, at long last, to call to him.

Meanwhile, he learned of a stunning event eastward—and a new politi-cal hero. For while young Madison and Bradford were cogitating about British oppression, Patrick Henry was taking arms against it.

6 "If This Be Treason, Make the Most of It!"

O N MARCH 20, 1775, PATRICK HENRY TOOK HIS SEAT IN ST. JOHN'S CHURCH in Richmond as a representative in a convention that had been called to devise Virginia's approach to the ongoing tensions with Great Britain. Lantern-jawed and heavy-browed, Henry was six feet tall and imposing. He walked with a pronounced stoop, as if bearing a heavy load he wanted everyone to know about. He affected an unschooled manner of speaking, and seemed to relish playing the role of avatar for the common man. But any ponderousness in his gravelly voice was quickly eclipsed by the quicksilver humor that flashed in his speech like sunlight on water.[1]

When a debate began about whether or not Virginia should support more independence for the colony of Jamaica, Henry saw an opportunity to advance a more militant vision of colonial freedom. He abruptly stood and introduced resolutions declaring the right to a "well-regulated militia" and asking the convention to put Virginia into an immediate state of defense.

His resolutions sparked a firestorm in the chamber. Their voices rising like thunder, Tory delegates shouted that his ideas were too provocative toward the British. Henry rose in response. "And what have we to oppose them?" he asked sarcastically. "Shall we try argument? Sire, we have been trying that for the last ten years."

He was attacking reason itself. The men had the vertiginous sensation of riding along with him into battle. "Gentlemen may cry peace, peace," he declared, looking around with flashing eyes. "But there is no peace." He resonantly pronounced his verdict: "The war is actually begun! The next gale that sweeps the north will bring to our ears the clash of resounding arms. Our brethren are already in the field! Why stand we here idle? What is it the gentlemen wish? What would they have? Is life so dear, or peace so sweet, as to be purchased as the price of chains and slavery? Forbid it, almighty God!"

And then he came to the deathless proclamation that would ring centuries later: "I know now what course others may take. But as for me," he declared, "give me liberty or give me death!"

For a moment, the men around Henry were suspended in time. Edmund Randolph later wrote that Henry's oratory "blazed so as to warm the coldest heart"—that he was "thought in his attitude to resemble St. David, while preaching at Athens, and to speak as man was never known to speak before." His gathered force—his posture, the broad embrace of his arms, the gravelly tone of his voice, his anger, his stark challenge to them—united to make him seem above their time somehow, as if he were emanating from, or perhaps driving, history itself.

The entranced delegates voted for the resolutions and to appoint a committee to arm the colony and elected Henry chair. His transition from lawyer to orator to revolutionary was fully in motion.[2] News of the "liberty or death" speech quickly spread. James Madison was electrified.

Who was the man who had delivered America's most famous declaration regarding political freedom, regarding revolution itself?

THE STORY OF HENRY'S REVOLUTIONARY SPIRIT WENT BACK AT LEAST A decade, to May 29, 1765, when he rose before his fellow members of the Virginia House of Burgesses. The men watching him didn't know Henry well; as a first-term delegate, he would not ordinarily have traveled in their social circles. He seemed to have a grittier background than them. Most were wealthy and accomplished. Four out of five had already served as justices of the peace, and nearly half had a college education. Half were related by birth or marriage to the "First Families of Virginia"—the Randolphs, Carters, Beverlys, and Lees. But Henry, they knew, had been largely educated at home by his father, had then worked as a bumptious tavern keeper, and only afterward took a rocky path to the law and then politics.

They also knew that five years earlier, in his quest to become a licensed attorney, Henry had been examined by a panel of four preeminent lawyers, including George Wythe, Virginia's foremost lawyer, and two of the famous Randolphs. Henry only passed the examination over great reluctance from two of the examiners, and despite his manifest ignorance of the laws, because of what the other two called his obvious genius, his powers of "natural reason."[3]

They were about to learn just what that meant.

One after the other, Henry introduced five resolutions defying Great Britain's hated Stamp Act, which levied new taxes on all printed paper goods. He declared that Virginia's General Assembly possessed the "*only* and *sole exclusive* Right and Power" to lay such taxes. In turn, several of the men rose to attack Henry's motives, his evident ambition, and his recklessness.

Henry, rising to defend his resolutions, said angrily, "Tarquin and Caesar had each his Brutus, Charles the First his Cromwell, and George the Third—" Henry's inflammatory words likened the British king to an emperor about to be deposed, alarming many of the wealthy men watching him, who rather *liked* their reassuring British ancestry. Suddenly, the Speaker of the House, John Robinson, interrupted—standing up, pointing at Henry, and shouting, "Treason! Treason!"

But the rumpled younger man ignored Robinson. "—and George the Third may profit by their example," he continued. "If this be treason," Henry pronounced, "make the most of it!"

Like lightning, his proclamation clarified the stark contrast between the revolutionaries and the Tories. And it succeeded. His resolution passed narrowly over bitter opposition from the same men who had called him a traitor. His fame quickly began to spread throughout Virginia, and then to the other states.

A mob burned a stamp distributor in effigy in Boston, and another group of men destroyed the coach of New York's lieutenant governor. Stamps were looted and burned in piles around the colonies.[4] In the following months, a French traveler who heard Henry's "treason" speech observed that "if the least Injury was offered" to Henry, that the "whole inhabitants" would "stand by him to the last Drop of their blood."[5] A century and a half later, Woodrow Wilson would write that Henry's speech was the "first words of a revolution, and no man ever thought just the same after he had read them."[6]

But while he made many friends, he made enemies as well.

THOMAS JEFFERSON, FOR ONE, KNEW HENRY WELL. THE TWO MEN HAD been opposing lawyers in central Virginia courts for several years, and while Jefferson admired Henry's oratorical gifts, he disliked him personally. When the courts adjourned for winter, Jefferson satirically recalled that

Henry would "make up a party of poor hunters of his neighborhood" and "go off with them to the piney woods of Fluvanna, and pass weeks in hunting deer, of which he was passionately fond, sleeping under a tent, before a fire, wearing the same shirt the whole time, and covering all the dirt of his dress with a hunting shirt."[7]

Jefferson found this pose inauthentic, and egregiously so. After all, Henry was deeply familiar with elite Virginia society, even if he chose not to join it. His father, John, had attended King's College in Scotland, receiving a classical education and achieving a deep familiarity with Horace.[8] Henry's maternal grandfather probably was related to the Duke of Marlborough, while his maternal grandmother belonged to the prosperous French Huguenots who settled near the James River.[9] Henry's aunt Lucy—his mother's sister—was the grandmother of Dolley Madison. His great-uncle, in fact, was Donald Robertson, Madison's tutor.[10]

Henry's father was a prosperous plantation owner as well as a colonel in his local militia.[11] He tutored his son at home, where he learned Latin, Shakespeare, and ancient history and mythology. Henry read Virgil and Livy in Latin when he was fifteen years old. Decades later, he would easily allude to Rhadamanthus and Nero in speeches.[12]

His father constantly pushed Patrick to become self-sufficient. When he was sixteen, John Henry put him and his brother William to work, giving them Indian spices, coffee, tea, molasses, wool, silk, and cloth to stock a household goods store. But the store was shunned by the wealthy—it only succeeded among the poorest customers. Henry, laughing and telling stories at the counter, came to regard them as his adoptive people, but they were not enough to sustain him. Business dried up, the store closing within a year. Two years later, when he was nineteen, he married the sixteen-year-old Sarah Shelton in a lavish, raucous ceremony featuring powdered wigs, high stockings, and hoop skirts, guest drunk on mint juleps and eggnog.[13]

The couple moved into a cottage named Pine Slash, where Henry defiantly farmed for tobacco with his own hands—unheard of for the descendant of a prosperous and well-educated home. The wealthy laughed at the classically educated young man hoeing alongside his own slaves. A surveyor described the couple as "obscure, unknown, and almost unpitied."[14] A fire then destroyed the cottage, along with just about everything Henry had earned and built. Undaunted, he sold some of his slaves, rebuilt the house, and purchased goods to start a new store. Ever gregarious, he talked on and on with his customers.

Thomas Jefferson met Henry that winter, during Christmas festivities. Jefferson, then seventeen, would later say of Henry, "His manners had something of coarseness in them; his passion was music, dancing, and pleasantry. He excelled in the last, and it attracted every one to them."[15] The next year, the store failed. Henry decided to head into the law, and then into politics, where he enjoyed considerably more success with his storekeeper persona.

His true genius was resonating with his audience, communing with the tender feelings that unite people despite education and sophistication. He gradually adopted a severe persona; contemporaries described his appearance as "grave, penetrating, and marked with the strong lineaments of deep reflection."[16] He had, in the words of one biographer, a "Roman cast," with piercing blue eyes that could change to a deep gray, a strong nose, a high and straight forehead, a heavy brow, long, black eyelashes, and dark eyebrows that made his eyes seem especially penetrating.[17] He had begun balding when young, but that didn't seem to affect his confidence one iota. On the contrary, overweening assurance became his forte.

He honed in on people's passions—their hopes and fears, their infatuation with the battle between good and evil, their vulnerability to his charisma. He could talk a jury into anything. A friend described his "perfect command of a strong and musical voice, which he raised or lowered at pleasure, and modulated so as to fall in with any given chord of the human heart."[18] Once, a man watching Henry's performance from an upper gallery became "so much enchanted with his eloquence" that he accidentally spurted tobacco juice on the heads of the members of the House.[19]

Henry's warmth had an animal element; he drew others toward him. After his death, Thomas Jefferson would say, "I think he was the best humored man in society I almost ever knew and the greatest orator that ever lived." In Jefferson's view, it was Henry's "consummate knowledge of the human heart" that allowed him to "attain a degree of popularity with the people at large never perhaps equaled." But even after death, Jefferson derided Henry as "avaricious" and "rotten hearted" and possessed of "two great passions"—the love of money and of fame.[20]

Patrick Henry inspired great love and great hate, sometimes all at once, sometimes even in the same person. And so it would be with James Madison, who began, at first, with love.

A FTER HIS "GIVE ME LIBERTY OR GIVE ME DEATH" SPEECH, HENRY returned to Virginia, hurling himself into building the volunteer militia company in his home county of Hanover. His law practice suffered, his cases flagging and revenues dropping. And then tragedy struck.

His wife, Sarah, suddenly developed a "strange antipathy" to both Henry and their children. Doctors soon declared her insane. Henry, distraught, brought her to Williamsburg for advanced treatment, but the doctors there were unable to quiet her disturbance. Henry's friends pled with him to institutionalize her in a newly constructed insane asylum in Williamsburg, but he refused. Instead, he installed her in an "airy, sunny" room in his house's half-basement. She died after several horrible months, in early 1775.[21] And so Henry was catapulted into the American Revolution not only by the hated British, but by his need to escape misery.

His moment arrived on April 20, 1775, when Virginia's British puppet executive, Lord Dunmore, stunned the Commonwealth by suddenly seizing fifteen half-barrels of gunpowder from the colony's magazine in Williamsburg. He ordered his men to carry the kegs onto a ship of war anchored off the shore. The result was a firestorm in war-ready Virginia.

Six hundred armed men quickly assembled in Fredericksburg. Although the assembly included notables like George Washington, Edmund Pendleton, and Richard Henry Lee, it still collapsed into bickering volleys about the potential backlash of an attack. Some men shouted in favor of a march to Williamsburg to retrieve the powder and, in Madison's words, "revenge the insult." Others worried about provoking an armed conflict too early. A letter from Randolph was read out loud, advising that Dunmore would yield the powder when it was needed. The gathering soon dispersed.[22]

The temporizing infuriated Henry. He returned home to Hanover County, where he convinced his local militia to take up arms and challenge Dunmore to yield the gunpowder directly. At the head of the company, Henry left that very evening.

Word of the country lawyer rebel spread quickly. Back in Montpelier, Madison longed to throw himself into the action. The nearby Albemarle County militia had missed the Fredericksburg meeting, but Madison brashly decided to join Henry to "enforce an immediate delivery of the powder, or die in the attempt." Madison and his brother Francis secured permission from the Orange Committee for Public Safety (led by his father) to join the Albemarle Committee. The young men left on horseback the next day, rushing along the road to Albemarle County.[23]

Meanwhile, Henry made astonishingly fast progress—too fast for the Madisons to catch up. Confronting Dunmore and his troops, Henry succeeded in convincing Dunmore to pay Virginia 330 pounds in exchange for the gunpowder. To the angry colonials, eager for a practical sign of progress against the British, that achievement felt like the first victory of an infant rebellion.

On his victorious return from Williamsburg, Henry collided with an eager company from Albemarle County, and a slender young man named James Madison. Despite his apparent shyness, Madison introduced himself to Henry with the same directness that had so impressed Witherspoon. Talking to Henry, he learned that he would soon be traveling to Philadelphia, and he asked Henry whether he would deliver a letter to Bradford for him. The older man agreed.

Henry took the letter along with him on the long road to Philadelphia and handed it to Bradford. Opening the sealed envelope, Bradford read his friend's description of the bulky older man who had served as letter-carrier. Henry's decision, Madison said, had already followed his signal pattern. It had "been contrary to the opinion" of the other delegates and would be "disapproved of by them," Madison wrote. But Henry had gained "great honor in the most spirited parts of the Country." Those "spirited parts" would stick with Henry for years to come.

As for those who disagreed with Henry's bold action—specifically the wealthy doves whose business interests would suffer from British reprisals— Madison had much harsher words. Theirs was a "pusillanimity," he spat, "little comporting with their professions or the name of Virginian."[24]

R ETURNING HOME, MADISON URGED THE ORANGE COUNTY COMMITTEE on Public Safety to write an official commendation of Patrick Henry.

They readily agreed, publishing a declaration that complimented Henry's "seasonable and spirited proceedings." Either Madison or his father—or both—inserted an aside zealously declaring the recent British aggression in Lexington and Concord, Massachusetts, a "hostile attack on this and every other colony, and a sufficient warrant to use violence and reprisal, in all cases where it may be expedient for our security and welfare."

Madison was enthusiastically heading into war. He took to the road to hand deliver the document to Henry himself.[24] Just two days later, Henry responded, grateful for the "Approbation of your Committee," assuring them that he had only been motivated by "Zeal for the public Good," and promising to print copies of the resolution.[25]

For Madison, the rough orator seemed to be a natural face for America's revolution. Little did Madison suspect that just when the revolution would most need to evolve, Henry would refuse. Madison, in the end, would be left to defend the republic—from Henry.

7 Suspending His Intellectual Functions

EVENTS BEGAN GATHERING TO A HEAD. THE SITUATION PROMISED TO propel Madison from his deadening life at Montpelier into the revolution threatening to break the country's chains. Then, Madison, at long last, received a clear advancement from the profession of tutor. On October 2, 1774, he received a letter signed by seven men on the statewide Committee of Safety. The committee, Madison read, placed "especial Trust and Confidence" in James Madison's "Patriotism, Fidelity, Courage, and good Conduct," and appointed him colonel—the same rank as his father. The advancement testified to Madison Sr.'s power and to the confidence of the leading men of Orange County advocating for the small but strangely prepossessing young man. Yet the appointment also careered Madison into a shame that would haunt him for the rest of his life.

ON JULY 28, 1775, HE EXCITEDLY WROTE BRADFORD THAT VIRGINIANS were raising an army of three to four thousand men—"The Preparations for War," he wrote, were "every where going on in a most vigorous manner." The issue of army supplies particularly preoccupied him—the "Scarcity of Ammunition," he told Bradford, was "truly alarming."[1]

He hurled himself into the effort. That summer, he practiced firing a musket for the first time. Tearing open gunpowder packets and ramrodding in bullets and powder—and pulling the trigger for a shocking blast—thrilled him. He boasted to Bradford that the "discipline & hostile preparations is as great as the Zeal with which these things were undertaken." He quickly came to view himself as a military man, becoming a bit haughty in the process. "You would be astonished," he confidently advised his friend, "at the perfection this art is brought to." A man, he declared, should be able to hit "the bigness of a man's face" at a hundred yards. The militia's men were so strong and well trained that they would demolish the officers of the enemy "before they get within 150 or 200 yards." His own aim was good, and he boasted that he "should not often miss it on a fair trial" at that distance.

But Madison—ever his father's son and Witherspoon's student—was vigilant against vanity. "I am far from being among the best," he quickly said.[2]

Madison began his service by joining the other men in a simple firing drill. Looking on, the younger men were ordered to practice their advances and fire their weapons. Performing before his father and the other men, Madison was suddenly struck by an overwhelming self-consciousness. As he moved from musket practice to actual company maneuvers, he anxiously felt a wrenching stomach-ache begin. Suddenly, he was unable to stand. Mortified, he then collapsed. The other men were forced to help him off the field.

The event was humiliating, and the shame stayed with Madison for his entire life. Writing about it when he was eighty years old, he masked his embarrassment, but his pain was apparent. "He was restrained from entering into the military service by the unsettled state of his health," he recounted in third person about himself, "and the discourageing feebleness of his constitution of which he was fully admonished by his experience during the exercises and movements of a minute Company which he had joined."[3]

What happened to Madison on that battlefield?

S CHOLARS HAVE HEATEDLY DEBATED EXACTLY WHAT WAS WRONG WITH Madison. Ralph Ketcham, his authoritative modern biographer, notes that Madison's parents ordered drugs for "an Epilepsy" in October 11, 1753, when their son was in his second year.[4] Lynne Cheney notes that these medications included two laxatives—Anderson's Pills and *pulvis basilicus*. Because he was the "only member of his family for whom there is any indication of epilepsy," Cheney concludes that the medicines were for the toddler James.[5] However, this could just be a false negative; the medication could very well have been for another member of the family with unrecorded symptoms of epilepsy, or for a slave with epilepsy whom Madison's parents were treating, or not for epilepsy at all (but for constipation).

Cheney takes her evidence to suggest that Madison, from a very young age, suffered from classic epilepsy, a nervous disorder that causes seizures. She suggests that Madison's confusing symptoms can be squared with classic epilepsy because he may have experienced "complex partial seizures," whose symptoms may include "dreamy states" and "automatic movements," such as plucking at clothes, as well as generalized "partial seizures" resulting from electricity in one part of the brain spreading to another, which can cause a victim to lose consciousness and fall to the ground, convulsing.[6]

These explanations all depend on what psychiatry deems an "organic" explanation of Madison's sickness, meaning that it was caused by a physical condition causing the symptoms. If, on the other hand, symptoms are based on psychological problems, one can have symptoms but not have a cause. There can be nothing functionally wrong with the body. The symptoms are psychosomatic (a word whose Greek roots are *psyche*, for" mind," with *soma*, for "body").

And this is what evidence suggests: that Madison suffered from severe anxiety-driven panic attacks that made him ill. In other words, his illness was a bodily condition driven by mental problems. In the parlance of modern psychiatry, he suffered from "psychogenic nonepileptic seizures." He did not, in other words, suffer from classic epilepsy; he suffered from crippling anxiety.

Why did he suffer such anxiety? There, again, we have to approach the problem like detectives, for the record is so fragmentary, and Madison was himself hardly transparent or fulsome about his condition.

Here is what we know.

We know that throughout Madison's life, the affliction would appear, as Ralph Ketcham notes, at "times of strain and tension."[*7]

---

* Irving Brant, Madison's most exhaustive biographer, also wrote in 1941 that the best explanation was not the "organic" disease of epilepsy, but instead the "functional" ailment of "epileptoid hysteria." He noted the then recent scholarship of Freud had followed the findings of the French psychologist Jean-Martin Charcot in discovering that "epileptiform convulsions" could mimic epilepsy, but instead resulted from the "impress upon the mind either of a physical injury or a mental experience corresponding to it." Brant noted the "common connection" of this sort of hysteria was "overstudy, day-dreaming, hypochondria, and a sense of physical inferiority." Irving Brant, *James Madison: The Virginia Revolutionist*, 1751–1780, vol. 1 (New York: Bobbs-Merrill, 1941), 107.

We know that after Madison died in 1836, his brother-in-law, John C. Payne, tried no less than three times to capture the problem in a short biography. First, Payne wrote:

> "But a constitutional liability to sudden attacks, of the nature of epilepsy, deterred him from—"

Payne was understandably reluctant to darken a great man's legacy with a sickness like epilepsy, which was then thought to attack its victims, taking advantage of their weakness. So Payne altered the description to read:

> "But a constitutional liability to sudden attacks, ~~of the nature of epilepsy, deterred him from~~ of a character and effect which suspended his powers of action."

But that wasn't good enough, either. Now, a "suspended" Madison appeared to be paralyzed—unable to move. Payne wanted instead to describe Madison as a combatant, as a survivor who otherwise would have bravely pursued military service, so he tried a third time:

> "But a constitutional liability to sudden attacks, ~~of the nature of epilepsy, deterred him from of a character and effect which suspended his powers of action~~ the feebleness of his health which he had experienced in training restrained him from entering the military service."[8]

That version was not perfect, but it better described Madison as having valiantly "experienced" an impartial "feebleness of health" *while training,* than as some frail weakling *unable even to try.*

We know that the ailment became a leitmotif for Madison. From his twenties to his eighties, he would complain almost constantly to family and friends alike about the problem that surfaced on the militia training field. In the fifteen-page document commonly cited as his authoritative biography, which he wrote in retirement, he recounted his sickliness no less than ten times, using terms like "very infirm health," "very feeble health," "unsettled state of his health," "confinement with bilious fever," and "detained by sickness." The fits seemed to arrive with any activity that made him feel self-conscious or anxious, particularly when he needed to seem successful in front of others, and most particularly when his father or other men were watching. The attacks could last for hours, even days, often sending him into bed where his sole thought was to recover through quiet and stillness—though he would remain pale and tremulous.

We also know other things Madison said more quietly about his condition. In his unpublished scribblings, Madison was explicit about the experience of his condition. In a memorandum requested by a Mr. Delaplane in 1816, Madison describes the "unsettled state of his health and the discouraging feebleness of his Constitution."[9] However, there was much more to it than that. In a version of the autobiography that Madison's presidential secretary Edward Coles recorded after interviewing Madison in 1828, Coles noted that as a young man he had an "affection of the breast and nerves."[10]

We know that there was another, more drastic symptom of the disorder, which Madison went to great pains to hide. In the Princeton University archives rests a mysterious version of his autobiography, written in Madison's own hand. This autobiography contains an extra handwritten sentence in smaller, more disorganized script than usual. After recounting his failure to "enter the army," Madison added the following sentence:

> viz. his feeble health, and a constitutional liability to sudden attacks, somewhat resembling epilepsy and *suspending his intellectual functions*. These continued thro his life, with prolonged intervals.[11]

In other words, his disorder not only caused him shame, it made him think he was going crazy.

We know from this description that the attacks, in his words, were "sudden"—as if he was being seized and shaken. Yet Madison carefully emphasized a confusing fact: that the attacks only "somewhat resembled" epilepsy itself. The attacks, in other words, were not a familiar illness. There was something *alien* about them. Madison wrote the notes describing the "suspension of his intellectual faculties" sometime between 1816 and 1831.[12] In every other version of his autobiography, the crucial phrase disappeared, and he said instead that he was "restrained from" entering into military service because of the "unsettled state of his health" and "the discouraging feebleness of his constitution."[13] It was almost as if he felt compelled to disclose a secret that he later tried, like Pandora, to recapture.

T HE FACT IS THAT HE WAS EXPERIENCING ANXIETY ATTACKS. THE MODERN *Diagnostic and Statistical Manual of Mental Disorders*, which mental health practitioners use, includes nine criteria for diagnosing panic attacks: heart palpitations; sweating, trembling or shaking; shortness of breath or smothering sensations; the feeling of choking; chest pain or discomfort; nausea or abdominal distress; feeling dizzy, unsteady, lightheaded, or faint; feelings of unreality or detachment; fear of losing control or going crazy; numbness or a tingling sensation; and chills or hot flashes.[14]

A patient who experiences four of these symptoms at once has anxiety attacks, and Madison routinely experienced many more. From his own descriptions and those of his friends, his "bilious" or "epileptic" fits included palpitations, trembling, choking, chest pain, abdominal distress, fainting, and the fear of going crazy.

Taken together, these frameworks perfectly describe what James Madison experienced, not just on the battlefield in Orange County performing military exercises, but throughout his life. "Think of anxiety like a continuum," Dr. Joseph Cooper, an expert in psychodynamic counseling at Marymount University, told me.[15] In what's known as a psychogenic nonepileptic seizure, a patient's anxiety takes physical form by tensing the smooth muscles that line the intestines and the stomach (leading to cramping and upset stomach) and the blood vessels (creating high blood pressure and headaches).

Along these lines, Edward Coles's reference to Madison's "breast and nerves" as the physical location of the attacks is especially meaningful. Madison's anxiety might have begun with a flutter of tension in his hand and jaw. As it increased, his anxiety would move into his body. His heart might have raced, his breathing becoming faster. Then his stomach would become upset. As his anxiety further escalated, he might start to feel dizzy, to get "foggy" in his head. He might have gotten "jelly legs." As the anxiety moved further into the body, he might then actually faint or even collapse.[16]

These symptoms would all have been made worse by repression. If someone has experienced trauma, but fears expressing it—for example, someone who feels anger or fear as a result of some trauma, but does not feel comfortable sharing those emotions—a "conversion disorder" can result.*

Even in an age far before therapy, Freud, and the invention of the ego, many of his contemporaries were writing introspective letters full of descriptions of their own emotions, whether John Adams or Alexander Hamilton or Thomas Jefferson. Among them, Madison was unusual for his remarkably adamant disinterest in his emotional or psychological well-being. As for what exactly happened on that battlefield, we can only speculate. Madison loved his father but felt controlled by him. By the descriptions of most people who met him but did not know him well, he was extremely reserved. His friends described him as deeply sensitive and easily wounded. Madison may have felt deep anger at his father (watching him attempt to perform military exercises in front of the entire company), and his anxiety could have resulted from the conflict between that anger and his inability to express it.

When people have conflicted feelings toward "attachment figures," such as a parent, this can produce feelings of anger and rage toward the parent. In this case, Madison's father might have been communicating that his son was not good enough, that he needed to be who his father wanted him to be. Such feelings can be "threatening to a child because they threaten to break the attachment relationship, the bond," Dr. Cooper suggested. That creates feelings of guilt that are highly uncomfortable and can create physical and psychological symptoms." Anxiety and then collapse could result—as they did.[17]

We cannot, of course, know the truth. On such questions, the historian is like an archaeologist assembling a window from shards of glass. The missing piece of the puzzle is whether childhood trauma played a role in the trail of events leading to Madison's seizures. Some form of childhood trauma is strongly associated with nonepileptic seizures.[18] Unsurprisingly, many patients are

---

* One recent study found that psychogenic nonepileptic seizures were correlated with problems with "emotional regulation," which means the ability to control one's behavior while experiencing intense emotions. Amanda A. Uliaszek, Eric Prensky, and Gaston Baslet, "Emotional Regulation Profiles in Psychogenic Non-epileptic Seizures," *Epilepsy and Behavior* 23 (2012), 364–69. Another recent study found the seizures stem from "conversion disorders," which is when psychological stresses develop (or "convert") into physical symptoms. See endnote 18.

"unaware of psychic conflict that might be related to the symptom" and often "doubt that their symptoms are related to internal psychic processes."[19] Among these patients, nonepileptic seizures are strongly associated with depression, panic disorder, and chronic anxiety.[20] Did Madison, as a young boy, experience some trauma—whether emotional, sexual, or physical? Again, we cannot know. Perhaps he had no childhood trauma at all. But he certainly acted as if he did.

At any rate, the most remarkable aspect of Madison's seizures was not his struggle, but his victory. Regarding Madison's symptoms, Professor Jim Coan of the University of Virginia's Department of Psychology, an expert in neuroscience, told me, "It's the response to the panic attack that sets the stage for the future." He explained, "Humiliation is a key risk factor for developing the full-on disorder. From there, fear of bodily sensations combine with a fear of further humiliation to place the sufferer in a choke hold of chronic insecurity." People with panic disorders seek out anything they can hold onto, to explain the panic attack(s) they have experienced. They often avoid those things, which is one reason so many are agoraphobics as well. "You isolate yourself in order to avoid humiliating displays of panic," Coan said. "Consequently, your anxiety diminishes when you're alone, so being alone is further reinforced by a decreased frequency of panics. The cost of isolation of course is extreme loneliness—it's own kind of emotional hell."

For these reasons, the humiliation that Madison likely suffered about his attacks, Coan said, "offers insight both into Madison's disorder and—and I think this is important—his courage and strength."[21]

For the most part, Madison outmatched the rebellion of his body, just as he mastered the country's most riotous elements. It's no coincidence that his greatest contribution to the Constitution was his philosophy of how to govern the seemingly ungovernable.

A FTER HIS MORTIFYING COLLAPSE WITH THE MILITIA, MADISON SPENT the next year before the Virginia Convention, wielding weapons not in military exercises, but on more scholarly terrain. He believed another battle, perhaps more important than the one with muskets, would soon play out on the field of ideas, where he could make his mark, if he prepared as he had at Princeton.[22] And so he plunged in.

8 All Men Are Equally Entitled

MADISON PLOWED INTO THE BOOKS HE HAD ORDERED FROM ENGLAND on liberty and political theory. He combed the texts for insights into how government could protect—rather than destroy—freedom.[1] In July 1775, he asked his Princeton friend Stanhope Smith, traveling north, to find him two more pamphlets: Josiah Tucker's "An Apology for the Church of England as by Law Established" and Philip Turneux's "An Essay on Toleration."[2] He burrowed deeper into his study at Montpelier.

Everything was escalating around him. In November, Lord Dunmore announced martial law in Virginia, seized Norfolk and Princess Anne Counties, solicited Virginia's slaves to enlist in the British army, and established a new oath of allegiance. Congress then declared that Dunmore was "tearing up the foundations of civil authority" and ordered three companies of Pennsylvania troops to Virginia.[3] On New Year's Day, Dunmore retaliated by burning Virginia's largest city, Norfolk.

With the strong support of Patrick Henry, another convention was called to meet in Williamsburg in May 1776 to formally declare independence from Great Britain and to draft a new constitution for Virginia.

Meanwhile, Madison's father helped to restore his son to a new kind of service. In April 1776, the property-holding men of Orange voted for James Madison Jr. to serve as one of their two delegates to the Virginia Convention. On April 25, Thomas Barbour, the sheriff of Orange County, formally certified Madison. He did not intend to waste the opportunity.

YOUNG MADISON EXCITEDLY TRAVELED TO WILLIAMSBURG. UPON ARRIVING, he again saw Patrick Henry, wearing his homespun persona—buckskin, yarn stockings, unpowdered wig.[4] On May 6, 1776, the delegates took their seats.

The committee's first task was to draft a Declaration of Rights. The initial draft, written by the prosperous, self-educated planter George Mason, stated, "all men should enjoy the fullest toleration in the exercise of religion, &c." Government remained in the superior position of reviewing applications from an individual citizen, as a king received his supplicants on their bended knees.

This was Madison's moment—the culmination of his two years of study on religion, conscience, and morals at Montpelier. He stood to introduce a new version of the declaration. In his trembling voice, nervously seesawing back and forth, he read aloud a change. All men, he said, should instead be "*equally entitled* to the full and free exercise" of religion, "according to the dictates of conscience."

George Mason's draft:
That religion, or the duty we owe to our Creator and the manner of discharging it, can be directed only by reason and conviction, not by force or violence: and therefore, that all men should enjoy the fullest toleration in the exercise of religion, according to the dictates of conscience, unpunished and unrestrained by the magistrate unless, under color of religion, any man disturb the peace, happiness, or safety or society.

Madison's draft:
That religion, or the duty we owe to our Creator, and the manner of discharging it, being under the direction of reason and conviction only, not of violence or compulsion, all men are equally entitled to the full and free exercise of it, according to the dictates of conscience, and, therefore, that no man or class of men ought, on account of religion, to be invested with peculiar emoluments or privileges, nor subjected to any penalties or disabilities unless, under color of religion, the preservation of equal liberty and the existence of the state be manifestly endangered.

The gravity of Madison's seemingly small alteration dawned on the other men. In Mason's draft, conscience had merely impelled an individual to plead with his government for toleration. But Madison's extraordinary new idea recognized an individual's *private* conscience with a new *political* right to the full and free exercise of religion. That made private conviction a new and powerful force in the state.

Madison then went even further, prohibiting the government from using religion to give out any "peculiar emoluments or privileges" and from delivering "any penalties or disabilities"—unless the "preservation of equal liberty" itself, or, worse, the "existence of the state," were "manifestly endangered." Unless there was an *existential* threat against the state, in other words, government must stay within its bounds.

His call for consciences that would seize power from the government, rather than beg for it—for an additive rather than subtractive idea of religious freedom—joined a national chorus. Later that winter, Thomas Paine's December 23, 1776, letter titled "The Crisis" began with the famous words, "These are the times that try men's souls." "He whose heart is firm and whose conscience approves his conduct," Paine proclaimed, "will pursue his principles unto death."[5]

O N THE HEELS OF HIS "GIVE ME LIBERTY OR GIVE ME DEATH!" SPEECH, and his triumph against Dunmore, Henry played a far mightier role than Madison at the convention. He boasted to John Adams that the convention was "employed in the great work of forming a constitution" and noted that his "esteemed republican plan" had "many and powerful enemies." But he did not see his equal in the crowd, certainly not in the very young and slight man from Orange. Indeed, he sniffed at the lesser talents arrayed around him. "I cannot count upon one coadjutor of talents equal to the task," he wrote Adams. "Would to God that you and your Sam Adams were here!"

After two months of work and the finalization of a new constitution for Virginia, the delegates elected Henry to be Virginia's first free governor. Forming a new government was a heady time for all. In Henry's letter of acceptance, he pledged to rely upon the "known wisdom and virtue of your honorable House," which would give "permanency and success" to Virginia's new democracy, and which would, in turn, help "secure equal liberty" and "advance human happiness."[6] In the last days of the convention, Madison was selected to be one of four trusted "tellers" who administered the counting of votes for the government's new officers. After electing Henry governor, Madison, along with all the other delegates to the convention, was deemed a member of the new House of Delegates, with a term expiring six months later. The men adjourned on July 5, with plans to meet in Williamsburg in October as delegates in the new government.

For his part, Madison had already begun plotting to join the man he first met on the road to defy Dunmore—the revolutionary who had become the mirror not only of Virginia, but the nation—and the man who would end up his sworn enemy.

M EANWHILE, BACK IN NEW JERSEY, JOHN WITHERSPOON CONTINUED TO agitate for armed revolt. In 1776, writing under the pseudonym of the "Druid," he began a regular series of essays in *The Pennsylvania Magazine*. In his first installment, he poignantly described himself as "toward the end of life." Although he could not take to the battlefield in the revolution about to erupt, he declared that he felt he still must play a role, as there would be "greater need than ever in America" for the "most accurate discussion of the principles of society, the rights of nations, and the policy of states."

The teachers, in other words, would still matter. The politicians devoted to principles would be more crucial than ever. Above all, he said, his "ultimate object" in the Druid essays would be this: "He who makes a people *virtuous* makes them *invincible*."[7]

The more Witherspoon's fame grew, the more his enemies hated him. On July 30, 1776, British soldiers on Long Island burned an effigy of Witherspoon preaching to George Washington and other generals, whose likeness was also torched. After the battle of Trenton, a Hessian, mistaking a Presbyterian minister named John Rosborough for Witherspoon, ran him through with a bayonet.[8] Across the Atlantic, Witherspoon's reputation was magnified until he bestrode the colonial land like a colossus. A classmate of his from Edinburgh wrote a letter saying, "We have 1200 miles of territory occupied by about 300,000 people of which there are about 150,000 with Johnny Witherspoon at their head, against us—and the rest of us."[9] Another British officer, writing in the war's last years in 1783, would single out "*Dr. Witherspoon* . . . the political firebrand, who perhaps had not a less share in the Revolution than Washington himself. He poisons the minds of his young students and through them the Continent."[10]

And perhaps his effect was not exaggerated. One hundred thirty-eight of Witherspoon's students, including two of his sons, would go on to hold some rank in the Continental army. Only five students were loyal to England.[11]

But Madison, deprived of the opportunity to take up arms, was leading the charge of conscience on a new front: the revolutionary government itself.

9 Councilor to Governor Henry

O N OCTOBER 7, MADISON TRAVELED BACK TO WILLIAMSBURG TO BEGIN working in the new government. His early biographer William Rives believed this was when Madison and Jefferson first met. Jefferson had been in Philadelphia that summer serving in Congress and had resigned his seat to join Virginia's House of Delegates where, Rives wrote, he became "naturally and properly the leader."[1] Jefferson was immediately struck by his impatient and anxious young colleague. He later described Madison as "a new member and young" and recalled that "his extreme modesty . . . prevented his venturing himself in debate."[2]

Madison may have been quiet, but he did not shrink from the challenges ahead. On the contrary, he dove further into the apparatus of the new government. He was appointed to the Committee of Privileges and Elections, the Committee for Religion, and three special committees dealing with unsettled claims against the state related to Dunmore's war, Virginia's disputed boundary with Pennsylvania, and abolishing special privileges for the Anglican Church.[3] The six-month term flew by. The delegates could only return if they were actually elected by their constituents, and so Madison traveled the long road home to stand for election.

The wind seemed to be at his back. His experience in Williamsburg had been extraordinarily heady for the twenty-six-year-old. He had single-handedly changed the course of freedom of religion in Virginia. He felt he might tackle the integrity of democracy in Orange County as well. But that indulgence in idealism was about to deliver Madison a crushing defeat.

T HE CUSTOM IN ORANGE COUNTRY WAS FOR CANDIDATES TO BRING LARGE quantities of cider and liquor to voters at polling places. Whoever kept the voters drunkest in this extramural political competition would win. Voters, who often had to travel long distances to vote, loved the tradition, which created a kind of competitive drunken party between candidates' supporters at the court house where voting was taking place. It was a messy, happily vulgar tradition, with voters growing more raucous as the day progressed.

Madison had always found the practice beneath Virginia's dignity and his own concept of public service. The Commonwealth, he thought, was aspiring to become a land of achievement and nobility. How could an aspiring office-holder win through such a quid pro quo? Why should he have to trade liquor for votes? He should, he felt, be able to lead public opinion, to change how people thought about such a retrograde practice. And so Madison decided to buck the long tradition.

He not only let it be known that there would be no free booze for Madison supporters at the courthouses. He went on to publicly attack the "corrupting influence of spiritous liquors" in his campaign. He felt positive about his decision, but he noticed quickly less applause than he had hoped, particularly because one of his opponents, Charles Porter, also happened to run a tavern. The vote was held on April 24, 1777. Voters filed into courthouses to cast their ballots, cheerfully accepting free cups of punch and cider from Porter's supporters. They jawboned about the candidates' strengths and weaknesses, drinking more, trading stories about their upcoming planting season and the progress of the assembly in Williamsburg, drinking even more. And they collectively decided to throw the young Madison out of office.

He lost not only to Porter but to another candidate as well. He was stunned. One day, he was an elected official, mirror of his father's long-earned prestige, and his home county's designate to the colony's precious new government. Now, he was a private citizen with no power.

Later, Madison's supporters would allege that Porter had used bribery and corruption in the election.[4] But whether it was a fair fight or not, Madison soon realized he had lost his grasp on the public's favor. Later in life, he described the experience with uncompromising candor, castigating himself rather than the voters for obtuseness. He had regarded the liquor custom, he remembered, as "equally inconsistent with the purity of moral and of republican principles." He was "anxious to promote, by his example, the proper reform." But he made, he said, the mistake of trusting that his "new views of the subject" would "prevail with the people; whilst his competitors adhered to the old practice."[5]

At some point, Madison wrote a mysterious "paper containing some reflections on the importance of maintaining the purity of popular elections." The paper, nowhere to be found today, was cited verbatim by Rives in his nineteenth-century biography of Madison. In it, Madison provided a richer and angrier account of the episode, revealing his raison d'être in politics: to elevate the government rather than flatter the people. In Virginia at the time, Madison explained, the people "not only tolerated, but expected and even required to be courted and treated. No candidate, who neglected those attentions, could be elected." Madison's decision was therefore "ascribed to a mean parsimony" and to a "proud disrespect for the voters."

He had, he recalled, erroneously believed that the "spirit of the revolution" would support a "more chaste mode" for elections. But he had collided with "old habits" that were "too deeply rooted to be suddenly reformed." He took a swipe at the candidates who had stooped to conquer. He was outvoted by candidates, "neither of them having superior pretensions, and one particularly deficient in them," but both men, he said, were willing to use "all the means of influence familiar to the people." After he lost, the hypersensitive Madison added insult to his own injury by appearing highfalutin and aloof when asked about his defeat. The elderly Madison explained that the "reserve" he expressed to others after his loss was mistakenly "imputed to want of respect for them."[6] But his protective measure was simply self-defense.

Madison decided he would never again allow a fickle public to determine his destiny. He would control public opinion, lest it control him. And he learned another, more personal, lesson. He must always connect with others. They must *like* him. And nobody could ever think he saw himself as above them—ever again.

M ADISON BELIEVED EACH YEAR CONTAINED A "SICKLY SEASON" THAT ran from mid-July to early November, so the odds of an enjoyable year after his loss were already low. He likely spent the following months holed up at Montpelier, away from the disease and the public and the world in general.[7] But in November, with the humid sickly season passed, a new political opportunity opened up. Madison, restless as always, seized it.

ARTICLE 9 OF VIRGINIA'S NEW CONSTITUTION REQUIRED THAT THE governor exercise his executive powers "with the advice of a Council of State" (as well as that he not, "under any pretence, exercise any power or prerogative by virtue of any law, statute, or custom, of *England*"). The Council of State was elected not by regular propertied voters, but by elected officials. For the colonial Virginians by now deeply suspicious of centralized power, the council was intended as a profound check on a governor—even one as popular as Patrick Henry.*

The election was held in the House of Delegates. When Madison's name was announced, sixty-one men voted for James Madison, and only forty-two for Meriwether Smith, his opponent.

Madison was back in power.

IN JANUARY, HE TRAVELED TO WILLIAMSBURG TO BEGIN HIS SERVICE. ON THE unseasonably warm day of January 14, 1778, he stood before Patrick Henry, placed his small hand on a Bible, and followed as Henry read these words out to him: "I, James Madison Jr.," he said, "do solemnly promise and swear, that I will, to the best of my skill and judgment, execute the said office diligently and faithfully according to law."

Dudley Digges, John Blair, Nathaniel Harrison, and David Jameson, the four other members of the council, looked on. Three were older and far more august than Madison. Digges, sixty, was a member of a storied Tidewater political family. Blair, forty-six, was a prominent lawyer. Harrison, almost seventy, was a state senator.[8] The only one near Madison's age was Jameson,

---

* By the Virginia Convention of 1829, the Council's power had become so controversial that one delegate said, "I am not going to say any thing more about the Executive Council. God help me, I sometimes think I am labouring under a partial insanity and that this must be one of the subjects in which it runs." David Robertson, *Debates and Other Proceedings of the Convention of Virginia* (Richmond: Enquirer-Press, 1805), 181.

a twenty-one-year-old prodigy who had already built a successful merchant business in nearby Yorktown.[9]

Madison liked Jameson, and bonded as easily with him as Bradford. The young men shared a contagious enthusiasm for ideas that easily spilled over into conversation. Their marked lack of pretense allowed them to surmount the barriers usually separating the politically ambitious. They even shared the same melodramatic hypochondria. Years later, after Madison had moved to Philadelphia as a congressman, Jameson would mourn the "thin putrid state of the Air" of Richmond, looking back to their time in Williamsburg for comfort: "I have been long used to the Salt Air," he wrote Madison, "and think I cannot enjoy health without it."[10]

Digges, Blair, Harrison, and Jameson would be Madison's partners in a new venture. Madison completed his oath: "[I] will be faithful to the commonwealth of Virginia, and will support and defend the same, according to the constitution thereof, to the utmost of my power."[11] They politely applauded—and got to work. They quickly had to deal with matters of life and death.

I N VALLEY FORGE IN PENNSYLVANIA, WASHINGTON'S SOLDIERS WOKE UP HUN-gry and spent their days that way, with precious supplies of pork, beef, and bacon achingly slow to arrive, and limited when they came. Night after night, they ate only fire cake—water and dough cooked over a campfire.[12] Their feet cracked and bled as the cold and snow ate them alive. A brigadier general described their condition: "near one half of them destitute of any kind of shoes or stockings to their feet, and I may add many without either Breeches shirts or blankets exposed." He observed many living in log huts without doors or floors.[13]

On December 31, Governor Henry received a letter from Congress with "alarming Accounts of the Distresses of the American Army for the Want of provisions." Washington warned Congress that unless supplies were sent immediately, the troops would *Starve Disolve or Disperse.* Madison and the others urged Henry to instruct the Continental commissary to send an "active intelligent & proper person" to Virginia's northwestern counties to buy up all the available pork, beef, and bacon, along with wagons for sending salt and other necessities—and quickly. Henry agreed, immediately putting the order in place.[14]

Madison was hooked on the problem that has long tormented military strategists—supplying troops in an extended war. But he was infuriated to find the council's efforts disappearing into Virginia's bottomless bureaucracy. The deputy commissary refused Henry's request for a mission northwest for provisions, advising the governor that he should ask his deputy instead. Henry, learning that eight or ten thousand hogs and several thousand cows were available to be driven to the camping soldiers, employed three "Gentlemen of Character" to instantly purchase the livestock and drive them up to Washington's camp.[15]

But, for Madison, the broader problem remained: the governor did not control, or even fund, the commissary. Congress did, and Congress was dysfunctional. On December 31, 1777, Congress allocated Virginia's delegates a paltry $50,000 to buy goods for the army.[16] That still left Henry in the constant position of begging for more money whenever it was needed, which it always was. Henry was livid. The commissary's refusals to act with alacrity, he told Virginia's congressional delegates (in a letter Madison probably drafted), "filled me with Concern & astonishment."[17] "The Genius of this Country," he angrily wrote, "is not of that Cast."[18]

Meanwhile, George Washington bitterly complained about the suffering of his troops. Early the next spring, Madison joined the other councilors in advising Henry that the "great fatigues to which he is constantly exposed" were placing Washington's *own* health at risk. Because necessary items were unavailable in the "exhausted part of America" where the troops were stationed, the five men asked the governor to direct the commissary to send Washington good rum, wine, and sugar.[19] Henry gladly complied.

EVEN THOUGH HE WAS MAKING WAR POLICY, MADISON WAS INSULATED from the dangers and violence of the battlefield in the quiet college town. The pillar of his comfortable world was his cousin, the Reverend James Madison, who had recently become president of the College of William and Mary. Madison moved into a room at his cousin's house, which was a "much better accommodation," he told his father, "than I could have promised myself."

His cousin taught natural and moral philosophy at the college and was an Anglican minister, which put him at good-natured odds with James's father. The reverend had always had a warm spot for his scholarly young cousin, and he was gentle and uncritical toward his houseguest. He admired James's fortitude and intellect, his humor and conviction, and his plain commitment to the common good. Madison, in turn, was moved by his cousin's steady moral compass; as an old man, he remembered the reverend as a man of "intellectual power and diversified learning" and recalled his "benevolence," "courtesy," and commitment to "our Revolution, and to the purest principles of a Government founded on the rights of man."[20]

However, as much as he enjoyed his cousin's companionship, he found himself longing for the everyday comforts, even the foods, of Montpelier. He wrote his father to ask for some of the local dried fruit he loved, explaining, "It would be very agreeable to me if I were enabled by such rarities as our part of the Country furnishes." He missed his family; he reminded his father, with some urgency, "I hope you will not forget my parting request that I might hear frequently from home."

And the eldest brother worried, too, about his younger brother Ambrose, who had left to fight the British. After hearing nothing about Ambrose's safety for too long, he became deeply anxious. "Whenever my brother returns from the Army," he pleaded with his father, "I desire he may be informed I shall expect he will make up by letter the loss of intelligence I sustain by my removal out of his way."[21]

Although Madison's bruising electoral loss still haunted him, his family and friends back home were plotting his restoration. On April 23, 1778— exactly a year after his loss—his neighbors reelected him, in absentia, to the House of Delegates. Virginia law prevented one man from simultaneously serving in the council and the legislature, and so the House of Delegates, by resolution, voided the election.[22] But Madison took satisfaction in the victory all the same.

H ENRY'S TERM AS GOVERNOR WAS SPEEDING TO AN END. IN JUNE 1779, Thomas Jefferson was elected Virginia's new governor. Madison stayed on as councilor to the new governor.

These were increasingly precarious times for the country, and especially for Virginia. As the most populous and prosperous of the states, Virginia had previously enjoyed unparalleled national prestige. But constant British attacks and a rapacious inflation crisis were sapping her strength. Even worse was the growing fatigue among Virginia's leadership class for tackling the problems themselves, through public service. Virginia had previously sent her very best people to Congress, including Jefferson himself; Edmund Pendleton, a lawyer and judge who had been president of the Virginia Convention and then the first judge of the Supreme Court; and George Wythe, the so-called first law professor, who taught Jefferson, James Monroe, and John Marshall at William and Mary, even designing the "*Sic semper tyrannis*" state flag with George Mason.[23]

Yet they all had departed Philadelphia, disgusted with the ineffectiveness of the Continental Congress. They left behind a cavernous emptiness. George Washington watched their replacements in Congress fritter away their power. He described with distaste to Benjamin Harrison, the speaker of Virginia's House of Delegates, their "idleness dissipation & extravagance." Most of the men, he spat, were infected by an "insatiable thirst for riches." He watched in disgust as they poured worthless money into Philadelphia's taverns and fleshpots. The delegates routinely spent three or four hundred pounds on a concert, dinner, or a supper; such decadence, he wrote, would "not only take Men off from acting in but even from thinking of this business." As a consequence, "party disputes and personal quarrels" had become the "great business of the day."[24]

Washington implored Harrison to present his letter to the best men in Richmond as a tool for recruiting them to travel to Philadelphia. As "ever the Sun did in its meridian brightness," he declared, the country had never been in such "eminent need of the wise patriotic and spirited exertions of her Sons than at this period." His "pious wish" for the county was, he told Harrison, that each state would "not only choose but absolutely compel their ablest men" to come to Congress, and that they would then launch an investigation of the causes that had produced "so many disagreeable effects in the army and Country."[25] That was precisely what Madison began planning to do.*

---

* Washington was not alone in bemoaning Virginia's men in Philadelphia. Richard Henry Lee, who seconded the motion in the Continental Congress calling for independence, had fled Congress along with Jefferson. In 1778, he wrote a letter mocking

With Madison's prestige continuing to rise, his older colleagues looked to the compelling young man to fill the void. When the General Assembly met on December 14, 1779, they elected James Madison one of four new representatives to serve in Philadelphia.

Madison was electrified. He wrote an ecstatic, unctuous letter to Speaker Harrison, assuring him that "as far as fidelity and zeal can supply the place of abilities the interests of my country shall be punctually promoted." The eager young man inadvertently dated the letter "November" instead of "December."[26] But as much as he wanted to leave for Philadelphia, he was restrained by that old friend—his conscience.

Throughout the thirteen states, new congressmen were saddling their horses and taking to chilly roads, in an attempt to outrace winter to the capital. They were excited for the fervor, chaos, and intrigue of Philadelphia. An unusual chill had begun to appear in the air. From New Jersey, Washington said the frost exceeded anything "that had ever been experienced in this climate before."[27] By January, heavy snows began to fall. A great winter descended on Virginia, locking Madison in a snowy prison. He had stayed behind on purpose.

The congressman-elect was already hard at work in his parents' home, refusing the seductive capital as he tried to save it.

---

the no-names who were replacing Virginia's statesmen in declamatory sarcasm. "The Virginia delegates in Congress are James Mercer! William Fitzhugh of Chatham! Flemming! Cyrus Griffen! Mery Smith!" By the next year, even those embarrassing men were gone. Fleming and Smith resigned in disgrace. Randolph retired under a cloud of financial impropriety. Fitzhugh dug in his heels in Virginia, effectively resigning. Patrick Henry refused to serve. Cyrus Griffin was the only one left in Philadelphia, but he could not even technically represent Virginia under Virginia's own law, which required three members as a quorum. Irving Brant, *James Madison: The Virginia Revolutionist, 1751–1780*, vol. 1 (New York: Bobbs-Merrill, 1941), 362.

10 "Distrust of the Public Ability"

MADISON SAT IN THE LIBRARY OVERLOOKING THE FARAWAY MOUNTAINS, their familiar blue gauze powdered by snow. His purse was filled with Virginia currency that galloping inflation had rendered virtually worthless. The crisis had started the year before. In December 1778, Washington had observed that money was sinking "five percent a day." Ominously, he said, "I shall not be surprised if in the course of a few months a total stop is put to the currency of it."[1]

Madison spent the winter plowing through advanced texts on economic theory. A half-century later, he would describe this as an "unavoidable detention"; the call came like a force of his own nature. His research ineluctably drove toward an answer, which he began sketching out in a magisterial, 3,500-word essay confidently challenging the major macroeconomic assumptions guiding the country, with all the impatience and tenacity of a young John Witherspoon.

Madison launched his essay with a broadside against public opinion. While it was commonly supposed that the value of money should be regulated by quantity, he proposed to submit to the public a counterargument. Inflation, he declared, was not about paper money itself; printed bills were collapsing because of an underlying decay in the common "distrust of the public ability" to redeem the dollars in the future. The real question, therefore, was not only whether paper money could be exchanged in the future for actual gold or silver—it was whether people *believed* it could be.

The story of how the country had reached this point of mass disbelief in the redeemability of currency was, according to Madison, as simple as it was insidious. In the early years of the war, the "sinister events" of Congress's incompetent management of army supplies had increased the "distrust of the public ability to fulfill" the country's commitments. Misconduct by the nation's purchasing departments—federal subsidies—had dramatically raised the price of articles like clothing, machines, and grain. That, in turn, had triggered the need to print more money so the public could afford the items. And that, in turn, forced the people—quite rationally—to doubt that the paper bills in circulation would be worth their face value in the future. The amount of currency required to purchase goods then naturally skyrocketed, because the people didn't believe their stated value.

In other words, the inflation catastrophe had been driven by a crisis in confidence in the very prospect of collective action through a federal center. Madison drew an ominous metaphor of a hapless entrepreneur who pursues a costly business, but lacks sufficient cash to finance the project. Instead, he uses bonds and notes secured by an estate to which he has a questionable title. Even worse, his enemies employ "every artifice to disparage that security."[2] The country's situation, like the entrepeneur's, was untenable because of the failure of leadership and the vacuum of united national purpose. Any policy that did not directly attack those problems was boxing at shadows.

Strangely, Madison felt no need to publish the essay. He took twelve years before placing it in his Princeton friend Philip Freneau's *National Gazette*. It was a private document that powered his entry into Congress, that helped him become, on the issue of federalism, a man of conviction, superior knowledge, and an unswerving theory of his case.

H IS ESSAY WAS COMPLETE. SPRING ARRIVED. AT LAST, MADISON LEFT Montpelier. He traveled for twelve difficult days to Philadelphia. He came into the city on Saturday, March 18. On Monday, he wrote his father a rushed, excited note describing the "extreme badness of the roads and frequency of rains." From the moment he stepped off his carriage and entered his boardinghouse, the threat of war rumbled in Philadelphia. Tom Paine was busily distributing his ninth pamphlet in his *Crisis* series. England, he warned, was about to reap the bitter fruit of its own cruelty. He issued bloodthirsty threats: "The world awakens with no pity at your complaints. You felt none for others; you deserve none for yourselves."[3]

In the chilly March air, Madison thrilled to the wartime city's vitality. He watched well-made carriages bounce past, women in fashionable dresses hurry by, and gentlemen, lobbyists, and foreign diplomats throw back mugs of ale in taverns, plotting for each legislative session. In his first days in the chamber, he watched with barely concealed disgust as the legislators bickered on matters they barely understood. The fiscal situation was even more dire than he had imagined, the public debt an anchor dragging down the nation's monetary system.

Years before his arrival, Congress had thrashed around the problem, eventually establishing a debt ceiling on September 1, 1779, with a resolution that stated that "on no account whatsoever" should the nation exceed $200 million.[4] Now, he watched with disgust as the men in Philadelphia dreamt up another scheme to escape the debt limit by changing old dollars for new currency.

The situation affected Madison's quality of life as a new arrival in the expensive city. He had brought to Philadelphia ludicrously complicated money: pounds printed in Virginia (which, like all states, had its own currency), the old federal Continental dollars, and the new federal currency called specie. But his two thousand Virginian pounds were declining in value every week and either had to be spent with the few merchants who would accept them or exchanged for federal currency at awful rates. Meanwhile, the bill from March 20 to September 20 at his boardinghouse alone would come to a staggering $21,373 in Continental dollars. He spent over a thousand dollars alone on haircuts.[5] By April, he would feel he had no option but to ask for a loan from the federal treasury for eight thousand dollars in specie to try to pay his expenses in nondeflated currency.[6]

Now, he watched with amazement as Congress voted for a system to convert the 200 million dollars currently in circulation into a new public debt of 5 million dollars. Their scheme would exchange forty old dollars for a single dollar of specie and a note of credit entitling holders to an additional 5 percent interest in six years. But because the actual return on specie was already plunging due to inflation, the resolution instructed states to pay their quotas to the federal government in hard currency, with "one Spanish milled dollar in lieu of forty dollars of the bills now in circulation."[7]

This was *precisely* the sort of madness Madison had diagnosed the previous winter at Montpelier, one that ignored the underlying crisis of confidence in government itself. Even worse, Congress would fill its *own* coffers with real

money—Spanish milled dollars—rather than the bogus currency it was printing, rather fecklessly showing its hand. Finally, he told his father, the scheme
would almost certainly backfire, creating "great perplexity and complaints in
many private transactions."[8] The nation was marching, arms locked, over a
cliff of its own making.

Angry and well informed, he was well prepared to take on the preposterous money exchange proposal. But as a brand-new congressman, he knew he
would need to bide his time and pick his moments. He chose to vent to confi-
dantes instead. Madison wrote to Governor Jefferson. Out of all the "various
conjectures of alarm and distress," he cried, nothing was more critical than
the parade of horribles in Philadelphia. The army faced an "immediate alternative of disbanding or living on free quarter." The treasury was "empty." The
government's credit was "exhausted." Even private credit had been extended
"as far as it will bear." The weak men of Congress, meanwhile, were "complaining of the extortion of the people," while the people bewailed "the
improvidence of Congress." Meanwhile, the army's military leaders blamed
both the people *and* Congress for failing to support soldiers on the front.

The country required, in other words, "the most mature & systematic
measures," but instead they were getting harebrained schemes like Congress's
"untried & precarious" currency exchange. The end result, he predicted,
would be a "total stagnation in prospect."

He tied these strands together in a diagnosis that would serve as his own
beacon for the remainder of his long public life. "Congress from a defect of
adequate Statesmen," he told Jefferson, was "more likely to fall into wrong
measures and of less weight to enforce right ones."[9]

Madison's damnation of Congress was so controversial it was omitted in
both the 1840 and 1900 versions of his papers.[10] Now that we know what he
said, "adequate statesmen" is the phrase that rings loudest in Madison's litany.
A legion of small men was collectively failing to rise to the occasion. Only
statesmen could save America from herself. And extraordinary statesmen were
not even needed. "Adequate" ones would do—ones with the humility of Madison himself.

At twenty-nine, James Madison had discovered, at long last, his calling.

PART II

11 A Defect of Adequate Statesmen

MADISON SCOURED THE NEWSPAPERS IN THE TAVERNS. HE SLICED OPEN the envelopes arriving daily from home. He eyed the exhausted soldiers returning from the front with musket wounds, amputations, and frostbite. Their plight galled him. The states' coffers simply did not hold enough currency to pay for the boots, blankets, flour, bacon, and rum that would get soldiers through battle. He fretted that General Washington was "weak in numbers beyond all suspicion" and facing as great a threat "from famine as from the Enemy." Unless reinforcements were sent, he said, the campaign would become "equally disgraceful to our Councils & disgus[t]ful to our Allies."[1]

As a delegate in Virginia, he had been fascinated by the issue too demonically complicated for many other delegates: supplying the troops. Madison loved wrangling with the issue of military supplies because it united, so concisely, all his preoccupations—the nation's money supply, his failure to serve as a soldier, and the home front. Even better, for a mind drawn to nettlesome paradoxes, the issue presented an almost perfect quandary. The Scylla and Charybdis were these: The states could print more dollars to pay merchants for the goods, but that would quickly deflate their currency. Or they could "requisition" (the polite term for "seize") wealthy citizens' private assets to supply the troops, but that would further cripple confidence in the government. And the federal government, of course, was too toothless to solve the problem on its own. In early 1780, Congress faced the astounding option of requesting that the states contribute to the federal treasury not in currency but *in kind*: with flour, beef, hay, and corn. It was as if the nation was returning to an ancient time where tribes exchanged goods for peace.[2]

If he was an impatient young man ready to unleash change on an immature nation *before* he arrived in Philadelphia, Madison's frustration only redoubled when two of Washington's regiments threatened to mutiny because their nation would not pay, feed, or clothe them.[3]

Two days after he first started his service in Congress, he was appointed to the three-member Board of Admiralty. This was a difficult assignment, for the navy was tiny and barely functioning and full of complaints to Congress.[4] Madison eventually resigned the assignment in early June, but not before drawing notice for the quality and precision of his commentary.

Barely half a year into his Philadelphia stint, the frenetic figure, silent on the floor of the legislature, was already eliciting remarkable respect. Madison pulled focus. Everyone listened when he spoke, watching him for cues, as he offered the piercing intelligence, leavened with wry humor, that had been his métier since college. By the summer, leaders in Congress suggested him for an appointment to a foreign embassy, most likely Spain or France, an extraordinary recognition for a first-term congressman. But he quickly declined. We do not know why, but he later expressed mortal fears that European travel would endanger his health. Through his long life, he would never visit the Continent, and anxiety again seems to be a likely culprit.

The Madisons of Virginia eagerly consumed news of his advances in Philadelphia. His cousin wrote him from Williamsburg, "We hear that you have refused an important Place in a foreign Embassy." Plainly devastated, the reverend desperately tried to reframe Madison's choice as courage. The "Refusal does you Honour," he said, but could not refrain from delectating upon the lost honors Madison would have gathered. His cousin confessed that he himself could not have "withstood so alluring a Prospect." But he conceded that Madison's noble nature insulated him from self-gratification; "ambitious motives," he said, did not "have any Influence with you."[5]

Madison was the avatar of his family's dreams. In assuaging his own anxiety, he also increased theirs. On that front, victory must have seemed impossible.

B Y OCTOBER 1780, THE RAGGED TROOPS WERE EYEING YET ANOTHER brutal winter. Madison predicted the supply trains would bring not relief but "infinite disappointment." He told his friends the states needed to own up to the unpleasant duty of taxing their citizens in real currency to fund their military operations. If the states refused taxation and relied on printing money, he said, "what was intended for our relief will only hasten our destruction."[6]

He responded to this dysfunctional situation with imagination. *Brainstorming* is the apt metaphor; he loved to let ideas rain, to splash with new concepts, or to let them splash with him. And like a great storm, his intellectual play could swamp conceptual ramparts, sweep away fences, and leave in its wake a fresh intellectual landscape reflecting his impatience.

One idea in particular now fixated him, which he quickly sent to his friend Joseph Jones, an ally sitting in Virginia's General Assembly. Madison had found a solution to attack the lack of confidence in the government itself, to bind the people to the government through a *nexus imperii*. He proposed to Jones that Virginia begin issuing war bonds—certificates that could be redeemed after the war ended, with interest. The scheme, he explained, would "anticipate during the war the future revenues of peace," driving a war-weary public to strive, even more urgently, to win the war. It would also "compel" the people, he said, to "*lend* the public their commodities, as people elsewhere lend their money to purchase commodities." The bonds would stop the collective enterprise from disintegrating into its constituent parts.[7]

But he heard only silence in response. Whether Jones was disinterested or the scheme fell flat when it was introduced on the floor, Virginia again failed not only to lead, but even to take a stab at resolving its fatal problem.

The situation frustrated Madison to no end. As winter approached and the days grew shorter, he complained to Edmund Pendleton that recruiting troops was not actually Virginia's greatest problem. Instead, the lack of food, munitions, and clothing stemming from the lack of money, he said, "gives the greatest alarm."[8]

WHILE MADISON WAS ANGERED BY AFFAIRS IN CONGRESS, HE WAS becoming strangely popular among the chattering classes in Philadelphia, who were fascinated by him. Attending the dances and gatherings required for a member of Congress, he displayed his customary chill among throngs of unfamiliar people—a shell noticeable to almost everyone. During his first year in Congress, he was attacked by Martha Bland, the wife of a dull, rival Virginia delegate named Theodorick Bland, as a "gloomy stiff creature." "They say he is clever in Congress," she reluctantly conceded, "but out of it he had nothing engaging or even bearable in his manners." He was, she sniffed, the "most unsociable creature in existence."[9] He probably couldn't have cared less what Martha Bland thought of him, and probably let her know it. He could turn hard and cold with those he did not like or know, and she was both.

His instinctive reserve had previously prevented him from speaking out in front of the hard-eyed, demanding men of Congress. But in November, the urgency of the moment finally spurred him to rise on the floor. The other men watched their young, bright-eyed colleague with curiosity; what could the tiny rural Virginian have to say?

H E BEGAN SPEAKING SO QUIETLY THAT IT WAS EXTREMELY DIFFICULT FOR the other men to hear him. He attacked the "evils arising from certificates & emissions" from the states. He then introduced a motion to prevent the states from printing any more money. The other congressmen did not applaud. Many appeared openly sour toward his idea. Several stood, in quick order, to attack his motion as "manifestly repugnant" to the nation's existing financial system. Madison, hard-bitten student of public opinion as he was, realized the opposition was too great. He allowed his motion to die. He later bemusedly recounted to his friend Jones that his idea met with "so cool a reception" that he "did not much urge it."[10]

But it was a small setback. His appetite for great change had been whetted. Meanwhile, a disorienting fog of war further cloaked the nation. Deep within, even crazy ideas were starting to appear reasonable.

A S AUTUMN CHILLED PHILADELPHIA AND WINTER FAST APPROACHED, Madison heard about a staggering proposal circulating Richmond to address Virginia's flagging troop recruitment. The idea was to reward each new man who joined the army with a male slave between ten and forty years old, requisitioned from anyone who already owned over twenty slaves. Jones—normally a stable, trustworthy fellow—relayed the plan with qualified enthusiasm.[11] The grossly inhumane plan appalled Madison.

But something about the idea did catch his attention. Brainstorming, he hit upon a new formulation. Virginia, he imagined, could "liberate and make soldiers at once of the blacks themselves" instead of making them instruments for the enlistment of white soldiers. In other words, slaves would be recruited to the army with the promise of their freedom. Writing Jones, he suggested that his new scheme would certainly be more "consonant to the principles of liberty," which, after all, "ought never to be lost sight of in a contest for liberty."

His system, he thought, would also be more pragmatic. The new black soldiers, so grateful for their freedom, would be courteous and obedient. As for the concern that the new soldiers might try to free family members and friends who were still enslaved, he was not worried. He confidently argued that in his experience slaves, once freed, lost all "attachment & sympathy" with former fellow slaves.[12]

Back in Richmond, the idea of enticing white soldiers with the promise of personal slaves quickly capsized when slaveholders attacked it on the grounds that it would illegally seize their property and liberal legislators called it "inhuman and cruel." But Madison's idea fared no better. Jones politely informed Madison that enlisting black men with the promise of liberation would not only require the immediate abolition of slavery—which was impossible—but would probably also lead the British to reprise Dunmore's earlier attempt to recruit black soldiers en masse. Just as bad, Jones said, would be the simple economic impact on Virginia. Without slaves, the southern states would collapse.[13] Jones apparently refused to carry Madison's measure at all.

While enthusiastic, Madison's creative proposal exposed a flaw in his thinking. Too confident in the power of a logical idea, too committed to control as an end in itself, he completely outthought himself. For how could such a scheme ever work in practice, really? But Madison, undaunted, kept brainstorming.

RESTLESSLY WALKING THROUGH THE COBBLED PHILADELPHIA STREETS, Madison seemed powered by an internal energy source. He sustained an intense pace of activity in Philadelphia, making friends with like-minded delegates around the capital who collectively took a perverse pleasure in bemoaning the country's precarious state. But as a collapse seemed increasingly imminent, the drama became less beguiling, and his sensitivity returned.

During the autumn of his first year in Philadelphia, he fell ill.[14] There were no soothing hot springs in Philadelphia, only the respite of the guest house, and so he retreated to bed. He complained bitterly about his health to his friends, and word quickly spread back to Virginia that Orange's precocious yet fragile son again stood on a brink. In early March 1781, his cousin the reverend wrote worriedly from Williamsburg, "I have heard of a severe Attack."[15] It was only by late March, a year after he arrived in the city, that his health was finally, in Madison's words, "re-establish'd."[16]

I N VIRGINIA, THE BRITISH GENERAL CORNWALLIS LAUNCHED A RENEWED assault, reasoning, "Until Virginia is reduced we could not hold the more Southern provinces." Patches of Tory resistance to the revolution broke out. In the spring of 1781, when the General Assembly met for a single day in Richmond, word spread that Cornwallis was poised to seize the city and capture the delegates.

The assembly, including Patrick Henry, fled on their horses for Charlottesville, sixty miles away. After a short respite, they learned the British were in close pursuit. Henry and three other men left for Staunton, another forty miles away. Once there, they hid in a deep gorge. When night came, they sought shelter from an older woman living in a lone cabin, whose husband and sons had just left to fight in Charlottesville. Henry explained that they were members of the legislature. "Ride on then, ye cowardly knaves," the woman retorted. Henry asked her whether she would shelter even Patrick Henry, if he had fled. "Patrick Henry would never do such a cowardly thing," she indignantly responded.

He then explained that he was, in fact, Patrick Henry. The old woman gaped. The revolutionary hero—there on her porch! "Well, then, if that's Patrick Henry, it must be all right," she exclaimed. "Come in," she cried, waving the four men in, "and ye shall have the best I have in the house."[17] She fed and protected the men that night.

She was one of Patrick Henry's sworn people—just one in a legion.

IMAGE 11.1. *PATRICK HENRY*, BY THOMAS SULLY.
COURTESY OF HISTORICAL SOCIETY OF VIRGINIA.

BACK IN PHILADELPHIA, MADISON WAS DEALING WITH MUCH MORE mundane matters, and with considerably less flair. Like the nation, he found himself occupying an unfamiliar economic stratum in the busy city, where the richest 10 percent of the population owned over half the wealth. Most of them were merchants who usually kept a town house in the city as well as a country estate within about ten miles. These homes were filled with mahogany furniture and silver services and were reached not on horseback but by expensive four-wheel carriages.[18]

To succeed in Philadelphia, Madison knew he must travel among those people. He would need to buy good wine and fine dinners, maintain horses and footmen, and keep clean and fashionable breeches, waistcoats, ruffles, buttons, and boots. He also would need to buy cord upon cord of precious firewood to heat his room in the city's frigid winter. But he had no income other than what his father and the Virginia government sent him, and he had to beg for both on a continual basis. He was humiliated by his father's refusal to send him an adequate allowance.

Worse, he could not collect on a loan he had made to his friend Edmund Randolph, then Virginia's attorney general. Randolph was Madison's complement in some respects, but they were also quite different men. Randolph's face was broad and calm, his demeanor open, but his pleasant persona concealed considerable tumult. After the Declaration of Independence, Randolph's father sided with the British and returned to England. Randolph endured continuing shame about his father's treachery. He was charismatic and intelligent, but unusually emotional and sometimes tendentious, more raw and unpredictable than more studied politicians—in other words, he needed cipher even more than Madison did.

In early 1781, Randolph had asked Madison for a loan of twenty pounds—perhaps two thousand dollars in today's currency. His prestigious position did not pay enough for Randolph to live on and pay the ignominious debts of his father. He was forced to maintain a private practice, staying on as attorney general to prevent his father's debtors from pursuing him, because, as a sitting state official, he could not be sued.[19] By the next year, Madison, struggling to stay afloat in the capital, asked Randolph to repay him.[20] At the same time, he pleaded with Randolph to work in Richmond to increase the salary for Virginia's delegates.[21] Randolph responded a little tartly, noting that "the great fulcrum of life in the extravagant city" of Philadelphia was to blame, and promising Madison nothing.[22]

Madison had no other options left. He reluctantly trudged down Front Street to a little office near a coffeehouse to visit a well-known lender named Haym Solomon to ask for a private loan. To hock himself seems beneath his station. But he simply had no choice.

A friendly, stooped man even smaller than Madison greeted him. Madison's embarrassment quickly dissolved in the face of Solomon's humility. After listening to his problems, Solomon told Madison that he would loan him the money he needed, but from his personal funds, and at a below-market interest rate. He explained to Madison that customarily high interest rates were "so usurious" that nobody should use them except, perhaps, speculators.

IMAGE 11.2. *EDMUND RANDOLPH.*
COURTESY OF THE LIBRARY OF VIRGINIA.

A strange kinship quickly developed between the two men. Madison was soon recounting to Edmund Randolph the "kindness of our little friend."[23] Anti-Semitism was as rife in America as anywhere else. The European stereotypes evident in the Shylock figure in Shakespeare's *The Merchant of Venice* were familiar to Madison and other colonial Americans. Yet in the months to come, Madison decidedly avoided anti-Semitism in his dealings with Solomon. By contrast, Randolph, who also borrowed from Solomon, mocked him as the "little Levite," complaining that he felt "most sorely" the "wounds" inflicted by "Haym Solomon, and divers other jews." Randolph even saw little Solomon as a menace, worrying that the moneylender and his brethren might throw him into jail if he failed to repay his debts with interest.[24]

Madison's affection toward Haym Solomon, as contrasted with Randolph's embrace of virulent stereotypes, reveals Madison's fundamental generosity, his capacity for sympathy with the downtrodden. Solomon lived only a little while longer. He used his own money to set up a business purchasing military supplies and selling them to the government, but he only rarely demanded the government repay him. He died in 1784, leaving behind no property other than his unpaid claims against the government, which were discovered and validated posthumously by Congress.[25]

The loan from Solomon relieved Madison's circumstance only temporarily; he continued to feel vulnerable financially. When he wanted to purchase a library full of scarce and necessary books, available for about a quarter of their normal price, he pleaded with his father to help pay for them.[26] Over a month later, when his father still had not responded, Madison rashly bought the books with a draft on his father's name. He wrote his father afterward, "I hope you will be able to find means to satisfy it," suggesting that if it could "not be otherwise done," then the elder Madison could deduct the amount from any "further supply you have in contemplation for me"—his inheritance. Of that drastic scenario, he wrote, "I must submit to it."[27]

Thirty years old, Madison still saw money as an instrument of "submission" to his father. He complained about his "arrearages." He even threatened that unless "liberal principles" prevailed, he would be "under the necessity of selling a negro"—a particularly fraught threat, for his father knew that his son did not view his slaves as only property.[28]

Madison escalated matters by employing what we might call today emotional blackmail. He informed his father that the state of his finances could even prevent him from coming home after the legislative session. He needed a new carriage, he said, but could not afford it.[29]

Finally, he had hit upon an argument that would work. His father, probably anxious about the effect of a long absence on Madison's doting mother, at last relented—and sent the money.

MADISON MUST HAVE LOOKED DOWN AT HIS BLACK BREECHES IN EMBARrassment as yet another delegate blasted the federal government where they all sat. He pondered the problem of how to convince, or induce, or force, the states to fund the government fighting their war for them. In January 1781, Madison had decided he was finished waiting. On February 3, less than a year after arriving in Congress, he rose on the floor and, in his soft voice, read out a measure that "earnestly recommend[ed]" that each state implement a new 5 percent tariff on all imports, with the monies going directly to the federal government.

John Witherspoon had become, by this time, a delegate to Congress from New Jersey. Madison saw him often in Philadelphia, and the two men had maintained their easy friendship from Princeton, ballasted by their mutual frustration with Congress. Madison met with his former professor and pressed him to support the tariff. Witherspoon not only agreed with his former student but took his idea a step further. He soon stood to introduce a motion that would empower Congress to regulate all commerce in every state, establishing a new and exclusive federal right to tax all imported goods.

Witherspoon's radical resolution was defeated by a narrow vote of five states to four. But he succeeded in creating political space for a more moderate measure. Madison quickly stepped into the gap, proposing a version that would pass the funds through state governments first, rather than allowing Congress directly to collect the monies. And that version passed.

At first blush, Madison's victory seemed hugely significant. The novice from Virginia had given Congress new power to govern both monetary policy and military supply, with a system uniquely designed for the country's unique politics. But nothing was that easy in the Continental Congress. With Massachusetts taking the lead, the states rebelled against Madison's nuanced solution.[30]

Madison pondered his loss, and he plotted.

12 The Coercive Power

MADISON WAS DOING BATTLE ON TWO FRONTS SIMULTANEOUSLY IN Philadelphia. On the one hand, he was fighting in Congress to strengthen the federal government and supply the soldiers. But he was also orchestrating support for the federal government back home in Virginia. Both contests usually felt exhausting and fruitless, and he gradually recognized that they both demanded a unified solution: coercion.

The federal government, he decided, must be able to *coerce* the states. His new ambition wove control as a *philosophical* matter into his *political* ambitions for the country. Searching for an opportunity to present his case, he seized on a new committee charged with giving Congress the "necessary powers" for executing the Articles of Confederation in the states. In essence, Congress wanted to give itself the power to actually govern based on its own laws, which would require federal officials to overrule their state counterparts. Madison quickly went to work, within a week helping to draft a startling new amendment to the Articles of Confederation that would give sweeping new powers to Congress—and, at long last, simply force the states to obey.

Madison's shocking amendment stated that if any of the states "shall refuse or neglect to abide by the determinations of the United States in Congress assembled," that Congress would be "fully authorized to employ the force of the United States as well by sea as by land to compel such State or States to fulfill their federal engagements." The amendment even gave the federal government power to prevent dissenting states from "trade and intercourse," both domestic and foreign—meaning Congress could bend a state to its will by choking off its commerce.[1]

Madison desperately needed allies for his bold new idea. He thought of his friend Thomas Jefferson, who had only recently made the startling decision to step down from Virginia's governorship.[2] Madison mailed Jefferson an envelope, including the amendment. Despite a rocky end to his governorship, the author of the Declaration of Independence still wielded substantial political authority. His support of coercion, Madison fervently believed, could help tip the balance. The "delicacy and importance of the subject," he urged his friend, required his support in Congress.[3]

Madison tensely awaited Jefferson's answer. But the former governor simply refused to respond. Two weeks after Madison asked Jefferson for his approval, he again wrote Jefferson, with labored politesse. "I hope your Excellency has recd. my letter inclosing a copy of a plan reported to Congress for arming them with co-ercive authority," he wrote. "Your first leisure moments," he continued, "will I flattered myself favor me with your idea of the matter."[4]

But there was still no response.

Five months passed before Jefferson wrote Madison back, but he did not even acknowledge Madison's springtime request for support of the amendment; he obliquely asked for the "opportunity of saving the right of correspondence with you which otherwise might be lost by desuetude," while complaining that he was "so far from the scene of action and so recluse" that he simply was unable to comment on current events.[5]

Winter passed, but still no word from Jefferson about coercion. On January 15, 1782, Madison *again* wrote Jefferson, this time to plainly complain, "Pray did you ever receive a letter from me inclosing a proposition declaratory of the coercive power of Congress over the States?" He prodded him further: "It went by an Express while you were at the head of the Exec."[6] But Jefferson never responded. Two years would pass before Madison finally dropped the matter.

These events revealed young Madison's impetuosity, the radicalism of his ideas, and how committed he had become to control. He was advocating a Continental Congress that would be able essentially to make war on the states. Jefferson's unsaid resistance probably stemmed from his skepticism that such an idea could actually exist in practice. Madison, undeterred, determined to refine his approach.

Meanwhile, at long last, Madison saw the end of the war approaching—and with it a new opportunity for the national order he craved.

I N OCTOBER 1781, WASHINGTON'S TROOPS ENCIRCLED EIGHT THOUSAND British troops in Yorktown. When news of General Cornwallis's surrender reached Madison in Philadelphia, he was exhilarated. But he recognized that one surrender, however commanding, would not end a war. The British command and allies were diffuse, the delays long and tactically significant, and the gray area between war and peace—the negotiations—as knotty and intricate as any battle plan.

The war would *have* to end sometime, but he knew the terms of peace could also end up being a cure as bad—or even worse than—the disease. Brainstorming, he again came up with a scheme to break the back of British resistance: to reestablish trade relations with Great Britain (thereby expanding relations with and the sympathies of the kingdom's influential commercial class), while expanding federal control over the western territories (thus increasing America's territory, population, and tax base at the expense of Great Britain).[7] Again, he saw his old professor as key to his strategy. He traveled to Princeton, sat down with Witherspoon, and presented his idea. The bearish, lugubrious man, now almost sixty, heard out his energetic former student. Madison amusedly recounted to Randolph his effort to get the phlegmatic man "to move in the business."[8] Under Madison's cheerful pressure, the professor relented and agreed to introduce the motion in Congress.

But opponents both of western expansion and trade dealings with the kingdom came together to defeat the motion.[9] The status quo again proved too powerful for Madison's rear guard actions. He would have to shake the country out of its torpor himself.

M EANWHILE, AS MUCH AS MADISON LOATHED THE BRITISH, HE WAS darkly impressed by their devious extension of the war, which should have concluded by then, in Yorktown. They seemed to intend infinitely to drag on negotiations about what would actually constitute peace. In May 1782, the Virginia House of Delegates passed a unanimous resolution instructing its congressmen—Madison included—to continue the war with "Vigour and Effect" until peace was obtained "in a Manner consistent with our National Faith and Foederal Union." Any peace that separated the United States from her allies, the resolution emphasized, would be "insidious and inadmissible."[10]

Madison was incensed by how the British exploited every appearance of weakness. The federal government could not fight the British if it could not fight its own states. And the troops' ragged and mutinous condition suggested the war could indeed be drawn out for years. With the New Year of 1783, Madison and many others decided they could close out the war by funding it adequately and by compelling the states to cooperate.

On January 27, 1783, Madison watched with great interest as a bespectacled Scottish lawyer named James Wilson rose on the floor. Two years before the Revolution, Wilson had published a famous pamphlet boldly arguing that the British Parliament lacked the authority to pass laws for the American colonies because the colonies lacked representation in Parliament. Madison respected him immensely. Standing, Wilson praised his adoptive country's intrepidity and remarkable optimism against the hated British. However, one area where his new countrymen had fallen short, he declared, was in the "cheerful payment of taxes." Given Americans' "peculiar repugnance" to taxation, he argued that Congress needed at long last to collect *general* taxes.

For Madison, the word *general* was the key. Congress would not be limited to asking for *specific* money for *specific* causes; it could finally tax *all* the states to fund the federal government itself. Madison also liked that Wilson employed actual facts in his argument. Before the war, Wilson continued bluntly, the British people had each paid about twenty-five pounds sterling per year to their government. But the United States rate was the equivalent of only ten pounds per person. How could an ambitious new country keep up with her oppressor on such shaky financial footing?[11]

Theodorick Bland, with whom Madison would frequently clash in later months and years, indignantly rose. Madison watched with disbelief as Bland argued that even if Wilson's facts were right, the delegates should still oppose his plan because Congress, even with a general taxation power, would still treat the states unequally, burdening the poor more than the rich. Bland suggested a deceptively mild replacement—to base the states' tax burden instead on the value of their lands.[12] Madison saw a poison pill in Bland's seemingly innocuous proposal. By allowing wealthy states to dominate poorer ones, the latter would then revolt against the coalition. That would replicate the very problem already preventing the states from yielding some measure of their sovereignty to the federal government.

The assembly adjourned without making a decision. That night, Madison finalized his notes, collected his thoughts, and prepared to dive into the fray.

What he had decided to do would mark the marriage of his evolving character and his emerging ideas. All of Madison's preparation in Virginia, and his self-forced march from sensitivity to assertiveness, was a prologue for what was to come: his demand that the states be *required* to pay a fixed percentage of their revenues to the federal government.

In the parlance of the time, this was known as an impost, but that obscure word has lost so much of its meaning over the years that it is simpler and more direct for the purposes of our story to describe the proposal's effects rather than its label. What Madison wanted was a *forced contribution*, and it was for that purpose—that form of what could only be called coercion—that he employed what I am describing as his "Method":

> *Find passion in your conscience. Focus on the idea, not the man. Develop multiple and independent lines of attack. Embrace impatience. Establish a competitive advantage through preparation. Conquer bad ideas by dividing them. Master your opponent as you master yourself. Push the state to the highest version of itself. Govern the passions.*

STANDING THE NEXT DAY, HE INTRODUCED IN HIS QUIET BUT FIRM VOICE A motion stating the "opinion of Congress" that the "establishment of permanent & adequate funds" that would "operate generally throughout" the country was "indispensibly necessary for doing complete justice to the Creditors of the U.S., for restoring public credit, & for providing for the future exigencies of the war." Those delegates paying attention noticed Madison was really offering only a preamble to something much larger he seemed to have in mind. He was not only refusing to back down in the face of Theodorick Bland's argument from futility; he was going to war for an absolute new federal power.

In a huff, his fellow Virginian, Arthur Lee—a small-minded nemesis of all things federal—stood. The states would never agree to a general power, he said. Putting the purse "in the same hands with the sword" would totally destroy the country's "fundamental principles of liberty." Lee boasted that he had helped torpedo the forced contribution on those very grounds in Virginia.[13]

The battle lines were taking shape, for giving the power of the purse to the power of the sword was *exactly* what Madison wanted: to invest the federal government with coercive power by funding it. The whole matter was now in the open, and Madison began with a broadside. For the nation's independence to rest on the "ruins of public faith and national honor," he said impatiently, should be "horrid" to anyone with "either honesty or pride."

He then posed a stark question to the audience. How would *they* pay the country's debt? There were two, he explained—and only two—possible answers: Either the principal must be paid, or the interest that was accruing. There was no other option.

The first possibility, he explained, was simply "impossible on any plan." There was not enough money in the federal treasury to pay off the entire war debt at once. That left Congress with only the second option—paying the interest.

Then he pushed his audience toward a second fork in the road. To pay the interest, there were again only two possible plans. There could be occasional "requisitions" on the states allowed by the Articles of Confederation. Or, each state could establish a permanent fund to regularly pay its share of the debt. But both possibilities had fatal problems. No one would lend to America if the government had to beg the states, over and over, for funds. As for the second path, he pointed out that the states would demand endless perks from the federal government in exchange for their permanent funds. This would erode the central government while leading to violent jealousy among the states—an outcome, he said, that was "too radical."

The opponents of a federal power must have stared sullenly as the small man informed them that they simply had no choice, that their only option left was to "examine the merits of the plan of a general revenue operating throughout the U.S. under the superintendence of Congress."

He then launched a numbing series of proofs for the superiority of the forced contribution.

It would reduce jealousy among the states. It would prevent them from diverting money from the federal government to their own capitals. It would give "instantaneous confidence" to the country's creditors. It was, further, legitimate and authorized, as the states had *already* given Congress the constitutional authority over both purse and sword.

Yes, he granted that some states did oppose the new power. Yes, the prospects for a forced contribution were "less encouraging than were to be wished." But still, he stated defiantly, several states had *already* agreed to send their 5 percent. And that logically meant all of them eventually could.

He paused to acknowledge a painful point: the recent collapse of the campaign for a forced contribution in Virginia. The Virginia legislature had appeared to support the contribution, but word had only recently reached Philadelphia that the Virginia legislature would now oppose it. This is what Arthur Lee had taken credit for.

Madison admitted that his home state's withdrawal was an "embarrassment." But he was determined to fight on—he *must* fight on. He owed allegiance not only to Virginia, but to the "collective interests of the whole." A congressman, he said, "ought to hazard personal consequences" out of respect for "what his clear conviction determines to be the true interest" of the state.

Finally, he *knew*, from the "knowledge of public affairs which his station commanded," that the Virginia legislature would not have repealed the forced contribution, if they knew what he knew. Madison simply asserted his will, because he knew his conscience.

The end result, he concluded, was that Congress had a *duty* to implement a general tax to pay the debt.[14] They simply had no choice.

F INISHED, HE SAT DOWN. WHEN HIS STUNNED OPPONENTS GOT BACK ON their feet, they found themselves playing on a battlefield drawn, defined, and controlled by Madison. Arthur Lee redundantly blustered that nobody who had ever "opened a page or read a line on the subject of liberty" could ignore the "danger of surrendering the purse into the same hand which held the sword."[15] But Madison's motion was seconded.

Later that night, scribbling in candlelight at the boardinghouse, he summarized the state of affairs to Randolph. He had done his best. If the forced contribution did not pass on a full vote, he wrote, "the foundations of our Independence will be laid in injustice & dishonor." He confided his fear that the failure to fund the federal government would make the union "of short duration."

He was cruelly disappointed when Congress, in its dysfunction, threw up its collective hands and tossed his motion into a committee. In that sausage mill, his clear and principled bill was ground into an "earnest recommenda-tion" that the states impose a 5 percent tax on only foreign goods, with the proceeds only put toward debts and war efforts, and then only for twenty-five years.[16] Lee, of course, seconded the butchered motion. The replacement dismayed even Theodorick Bland, who said it was "replete with injustice & repugnant to every idea of finance."[17]

Madison realized that he could not simply send a fragile idea into the jungle of public opinion and hope it would survive. More militant measures were required. One idea he excitedly shared with Randolph was for a "free & well informed gazette" that would "sufficiently counteract the malignant rumours." Setting up what he described as an "antidote" would, he explained, be an "easy & oeconomical task" that would dispel the "state of darkness" resulting from a "want of a diffusion of intelligence."[18]

Aside from his brainstorm of a sophisticated media arm for the allies who would soon enough describe themselves as Federalists, Madison also knew he must improve on what he had employed in his promising but unsuc-cessful campaign for the forced contribution—what I am describing here as his Method.

In the coming years, he would implement this Method every time he launched a war against a bad idea and erected, on the ruins, his own ideas. He devised the Method intuitively as a replacement for the derisive and imbal-anced Socratic Method that he had criticized so harshly as a teenage student. He never named it. Indeed, he rarely reflected on his strategies at all. But his approach always had nine key elements:

First, *find passion in your conscience.* From his lessons at the elbows of his fierce Scottish mentors, Donald Robertson and John Witherspoon, to his earliest response to religious repression in Virginia, he never wavered from the gravitational pull of his conscience. The almost physical impulse of his sense of right and wrong drove his political decisions as surely as a magnet pulls a compass's needle. By a conscience inspired by *general* matters of right and wrong—by those issues affecting entire states or the whole country—he brought tremendous conviction to his arguments about policy, at the same time illuminating the motives of opposing politicians as selfish and short-sighted. Thus, Chief Justice John Marshall, toward the end of his life, when asked who, of all the orators he had ever heard, was the most eloquent, said,

"Eloquence has been defined to be the art of persuasion. If it includes persuasion by convincing, Mr. Madison was the most eloquent man I ever heard."[19]

Second, *focus on the idea, not the man.* As powerful as politicians and citizens were, he saw ideas as the primary agent of history. A powerful idea could structure a vision of a future, spark men's passions, and overpower political alliances. He knew that if he destroyed the idea, the man behind it would not matter. Conversely, the right idea could be as radiant and generative as the sun. And so he concentrated on demolishing destructive ideas and elevating good ones. While that approach deprived him of the sweeping emotion customary to interpersonal political dramas, it lent his arguments a purity and force that was vastly more compelling to an observer.

Third, *develop multiple and independent lines of attack.* He appreciated clean, elegant, simple ideas—the singularity of religious freedom, the need to balance factions—as much as any man. But he also believed that killing a noxious idea required diverse and overwhelming force, not conceptual or tactical parsimony. As a *political* matter, then, Madison deployed a wide range of differentiated attacks—historical, logical, moral, emotional. Any one of these could be persuasive in its own right, but together they comprised a devastating assault.

Fourth, *embrace impatience.* Many forces conspire, in politics, to favor the patient. Legislation moves slowly; coalitions take time and steadiness to build and bond; public opinion must be shifted; and, perhaps most importantly, leaders who are too restless, who resist the proven benefits of steady pressure, will burn out. Yet time and again, Madison defied those proven patterns and instead embraced the power of impatience. Madison exposed the vulnerability of his opponents; while inertia was daunting, it was also lumbering and inept. With urgent, even fierce action, he could hammer a flawed system at its weakest points and conquer it.

Fifth, *establish a competitive advantage through preparation.* As both an eager student and bruised competitor in politics, Madison understood all too well the need to dominate an opponent. But because he lacked, himself, the rhetorical skills and the emotional magnitude of more theatrically impressive enemies, he developed his advantage on different grounds—through information and through preparation. With greater depth than his competitors, he could defeat their arguments on substantive grounds. By designing his battle plans ahead of time, he could anticipate his enemy and force them to play on his ground.

Sixth, *conquer bad ideas by dividing them*. Beginning in his college days at Princeton, Madison developed a disarmingly simple habit of isolating a question into two—and only two—options. By analyzing only two sides of a question, he could play each against the other. By making his audience consider *only* two options, he gave himself profound control over their own consideration of his problem. He would lead others down an intellectual path where their landscape narrowed, step by step, putting them increasingly within Madison's control.

Seventh, *master your opponent as you master yourself*. Madison developed, over the years, habits of mind and patterns of discipline to deal with his own hypersensitivity. His tenacity and his durability were strikingly similar to the posture he urged upon the country to address its own weaknesses. While he was not above bemoaning his situation—indeed, his melodrama about his health became a leitmotif until his old age—as a practical matter, he managed his sensitivity by concentrating on achievable objectives, subordinating the complaints of his mind and body to the dictates of political necessity, and forging ahead.

Eighth, *push the state to the highest version of itself*. It was the achievement of the state—the form of the state and national governments, the sort of men who took positions within government, and the actions government took—that most concerned Madison. And so he focused on the state above all else—above personality, culture, region, even family. He was unwilling to compromise on the overarching goal: that democratic government should achieve its greatest potential, that it should become the greatest and most noble version of itself. This common thread united his many projects— whether to reform aspects of government or overhaul entire sections of government itself. Government itself *could* and *must* always improve.

Ninth and last, *govern the passions*. The greatest danger Madison saw for America lay within the body politic itself. The passions were native to human beings and thus to democracy. His project since youth had been to discipline, tame, and channel the passions. The checks and balances Madison ultimately proposed in his constitution would help *contain* the passions, preventing them from taking over entirely. But to *channel* and *govern* them would require leaders like Madison—individuals with the mission of steering the anger and love and hatred and enthusiasm of the country's people toward governance of themselves.

To AN ADVERSARY, MADISON'S METHOD WAS MADDENING AT BEST AND infuriating at worst. As physically slight as he was, Madison seemed indefatigable, almost to burn with an inner intensity. He always knew more than you. He had anticipated most of your moves and seemed to have planned out everything he would say. He dragged his audience through a series of choices they had no option but to make, toward conclusions they had no choice but to accept. If you responded to one point, there were always countless others to deal with as well. It was a Socratic dialogue without the question marks—a symphony of preparation, discipline, and control. Every attempt you made to bait him—to trick him or play to his ego—would be avoided by a return to the plan. And, most importantly, if you ever revealed yourself to be combating for any selfish or special interest, that fact would become garish in contrast to his self-evident conscience, in contrast to the fact that he really did seem to have the common good at heart.

THREE MONTHS AFTER THE INITIAL COLLAPSE OF HIS FORCED CONTRIBU- tion, Madison rose to deliver the results of a committee Congress had convened to further study the proposal. In those three months, he had sharpened every aspect of his Method.

Find passion in your conscience. Focus on the idea, not the man. Develop multiple and independent lines of attack. Embrace impatience. Establish a competitive advantage through preparation. Conquer bad ideas by dividing them. Master your opponent as you master yourself. Push the state to the highest version of itself. Govern the passions.

Standing, Madison coldly laid out the facts of the debt, speaking almost as a teacher to a student, educating and disciplining at once. The total amount, he announced, was a stunning 42 million dollars. Interest payments alone demanded 2 million dollars annually. Only a 5 percent contribution from each state would be worthy of the Revolution—"a full reward for the blood, the toils, the cares and the calamities which have purchased it." Most important, the scheme must *require* the states to comply. They could be allowed no choice in the matter.

By so openly employing his own conviction, he at once elevated the debate and threw his opponents off balance. The "pride and boast" of the American experiment, he explained, was the fight for rights basic to human nature. The delegates could achieve that promise through the forced contribution. If it passed, he promised, the revolutionary cause would acquire "dignity and lustre." The nation would stand as a city on a hill, with the "most favourable influence on the rights of mankind."

But if the federal government disintegrated because it could not even fund its own operations, he ominously predicted that the "last and fairest experiment in favor of the rights of human nature" would be "insulted and silenced by the votaries of Tyranny and Usurpation."[20]

While he again failed to gain a majority for the forced contribution, his eloquent, puissant speech earned Madison his first truly national audience. His supporters in Congress reprinted the speech in a pamphlet along with exhibits and a plan of the new revenues the forced contribution would generate. They then mailed thousands of copies around the country. Private reprints were made in Massachusetts, Connecticut, New Jersey, and Virginia—and England and France. General Washington wrote a circular praising Madison's address for "so much dignity and energy that in my opinion, no real friend of the honor and independency of America can hesitate a single moment." If Madison's speech did not "produce conviction," Washington warned, a national bankruptcy, "with all its deplorable consequences," would occur.[21]

By the summer, the pamphlet had spread to his cousin the reverend in Williamsburg. "I have seen with much Pleasure the Pamphlet," he beamed, and praised the speech as "well calculated to direct the mind to important Objects."[22]

Meanwhile, that same spring, Madison was appointed to a prestigious peace committee whose members also included Alexander Hamilton and James Wilson.[23] He would now be on the front lines of finalizing the whole nation's standing with her former oppressor—at last closing the nation's bloody first chapter, while opening her hopefully promising next one.

T HE MORE MADISON'S REPUTATION AS A WARRIOR FOR THE FORCED contribution grew in Philadelphia, the more Henry, back in Virginia, sensed a threat.[24] In May, Jefferson wrote Madison in cipher that Henry "as usual" was "involved in mystery." "Should the popular tide run strongly in either direction," Jefferson predicted, Henry would "fall in with it."[25] The legislature scheduled debate on the forced contribution for early May in Richmond. A heated whisper campaign began among both friends and foes, triggering waves of political organizing. When the day came, hundreds of men turned up—more than had appeared in the legislative chamber at one time for many years.[26]

Henry strafed the measure for its short-term financial cost to Virginians. Randolph listened in disbelief as Henry argued to the chamber that taxes should actually be *lower* than they currently were. Heads nodded; Henry's antifederal invective seemed to be catching fire in the chamber.[27]

But after the meeting, public opinion on the topic turned so volatile that it slipped through even Henry's nimble fingers. Virginians appeared torn between their loyalty to their state and the obvious dysfunction of the federal government. A sizable plurality emerged in favor of the forced contribution as a distasteful but necessary means to fund a distasteful but necessary federal government. Trimming his positions accordingly, Henry began a pattern of dizzying reversals. A week later, he suddenly announced he had become a "strenuous supporter" of the forced contribution, albeit with certain restrictions, such as preventing federal tax collectors from tramping through Virginia to collect new monies. Henry, Randolph recounted satirically, "ludicrously offered an easy remedy" of "drawing the teeth and cutting the nails of the officers of revenue."[28]

The contrast with the fixity of Madison's principled stance—his conscience—could not have been starker, especially to Madison. But Henry's facility with words and politics gave him advantages in the roiling democratic sea; Madison admitted to Randolph his deep concern about the powerful influence of "eloquent mouths" like Henry's. But he also felt he had earned the upper hand over such vulgar appeals. Unless the forced contribution's enemies could come up with another option "equally consistent with public justice & honour," he brashly predicted to Randolph that "all those who love justice and aim at the public good" would support his plan.[29]

Two weeks later, Henry took up a populist banner and argued that, instead of approaching the general populace for the revenue, Virginia should instead aim for the "pockets of the wealthy consumer"—in other words, soaking the rich.[30] He festooned the forced contribution with even more conditions certain to doom it, arguing that the federal government should compensate Virginia for any amount that was over her quota—a plainly unworkable idea for a transparently broke Congress.[31] Virginia's legislators tried to follow Henry's looping lead, asserting that it was the *federal government* instead that owed Virginia 1 million pounds.[32]

Having unleashed this chaos, Henry summarily departed Richmond for Leatherwood, his estate in Hanover County. Randolph was appalled by the wreckage Henry left in his wake. He wrote Madison that Henry had intentionally made an "abortion" out of the forced contribution.[33] The saving grace, he said bemusedly, was that Henry's "sight for home" had exposed him "to a daily loss of his popularity." But that was precious little consolation; for Randolph admitted that the master of the people could "always recover himself in interest by an exertion."[34]

He was more public than ever; but with his escalating radicalism, his increasing seniority, and his penchant for control, he also began to move into the shadows.

W HETHER IN CANDLELIT TAVERNS OR THE FLICKERING FIRELIGHT OF boardinghouses, Madison realized he needed secrecy to communicate effectively and to broker deals. With their single drivers and exposed cargo, the mail carriages traveling from Philadelphia to Virginia were easy targets for bandits and spies. Congress had formally mandated cipher—the composition and decoding of written text through complex numerical codes—for sensitive wartime correspondence with a resolution stating, "If an original page is of such a nature as cannot be safely transmitted without cyphers, a copy in cyphers, signed by the Secretary for the department of foreign affairs, shall be considered as authentic."[35]

As he began taking committee assignments covering such delicate matters as the naval budget and negotiations with the French, Madison became militant about secrecy in both his official business and his private correspondence. He started writing significant portions of his letters to his friends in cipher, which required him to meticulously compose blocks of text in letters or numbers, often in candlelight, glancing back and forth from long sheets of paper, as he wrote words by characters, phrases by words, paragraphs by sentences, all one by one.

On May 28, 1782, he told Joseph Jones (italics show the words that he composed in code), that Virginia should announce "*the sense of the people*" for a strong peace, which would be "*regarded as more authentic than a declaration from Congress.*"*[36] The code enabled Madison to speak honestly about Congress's weakness, while controlling the consequences.

That same summer, hunched over his desk, Madison laboriously decoded a letter from Edmund Randolph. Meticulously parsing three-numeral sequences for their lettered equivalent (344, for example, was the code for *nd*), Madison learned that Randolph suspected there was a plot to eject both men from office by raising fears that they were both too compromised to serve Virginia effectively—specifically, Madison's enemies were charging that his notorious study of the law was distracting him. His enemies had attacked him under the "garb of friendship," Randolph wrote, "It was lamented, that the rigour of law *should cut off so* [here, Randolph forgot to insert an adjective for "well-deserving"] *a servant* from *public employment.*"[37]

Randolph and Madison retreated further into the darkness. As the wartime negotiations went on and as their suspicions about spying increased, Randolph suggested to Madison that they continue to use the official government cipher when talking about intelligence on public policy, but switch to a new cipher to communicate about individuals. Madison agreed and suggested a new cipher invented by James Lovell, a highly regarded delegate from

---

* The letter was a ship in the night, however; unbeknownst to Madison, Virginia had already passed the instruction. "To Joseph Jones," May 28, 1782, Robert A. Rutland et al., eds., *Papers of James Madison*, vol. 4 (Chicago: University of Chicago Press and Charlottesville: University of Virginia Press, 1962–), 291n.

Massachusetts. For a keyword, he proposed the name of Cupid, one of his cousin the reverend's young slaves.[38] Randolph readily agreed, admitting, "I have been in some pain from the danger incident to the cypher we now use." The British, he knew, were intercepting and even publishing ciphers.[39]

Secrecy, for Madison, was fast becoming not only a means but the end itself. When evaluating Virginia's proposed scheme to redeem old paper currency for new specie, for instance, Madison found the "defect of information" made it impossible for him to "deduce the general interest." He proposed a solution to Randolph: that he gather the sense of the legislature through a private meeting of its leading men. The stakes of secrecy were incredibly high; Madison told Randolph that if anyone got word of the new currency schemes, they would snap up specie in even greater amounts, in a "revival of Speculation."[40] That could push the nation even more quickly over a fiscal cliff.

I N THE NEW IMPERATIVE OF SECRECY, CONTROL WAS BECOMING NOT JUST A matter of political philosophy for Madison. It was the substance of his very being. But despite his best efforts, the passions he had so carefully cabined were about to wreak havoc in his tightly wound life.

13 A Sad Reunion

THE TRAIN OF EVENTS BEGAN WITH A HORRIBLE EVENT IN HIS FRIEND Jefferson's life. In late September 1782, Madison learned that Jefferson's long-suffering wife, Martha, had died. Jefferson, he knew, had loved Martha completely, and the prior year had already been convulsive for the couple. In flight from the British, Martha had given birth to a baby daughter, Lucy, but the infant died after four months, breaking her parents' hearts. Just three months ago, Jefferson had retired from the governorship to Monticello to be a husband, father, farmer, and lawyer.

Randolph visited with Jefferson and wrote Madison with alarm that the man's grief was "so violent" that he was "swooning away" whenever he saw his children.[1] Madison had a difficult time envisioning his friend out of control. He responded coolly, as if Jefferson's trauma was just another challenge to dissect and control. "I conceive very readily," he wrote, "the affliction & anguish which our friend at Monticello must experience at his irreparable loss." But Jefferson's "philosophical temperament," he confidently told Randolph, made the report of his swooning at the sight of the couple's children "altogether incredible."

Not only did Madison refuse to mirror Jefferson's passion. He saw a political opportunity in his tragedy. He had already felt that Jefferson's talent was being wasted on domestic life. He now asked Randolph to approach Jefferson to serve as a peace commissioner in Europe as "soon as his sensibility will bear a subject of such a nature."[2] Madison passed the idea to other legislators, and it spread quickly. In November, Congress unanimously supported reappointing Jefferson as minister plenipotentiary for negotiating peace. Congress openly discussed his domestic situation. Madison, taking notes, wrote that many hoped "the death of Mrs. J. had probably changed the sentiments of Mr. J with regard to public life."[3]

Madison then heard what was, for him, another kind of death: the crushing news that the Virginia legislature had defeated the forced contribution once and for all.

R ANDOLPH ADMITTED HE HAD WAITED TEN DAYS TO TELL MADISON THE news because it "was not a fit season." "I commiserate your situation indeed!" he told Madison.[4] The defeat took on a biblical cast in Virginia. Just after the New Year, Governor Harrison wrote to Madison that "the cloven footed monster" was roaming in Richmond—a beast, Harrison wrote (no poet, but trying) "cover'd with the thickest covering." The forced contribution's foes, through "silken words" and "high sounding patriotic speeches," were tempting men to error and to sin—even those "who think they know and are on their guard against him."[5]

The defiant states continued to sap the country's strength. Madison was delighted when Jefferson agreed to return to public life in his reappointment. The peace negotiations with Great Britain were dragging on, the countries still technically at war. Madison returned to the *nexus imperii* he had proposed to Witherspoon: to bind the two countries through their mutual interest in money. He introduced a motion instructing the ministers plenipotentiary—John Adams, Benjamin Franklin, John Jay, and now Thomas Jefferson—to establish "direct Commerce" with the British empire.[6] By tethering the United States and its parent through trade, he thought, the two countries would be forced to heal their war wounds through mutual interest. His motion passed unanimously.[7]

By January, Jefferson moved back into the boardinghouse run by Mary House, a popular Philadelphia house where Jefferson, Madison, and several other congressmen regularly stayed for long stretches at a time. The reunion with Madison, despite Jefferson's bottomless pain, was joyful for both men. Fermenting ideas excitedly, they quickly landed on a project suitable to their personalities. The prior summer, Theodorick Bland—in a rare forward-looking move—had successfully motioned that Congress compile a "list of books to be imported for the use of the United States in Congress Assembled." The committee charged with that mission again brought together Madison (as chairman) and John Witherspoon, as well as John Lowell from

Massachusetts. But with Witherspoon and Lowell both leaving Congress, Madison had continued the work mostly on his own.[8]

With Jefferson in Philadelphia, he could attack with renewed force the project of building a world-class library for a reimagined nation. The list Madison and Jefferson worked up was sweeping in its ambition and strikingly particular in its scope. The books included many volumes that Madison studied with Robertson and Witherspoon, major works of intellectual history, moral philosophy (Francis Hutchinson), collections of laws (Hugo Grotius), and collections of treaties and of laws. It featured works on French international law and diplomatic history; books of general history, from Voltaire to Sir Walter Raleigh, geography, and maps; and Greek, Roman, Italian, German and Dutch, French, Russian, Spanish, Prussian, Swedish, and, of course, British history. It also held journals of travels to foreign lands, such as India; synoptic works on law (Blackstone); and books of articles about the American states and territories.

Most critically, they tilted their list toward political theory. For the perusal of the United States Congress, Madison put down Plato's *Republic*; Aristotle's *A Treatise on Government*; Sir Thomas More's *Utopia*; Thomas Hobbes's collected works, including *Leviathan*; John Locke's *Two Treatises on Government*; Niccolò Machiavelli's collected works, including *The Prince*; Montesquieu's collected works; Adam Smith's *An Inquiry into the Nature and Causes of the Wealth of Nations*; and David Hume's *Essays and Treatises on Several Subjects*.[9]

What was missing from the list was as notable as what it included. There was no Jean-Jacques Rousseau, whose idealistic, passionate exposition of society's "general will" and the individual necessity of enlightenment had captivated the French revolutionaries. There was no Cicero, whose Platonic assertions about statesmanship contained little imagination but stern admonitions about ethics in politics.

And there was no Shakespeare. The playwright was beginning to loom large in America's political thought. John Adams, for instance, praised Shakespeare's "knowledge of nature, of life and character," employed *Macbeth* to attack England's treatment of colonial Americans, and used *Henry VIII* to question unfair tax policy and *Coriolanus* to undermine internecine politics.[10] On the afternoon of July 14, 1787, George Washington left the floor of the

Constitutional Convention to watch a performance of *The Tempest* at Philadelphia's Opera House—a play which many scholars have suggested could be about the plight of an iconic marooned colonial American.[11] But Madison included no Shakespeare in the plan.

The list was a visionary but logical and even harsh armory of political ideas. But despite all of this intellectual preparation, Madison was about to succumb to the least intellectual experience of all.

14 Kitty

IT ALL BEGAN IN THE DARK, IN MRS. HOUSE'S FLICKERING SITTING ROOM, where Madison and Jefferson, sheltered from the cold outside, mulled the day's developments in the legislature with other guests and visiting friends. William Floyd, a delegate from New York State, arrived with his wife and three daughters. The youngest, Catherine, was nicknamed Kitty. She had large, wide-set eyes, a strong chin, soft hair, gentle cheekbones, and delicate lips. When Madison had met her a year earlier, she was fourteen. Now fifteen, Madison was entranced.

Madison had become his own man in Philadelphia. He was respected in most quarters, and revered in others. Since arriving, he dressed more finely, and he had become more assertive. His insecurity about his vocation had receded, as he had put to rest—or at least silenced for a while—the infernal question of whether he would ever become a lawyer. Now, he felt ready to fall in love.

The house was close, lit by candles and firelight. Sharing meals with Kitty and her family around a common table, he stared at the girl. His heart pounding in bed late at night, he thought about her obsessively. Jefferson noticed his friend behaving differently around the girl, at once more awkward and more manful. Kitty was charming, effervescent, intellectual, and composed. She was also young, unformed, and, in many respects, a foil for Madison's broader aim for normalcy, for his intense desire to terminate his nomadic political life and join polite society as a married man.

But as with some of Madison's more ambitious brainstorms, he was vulnerable to making castles out of concepts. He likely had not had a romantic relationship since his abortive affair at Princeton. Barely out of childhood, Kitty seemed to perfectly mirror Madison's adolescent fantasies about both a wife and a sexual partner. But in the end, the events that unfolded were perhaps no more complicated than the oldest passion of them all.

Madison was not experienced in seduction or even flirtation, but he understood politics. He had real power now in Philadelphia, which he knew he could leverage to gain the crucial approval of Kitty's father. He and William Floyd had much business to discuss, and the Virginia congressman's growing prestige impressed Floyd. Pretty soon, Madison was sure that Kitty's family would approve his eventual proposal of marriage. His enthusiasm began to color everything. He almost never described his personal situation in his letters to his family, particularly to his father, yet on February 12, he wrote, "[I] have little more to say to you than that I hope you & the family may be as well as I am myself."[1] He might as well have added exclamation points.

The courtship seemed to go well through the late winter months. For Jefferson, the pursuit was more than diverting; it was life-affirming. He cheerfully encouraged Madison's quest, even going out of his way to befriend Kitty himself. When Madison was absent from the house, Jefferson sat with Kitty, joking and praising Madison. They made a strange pair—the tall, debonair, silver-tongued Virginian, haloed by melancholy, and the cheerful, fanciful teenager. Kitty liked literature; she gave Jefferson a poem, which he later returned in a letter to Madison. "Be so good as to return with my compliments to miss Kitty," he wrote his friend. "I apprehend she had not got a copy of it, and I retain it in my memory." He fondly recalled the "pleasing society" of the house, including the teenager.[2]

Madison felt Kitty was warming to him. His letters—even those on matters of state—betrayed his happiness. On March 25, he updated Randolph on Congress's upcoming ratification of the peace treaty with Great Britain. He enclosed a newspaper article that described the "happy event," and explained, "Happy it may be indeed called whether we consider the immediate blessings which it confers, or the cruel distresses and embarrassments from which it saves us."[3]

In the meantime, Jefferson, tired of the dilatory appointment process for the ambassadorship to France, returned to Virginia. But he still tracked his friend's affair. In mid-April, Madison opened a letter from Jefferson that contained a large section in cipher, in which Jefferson recalled that the joking and laughing, the "raillery you sometimes experienced" at the boardinghouse, "strengthened by my own observations," had given him "hopes there was some foundation for" Madison's marriage to Kitty. Jefferson was himself, he said, an ardent advocate of the match: "I wished it to be so as it would give

IMAGE 14.1. *KITTY FLOYD*, BY CHARLES WILLSON PEALE, 1783.
COURTESY OF PRINTS AND PHOTOGRAPHS DIVISION, LIBRARY OF CONGRESS.

me a neighbor whose worth I rate high." At long last, his shy friend might find himself a wife: "I know it will render you happier than you can possibly be in a single state," he assured Madison, even confiding a curious fact—that he, Jefferson, had been pressing the case all along. "I often made" a relationship with Madison "the subject of conversation" with Kitty, he confessed. Indeed, he "was able to convince" himself that Kitty "possessed every sentiment in your favor which you could wish."[4]

Completing the decoding, Madison must have laid down his quill with satisfaction. Kitty *would* be his. His personal and professional life, so long divorced, were finally entwining, and at just the right time. His two terms in Congress were about to end. With his reputation as a leading political figure firmly established, Madison would return to Orange as a professional, married man. He might even become a lawyer.

Likewise in cipher, he composed an excited response to Jefferson. Even within the disguise of code, Madison wrote coyly, with an intricate weave of double negatives, about "Miss K." "Your inference on that subject," he told his friend, "was not groundless." Even before Jefferson left Philadelphia, he said—with a bit of swagger—"I had sufficiently ascertained her sentiments." Since Jefferson had left for Virginia, progress had accelerated; Madison had electrifying news. "Since your departure," he wrote, "the affair has been pursued." Kitty, in other words, had accepted his proposal of marriage. He said that "Most preliminary arrangements although definitive" would need to wait until the end of the congressional term in the autumn, when the couple would plan their triumphal return to Virginia.

He was so intensely grateful for the older man's support that he began gushing. Jefferson's "interest" in Madison's "happiness," he said, was a "pleasing proof that the disposetions which I feel are reciprocal."[5] Why should Jefferson's enthusiasm about the match have provided any information whatsoever about Kitty's feelings? Madison's excitement about the alchemical effect of marriage was at once so inexperienced and fervent that he confused applause and performance—to his peril.

O N APRIL 29, FLOYD, HIS WIFE, AND THEIR THREE DAUGHTERS STEPPED onto their coach to return to Floyd's district in New York. Floyd invited Madison to accompany them. For sixty miles, he traveled a journey of romantic promise, as the company bounced along the spring road through Brunswick, Trenton, and Princeton, with Madison pointing out familiar sights along the way. He had never left Congress for so long, and he wrote Jefferson afterward, unashamedly, that his long absence "disables me from giving you the exact information of their latest proceedings."[6]

His long habit of overwork had always provided him with a perverse equilibrium, but his new emotions were tilting him off his axis; losing his balance, he had never been happier. His hypochondria began to ease, and people commented that he seemed healthier. On May 24, Jameson wrote him, "I have the pleasure of being informed by Mr. Jones that you enjoy a good state of health—a close & constant application to business seems not to have been so prejudicial to you as I feared it would."[7] The floodgates to his heart were springing open. On May 27, he went shopping on the streets for presents for his little sisters Sally and Fanny and bought a piece of silk for Sally, which he wrote his father he would "send by the first opportunity." He even added, teasingly, "Perhaps I may make an addition to it," as "Fanny I suppose too must not be overlooked."[8] As an eldest brother, he was accustomed to being an authority. As a lover, he now saw himself as a caretaker as well.

With the Floyds back in New York for the time being, his engagement pending, and his term in Congress coming to an end, Madison settled in for a pleasant if open-ended summer. He was keeping Kitty a secret, planning on bringing home to his family a surprise bride in the autumn. He slyly wrote his father, "The time of my setting out is as uncertain as at the date of my last" letter, but "it will certainly take place before the fall."[9]

He had only to wait. But an unplanned obstacle was thrown into his path—mutiny.

MONTHS EARLIER, GOVERNOR HARRISON HAD CONFESSED TO MADISON and the other Virginia delegates his fears about a revolt by unpaid army officers, while conceding his inability to do anything about it. To pay them, he lamented, was "absolutely out of our Power." The state could not even revert to tobacco as currency, as the state treasury only held five thousand pounds' worth. He pathetically rationalized that the soldiers' situation was "not worse than it has been."[10] With such reasoning from the country's leaders, the contagion naturally began spreading across Virginia's state lines toward Philadelphia.

In mid-June, three hundred angry men marched toward Congress. Storming into nearby taverns, they gulped down strong ale, angrily rehearsed their grievances, then stormed outside, tankards in hand. They began stamping their feet and cursing at the State House that they must be paid, once and for all, the salaries they were owed. Several pointed their muskets at the windows and threatened to fire on Congress.[11]

The rally lasted for three hours. Barricaded within the building, the delegates fearfully looked through the shutters at the angry mob. They then fled through the building's exits to surrounding taverns and to their boardinghouses. With nobody to further assail, the drunken men began dispersing, mostly to fall asleep. By six o'clock, all was clear, and Congress reassembled in the State House. But nothing could ever be the same.

Dismayed, Madison noted that the delegates seemed deeply shaken. Three days later, Congress announced that the "Dignity and Authority of the United States" had been so "constantly exposed to a repetition of Insult" that Congress actually could not "continue to sit in this City"—and would move to Princeton.[12] Madison was embarrassed by Congress's weakness, particularly before such wayward opponents. But he had no choice; he needed to join the body to which he had been duly elected. And so he and his colleagues piled atop horses and into carriages and bolted the city, traipsing along the dirty, dusty road to Princeton.

In his humiliation, Madison branded the mutineers as vacillating opportunists—"in constant vibration" one moment, then "penitent and preparing submissions" at the next, and finally "meditating more violent measures." They could not even make up their mind about their goal—whether they wanted to topple the bank, or to kidnap members of Congress, or both. As he summarized for Jefferson, "The real plan & object of the mutiny lies in profound darkness."[13] Tellingly, after Congress left for Princeton, the insurrection quickly deflated, and their leadership, featuring such luminaries as a "deranged officer" named Carbery, escaped.

But even as any real threat dissipated, Congress remained mired in lethargy and cowardice. The Friday after the rebellion, only six states' representatives showed up in Princeton, meaning Congress lacked a quorum to do any actual business. Democracy's ancient foe was rearing; days later, Hamilton condemned to Madison the "passion" that led the legislative body to flee its own city and lamented the embarrassing "timidity" that lingered.[14] Congress's flight had become "a subject of much conversation and criticism." With nothing to do that weekend, Madison returned in his coach to Philadelphia on Friday night.[15]

In September, when Congress pardoned the sergeants who led the revolt, the affair became as pointless for Madison as it was humiliating. The revolt's only effect was to further paralyze Congress, who settled into an awkward life in its new Princeton home. Whether it would *ever* return to Philadelphia was, Madison sardonically wrote Randolph, an "interesting question."

His distraction by Kitty and his pending marriage, his lame-duck status in Congress, and his disgust at the body's ineptitude all combined to erode his prodigious work ethic. He had previously produced a nearly perfect record of congressional attendance, from March 20, 1780, to June 24, 1783. But after Congress moved to Princeton, he became less exacting. The first quorum assembled in Princeton on June 30. Between then and the expiration of his term on October 31, Madison voted only half as often as did two of the other Virginia delegates. He stayed in Philadelphia as often as he could, where he could write more easily, borrow books from friends, and meet with visiting Virginians.[16]

In Philadelphia, he could also avoid his preposterous living situation in Princeton, where his continuing poverty forced him to economize by sharing a room with Joseph Jones. He liked Jones, but that didn't mean he wanted to live with him in a single room "not 10 feet square." Madison had to write from his bed, in candlelight, "in a position that scarcely permits the use of any of my limbs."[17] He longed for the lambent memories of his future wife at his boardinghouse and returned as often as possible. He kept busy, making the necessary trips back and forth from Princeton to Philadelphia. He was particularly interested in one ongoing task—the location for the new capital. With the southern and northern states fighting for the territory, he favored George Town, midway between the regions.[18]

But this pleasant-enough plateau was about to come to a precipitous end.

I N AUGUST, MADISON FOUND A CURIOUS LETTER FROM KITTY IN HIS MAIL. He must have had a sinking feeling in his stomach when he noticed the letter was sealed not with the usual wax but with an ugly lump of raw brown material. He peered at the stuff more closely. It was, according to Floyd family legend, a lump of rye dough pressed onto the paper—as unceremonious and dismissive as what was inside.[19] He had no choice but to open the letter. The words were not at all in cipher, their meaning mercilessly clear. He read as Kitty, in her youthful script, brusquely ended their engagement, with what he drily described later as a "profession of indifference."[20]

That letter destroyed him. He would never speak to, or even see, Kitty again. He apprised Jefferson of the development with his familiar fretwork of technicalities, elision, and double negatives, this time not to channel his passion for Kitty, but to unveil his heartbreak. He described "several dilatory circumstances on which I had not calculated." He shared his "disappointment."

He tried to seem worldly. Kitty's rejection, he said airily, was "one of those incidents to which such affairs are liable." He admitted that he no longer knew when he would come back to Virginia, as his return—previously planned to reveal his bride—was suddenly "less material." He even held out hope that Kitty might change her mind; the situation, he declared, was in an "uncertain state," and a "more propitious turn of fortune" was still possible.[21]

To Jefferson, it was obvious that his sensitive friend had been deeply wounded. Jefferson responded quickly: "I sincerely lament the misadventure which has happened," he wrote, "from whatever cause it may have happened." He reassured Madison that the "world still presents the same & many other resources of happiness." Not only that, he told him, "You possess many within yourself." That recourse to self-reliance was new to Madison, who had no habit of introspection, but Jefferson explained that "firmness of mind & unintermitting occupations"—hardly unfamiliar to his driven friend—would "not long leave you in pain."

Jefferson himself lashed out a bit at Kitty. Nothing could have been "more contrary to my expectations," he said—and he prided himself as an expert on women—for his assurances to Madison had been "founded on what I thought a good knowledge of the ground." But females—the young as well as the adult—were just that way. Of "all machines," Jefferson mused, "ours is the most complicated & inexplicable."[22] But Jefferson's ruminations were thin gruel indeed for his grieving friend. Adding insult to injury, Kitty went on to marry a nineteen-year-old medical student who had also stayed at Mrs. House's boardinghouse, where he had "hung round her at the harpsichord."[23]

I N 1937, A FOLDED PIECE OF PAPER WAS DISCOVERED IN THE LOCKET containing Madison's miniature portrait, prompting the *Daily Princetonian* to publish an article titled, "Madison Paid Court to 'Sweet Dulcinea' Outside Old Nassau's Sequestered Walls." The piece was riddled with giddy undergraduate apocrypha. The student who wrote the article apparently interviewed William Floyd, a descendant of Kitty, who opined that Madison "met and lost his beloved" on Long Island, while accompanied by Thomas Jefferson on a mission directed by General Washington to investigate the Poosepattuck Indians. "We believe that both young men fell in love with the

Floyd girls," Floyd recalled, "and they, not knowing that their swains would become so prominent let them slip."[24]

There's no evidence that any of this was true. But overheated rumor can be a symptom of subterranean insight. There has long been a cartoon of Madison as a hollow, brittle man defined by his dryness and rationality. The Kitty story still fascinates us, as it did that Princeton undergraduate journalist, because it so violently ruptures that caricature.

No surprise that the collapse with Kitty sent tremors through every filament of Madison's life. During his time in Philadelphia, he had been living with a slave named Billey, whom his maternal grandmother had deeded to him when he was just a baby. Billey was eight years older than Madison, and Madison had a sympathetic relationship with him. Billey despised his enslaved condition so palpably that he seemed not to be a slave at all. His unforced humanity, combined with Madison's own unguarded conscience, sparked a surprising decision.

MADISON WROTE HIS FATHER, "I HAVE JUDGED IT MOST PRUDENT NOT to force Billey back to Va. even if it could be done." The enslaved man's mind, he explained, had become "too thoroughly tainted to be a fit companion for fellow slaves in Virga." He knew that he would not get "near the worth of him"; in this instance, he firmly declared, principle would have to trump economy. He could not "think of punishing him" for "coveting that liberty for which we have paid the price of so much blood," he told his father, "and have proclaimed so often to be the right, & worthy the pursuit, of every human being." In his mind, at least, one thing was settled—Billey was no longer a slave, but a *human being.* In his own upheaval, the principle of freedom could no longer be confined to whites. It was a right for all human beings, black and white alike.

Pennsylvania law made overt manumission difficult, so Madison sold Billey into a contract for "personal servitude or apprenticeship" for seven years, after which he would be freed.[25]

But while Madison was preoccupied by matters of the heart in Philadelphia, events were conspiring to give Patrick Henry his greatest powers yet in Virginia.

IT WAS THE SUMMER WHEN AMERICA BEGAN TURNING FROM ITS REVOLU-tionary chapter to the business of becoming an independent nation. In November 1782, Great Britain and the United States had signed a preliminary peace treaty. On April 15, 1783, Congress ratified the treaty. And on September 3, 1783, John Adams, Benjamin Franklin, and John Jay signed the Treaty of Paris at the Hotel d'York with Great Britain, Spain, and France, formally ending the Revolutionary War and recognizing the independence of the United States. The Mississippi River now formed the new country's western border, with British North America established as a separate territory, and all prisoners of war to be released by all parties.

Henry rose anew as the hero of a successful revolution; the looming question for Madison and thousands of others was what Henry would use his great prestige *for.*

George Mason sent Henry a letter congratulating him on the accomplishment of "the warmest wish of your heart, the establishment of American Independence and the liberty of our country." It was in Henry's power, Mason declared, to do "more good and prevent more mischief" than any one else; he hoped Henry would "exert the great talents with which God has blessed you" to promote the "general happiness and prosperity."[26]

Madison did not share Mason's optimism. Among his friends and him, concern began to grow. How *would* Henry use the tremendous authority he had earned of Father of the Revolution? Would he become Father of the Nation as well?

15 A Remonstrance

As 1783 drew to a close, Madison devised a plan to stay in Philadelphia all winter for "close reading." Just as at Princeton a decade earlier, he clung to an ambiguous present rather than return to Montpelier. But it seemed Congress might stay in Princeton, which left him tenuously situated—he would be all alone in the city, with no job and no role. His father had also let him know that his mother—a "tender & infirm parent"—wanted him back in Virginia. Deeply torn, Madison confessed to Jefferson his "anxiety on the subject" of whether to return to Orange.[1]

In the end, the eldest son again buckled under his family's pressure. He remained with Jefferson in Philadelphia through the expiration of his term in Congress. Three weeks later, the pair left for Annapolis, where Congress was scheduled to meet. A quorum did not show up, however, and so Madison was all too quickly back on the long road home.

He arrived at Montpelier on December 5. Three and a half years had passed since he had left the homestead. His father and his brothers Ambrose and Willey had been busy acquiring land, some sixteen thousand acres in what is now Kentucky. Looking around him, he saw a bustling plantation that felt like the headquarters of a family empire.[2] There was a busy, edgy feel in the ironworks and farm and cellars. A brutal winter was just beginning, with cold gray skies threatening to dump the greatest quantity of snow in anyone's memory.[3] He noted the dread on his family's faces as they contemplated the weather's impact on their revenue in the coming year.[4]

But all was not gloomy. The coming weeks were also filled with the merriment and chaos and fire-lit stories of a large, extended family shut indoors for a long winter. With the exception of Madison, the family was growing, his nieces and nephews scrambling around their grandparents' house at will. They all noticed the changes in Madison. The tender young man was tougher and more seasoned. He had survived the battles of a flailing nation and suffered the wounds of love. Most markedly, he was alone, and plainly not sure what he would do with himself. Yet they all knew he would need to do *something*. He would have to live up to his potential.

D URING THE ICED-OVER WINTER, MADISON RETURNED TO READING THE law, hating it more than ever. He could not return to subjects he loved more, because all his books from Philadelphia, which he had sent home by a separate carriage, had been delayed by the freezing slush. Madison desperately wanted to visit Jefferson's library at Monticello, but the weather turned so severe that he couldn't even leave Montpelier. It took until late March for the books to arrive, exasperating him.[5] He procrastinated on his legal study with long, looping letters to Jefferson. Perhaps trying to keep his forlorn friend busy, Jefferson, who was leaving soon for Paris to start his term as ambassador to France, asked Madison to start a meteorological diary, instructing him to record twelve pieces of data every day, including the direction of the wind at sunrise and the appearance and disappearance of birds. "It will be an amusement to you," Jefferson promised, "and may become useful."[6]

The spring thaw eventually came to Montpelier, along with morning birdsong, tender green buds on the dogwood trees, damp reddish patches of thawing clay, and a surprising letter in the mail. That great avatar of the people, Patrick Henry, enemy of the forced contribution and, seemingly, of all things federal, was writing his former aide about constitutional reform. Henry told Madison he wanted him to commit "further Services to our Country." Although Madison deserved "some Respite," Henry wrote, "Is not the federal Government on a bad Footing?" The situation required, he said, "Correction & Improvement." "How mortifying is it," Henry asked rhetorically, "to see a rich Harvest of Happiness, & Labourers wanting to gather it in?"[7]

Madison, flattered and restless to return to politics, put his name forward as a delegate from Orange. He won easily. He arrived in Richmond in mid-May. One of his first orders of business was to sit down for coffee at Formicola's in Shockoe Hill with Patrick Henry and Joseph Jones, as well as a friend named William Short.[8] He had a particular plan in mind. He wanted the former governor to support an effort he would lead to revise Virginia's outdated constitution, as a paragon for a similar federal project.

In dreaming up this project, Madison's self-confidence bordered on arrogance. Henry was so renowned for his singular passion for Virginia that it was almost delusional to imagine he would join Madison's federal cause. But Madison had been totally immersed in realpolitik in Philadelphia. Yes, he held Henry at least partly responsible for the death of the forced contribution in Virginia, and, by extension, for the country's catastrophic war policies. Yet Madison also saw Henry for who he was—Virginia's most powerful public figure and a vital artery to the people who would be crucial to any long-term solution.

Over coffee, the men discussed the dysfunction of Congress and the need for reform. To Madison, it seemed their minds had actually met, and he took a rare leap of faith afterward, enthusiastically informing Jefferson that Henry seemed "strenuous for invigorating the federal Govt." As for a new state constitution, he said of Henry that the "general train of his thoughts seemed to suggest favorable expectations."[9] A friend of Henry's wrote Jefferson the next day that Henry had declared that he "saw ruin inevitable" unless Congress was given a "compulsory process on delinquent States."[10]

For Madison, things were looking up. Henry seemed to be warming to the idea of a new federal government. Perhaps he had seen reason. Perhaps he could lead the nation after all. But the revolutionary hero was bound to disappoint Madison. The two men, driven as much by their personalities as their political philosophies, were destined to clash.

I N AUGUST, MADISON'S PROFESSIONAL ANXIETIES WERE ALLEVIATED SOMEwhat when his father again gave him land, 560 acres this time, attempting to bequeath to his son, at long last, a profession: planter. But the vocation felt like an ill-fitting costume. Madison made passing attempts at addressing an infestation of his wheat and corn crops by chinch bugs. But he yearned for intellectual stimulation and cosmopolitan company. He quickly sold off some land, which gave him capital and, for a time, the means for independent subsistence.[11] He left for Philadelphia, explaining to Jefferson his "need of exercise after a very sedentary period" and his desire of "extending my ramble into the eastern states which I have long had a curiosity to see."[12]

When he met his friend the Marquis de Lafayette in Baltimore, Madison found the adventure he was seeking. He was swept up in a three-week

journey with Lafayette to witness a treaty with the Six Indian Nations in
Fort Schuyler, New York, at the elbow of a man of action he deeply admired.
Wherever Lafayette went, Madison wrote, he was cheered with the "most
flattering tokens of sincere affection from all ranks." From New York, the men
took barges through punishing winds and choppy waters to Albany. They
stayed afterward in a Shaker village, where they watched a hundred worship-
pers convulse and commune with the spirit. Lafayette practiced hypnotism on
a willing man to sensational effect. They camped in the forest and welcomed
Indians bearing meat and chickens.

Arriving at Fort Schuyler, they stayed overnight at a judge's house.
The next day, they rode on horseback on a footpath through tall forest and
marshland in gloomy, rainy weather, then arrived at the Oneida's main village. Madison met a white man and woman who by choice lived among the
Indians, dressing and behaving as Indians. His party stayed for eight days,
witnessing the signing of the treaty.

He then headed back home, his head spinning with all he had seen.[13]

B Y NOVEMBER, MADISON WAS BACK IN RICHMOND. ALL CHANCES OF
collaboration with Henry disappeared when he introduced his assessment to support Christian churches, and Madison launched his year-long plot
to destroy the tax and build on its ruins a brilliant beacon of freedom. Jefferson anticipated the collision. In December, he wrote to Madison in cipher
that "*while Mr. Henry lives*," the only likely outcome would be another flawed
constitution" that would be forever saddled on Virginia. With bemused des-
peration, he declared, "What we have to do I think is *devoutly* to *pray* for *his
death*."[14] He was only half-joking.

As for Madison, he could find no joy in Virginia's capital city. The cold
earth was shellacked with snow, the weather cloudy and foggy.[15] He bemoaned
the barrenness of his life, the fact that in the legislature, "few occurrences
happen which can be interesting, and in my retired situation, few even of
these fall within my knowledge."[16] He complained to Monroe that the session
was simply tedious.[17] A window opened when he was nominated to serve in
the court of Spain.[18] But he *again* refused an exotic position in a foreign land.
His insightful friend Lafayette not unkindly chided his home-bound friend

for "Your obstinate plans of life,"[19] but something more serious was probably at work—Madison's anxiety about exposure abroad to foreign threats—both known and unknown.

Madison descended into a deeper funk. Jefferson urged him to visit France, promising to provide room, board, and shelter, with the only requirement that Madison "do me the favor to become of the family." For two hundred guineas, Jefferson promised, his friend would purchase the "knowledge of another world." Not only that, but Monroe was coming as well. Jefferson promised that, if Madison stayed from May through September of the following year, he would be back in Virginia for the beginning of any important business in the legislature.[20]

But Madison never seriously considered the offer. Again, his hypochondria and stubbornness combined to make such an open-ended trip, across the ocean and to a foreign country, unthinkable. Answering his friend, he provided an endless, mounting sequence of objections. "Crossing the Sea," he said, would be "unfriendly to a singular disease of my constitution." And if he ever visited Europe, he would need to be "less stinted in time than your plan proposes." And he had "a course of reading which if I neglect now I shall probably never resume." And as if those three excuses weren't enough, Madison unburdened himself of an omnibus complaint—his situation, he said, was "as yet too dependent on circumstances to permit my embracing" Jefferson's offer "absolutely."[21]

While this systematic approach would prove devastating against many public policies Madison opposed, in the context of a friendship, it was just rude. No wonder that Madison often gave the impression of being cold and aloof. Those habits were part of the protective shell the vulnerable young man devised to defend himself against a threatening world.

IN MIDSPRING, THE LEGISLATIVE SESSION CONCLUDED, AND MADISON trudged back to Orange County. He was now thirty-four years old, still a bachelor, still unemployed, and still pessimistic about his prospects in general. While he was energized by the coming fight with Henry on the assessment, that didn't answer the more existential question of what he should do while not a part-time legislator. Once again, he began wrestling with his old nemesis: the law. On a dreary March day, with an unseasonable mixture of rain and snow descending from a vault of thin clouds,[22] he complained to Lafayette that he was spending the "chief of my reading on Law." He moaned to the Frenchman, "I shall hear with the greatest pleasure of your being far better employed."[23] The spring months brought only more professional stress. He confessed to Randolph his growing desire to achieve a "decent & independent subsistence." He was reading the law with as much discipline as he could muster, he said, but he was still "far from being determined ever to make a professional use of it."[24]

But he was ironically receiving recognition in the law through politics. In February, George Wythe—Virginia's most prestigious teacher of law—had written Madison that William and Mary was giving him the honorary degree of LLD—doctor of laws. The other recipients included Benjamin Franklin and Edmund Randolph. Madison, flustered, responded to Wythe that the distinction was "so flattering" that he would "feel greater satisfaction in expressing" his acknowledgement "if I had less reason to distrust my title to it." He did not, he said, count himself among the "illustrious Votaries" of those "who so worthily minister in the Temple of Science," but was instead merely someone with "a zeal for her service." But he would accept the degree, he said, "in the most respectful manner."[25]

But the longer he battled the law books, the more determined he became on the essential point: He could not accept the compromises he thought were inherent to the legal profession. He would refuse to take unsavory cases and clients. He would not waste his precious time on the mind-numbing research and drafting.

But if not law, what profession could he take? In Orange County, he watched the enslaved men and women toil in his father's fields, bend and scrape and curtsy inside the mansion itself, and do their masters' bidding in town. He wanted no part of it. Despite the land he now owned, he decided he could not be a planter—at least not a *successful* planter with an ironworks and an active tobacco plantation. He had decided, he informed Randolph, "to depend as little as possible on the labour of slaves." But where did that leave him? He brainstormed on the problem constantly. He told Randolph that these issues had "brought into my thoughts several projects from which advantage seemed attainable."[26]

Peach, gooseberry, and plum trees were blooming, clouds of cherry blossoms floating to the ground.[27] He felt a new urgency arrive with the spring breeze. He wrote Jefferson to send "treatises on the antient or modern foederal republics—on the law of Nations—and the history natural & political of the New World; to which I will add such of the Greek & Roman authors where they can be got very cheap."[28] Jefferson might as well have mailed boxes of dynamite to his young friend so impatient to change the country.

F OR ONCE, MADISON SEEMED TO WANT TO STAY IN ORANGE. HIS FRIENDS kept trying to convince him to travel out of Virginia. Monroe missed Madison's company and asked him to take a trip to Indian country on the Ohio River sometime in August or September, pleading that he would be "happy in your company."[29] But Madison adamantly refused the invitation with a series of pointlessly emphatic factual and logical rebuttals. He did not have enough money, he complained. The time of the treaty was "extremely uncertain." "Great delays" would occur on the trip. Their return would be hampered by "the lowness of the waters" and by the "want of boats at our command" and by the "necessity of travelling back thro' the Wilderness via Kentucky." As for other trips Monroe had suggested, a journey to Montreal and Quebec was "objectionable" because of the "time it would require." And an "Eastern ramble" would require "carrying horses from Virginia."[30]

But one objection was the most telling. He could not leave, he told Monroe, because he might be called to public service. He had caught wind of a possible appointment to an interstate commission to negotiate with Maryland on the navigation of the Potomac.[31] He was unwilling to risk a lucky break for the nation's service for a traveling lark. His time might still come.

Another issue was also keeping him in Orange. Madison had a mysterious romantic relationship that summer—and perhaps even became engaged again. The clues lie in letters about his long-standing bachelordom. He had grown accustomed to his friends ribbing him about his solitary state. Caleb Wallace, a colleague who lived in the Kentucky territory, wrote Madison to catch up. Nine years older than Madison, Wallace had three children. "As you are yet a Stranger to the parental Tyes," he teased his bachelor friend, "I hardly know how to tell you" of both the "great amusements" and "serious

Cares" of the children. Therefore, he wrote, "I shall only remind you at present of the Taunts to which old Bachelors are justly exposed."

But more seriously, he told Madison, "But I shall not say more, as I have had an intimation that you are like to be in a more honourable State e'er long."[32] For this "intimation" to have traveled from Orange County to Kentucky, Madison had become involved with a local Orange County woman at least long enough to spread rumors of an engagement.

Madison wryly responded that although he was a "stranger to parental ties," he could "sufficiently conceive the happiness of which they are a source to congratulate you on Your possession of two fine sons & a Daughter." He completely ignored Wallace's nudge about his engagement, except for his oblique concession that he had "no local partialities" that could "keep me from any place which promises the greatest real advantages."[33] Self-controlled as always, he had already cabined the affair, his love interest became just a "local partiality."

Over the coming months, he settled into a posture of irony. After Monroe married, Madison wrote him on a cloudy day to wryly congratulate his friend on his "inauguration into the mysteries of Wedlock."[34] Soon after, Madison opened a note from William Grayson, in Philadelphia, listing no less than four congressmen who had recently married. The situation, Grayson laughingly wrote, seemed "to portend a conjunction copulative. In short, I think we have got into Calypso's Island." Turning serious, Grayson said, "I heartily wish you were here," as "I have a great desire to see you figure in the character of a married man."[35]

By now, Madison's romantic failures must have filled him with a sense of futility. But he was working on his grand project, contained in those two trunks Jefferson sent him from Paris. He continued forging ahead—alone.

16 Solitude and Reform

THE YEAR 1785 BECAME ONE OF ACTION. IN THE SUMMER, MADISON traveled to Williamsburg and defeated Henry's religious assessment with his Memorial and Remonstrance to friends, and it began spreading like wildfire, ultimately leading to the defeat of Henry's bill, as described in the introduction to this volume. In the fall, he returned to the sweeping project he had first proposed to Henry in their coffeehouse conversation a year earlier: the radical overhaul of Virginia's own laws.

Virginia's statutory laws were littered with medieval punishments and ancient commercial ideas. A decade earlier, Jefferson had launched a herculean effort to replace Virginia's Code. Under his pressure, Virginia's legislature had created a committee that recommended over a hundred changes, but Speaker Benjamin Harrison, no friend of enlightenment legislation, thwarted the plan. When Jefferson left for France, his reform effort floundered.

Now, Madison saw an opportunity to bring the project back to life. Entering the autumn session of the General Assembly, he launched a new campaign for reform, startling everyone with its speed and force. What was about to come was a rehearsal for his role in the Constitutional Convention and an object lesson in the profound power of his Method. Standing in his way were familiar foes of reform—the conservatives who thought any change to criminal law would only coddle criminals, the landed gentry who believed modernizing commercial regulations would threaten their pocketbooks, the narrow-minded who were hostile to rationalizing Virginia's government. Madison needed to overcome all of them. And so he turned to his Method.

Find passion in your conscience. Focus on the idea, not the man. Develop multiple and independent lines of attack. Embrace impatience. Establish a competitive advantage through preparation. Conquer bad

*ideas by dividing them. Master your opponent as you master yourself.
Push the state to the highest version of itself. Govern the passions.*

On October 31, 1785, he rose on the floor and introduced, in sequence, one hundred and eighteen bills. He began, fittingly, with an Act for Religious Freedom.[1] "Whereas Almighty God hath created the mind free," he read, all attempts to influence the mind by "temporal punishments or burthens, or by civil incapacitations," would only "beget habits of hypocrisy and meanness," and were a "departure from the plan of the Holy author of our religion."

With Henry in the governor's seat, safely lacking a vote, the General Assembly declared that no man could be compelled to frequent or sup-port "any religious worship, place, or ministry whatsoever" or be "enforced restrained, molested, or burthened in his body or goods" or otherwise suffer "on account of his religious opinions or beliefs." The bill provided the state with sweeping power to enforce this right, concluding, "All men shall be free to profess, and by argument to maintain, their opinion in matters of religion."

He dug the deepest foundation possible under the bill, declaring that any act later passed to repeal the Act, or even to "narrow its operation" would *itself* be "an infringement of natural right."[2] In other words, *any* limitation on the freedom of conscience would henceforth not be a crime against the government, but against human nature and against God. He would later boast to Jefferson that "I flatter myself" that the bill had "extinguished forever the ambitious hope of making laws for the human mind."[3]

He moved on to his other bills, which ranged from modernizing the standard of care for the insane, to giving the criminally accused the right to a trial of their peers, to creating the position of lieutenant governor in case the governor died or left office.

Of his 118 bills, the legislature passed a stunning 36—in less than three weeks. The other delegates regarded Madison with awe. Archibald Stuart wrote a colleague, "Can you suppose it possible that Madison should shine with more than usual splendor [in] this Assembly. It is sir not only possible but a fact. He has astonished mankind & has by means perfectly constitutional become almost a Dictator upon all subjects that the House have not so far prejudged as to shut their Ears from Reason & armed their minds from Conviction."[4]

Madison's preparation, his conviction, and his self-mastery lent him a bracing confidence. Although reform had been "assailed on all sides," he told Monroe in early December, "I think the main principle of it will finally triumph over all opposition."[5] Madison's impatience was palpable in a letter he sent Monroe on December 17, lamenting that his progress had only been halted by the "waste of time produced by the inveterate and prolix opposition of its adversaries & the approach of Christmas."[6] Under his barrage, conservatives in the House stood their ground on one major measure—to remove the death penalty for many crimes.[7]

But while others were awed by his apparent progress, Madison was deeply frustrated by the actual lack of it. After the conclusion of the legislative session, it turned out that though dozens of the bills passed, they did not implement much change at all. By the "proper criterion," he told Monroe dismissively, "no Session has perhaps afforded less ground for applause." The whole enterprise, he thought, cast shame on his state. "I am glad to find that Virginia has merit where you are," he told his friend, "and should be more so if I saw greater reason for it."[8] The following year, when it was clear that the legislature was going to undermine most of the paper victories with patchwork amendments, contradictions, and different dates of effectiveness, he was left to lambast the embarrassing "incoherence of the whole."[9] Going into the fight, he realized, he had underestimated the strength of the stubborn status quo.[10]

That problem continued to plague the federal government as well. In February 1786, *three years* after his stem-winder for the forced contribution in Philadelphia, he was enraged by the fact that Congress still hadn't finished the job. And the states were stuck as well; New York and Georgia had not complied with Congress's 1783 demand that they pass enabling legislation for the impost. A feeble Congress had been "earnestly recommending" to the remaining states that they take the impost bill "into their immediate Consideration."[11]

And so it was perfectly natural that, when Monroe asked Madison for his thoughts on the overarching "Question of policy"—whether they should "correct the vices of the Confederation" by "recommendation gradually as it moves along, or by a Convention," Madison told him emphatically that the answer lay on the most radical path. Congress's attempts had "miscarried," he said, because of the "impotency of the federal system." He found it impossible to "remain skeptical" about the need for "infusing more energy into it." His conclusion was inescapable: "Let a Convention then be tried."[12]

The nation must overhaul itself. He began to prepare.

S URROUNDED BY THE DOZENS OF BOOKS FROM JEFFERSON, MADISON searched for clues of how to govern the passions that had plagued the United States since the Revolution.

He plunged into a confederation that had been founded in Greece in 1522 BC to protect a union of cities from the terrorizing raids of barbarians. Like the American states, he learned, each of those cities would send two deputies to spring and fall central meetings. Those deputies were bound by oath to defend the union, and to avenge anyone who harmed the temple of Delphos. They enjoyed other federal powers, such as commissioning a federal military general with "full powers to carry their decrees into execution."

But what most interested Madison wasn't what tied the Greek cities together, but what drove them apart. Just as in America, the Greeks' main problem was their lack of measures to prevent the strong from preying on the weak. The "Deputies of the strongest Cities," he learned, too often "awed and corrupted those of the weaker," and so the powerful cities almost always won in disputes.

Radiating outward, that inequity infected foreign policy—the great example being Sparta's conquest of Athens, which the large cities supported. The confederation, sapped by the constant battle of weak against strong, was easily conquered by Philip II of Macedon. Later, the confederacy succumbed to the Roman Empire. Had the confederation been "stricter," Madison wrote, she might have been able to stop the "vast projects" of Rome.[13] The lesson was that the American states' squabbling, like that of the Greeks, could destroy the country itself.

Plowing further into his library, he unearthed yet more startling parallels. In early Switzerland, he found several disparate communities had organized themselves to defend against invasion by the Austrians. One deputy from each would attend an annual meeting of a diet. Each canton also had its own diet, just as in the United States.

The forces that ripped the Swiss confederacy apart resembled America's. The cantons, he observed, were only "so many independent Commonwealths in strict alliance." Each canton individually maintained its own ambassadors, money, and treaties. Any canton could call on the others for its defense, but the union had no common treasury, troops, currency, or court. All this, Madison discovered, resulted in a "perpetual defensive engagement agst. external attacks, and internal troubles." The older cantons claimed superiority over the younger ones, leading to inequitable common decisions. As in America, the mess stemmed from four great factors: the radically different sizes of the cantons, their different governing systems, their intolerance of religious differences, and the union's overall weakness. And so their mutual obligations, meant to serve as "a Cement," instead became "occasions of quarrels"—just as in the thirteen American colonies.

He continued to accumulate evidence that the fallen classical confederacies strikingly mirrored the American states—that their ancient disease had infected America. But with conscience, conviction, and coercion, he believed America could channel the passions.

As DESPERATELY AS HE TRIED TO CRACK THE NATION'S PROBLEMS, HE WAS straining just as hard to resolve his continuing professional dilemma. Under great financial pressure, Madison embarked on a real estate speculation with Monroe that can best be described as loony. Both Madison and Monroe had separately visited the Mohawk River in upper New York and had been "equally charmed" by it. A tributary of the Hudson River, the Mohawk wound gracefully through upper New York, flowing through lovely rock outcroppings and gentle stands of clustered trees, opening to fill a gorgeous valley. George Washington had purchased land there, and during a visit by Madison to Mount Vernon, advised his young friend that if he had "money to spare and was disposed to deal in land," the valley was "the very Spot which his fancy had selected of all the U.S."[14]

Madison saw an opportunity to get rich quick. He hatched a plan with Monroe to purchase land for development. The two men bought a small parcel to anchor the project. But they were both too cash poor to drive the project themselves; they needed investors. In August 1786, Madison awkwardly approached Jefferson with the business proposition in a letter he mailed to Paris (written in cipher, of course). He not only proposed that Jefferson be their major investor; he asked him to recruit French speculators who would take advantage of favorable exchange rates. But he was far from his comfort zone. He admitted defensively that he was conveying the idea "freely because we trust that if it does not meet your sanction you will as freely tell us so." He asked Jefferson to invest "say, four or five thousand louis more or less." He urged Jefferson to take advantage of America's mad currency situation. Because specie was currently scarce in America, the land was incredibly cheap, but as the specie was "this child of extravagance," he told Jefferson, it would become "the parent of economy." That, in turn, would give the investors their "due share of the universal medium"—of wealth.[15]

But Jefferson had no interest in Madison's clearly speculative scheme. When he wrote back, he was several months late and apologetic but firm. He would not invest. He explained that he likely could not secure any French government funds because investors were already enjoying greater returns in France. And while there *was* the possibility of finding "monied men" who might take the risk—and while Jefferson gamely said he would "be attentive to propose to them this plan"—he was careful to say, "I consider it's success however as only possible, not probable."[16]

Madison must have read Jefferson's letter with embarrassment. Just two weeks before, Madison had painfully apologized to Monroe for being unable to pay him back some loans. Madison, humiliated by his poverty, had thanked Monroe for his "goodness on the occasion," which he confessed "only makes me the more uneasy at imposing on it."[17]

Madison's anxiety about money, his lack of vocation, his eternal bachelorhood—all his various incompetencies—seemed to be uniting against him. He escaped, again, to statecraft.

J UNE 22, 1786, BEGAN FOGGY BUT GRADUALLY CLEARED. THE ENSLAVED MEN and women at Montpelier brought fresh strawberries to Madison's table.[18] His quiet time was about to end. He left for the convention Congress had called in Annapolis to somehow resolve the catastrophic commercial disputes among the states. Without addressing the broader structural issues of federal power, he suspected the convention was a fool's errand. He was determined not to waste a good trip.

He was only due in Annapolis in September. That was over two months away, and he plotted a sinuous journey to his destination. His itinerary took him far north before coming back south, including visits with friends in Winchester, Harpers Ferry, and Philadelphia, where he stayed about ten days, then New York, where he remained for about three weeks, and then, finally, Princeton, where he visited John Witherspoon.

When he arrived in Princeton, after all his conversations along the way, his mood had become noticeably grim. He vented a litany of woes in a letter he sent to his brother Ambrose: "No money comes into the public treasury, trade is on a wretched footing, and the States are running mad after paper money."[19] Greeting his old student in the little town, it must have been immediately clear to Witherspoon that young Madison had reached his brink. Madison openly confessed his fears about the fatal weakness of the union and urgently presented his conclusion that a new federal constitution was required. Witherspoon, probably perceiving in the present Congress the same infuriating intolerance of the Moderates decades earlier in Scotland, saw the subject "in its proper light," according to Madison. He signed up and promised that he would speak freely when an "opportunity offers."[20]

In September, Madison stepped off his coach in Annapolis, feeling pessimistic at best. But there was a silver lining. As he had recently written Jefferson, Annapolis—when it failed—could ultimately lead to a "Plenipotentiary Convention for amending the Confederation." But though his "wishes are in favor of such an event," he told his friend, the odds were that Annapolis would generate only a handful of narrow commercial reforms. Indeed, he confessed to Jefferson (in cipher), "To speak the truth *I almost despair even of this.*"[21]

Annapolis was instructive in the way of many rehearsals—as practice against disaster. For that is what it became. Although the meeting was taking place in Maryland, that state's delegates, believing the convention was transgressing on the powers of Congress, boycotted the convention. Connecticut also refused to attend. South Carolina and Georgia's delegates argued that the event would be redundant and pointless because prior agreements focused on commerce, and also did not come.[22] Madison was not exempt from the squabbling; Rufus King criticized him for going to Annapolis without an attempt to "discover or propose any other plan" than a commercial one.[23]

On September 5, as the convention began, Madison billed Virginia for a dinner where large quantities of wine, punch, *and* porter were served—a boozy way to enter a conclave destined to fail.[24] Madison has had a long reputation for sobriety. As Paul Jennings, his White House slave, later wrote, "He was temperate in his habits. I don't think he drank a quart of brandy in his whole life" and recalled that at "hearty dinners," Madison had "invariably but one glass of wine." When "hard drinkers" were making numerous toasts at his table, Jennings remembered, his master would "just touch the glass to his lips, or dilute it with water, as they pushed."[25]

Madison's self-control was legendary—and perhaps, at times, a legend. Might it be that he indulged in times of intense stress? Only the flies on the wall of that Annapolis restaurant know, but it's possible that the drinks he bought that evening were not only for others.

Hungover or not, his head must have hurt the next day as he watched the convention begin to unravel almost as quickly as it had started. The eastern states' delegates, already angry at having to travel to Annapolis and impatient to return home, departed abruptly, destroying the required quorum. In cipher, Madison snarled to Jefferson that their "*regard for their private characters*" prevailed over "*their public duty*"—almost the worst sin he could imagine.[26]

L IKE A FUSE, THE ANNAPOLIS EXERCISE WOULD PROVE VALUABLE ONLY IN burning out. The only positive thing the gathering produced was a recommendation for a true convention on the entire federal problem—on "extending the revision of the federal System to all its defects." At long last, there would be a constitutional convention, and it would meet in Philadelphia on May 2, 1787.[27]

Madison returned home, intent on planning for what he knew would be an epochal gathering. But just when it seemed to him that the fragile nation could not bear any more strain, he learned with panic about a political earthquake in New England.

17 "A Little Rebellion"

UNDER A NEW CONSTITUTION PASSED IN 1780, MASSACHUSETTS HAD launched a wave of oppression of the poor by the rich. The state had severely limited political participation (including both voting and running for office) to men who owned certain amounts of property. In several western towns, not one single citizen was qualified to hold statewide office. Supported by state law, landed interests had also been loaning money to farmers at usurious rates, which they could not afford to pay back in the current recession. Bankrupt farmers were being thrown into debtors' prisons by the hundreds.[1]

On August 29, 1786, the resentment at this onslaught erupted. A veteran and farmer named Daniel Shays led an angry crowd of 1,500 men to a courthouse in western Massachusetts where judges were meeting to imprison debtors. Shays strode up to the courthouse doors and delivered a petition demanding that the judges shut down the proceedings.

Terrified by the mob outside, the judges shut their doors. Massachusetts soldiers were summoned, who quickly repulsed the rebels. Regrouping, they marched thirty miles through the bitter cold to the town of Petersham. After launching a second rally, they were again overtaken by a small state army while they were sleeping. One hundred and fifty prisoners were taken; the rest of the rebels (including Shays himself) scattered and escaped.[2]

That was the real extent of what came to be known as Shays' Rebellion. The rebels never again appeared in any collective force, instead disappearing into dispersed cells. Those were gradually suppressed by soldiers and prosecuted in the courts.[3] But the revolt radiated alarm through the colonies. Four days after the courthouse rally, Massachusetts governor James Bowdoin issued a proclamation condemning Daniel Shays for introducing "riot, anarchy and confusion" and for "destroying the fairest prospects of political happiness."[4] From Congress's seat in New York, Henry Lee wrote Madison that the rebel force was attracting more and more men in the east and was "becoming very serious."*

Madison felt his research had predicted the rebellion. But his overheated imagination exaggerated the speculation in the gossip traveling the country. Calculating that Massachusetts' overall population was 75,000, and that of several Berkshire counties 40,000, he estimated that over half of Massachusetts' population could be involved in sedition.[5] A week later, he agreed with Lee's prediction that the rebellion would "portend extensive national calamity." Lee predicted, "The contagion will spread and may reach Virginia."[6]

Madison swallowed that rumor whole. He wrote his father, "We learn that great commotions are prevailing in Massts." The "appeal to the sword," he said, was "exceedingly dreaded." In fact, the rebels were "as numerous as the friends of Govt." Not only was a minority of the lawless becoming a majority—the tipping point in Madison's calculation of checks and balances—they were fiercer than their foes, "more decided in their measures."[7]

Despite Madison's fears, the rebellion was quickly put down. On February 12—just five weeks after its beginning—the rebellion was "on the point of being extinguished."[8] Three days later, Madison wrote Randolph a letter stating confidently that the "insurrection will be effectually quelled."[9]

In Paris, Jefferson got wind of the rebellion, whipping up in him a cyclone of new thoughts. He sent Madison a famous letter on January 30, 1787, admitting that he was "impatient to learn your sentiments on the late troubles in the Eastern states." He argued that as far as he had seen, the rebels "do not appear to threaten serious consequences." On the contrary, he said, "*Malo periculosam libertatum quom quietam servitutem*"—"I prefer dangerous freedom to peaceful slavery." He explained that "even this evil" was "productive of good."

Jefferson expanded in what would become one of his most famous dicta: "I hold it that a little rebellion now and then is a good thing, & as necessary in the political world as storms in the physical." Not only did Jefferson believe the Shaysites' actions were salutary, he also advised amnesty for them. The

---

* Henry Lee is not to be confused with Richard Henry Lee. Henry Lee served as a cavalry officer in the Continental Army, where he earned the moniker "Light-Horse Harry." Henry Lee attended Princeton with Madison, graduating a year later and greatly admired his senior fellow student.

"honest republican governors," he declared, should be "so mild in their pun-ishment" so as "not to discourage them too much."

Madison, reading Jefferson's letter, could not have disagreed more. A breach opened between the two friends. Despite their agreements on the need for federalism, they had perpendicular opinions on rebellion *against* the government, with Jefferson seeming to countenance rebellious attacks against both state *and* federal institutions.

And that got to the very point, for Madison, about what Congress ought to be able to do about its own security. In Richmond, he listened as debate among the delegates swiveled to the question of whether *Congress* could direct federal troops to repulse a rebellion against a *state* government. Madison rose to argue that "popular commotions if not thoroughly subdued" did, in fact, threaten the "tranquility of the Union." When faced with internal rebellion, he said, the states essentially belonged to a federal alliance for self-defense; they must act accordingly.[10]

Yet he found Jefferson's argument lingering with him. Weeks later, as the dust from Shays' Rebellion settled, Massachusetts began taking precisely the punitive approach Jefferson had warned about, disenfranchising most of the rebels, creating a new state-run militia to maintain "tranquility," and asserting a right to federal support to quash future insurgencies. Madison thought these steps would render the rebels more "silenced than subdued."[11] He wrote Wash-ington in cipher that although the rebellion was "nearly extinct," the efforts for "*disarming and disfranchising*" the rebels could indeed spark a new crisis.[12]

In fact, the Massachusetts legislature eventually chose Jefferson's toler-ant path, pardoning most of the rebels and not even requiring them to refrain from rebellious activity as a condition of their amnesty. Intellectually, Madi-son appreciated the policy's strategic intent; emotionally, he still despised the beneficiaries. As a consequence, for their "insolence," Madison sniped, some rebels were even claiming their insurgency as "badges of their character."[13]

The clash between Madison and Jefferson on Shays' Rebellion, though muted by long distances and the passage of time, was revealing. Madison, the control freak, saw disaster in rebellion. Jefferson, the free spirit, saw raw potential instead. For Madison, the passions posed an existential threat to the state; for Jefferson, the state's resiliency lay in its *embrace* of them. That ten-sion has never been resolved in American democracy. Over time, Jefferson's permissive approach would prevail on Shays' Rebellion. But the event would also help prompt the total constitutional overhaul that Madison was demanding. Madison wrote a friend that though the "melancholy crisis of things in Massachusetts" was "distressing beyond measure," it did provide even more proof for the "necessity of vigour" in the federal government—and of the need to "restore health to any diseased part of the federal party." A federal convention, he declared, was the *only* solution.[14]

O N NOVEMBER 1, 1786, MADISON WAS STUNNED TO SEE A PROPOSAL ARISE to print yet *more* paper money in Virginia. Reprising his Method, he sat down and scribbled out an elaborate outline for a series of assaults that would destroy the noxious weakness once and for all. It included categories he titled "Unjust," "Unconstitutional," "Antifederal," "Unnecessary"—and "Pernicious."

> *Find passion in your conscience. Focus on the idea, not the man.*
> *Develop multiple and independent lines of attack. Embrace impatience.*
> *Establish a competitive advantage through preparation. Conquer bad*
> *ideas by dividing them. Master your opponent as you master yourself.*
> *Push the state to the highest version of itself. Govern the passions.*

Rising in the assembly, he began his performance, using his blueprint as a script. But he reserved his harshest attacks for the flaws he had enumerated under the category of "Pernicious." He assaulted paper money as a symptom of Virginia's deeper spiritual failings. It was, he railed, "fostering luxury," "serving dissentions between States," "destroying confidence between individuals," "vitiating morals," "reversing [the] end of Govt which is to reward best & punish worst." It was a "disgrace" of republican governments "in the eyes of mankind."[15]

Word about Madison's powerful speech quickly circulated around Virginia. On November 1, Washington sent his young colleague an approving letter from Mount Vernon. "Wisdom, & good examples," Washington wrote, were necessary to "rescue the political machine" from the "impending storm." Only a radical overhaul would do. "Without some alteration in our political creed," he concluded, the "superstructure we have been seven years raising," which had cost so "much blood and treasure," would fall. With thirteen separate states pulling each other apart, the center would not hold. But a "liberal, and energetic Constitution," that was "well guarded, & closely watched"— that, he said, would restore the nation to "respectability & consequence."[16]

Madison barely looked back. On November 6, he stood in Richmond to introduce a bill to send delegates to a *real* national convention. Virginia must support and attend the convention, he urged, for the "crisis is arrived" to address the "solemn question" of whether America would "by wise and magnanimous efforts reap the just fruits of that Independence which they have so gloriously acquired." He directly challenged the other men. Would the country yield to "unmanly jealousies and prejudices" and the "partial and transitory interest" that would "renounce the auspicious blessings prepared for them by the Revolution"?[17]

1786 WAS THE YEAR BEFORE EVERYTHING HAPPENED, THE YEAR when the grandest questions played themselves out as leading men struggled to divine the basic purpose of their half-born confederation. Madison's frustration now bordered on a frenzy. In December, he wrote Jefferson to ridicule the Virginia legislature's failure to fund the government through taxes. He exclaimed that "our internal embarrassments torment us exceedingly."[18]

His predicament mirrored that of the nation. He was forced into joining sordid compromises precisely when there was a clarion need for statesmen. Embarrassed, he admitted to George Washington that he had joined the state assembly's absurd but unavoidable decision to allow Virginians to pay the "Specie part" of their taxes with tobacco. He had done so, he said, from purely political motives, as a "prudential compliance with the clamours within doors & without" and to avoid "more hurtful experiments."[19]

John Blair Smith, from Virginia's Hampden-Sydney College, wrote Madison that "virtuous & enlightened statesmen" might still "devise the means of extricating us from our embarrassments."[20] Madison now saw Washington, the nation's most prestigious leader, as the key to victory. He began courting the general with his usual cheerful assiduity. In October, on the way back from the Annapolis convention, he stayed at Mount Vernon for two nights. He tried to convince Washington to both attend and support the constitutional convention. On November 18, Madison received a letter from Washington that suggested his campaign was working. Although the general said he had "bid adieu to the public walks of life," he told the younger man, from the "sense of the obligation I am under for repeated proofs of confidence in me" in the "business of revising the foederal system," he could envision having "obeyed its call."[21]

But what did the oblique construction mean, exactly? Would Washington *actually* attend, speak at, and endorse the convention? Madison again visited Washington in late January. He argued carefully and forcefully for the need for federal coercion in a new constitution. During his visit to Mount Vernon, Washington "prudently authorized no expectations of his attendance." But he left open the possibility that he could step "into the field if the crisis should demand it."[22]

Gradually, steadily, Madison continued to wear down the general's resistance. Two months later, Washington wrote Madison to express doubts about "whether any system without the means of coercion in the Sovereign, will enforce obedience to the Ordinances of a Genl. Government." Without such a general government, he concluded, "every thing else fails." Even better for Madison, when it came to specifics, Washington demurred to Madison, asking him, "But the kind of coercion you may ask?" and answering his own question, "This indeed will require thought."[23] Washington seemed happy to allow the younger strategist to fill in the details, and Madison was happy to do just that.

AFTER THE LEGISLATIVE SESSION IN RICHMOND CONCLUDED, MADISON returned to Orange for about a week, then left for New York, where Congress at long last formally authorized the constitutional convention in Philadelphia. Throughout his travels, he was preparing himself for the battle ahead. In the pattern that began at Princeton, where he took a double load of courses and made himself ill by overstudying, he planned to bunker down in New York among his books and his thoughts to apply his Method to the battles to come.

As the country's new capital city, New York was rich with the seductions and intrigues he had come to know from Philadelphia. He recognized that the catholic militancy of his preparation for the convention would isolate him not only from the world but from women, extending his sad bachelorhood. He admitted to the ever sympathetic Eliza Trist that his "unsocial plan" would probably expose him to "greater reproach" from society. But he could see no other option. He resigned himself this bitter fruit of his self-appointed role as savior-statesman.[24]

He arrived in New York City on February 9 and settled into his boardinghouse. He established his day-to-day routine in Congress. But his mind wandered to the project waiting in his private quarters—a majestic memorandum that would tear away, once and for all, the restraints on America's greatness. He was so distracted by the endeavor that he could only summon muted disgruntlement when he learned that a large majority in Virginia's Senate had put a "definitive veto" on a proposal to support a new federal government. "It would seem," he murmured, Virginia's politics were being "directed by individual interests and plans," which would be "incommoded" by the "control of an efficient federal government."[25]

In February, debate again erupted in Congress about whether to actually go through with the constitutional convention, now mere months away. He jotted down notes as the convention's foes blasted away with amendments. But amid the dissension, he also observed a collective soul-searching. The "reserve of many members," he wrote, "made it difficult to decide their real wishes & expectations from the present crisis of their affairs." He perceived general agreement that the status quo was "inefficient & could not last long." The "southern and middle" states wanted "some republican organization" of the country that would preserve the union" and give "due energy to the Governmt. of it." But the eastern members were "less desirous or hopeful of preserving the Unity of the Empire."[26] The final verdict would depend on each state, one by one.

Back in his room, he toiled away, hunting for ways to make democracy succeed in America's unique nation-state. As momentum gathered for the convention, his anxiety grew. While it seemed the meeting would take place, and be "pretty full," he felt its actual result belonged "among the other arcana of futurity" and was "inscrutable." The country's rope was fraying. Shays'

Rebellion, he said, had done "inexpressible injury to the republican character," even creating "a propensity towards Monarchy" among leading men.

Worse, he observed the idea of splitting the country—of partition—was
spreading. He predicted that the majority could turn toward breaking the
country into "three more practicable and energetic Governments"—south,
north, and west. In that terrifying event, he gloomily concluded, it was "not
possible that a Government can last long."[27]

He amplified on his concern to Monroe, predicting that without a "radical amendment" of the movements for monarchy and for partition, one of
those "revolutions" could very well take over. He urged his friend, "I hope you
are bending your thoughts seriously to the great work of guarding" against
both.[28] For that is what Madison was doing back in his room amid all those
books. He knew, back in Virginia, Henry was stamping and stirring.

ON MARCH 5, JOHN MARSHALL TOLD MADISON THAT HENRY, WHOSE
"opinions have their usual influence," was preparing for war against
the new Constitution. He was publicly threatening that he would leave the
confederation before relinquishing any navigation of the Mississippi.[29] It was
absolutely crucial to Henry that Virginia be able to unilaterally control the
country's most important river and all the trade and commerce that came
along with it. Many also suspected Henry had commercial interests in the
region that were the real root of his passion. Randolph predicted that Henry
would only support a "negative with some emphasis" on the idea.[30] In late
March, when it became clear to many that Henry's concerns were overblown
and speculative, because there was no general intent among the Federalists to
yield the Mississippi, the damage was already done. Madison angrily predicted
to Jefferson that Henry's implacable disgust, which "exceeded all measure,"
would create "very serious" consequences.[31]

With such wreckage strewn around him, Henry loomed ever larger. In
March, Madison learned that Henry had "positively declined" to attend the
convention. By boycotting, Madison suspected Henry intended to "leave his
conduct unfettered on another theatre." Unsullied by his personal participation in what he saw as a corrupt conclave, Henry would remain pure in

assailing the product of Philadelphia. The convention, Madison darkly predicted, could "receive its destiny from his omnipotence."[32]

Meanwhile, however, Henry was suffering in his own right. Short on cash, he was being hounded by his creditors.[33] Those troubles did not diminish his fury against the Federalists—perhaps they even aggravated it.

Madison kept his promise to himself and redoubled his ambitions for the convention. He wrote Jefferson a long letter praising the "political experiment" the nation was about to enter. The principle that must tower "Over & above" all else, he said, was the need to give the federal government "a negative *in all cases whatsoever*" on the states. Arrayed around that coercive authority, the other elements would fall into place. The nation would be protected from invasion, the states prevented from "thwarting and molesting each other," and minorities insulated from "unrighteous measures which favor the interest of the majority."[34]

The only piece missing was a statesman to drive the scheme home.

18 The Vices

⎯⎯⎯⎯⎯⎯⎯◆⎯⎯⎯⎯⎯⎯⎯

THE PREPARATION FOR PHILADELPHIA ENERGIZED MADISON LIKE A TONIC. He was back in good health.[1] Although he expected a "very full and respectable meeting," he did worry that he should not indulge such "sanguine expectations." There were too many opinions and prejudices, too many "supposed or real interests" among the states. The "only ground of hope," he wrote his father, was the simple, inarguable awfulness of the status quo—the "existing embarrassments and *mortal* diseases of the Confederacy."[2]

His monastic research was on two parallel projects—the first negative, the second positive, and both perfectly complementary to each other. The first would root out every last one of the existing system's vices. The second, on the other hand, would unite all his findings into a design for how the nation could remake itself. The first project would become Madison's celebrated memorandum, "Vices of the Political System of the United States." The second would become his constitutional blueprint, the "Virginia Plan." The scale and scope of both ventures thrilled Madison as befitting Virginia's own greatness. "I will just hint," he told Randolph, at "my ideas of a reform," but couldn't help but boast. He promised they would "strike so deeply at the old Confederation" that they would lead at last to "systematic change."[3]

He began his "Vices" essay in February, taking notes on the first of what would be forty-one pocket-size pieces of paper.[4] He finished in April. Like his speech for the forced contribution, and his Memorial and Remonstrance, and his campaign to reform Virginia's antiquated code, and his attack on paper money, he employed his Method.

Find passion in your conscience. Focus on the idea, not the man. Develop multiple and independent lines of attack. Embrace impatience. Establish a competitive advantage through preparation. Conquer bad

ideas by dividing them. Master your opponent as you master yourself.
Push the state to the highest version of itself. Govern the passions.

In "Vices," he deployed a diverse arsenal of weapons to attack the confederacy's well-known vulnerabilities while exposing new ones—all while laying the foundation for the Virginia Plan. His approach was deceptively simple.
He walked through twelve individual vices of the American political system.
Each vice, on its own, was debilitating to the confederacy. But together, they
were devastating.

He began by charging the states with violating the country's own Articles of Confederation, an "evil" that was, he said, "fatal." His next four vices
were pinprick attacks. The states were making treaties with Indians, developing compacts among themselves, and raising their own troops, as Massachusetts had in response to Shays. They were passing laws that violated
international peace treaties, such as the treaty with France. And they were
routinely trespassing on each other's territories. All this, he concluded, was
making public projects impossible, whether uniform laws on naturalization,
literary property, or the building of canals.

He then spun to a fresh, more expansive topic, attacking prevailing
republican theory as "fallacious" for holding that "right and power being
held in the majority" were "synonymous." The might of the larger states, he
pointed out, did *not* make right; the small states needed protection, especially
if a majority wouldn't support them, which was their untenable predicament
at the present moment.

He then turned to his great objective: coercion. "A sanction is essential
to the idea of law," he analogized, "as coercion is to that of Government."
That the Articles of Confederation contained "so fatal an omission" stemmed,
from the states' "mistaken confidence" that "justice," "good faith," "honor,"
and "sound policy" would, on their own, prevail. He pivoted to a litany of defi-
ciencies plaguing the states themselves. He castigated the multiplicity of laws
among all the states as a "nuisance of the most pestilent kind." He declared
that the "luxuriancy of legislation" was a "general malady." He reviled the
dangerous "mutability" among the states' laws, which only seeded chaos as
they were repealed and superseded.

Those were just the first ten vices, ranging from sweeping to specific, from annoyance to threat. But they were all really just a prelude for Madison's thundering conclusion—the "injustice of the laws of States." The foregoing problems, he stated, raised the most alarming defect of all: the absence of the "fundamental principle of republican Government"—of majority rule—in a new country where the states were actually part of a national whole.

Politicians, he coolly observed, are usually motivated by ambition and personal interest, rather than the common good. And the people themselves often join in a "common passion," becoming a majority and crushing the minority. Indeed, mass action can make people *worse* off, as "individuals join without remorse in acts, against which their consciences would revolt if proposed to them under the like sanction, separately in their closets." The answer, he said, was to *expand the republic*; the "enlargement of the sphere" would dissipate individual passions, thereby controlling the Daniel Shays of the country. Through a "modification of Sovereignty," the broad new nation—ever expanding toward the frontier he had known so well at Mount Pleasant—would have no choice but neutrality between factions, preventing majorities from dominating minorities and factions from undermining the nation itself.

It was a bold, counterintuitive case for expanding the empire and sweeping all thirteen states into a truly common government for their *own sake*. With that brilliance in place like a centering jewel, he concluded his "Vices" memorandum on a mysterious, longing note. The country would need elections that would "extract from the mass of Society" the "purest and noblest characters." These enlightened leaders, he promised, would "feel most strongly the proper motives" for public service, and would be "most capable to devise the proper means of attaining it."[5]

He plainly counted himself as one of those crucial figures—as one of those statesmen.

A S HE TORE DOWN THE ALREADY CRUMBLING PILLARS OF THE CONFEDER-acy, Madison simultaneously worked on the problem of what to erect on the ruins. He devised a fifteen-item-long blueprint that he included in a letter he sent to George Washington on April 16, 1787, advising the general that he had "formed in my mind *some* outlines of a new system" and that he would "take the liberty" of sending them "without apology, to your eye."

He told Washington, "A national Executive must also be provided," but was delicate in sending that idea to the man who would probably become that executive, hastening to explain that he had not formed his own opinion about the "manner in which it ought to be constituted" or the "authorities with which it ought to be cloathed." Washington himself would fill in many of the details—as president.

The legislative department, Madison said, should be divided into two branches, one chosen quickly, with rapid succession, and the other with a slower rotation, to "leave in office a large majority of old members." That would become the Constitution's bicameral legislature, the House and the Senate.

He wanted, he said, a middle ground between state sovereignty and a federal republic, through one legislative chamber that would give each state the same representation regardless of population. That would become the Senate.

The judiciary, he told Washington, needed "national supremacy." While not in the Constitution, that would emerge in another twenty-five years as the doctrine of judicial review, announced by Chief Justice John Marshall (one of Madison's allies) in *Marbury v. Madison* in 1812.

The federal militia, Madison said, needed to be governed by the federal government. That would become Article I, Section 8, Clause 15's authorization that the federal military "execute the Laws of the Union, suppress Insurrections and repel Invasion," and Article II, Section 2's authorization for the president to command the state militias "when called into the actual Service of the United States."

But Madison focused with greatest intensity on coercion: the subject that had preoccupied him for four years, since 1783, when he had tried to convince Thomas Jefferson to support a new amendment empowering Congress with great new authority over the states.

At the very least, he said, the new national government needed to be "armed with positive and compleat authority in all cases which require uniformity"—such as regulation. That would become the new Constitution's "Supremacy Clause," which declared, in the instance of conflict, all federal laws were supreme to all state laws.

But he also urged Washington to support a "negative in *all cases whatsoever* on the legislative acts of the States." That meant not that courts would strike down state laws when they conflicted with federal ones, but that Congress could itself peremptorily strike down state laws. Without such a congressional veto on state laws, he warned, the states would "continue to invade the national jurisdiction," to "violate treaties," and to "harass each other with rival and spiteful measures." While the "great desideratum" was a "disinterested & dispassionate umpire in disputes between different passions & interests in the State," no such umpire existed, or would ever exist. Congressional laws must simply rule over the states.

Madison urged Washington to support a stronger, even more militant enabling authority for the coercive rights of the federal government. The "right of coercion," he told the general, "should be expressly declared." Congress must be able to subjugate any state government, any militia—any resistance whatsoever—not just by laws and the courts, but by the federal military, federal personnel, and the collective will of national leaders signing, and binding themselves to, the new constitution.

He took pains to spell out how the right would work in practice; it would probably never actually need to be enacted, he explained, because of the "difficulty & awkwardness of operating by force on the collective will of a State." The right would still exist. And all parties would know about it.

Looking ahead, he told Washington, he saw three signal obstacles.

First, the convention in Philadelphia would have to agree with the constitution that emerged. Second, Congress would need to approve the new constitution. And finally, the states would need to ratify the constitution. He admitted that these barricades would "inspire despair in any case." But it was the last step that would be at once the most difficult and the most pivotal.[6] The constitution must be ratified by "the people themselves," wrote Madison, and not by the legislators in their elite assemblies. Only such a process, by reflecting and absorbing the vicissitudes of public opinion, would "give a new System its proper validity and energy."[7]

Madison, in other words, knew exactly what he was getting into with the states' ratification of the Constitution. It was, without question, the path most fraught with peril. But he also believed the journey, and the victory, would forever bind the nation.

But that noble aim was also certain to bring him again into a collision with Patrick Henry, the undisputed master of Virginia's people.

O N MAY 2, MADISON LEFT NEW YORK FOR PHILADELPHIA. AFTER THREE days of late spring travel over rutted roads, he arrived in the city of so many of his dreams and victories and dashed hopes. He was nervously thrumming with anticipation. He hoped for, he said, a "full and respectable showing" from the states. But he knew Rhode Island, defiant and uncooperative as always, had already decided to stay away, and he also knew that both Maryland and Connecticut seemed wobbly. But he was far more worried about "Disagreement in opinion among those present" than the absence of one or two states.

"The nearer the crisis approaches," he confessed, "the more I tremble."[8]

19 "On My Right & Left Hand"

SMALL PLANNING MEETINGS BEGAN ON MONDAY, MAY 14, WITH GROUPS OF delegates meeting in the taverns and guest houses of Philadelphia to plot strategy. The weather mirrored their turgid mood; the first week was plagued by frequent rain and rivers of mud.[1] Madison anxiously wrote Jefferson that the "number as yet assembled is but small."[2] By May 27, only seven states had sent delegates, and he wrote his father that he was "suffering" from the "daily disappointment" of the turnout. True, they had received word that three more states would come the next day. Nevertheless, he told his father, every "reflecting man" was "daily more alarmed at our situation."[3]

Washington arrived with quiet but unmistakable drama. Philadelphia's "City Troop," dressed in white breeches, high-topped boots, and round black hats decorated with silver bands, greeted him at his ferry. They walked along with him downtown, while spontaneous outbursts of clapping, shouting, and cheering broke out among people on the street.[4] But Madison also observed individuals quietly sharing with the general "more sober marks" of "affection and veneration."[5]

Madison was delighted that Washington had chosen to spend his considerable political capital on the event, but he was apprehensive all the same. He was hearing from Monroe that there was "great anxiety" back home in Virginia about the convention. Monroe painted its significance in almost celestial terms. "Indeed," he wrote, "it seems to be the sole point on which all future movements will turn."[6]

ON THE FIRST DAY OF DEBATE, MADISON AND THE OTHER MEN WALKED up creaking stairs to the creaking second floor of the State House. The building lacked a steeple, which had been removed for structural reasons years earlier. Set well back from the street, the State House had a peaceful and stable feel. A river flowed by six blocks to the east, providing at least a visual respite from Philadelphia's oppressive summer heat, which some said would be the worst in thirty-five years. Madison's boardinghouse was at Fifth and Market Streets, a few blocks away, so it did not take long to stroll there—which was good, because rushing was sure to cause him, in the heat and humidity, to sweat ceaselessly.[7]

In advance of the convention's first day, Madison had made an important decision. Throughout his research, he had developed a strong "curiosity" not only about what made successful constitutions work, but about the human drama behind their creation—about, as he put it, "the reasons, & the anticipations, which prevailed in the formation of them." And so he decided to create an "exact account of what might pass in the Convention" to satisfy others' "future curiosity."

To that end, on that first day, on the second floor of the State House, Madison walked forward through the delegates down before the chair in front of the room reserved for the convention's presiding member. As he described it later, all of the other members were then arrayed around him "on my right & left hand."[8] He took out his quill and inkpot and, as the others began to talk, began taking meticulous notes of every word said by every delegate present. With his omnipresent quill, Madison became, in some sense, the conscience of the convention. The other delegates, ever mindful of their reputations, were always performing for the young man at the center of the room. His act was even more important because of the convention's self-imposed decision to keep every word of the proceedings secret. Madison's record was not journalism or memoir, but history itself.

Years later, Randolph described his friend at the convention: "His lips were never unsealed, except to some member, who happened to sit near him; and he who had once partaken of the rich banquet of his remarks, did not fail to wish daily to sit within the reach of his conversation." In the same text, Randolph could not resist a jab at Henry. In contrast to the former governor, he remembered, "Madison was enviable in being among the few young men, who were not inflated by early flattery, and could content themselves with throwing out in social discourse jewels, which the artifice of a barren mind, would have treasured up for gaudy occasions."[9]

I N OFF-HOUR STRATEGY SESSIONS, MADISON WORKED WITH RANDOLPH AND George Mason to refine the Virginia Plan. With an open, unassuming face and a wealthy bearing, Mason was renowned as a man of principle who had lived an at-once rich and tortuous life. He and his first wife had twelve children, three of whom died; she then also died, pitiably, from complications of childbirth. Eight years later, Mason had remarried, but he had no more children. Unlike so many other men at the convention, he was self-educated and had earned his wealth as a planter. He lacked the polish and carriage of Madison and Randolph, but he burned with his own fully realized conscience, particularly for individual rights against the state.

The two other men agreed to include most of the ideas Madison had shared with George Washington in the spring—the bicameral legislature, the three branches of government, the "National Judiciary" as "one or more supreme tribunals," and the guarantee of a "Republican Government" by the "United States to each state."[10]

Madison also urged the two other men to include the aspiration he had revealed to Washington—a negative by Congress on the states "*in all cases whatsoever.*" Like Thomas Jefferson before them, Randolph and Mason balked. This profound measure of federal control over the whole nation struck them as too extreme. On May 29, Randolph stood on the floor to read out the fifteen elements of the Virginia Plan. While the version had most of Madison's ideas, he listened unhappily as Randolph announced their milquetoast compromise: that Congress would have only the power "to negative all laws passed by the several States, contravening in the opinion of the National Legislature the articles of Union." That formulation only enabled federal supremacy on *laws*, and then only when congressional *opinion* determined that those laws violated the Constitution's express *articles* (an arduous process that required debate, and then a majority vote). This was a far cry from Madison's ideal of unfettered federal legal authority supported by unhampered federal military supremacy.

For a couple of days, Madison stewed. He finally could constrain his frustration no longer. On May 31, he rose on the floor and openly confessed to the other men his concerns about the dilution of federal power. He declared his "strong bias" in favor of a constitution that would, for the first time, enumerate specific and superior authority for Congress. He admitted that he had doubts concerning the "practicability" of such a mandate, given the obvious reluctance revealed by Mason and Randolph. But he stubbornly stated he would "shrink from nothing" that would enable the new government to overcome its existing terminal weakness.[11]

He suspected that the quest for a resilient *nexus imperii* between the federal and state governments would become America's Sisyphean task. And true enough, in the decades since, for every upward advance the nation has made on that front, the boulder always seems to slip back down the slope.

W HEREVER HE COULD, MADISON TOOK ACTION TO PROTECT MINORITIES from tyrannical majorities. In June, for instance, he watched as Charles Pinckney, a young, wealthy, self-important South Carolinian, introduced a motion to require that state legislatures, rather than the people at large, would elect the House of Representatives—removing the people from voting for their delegates to the federal government. Madison stopped taking notes and rose. Seesawing back and forth in his self-calming way, he began in his quiet voice.[12] The election of at least one branch of the legislature by the people themselves, he said, was "a clear principle of free government." Anywhere a majority is "united by a common interest or passion," he explained, the "rights of the minority are in danger." Honorable motives would not restrain the majority—not honesty (which, he said, is "little regarded by bodies of men as individuals"), not integrity of character (which, he noted, is "always diminished" in large populations), and not even conscience— because, he argued, it is "inadequate in individuals." Even religion, he said, "may become a motive to persecution & oppression."

With Henry's incredible power in Virginia clearly in mind, he described the particular danger of demagogues—manipulative and ambitious leaders of the masses: an "influential demagogue," he said, can "give an impulse to the whole"; their passion could spread like contagion. He declared that large districts were far "less liable to be influenced" by factions and by demagogues than small ones.[13] The only answer was to "enlarge the sphere"—to embrace, as policy, national expansion. A constantly growing democracy would confuse the demagogues and the factions, pulling the boundaries they sought off into the horizon, rendering them small and ineffectual, just one of a cast of thousands, thus protecting the country from breaking apart.[14]

I N PHILADELPHIA, HE WAS PLAINLY FASCINATED BY THE MAJORITY'S CAPACITY for cruelty. Months later, during the battle to ratify the Constitution, Madison would tell Jefferson that no majority driven by a "common passion" would *ever* be able to refrain from crushing the minority. Religion was especially dangerous, "kindled into enthusiasm, its force like that of other passions," then "increased by the sympathy of a multitude." Even "in its coolest state," he said, faith had more often been "a motive to oppression than a restraint from it." The "only policy" against such a torrent, Madison declared, was "*divide et impera*"—divide and conquer.[15]

That is what he tried to do in Philadelphia through one particular new institution: the Senate. He believed an inflamed majority could be throttled by the house of the legislature designed for the wise and self-governing—the statesmen. When an effort developed to gut the elite body by populating it with many more members, he argued that the Senate *must* be designed for "enlightened statesmen." The whole *point* of the Senate, he insisted, was to "consist in its proceedings with more coolness" and with "more system" and with "more wisdom" than the "popular branch." Enlarging the Senate would infect it with the "vices which they are meant to correct."[16]

Madison seemed to be imagining himself sitting there. He soon went so far as to contend that senators should enjoy a nine-year term. The House, he explained, would be "liable to err" from "fickleness and passion." The Senate would provide a "necessary fence against this danger" precisely because it would house "a portion of enlightened citizens" whose "firmness" would "seasonably interpose" against "impetuous counsels," and would resolve the problem of majority tyranny. The body could defang the enemy within.[17]

D ESPITE HIS EARLY SETBACKS, AS THE SUMMER PROGRESSED, MADISON doggedly continued his pursuit of coercion. In early June, Pinckney moved that Congress should have the ability to negative all laws it judged "to be improper." That power would essentially declare illegal even a *potentially* disobedient activity by a state, and Madison quickly rose to second the motion. He pointed out that experience had shown a "constant tendency in the States to encroach on the federal authority," to violate treaties, and to "oppress the weaker party." The states' intransigence came pretty close to inviting actual violence. Shays' Rebellion had shown that. What if Massachusetts had been conquered? What if a rebel-led government had then conspired with rebels in neighboring states?

The only alternative, he concluded, was "an appeal to coercion." The congressional veto on state laws was, he said, the "mildest expedient that could be devised for preventing these mischiefs." Congress needed to be able to strike down any state law it chose, for any reason. That plenary authority would be, he declared, the "great pervading principle that must controul the centrifugal tendency of the States." Without it, they would "continually fly out of their proper orbits" and "destroy the order & harmony of the political System."[18] The Constitution, without coercion, would be chaos.

Madison's stance set him against Jefferson—not for the first time, and not for the last. Hearing about the proposed veto, Jefferson wrote Madison from Paris with barely concealed alarm, "Prima facie," he told his friend, "I do not like it." He went on, "It fails in an essential character, that the hole & patch should be commensurate." He noted that very few states' acts touched on federal law. To give Congress a veto on *all* state laws would upset the apple cart.[19] At a subconscious level, Madison probably recognized that Jefferson had exposed a central vulnerability in his adamant case for the veto "in all cases whatsoever."

Jefferson's challenge revealed the degree to which control, for Madison, had become an obsession. In other arenas, especially his own political campaigns, he had developed an appreciation for nuance and subtlety. But not here. Not when dealing with the contagious passions of the collectively self-destructive colonies. And so throughout the summer, Madison stubbornly adhered to his argument. Over a month after the contretemps with Jefferson, he was still trying to haul the convention in his direction. In July, with the Philadelphia heat grown stifling, he rose to contend that the federal negative was "essential." The states, he argued, had a natural "propensity to pursue their particular interests in opposition to the general interest." Their tendency to fly off on their own trajectories would continue to "disturb the system," he said, unless "effectually controlled," going on to say, "Nothing short of a negative on their laws will control it."[20] But he failed, as the convention rejected the negative by what Madison bitterly described as a "bare majority."

His mind was not eased by continued revelations of disintegration back home in Virginia.

FROM HIS HUMID ROOM, STIPPLED BY CANDLELIGHT, THE COBBLED STREETS outside quiet after the daytime drumbeat of delegates' shoes, he wrote Jefferson that the appetite for paper money in Virginia was growing stronger with each day. The people were hungering for a quick fix to their inflated money. "Mr. H—n—y," he wrote (as if the clever trick of removing letters from Henry's name would also elide his opponent), was the "avowed patron of the scheme." Most dangerously, Henry was (Madison wrote in cipher) "*hostile to the object of the convention.*" He "*wishes,*" Madison coded, "*either a partition or a total dissolution of the confederacy.*"[21]

A rage was starting against all financial support of government itself. Arsonists in King William County burned down a courthouse that contained tax collection records. Men were physically threatening tax collectors visiting their homes and businesses. A sheriff in Virginia responded by refusing to protect any tax collector. A sick feeling entered Madison's fevered imagination; the Shays epidemic, it seemed, had infected Virginia. A complete breakdown of law and order seemed within the range of possibility. Amid all of this, the hunger for paper money raged on, with the "people, in general" appearing "very much discontented."[22]

He dramatized the saga in a letter to William Short. There was "no hope" from the existing system, he scribbled, and so the "eyes and hopes of all" were set on Philadelphia. The delegates' decision would have a "material influence on our destiny," not to mention the "cause of republican liberty."[23] The *world* was the stage for Philadelphia.

No wonder Madison had anxiety attacks.

DURING THE LONG WEEKS IN PHILADELPHIA, MADISON BECAME INCREAS-ingly irritated by the convention's self-imposed gag order. He was, after all, irrepressibly honest, even voluble, with his close friends, and the rule interfered with the fluid relationships so central to his happiness. He admitted to Monroe that he felt "great mortification" at the "disappointment" the silence "imposes on me to throw on the curiosity of my friends."[24] A few days later, he apologized to his brother Ambrose that the rules were forcing him to "disappoint the curiosity you will naturally feel to know something of these proceedings."[25]

The secrecy edict heightened the proceedings' pent-up drama. After about six weeks, Madison wrote Jefferson that the "public mind is very impatient" for the release of the Constitution—and that rumors were, meantime, swirling, "which tend to inflame curiosity."[26] In Williamsburg, the eager reverend was no exception, writing Madison on August 1—after the reign of secrecy had lasted about eight weeks—"We are here, & I beleive every where, all Impatience to know Something of your conventional Deliberations." With exasperated whimsy—or whimsical exasperation—he exclaimed, "If you cannot tell us what you are doing, you might at least give us some Information of what you are not doing."[27]

But Madison, no stranger to self-control, managed to comply with the order.

FOR MADISON, THE MOST SIGNIFICANT EPISODE OF THE CONVENTION occurred when the formidable William Paterson rose to deliver what became known as the New Jersey Plan. The plan rejected almost every aspect of Madison's political philosophy. Instead of a bicameral legislature, with the populous House and the statesman-filled Senate, it provided for only one Congress with one vote per state. It allowed Congress to collect taxes, but only upon the states' repeated consent—permanently installing, rather than resolving, the tension that had driven the forced contribution fiasco. Congress—not the people—would elect the chief executive, and it would allow the president to be recalled by a majority of governors, further bending the federal executive to the states' will.

Six years older than Madison, Paterson was a fellow Princeton graduate who went on to become a Supreme Court justice and governor of New Jersey. He was composed, thoughtful, dignified—and dangerous. Madison was aware that Paterson's vision of the union differed so starkly from his own that the very sophistication of the Virginia Plan might appear radical by comparison.

No matter how well intentioned, the New Jersey Plan would invite the passions already jeopardizing the union to run amok. Yet Paterson himself did not appear radical, which made his proposal, and its messenger, doubly threatening. Madison planned the destruction of the New Jersey Plan with his Method.

> *Find passion in your conscience. Focus on the idea, not the man. Develop multiple and independent lines of attack. Embrace impatience. Establish a competitive advantage through preparation. Conquer bad ideas by dividing them. Master your opponent as you master yourself. Push the state to the highest version of itself. Govern the passions.*

He plotted eight distinct salvos, which he delivered with devastating precision on the floor. For his first attack, he headed straight for the heart of the New Jersey Plan. The danger of Paterson's proposal, Madison claimed, lay in New Jersey's own recent behavior. He described a current union that resembled the terrifying state of nature in Thomas Hobbes's *Leviathan*. If the men there had not read Hobbes recently, they were familiar with his argument: to save themselves from a state of nature that was "solitary, poore, nasty, brutish, and short," free men must yield their liberty to a collective center—to government. Madison recounted a "most notorious" instance when New Jersey herself had "*expressly refused*" to comply with a constitutional decision of Congress, only later deciding "barely to rescind" her refusal without "any positive act of compliance." By this point, it was obvious that Madison saw such opposition as insolence; his attack on the state, in turn, was almost ad hominem.

He next approached the New Jersey Plan's proposal of a Congress with one seat for every state. Madison bootstrapped everything onto his argument for the bicameral legislature. Government, he declared, could not be "feeble." The centrally weak coalitions of Sparta, Athens, and Thebes were "fatal" to the confederacy. And when men, and states, were "large, strong, and also nearly equal," they "immediately become rivals."[28] Carthage and Rome, he said, "tore each other to pieces" instead of uniting—meaning that powerful states needed the sort of *nexus imperii* the bicameral Congress could provide. As for the small states, he pleaded with them to renounce the obvious self-interest in the one-state-one-vote New Jersey Plan—which would "infuse mortality" into the Constitution and, he warned, force the confederacy to "go to pieces."[29]

His next assaults were equally damaging.

The New Jersey Plan, he said, would fail to prevent states from raising their own armies and from trespassing on each other.

It would lead to horrible administrative problems within the states.

It would expose the Union to infiltration by foreign enemies.

It would leave the smaller states *more* vulnerable to the predations of the majority. The "larger States will be impregnable," he predicted, while "the smaller only can feel the vengeance."

Finally, it would self-destruct; the states supporting the New Jersey Plan would, through "pertinacious adherence," lead the union either to dissolve or be divided into "two or more Confederacies."[30]

Altogether, Madison painted a picture of ruinous decisions, dismemberment and indulgence, failure and chaos. Finished, he sat down. The vote was soon counted. When the numbers were in, it came as little surprise that the stubborn, slender man from Orange had defeated august Paterson and his New Jersey Plan.

A FTER SIX WEEKS OF DEBATE, MADISON HAD BECOME EXHAUSTED BOTH by the constant quarreling and the daily and nightly task of recording the debates. Every day, the room started cool but became increasingly hot and stuffy. But when someone was speaking, he could never leave—not to relieve himself, not to have a conversation with a friend, not to step into the sun and the fresh (if humid) air. When someone wavered or spoke softly, he had to strain physically to capture their phrases. He complained to Jefferson that the task was a "drudgery," but he pledged he would finish it as long as illness did not stop him.[31]

Back in Virginia, he knew Henry and his friends were already throwing up barricades to whatever the convention might produce. Henry saw a ripe political issue in Congress's proposal to settle debts with the British. At the same time, he was agitating for yet more paper money. Prior to that summer, his county, Prince Edward, had opposed paper money, but with Henry's support, Madison learned that the county was clamoring for more.

Even worse, under Henry's machinations, a friend warned Madison, the "doctrine of three Confederacies"—of splitting the country into three parts—was gaining more traction.[32] While Philadelphia plodded along, Madison's worst nightmare seemed more real than ever—that Henry and his passions would rip the country apart.

I N LATE JULY, MADISON ROSE TO ARGUE IN FAVOR OF THE POPULAR ELECTION of the president. In doing so, he disclosed a powerful tenet of his emergent political philosophy—one that surely was not in place when he had defied the people of Orange County and their Election Day thirst for free liquor.

Of all the country's sources for political legitimacy, he declared to the men around him, the general populace was the "fittest in itself." Because only the people would "know & vote for some Citizen" who had earned "general attention & esteem," they would select a president of "distinguished Character."[33] Despite his long observation of the destructive power of simple majorities, Madison still felt that the *total* of the people would make good and just choices. The sort of man who earned their esteem, therefore, would be healthy for their democracy. In late July, he strove to enumerate for the other delegates the disastrous alternatives. He explained that if the state legislatures instead elected the president, he would "be rendered subservient" to the states. If the governors chose the president, that would be even worse, with the governors "courted, and intrigued with," by the candidates for president.

The Electoral College, he declared, was the answer. The people would select electors, who would in turn meet away from the seat of government and choose the president. The clever idea threw a barrier between any demagogue who might come into a popular election and the presidency itself, in a process he said would give "little opportunity for cabal, or corruption."[34]

By tethering himself to the people—by trusting in them and even looking up to them—Madison was taking a firm stance on an ancient dilemma that still bedevils us today. Do the people get it right most of the time, or not? Can the median of public opinion be trusted when it comes to electing politicians, or not?

That battle went back to ancient Athens. Plato, seared by the violent upheavals in Athens and the mob-led assassination of his mentor Socrates, proposed a fictional state run by elite Guardians that locked the people away from political power. Plato's student Aristotle rebelled against that harsh utopia, arguing instead that the "principle that the multitude ought to be supreme rather than the few best is one that is maintained, and, though not free from difficulty, yet seems to contain an element of truth."[35]

Madison's logic resembled Aristotle's: When the people come together, Aristotle believed, their collective effort was "better than the few good," just like a "feast to which many contribute is better than a dinner provided out of a single purse."[36] So it was with Madison, who had come to value the wisdom of the crowds over the opinion of any planter or merchant. And that belief, more than anything else, was at last making him the American statesman he had always sought to become.

A
S THE CONVENTION DREW TO A CLOSE, MADISON BECAME DISTRACTED by the information from his brothers that his father was sick. While robust, the man was still sixty-four, and Madison couldn't stop thinking about him. On August 12, he wrote his father a meandering letter, enclosing several newspapers, confessing that he didn't have "any thing worth communicating" and was writing from his "chief anxiety," which "is to hear that your health is re-established."[37]

When his father didn't write back, three weeks later Madison impatiently sent another letter plaintively accusing him of not responding. "I have been long anxious to learn the re-establishment of your health."[38] But still he heard nothing. His father did eventually recover, but not without reminding Madison of his unbreakable ties to Virginia and the fact that he was, as he had always been, his father's son.

T
HROUGH THE CONVENTION, MADISON HAD BEEN WRESTLING WITH THE paralyzing issue of slavery—how much to allow, when, and on what terms. As the convention neared its end, he responded to a proposal to extend the limit on the slave trade from twelve to twenty years by rising and declaring to the delegates that slavery was "dishonorable to the National character." Twenty years, he said, would "produce all the mischief that can be apprehended" from slavery. In a discussion of the taxation rate for imported slaves, he declared that there should be no rate at all. In fact, he proclaimed, there

should be no *taxation* on slaves whatsoever, because it was "wrong to admit in the Constitution the idea that there could be property in men."

In support of his argument, he advanced a clever logical defense: Slaves, he said, were "not like merchandize." They were "not consumed." And therefore they could not be treated as property.[39]

The other slave-owning delegates must have been deeply irritated by his épée. Indeed, how can we square such a claim with Madison's own slave-owning? Was it gross hypocrisy, or something more complicated? No answer will be satisfying or even reassuring. But we can still try to *understand* the paradox. One explanation is the following: Madison applied a different political philosophy to matters concerning the *state* to those concerning his own house. For him, the private was not the same as the public. To him, the stakes within the private realm of home and family of owning men and women and children were lower, the principle involved of a different kind and scope. At the national level, however, he believed slavery presented an existential threat to a country premised on freedom. At Montpelier, with slaves he felt he treated well, he saw no such conflict. In fact, he thought the men and woman he owned were better off with him than in the predatory violence of the freedman's life.

In the early 1830s, before he died, Madison received a series of urgent letters from his former White House secretary Edward Coles that culminated a campaign Coles had begun in 1819 to convince Madison to free his slaves. Coles took abolition particularly personally. He had moved from Virginia to Illinois, along with his own slaves, in order to free them in Illinois. He would later become governor of Illinois on an abolitionist platform.

Madison and his wife Dolley loved Coles. Madison saw him almost as the son he never had. But he firmly parted ways with him on the issue of manumission. In 1819, in response to Coles's first entreaties, Madison rebuffed him, citing "the habits of the slave." Without the "instruction, the property or the employments of a freeman," Madison wrote, freeing the men, women, and children he owned would make them worse off. He told Coles he wished the latter's "philanthropy" could succeed in "changing their colour as well as their legal condition." Without such a change, he said, they were "destined to a privation of that moral rank & those social blessings, which give to freedom more than half its value."[40]

For over a decade that followed, Coles never relented. In 1832, he implored the former president at least to free his slaves in his will, as George Washington had, telling Madison that keeping his slaves would be a "blot & stigma on your otherwise spotless escutcheon," whereas freeing them would be the "finale of your character & career, & to the consummation of your glory."[41]

But Madison wasn't interested in either finale or consummation, even from as loyal and principled a disciple as Coles. He again firmly declined Coles's plea. In 1834, he explained that the finances of Montpelier were so poor that he either needed to sell slaves or land to survive. He had been selling land, he said, but now could not afford even to support his slaves; therefore he had "yielded to the necessity of parting with some of them to a friend and kinsman who I am persuaded will do better by them than I can, and to whom they gladly consent to be transferred."[42]

These answers, over the span of fifteen years, tangle together all of the most frustrating aspects of Madison's approach to this issue of human justice. He cited the slaves' "colour" as the root of a social conditioning to which they were "destined"—separate from their "legal condition." But he did not seek to use the law to change those very conditions, and their destiny. He then sold his slaves to finance the maintenance of lands that he himself could not manage.

Perhaps it should come as no surprise that this son of his father, and this eldest brother, would be at once so paternalistic and so controlling on this one issue regarding the rest of his "family" at Montpelier. As a slaveholder himself, his lifelong anxieties about money and his professional difficulties in planting combined with his sense that he should determine and control the outcomes of those for whom he felt responsible. Yet that does not make his words and his actions any less disappointing to history, to Americans, and to his own legacy, as Coles so keenly recognized.

In Philadelphia during the convention, Madison was clearly torn by the conflict between his own slave-owning and the clear principle of equality for all men. Yet he joined the noxious compromise of counting slaves as three-fifths of a freeman on the question of how to count slaves for congressional districts. He defended his support later on the grounds that it was politically necessary to bring the southern states into the alliance.

He never seemed at ease with his own compromise. In his later years, he struggled to find an answer to slavery that would be as systemic and elegant as his other resolutions of the country's dilemmas. In 1816, when he was sixty-five, he joined the founding of the American Colonization Society, which sought to bring African Americans to the newly created country of Liberia. In 1833, three years before he died, he ascended to the presidency of the organization. Slaveholders and abolitionists alike saw value in the Liberia project—slaveholders wanted the problem of free American blacks solved once and for all, and abolitionists wanted a homeland for African Americans. For that reason, it seemed like an ideal Madisonian compromise—a *nexus imperii* between the warring factions.

Yet Liberia would not solve America's most crippling problem. It would not even come close. By the time the American Civil War ended, in 1867, the society had sent about 13,000 free American blacks to Liberia. By that same time, 750,000 Americans died in the failure of North and South to reconcile over slavery.[43] It was the singular challenge young Madison had been unable to resolve either in the Constitution or afterward—in his own life as in the country's.

O N SEPTEMBER 15, THE DELEGATES FILED UP THE WOODEN STAIRS OF THE State House—more worn than at the start of the summer—for the final vote on the Constitution. At about three in the afternoon, two dissenters made their final stands. Madison's friend Edmund Randolph rose first. The other delegates watched the notoriously open-hearted attorney begin to speak with great interest. Randolph was plainly troubled by opposing the majority in the room. Yet he decried the "indefinite and dangerous power" the Constitution would give to Congress. Scribbling, Madison recorded Randolph's announcement of an alternative: State conventions should be allowed to amend the plan, with those questions to be decided by *"another general convention."* If the men did not follow his proposal, Randolph declared, he would refuse to follow them.

George Mason stood next. He first seconded Randolph's motion. He then dramatically predicted that the new Constitution would "end either in monarchy, or a tyrannical aristocracy." He would not vote for it, he announced—either in Philadelphia or Virginia.

Pinckney then rose to attack the attackers. It was well understood that the Constitution, as drafted, would be approved, and the gravity of that decision was settling on the men. Looking around him, Pinckney noted their "peculiar solemnity." Although Pinckney admitted that he, too, objected to certain aspects of the plan,[44] he lambasted the idea of a second convention: Only "confusion and contrariety" could "spring from the experiment." "Conventions," he said, were "serious things, and ought not to be repeated."

The vote on the motions was called. Madison sat, quill poised. Randolph's motion was read. The delegates were polled, state by state. Madison wrote, with satisfaction, "All the states answered no." The motion of whether to "agree to the Constitution as amended" was then announced.[45] The states' delegates were again counted off. Every one voted aye.

It was six o'clock in the afternoon—the end of what had been the longest session of the summer. Autumn was coming, change was in the air, and Madison and his Virginia Plan had prevailed.

The next day, the men again filed up the stairs for the final day of the long session in Philadelphia. Only forty-one of the original fifty-five delegates had lasted this long. For the first time since the convention began, George Washington rose to speak. He declared his support for an amendment decreasing the size of House districts—then forty thousand—by one quarter, making the House of Representatives more numerous and populous—and his motion was adopted unanimously by the delegates. They knew they were looking at their future president.

Benjamin Franklin then made an epochal comment. Gesturing to the painting of a rising sun painted on the back of the convention's president's chair, he said, "I have often and often in the course of the session, looked at that behind the president without being able to tell whether it was rising or setting." He paused and then continued, "But now at length I have the happiness to know it is a rising and not a setting sun."

Every member except for Elbridge Gerry, George Mason, and Edmund Randolph then signed the document. The Constitution—provisionally—was now a certain kind of law. But they all knew—Madison more keenly than any—that it would become reality only if the states ratified it.

Washington then invited the entire group for supper at the City Tavern on Second Street near Walnut. The men walked over in a jumble of emotions—exhaustion, relief, somber reflection, and joy at their release. They "dined together," Washington recorded in his diary, "and took a cordial leave of each other."[46] But one man among them was neither joyous nor relieved.

M ADISON WAS TROUBLED BY HIS FAILURE TO ACHIEVE A CLEARLY COERcive power for the new federal government. In the days immediately following the Constitution's passage, he obsessively returned to that fatal flaw. It soon began poisoning his view of the whole summer and the whole document. He snapped to Jefferson that the plan would "neither effectually answer its national object" nor stop the "local mischiefs" that "everywhere excite disgust against the state governments."[47] He told others that the convention had made a mistake in incorporating an "infinite diversity" of views, which had become "as difficult as it was desireable."[48] It was a Constitution designed by committee, and looked like it. Instead of balance among its hinged parts, he saw instead a parlous yaw.

His pessimism deepened over the coming weeks. He returned again and again to the lack of coercion. In late October, he complained to Jefferson that without the "check in the whole over the parts, our system involves the evil of *imperium in imperio*"—of authority within authority, a divided center. He explained that if a "compleat supremacy" could not be achieved, at least the federal government should be enabled to defend itself against encroachments by the states. He cited England as an example. Take away the king's "royal negative," he said, and the system's unity, coherence, and internal order would be destroyed.[49]

The vote was beginning to seem to him like a mere pause in the country's disintegration. The criticism pouring in didn't help. His cousin the reverend wrote to say the Constitution had a "Defect" that "perhaps threatens Ruin to Republicanism itself." The system, he said, failed to ensure that all the government's branches were distinct and independent. Certain features would breed tyranny—especially the lifelong president who could veto Congress. That provision bore "so strong a Stamp of Monarchy or Aristocracy," the reverend warned, that the Constitution could not last for long.[50]

And then there was ratification to worry about. In late August, Lafayette confessed to Madison that the tumults in America were disturbing him deeply, that he was "Very Anxious" to know whether the Constitution could actually be implemented. The United States' reputation, he said, demanded immediate action. The country possessed the "Liberality, Wisdom, and Patriotism" to conquer its demons. But if it could not, Lafayette told his friend, "I feel that the tranquillity of My Life Will Be Poisoned."[51]

Madison felt the same way. But one beam of light pierced his gloom. People were so desperate for stability, he felt, that the momentum for ratification would overwhelm even local prejudices.[52]

IN LATE SEPTEMBER, MADISON LEFT MRS. HOUSE'S IN PHILADELPHIA TO attend the session of Congress in New York. He pulled up to the lodging house of Dorothy Elsworth at 19 Maiden Lane (today, just north of Wall Street in Lower Manhattan) and was soon greeting the other Virginians staying there. He hoped to get to work as quickly as possible. Congress needed to support the convention in Philadelphia by sending the Constitution to the states. To that end, he launched a blitz of meetings with Alexander Hamilton, John Jay, Rufus King, Gouverneur Morris, and Henry Lee.

Madison took his seat in Congress and joined other veterans from Philadelphia in a motion to send the Constitution to the states immediately for ratification. They quickly swatted down objections from Richard Henry Lee, and Congress unanimously supported the measure.[53] Another obstacle had been overcome, but it was minor compared with what was to come.

Patrick Henry, he predicted to Jefferson, would certainly "wage war against any reform whatever."[54]

20 The Campaign Begins

BY LATE SEPTEMBER, THE FULL EXTENT OF THE ACCOMPLISHMENTS IN Philadelphia had worked its way back to Henry in Virginia. By boycotting the convention, he had hoped to maintain the purity and force of his opposition. Yet he must now have understood that by absenting himself, he had allowed the movement to gain more traction. He betrayed his mounting frustration in September, when he "assembled, and harangued" a crowd of his constituents in Prince Edward County to support paper money. When it was clear that a large majority would defy him and oppose paper money, he lost his temper and shouted that "they should no longer consider him as their representative."[1]

In mid-October, Monroe warned Madison that the convention would "perhaps agitate the minds of" Virginians more than any topic since the Revolution itself. That Henry was against the Constitution, he told his friend, would ensure a "powerful opposition."[2] Monroe himself was, in fact, in the process of deciding to join Henry—a perilous development indeed.

Madison was coming to realize that the new Constitution would face blistering opposition around the country. He was particularly distressed by the prospects in Virginia where, he wrote his father (now healthy and cheering on his son) that for "obvious reasons opposition is as likely to arise in Virginia as any where."[3] He told George Washington, "I am waiting with anxiety for the echo from Virginia, but with very faint hopes of it corresponding with my wishes."[4] While the political developments in many other states seemed auspicious—Maryland was "well disposed," he thought, and Delaware would "fall in of Course"—his home Commonwealth, he said, "I fear will be divided and extremely agitated."[5] With disarming candor, he told his old friend Edmund Pendleton that it would be "truly mortifying" for a state that had "generally taken the lead on great occasions" to fail now.[6]

Madison wrote Washington, "Much will depend on Mr. Henry." He willed himself to believe Henry was still up in the air, arguing that his "favorable decision on the subject may yet be hoped for."[7] But then he learned that Henry was scheming, "however foreign his subject," to hit the Constitution with "a side blow."[8] Henry had initially wanted to abort the Constitution by preventing a ratifying convention in Virginia entirely. But by October, he realized that the momentum was too strong. So he quickly switched tacks, declaring that it "transcended our powers to decide on the Constitution; that it must go before a Convention." Washington ingenuously told Madison that "much pleasure was discovered" at Henry's announcement.[9] But Madison knew Henry's newfound enthusiasm for a ratification convention was, at best, a Trojan horse.

In Richmond, Randolph—who was starting to lean toward supporting the Constitution he had so painfully attacked on the convention's last day—confronted Henry several times on his opposition to the Constitution. The former governor became so upset during these exchanges that he actually could not continue speaking—"He recedes so far from me," Randolph recounted to Madison, "that we must diverge after a progress of half a degree further."[10]

Madison's anxiety spiked. In late October, Henry, joined by Governor Harrison, devised a stratagem to call a convention with the purpose "to adopt—reject—or amend—the proposed Constitution." This poison pill would allow the single state of Virginia, by amending the Constitution with one all its own—thereby replicating the very problem Madison sought to solve. After heated debate, Henry lost his motion.[11] But the loss only provoked him.

In the weeks to follow, Henry grew even more wrathful. Archibald Stuart wrote Madison that Henry was becoming "loud on the distresses of the People" and "makes us tremble" with threats of a rebellion if the people were "driven to despair."[12] In mid-November, Madison heard the enthusiasm for the new Constitution was "subsiding" in Richmond, giving way instead to "a spirit of criticism." To Washington, he confessed that he felt "fearful of the "influence and co-operation" of enemies like Henry.[13]

Henry Lee confessed to Madison his "real Grief" that Henry was successfully gathering a base of supporters in the Virginia legislature who "manifested hostility to the new constitution." His "art is equal to his talents for declamation," Lee declared, admiring Henry despite himself.[14]

Henry seemed to be approaching some sort of climax. Madison heard that his "anxiety was too great to be concealed." In debates, Henry's very body appeared agitated by his spite toward the Constitution; Archibald Stuart said his anger affected his "whole frame" and made him "sweat at every pore." But that was not a good thing for Henry, Stuart reported, for he then appeared at a "greater disadvantage."[15]

In perfect contrast to his younger nemesis, who seemed to have everything under control, Henry was losing his. The closer the men got to their duel, the more they resembled their respective political philosophies. Like a trimmed and well-captained schooner navigating swells, Madison's subtle checks and balances reflected his psychology and temperament and Method. Henry's gusty swells, by contrast, mirrored his tempestuous revolutionary ethos. The country could follow either course—the ship or the sea.

MADISON PLOTTED HIS JOURNEY TO THE RATIFICATION BATTLE WITH care. He would first need to be elected a delegate to the state convention in Richmond. He approached this seemingly minor hurdle with deadly seriousness. Although he still professed the humility drilled into him by his father—writing his brother Ambrose decorously, "I shall not decline the representation of the County if I should be honoured with its appointment"—he also asked his brother to spread the word. His false modesty dissolved entirely as he soberly instructed Ambrose to let him "know what competition there will probably be and by whom."[16]

Once he was a delegate, he had no doubt Henry would be his primary obstacle—as Madison put it, "the great adversary who will render the event precarious." Henry, he wrote Jefferson, was "working up every possible interest." He was latching onto any cause that might provoke the people. He began fulminating against the importation of all foreign goods, proposing new duties on popular items from foreign rum to British leather, which Madison derided as "little short of madness."[17] Yet there was a method to it. Through such machinations, Henry was nimbly recasting himself as a passionate nationalist in the months after the Philadelphia cabal and before the Virginia ratification battle.

But Madison clung to his faith that Henry's blustery manipulations would no longer suit the freshly enlightened nation. He *believed*, he said, that the "body of sober & steady people, even of the lower order, are tired of the vicicitudes, injustice and follies which have so much characterized public measures." The people, he told Jefferson, were "more likely to cherish than remove" the Constitution.[18] He was certain that reason would out. It must.

I N NEW YORK, MADISON UNDERSTOOD HIS RELATIONSHIP WITH ONE NEW Yorker in particular would have outsize importance in the mission ahead. He and Alexander Hamilton had first come to know each other five years earlier in Philadelphia, when Madison was entering his third year in Congress, and Hamilton was beginning his first term there. Hamilton, like Madison, had a fierce impatience with what he saw as the small-minded men who were throttling the country's potential. Yet the two men had traveled vastly different paths to their alliance.

Hamilton was born and raised on the Caribbean island of Nevis. His father was a fearsome, violent man; after giving birth to Alexander, his mother made the courageous but scandalous decision to flee the marriage. But she died when her son was just eleven. His vindictive father gave him little property, effectively leaving him an orphan. With stunning perspicacity, the slender, five-foot-seven, red-haired boy became an autodidact. He read everything he could get his hands on. He authored precocious essays, likely including one titled "Rules for Statesmen." (Madison was not alone in his early infatuation with achieving that ideal political type.) Hamilton caught the attention of the island's leading men, who sent him to the mainland, to New York, to gain an education and to enter society.[19]

At eighteen, the self-assured and ambitious Hamilton idolized John Witherspoon and set his sights on attending Princeton. He secured a meeting with Witherspoon. The Scot grilled the brash young man on his knowledge of the liberal arts. But then Hamilton announced he had his own condition for attending Princeton—he must be allowed to skip through all of his classes "with as much rapidity as his exertions would enable him to do." Witherspoon was taken aback; he did not like the young man's abrasive ambition. Weeks later, he rejected Hamilton.[20]

Chagrined, Hamilton quickly arranged instead to attend King's College in Manhattan (later Columbia) instead, where he excelled. He left school for

IMAGE 20.1. ALEXANDER HAMILTON. COURTESY OF THE LIBRARY OF CONGRESS.

a time to fight valiantly in the war, founding volunteer militia, then becoming aide-de-camp to George Washington, and spent a winter at Valley Forge. He married into the wealthy Schuyler family. After successfully commanding a battalion of Lafayette's at Yorktown, he moved with ease into law and politics. By adulthood, he had become refined and striking, with piercing eyes, volcanic intensity, and overpowering brilliance. A friend said that when he was animated by a subject, "you could see the very workings of his soul"—so different from the guarded, private Madison.[21]

In Madison's first term in Congress, he generally maintained an appreciative but critical distance from Hamilton. In April 1783, Congress debated a revenue scheme whose commissioners could allow states to make claims against federal tax revenue. Madison criticized Hamilton's "rigid adherence" to a different plan that Hamilton "supposed more perfect," that would have prevented states from spending the monies without federal permission.[22] Madison's cutting remark was revealing; he saw Hamilton, at the time, as a man who did not understand politics, persuasion, or compromise.

Much changed, however, in the coming years. Hamilton resigned from Congress in 1783 to open a private law practice, where he controversially defended Tories. The next year, he founded the Bank of New York. He also advocated for the doomed Annapolis convention, which he saw as necessary to a coherent commercial union.

At the Constitutional Convention, Hamilton became famous for a brash, six-hour speech where he proposed scrapping both the Virginia and New Jersey Plans for one modeled on the British king, Parliament, and courts. He proposed a lifelong Senate chosen by electors, a House of Representatives serving three-year terms, a twelve-member Supreme Court with lifelong appointments, and, most significantly, an "elective monarch." Madison wrote that Hamilton "had no scruple in declaring that the British Govt. was the best in the world and that he doubted much whether anything short of it would do in America."[23]

But when his plan failed to gain support, Hamilton gradually supported the compromise product of Philadelphia. On the last day of the convention, when Edmund Randolph, George Mason, and Elbridge Gerry refused to sign the document, Hamilton became visibly agitated. He rose before the assembly and argued that the refusals of even a "few characters of consequence" could do "infinite mischief," pointing out that he himself was signing the Constitution, despite the fact that "no man's ideas were more remote from the plan than his were known to be." He explained his decision as one between "anarchy and convulsion on one side" and the "chance of good" on the other.[24]

Hamilton and Madison were more like brothers in arms than brothers, their union a consequence of their cause rather than any deep sympathy between them. And it was in that spirit that they joined forces in a campaign to drive the country forward.

HAMILTON BOARDED A SINGLE-MASTED SCHOONER SAILING ON THE North River from Manhattan to Albany. With his quill wavering in his hand and the waves rolling underneath, he wrote the first installment of the long newspaper opinion pieces that would come to be known as the Federalist Papers.[25] Hamilton had concocted the plan to persuade the leading men of his state to support the Federalist cause. He hoped the essays would in turn spark a chain reaction throughout the colonies.

He began his first essay by beseeching his readers to recognize the gravity of their role. The subject, he wrote, "speaks its own importance." He described with venom certain enemies of the Constitution: those who had "begun their career by paying an obsequious court to the people, commencing demagogues and ending tyrants."[26] While he did not mention Patrick Henry's name, he might as well have; Hamilton cast popularity and flattery as grounds for suspicion rather than worship.

Thus began the familiar refrain in the Federalist Papers—an injunction for citizens to defy the passions, to defuse demagogues, and to join their nation at the frontier of reason and restraint.

Hamilton's essay appeared in New York's *Independent Journal* on October 27, under the name "Publius." Copies took days to travel from hand to hand down the coast. On November 9, Archibald Stuart clipped a copy in Richmond, folded it into a letter he sent to Madison, and declared himself "extremely pleased," because Publius had given him "the highest expectations."[27]

Madison was pleased as well, for he was joining Hamilton's campaign. Hamilton knew from the start that only a star team could address the dizzying range of questions ahead about how the new constitutional government would function, from foreign policy to the separation of powers to the new court system. He had first approached John Jay for assistance. Jay was a gaunt, brilliant, rheumatic New Yorker who had drafted the New York Constitution. Jay had readily agreed to participate. The two men worked up a blueprint of topics that Hamilton crisply meted out in Federalist Number 1: the "utility of the UNION to your political prosperity," the "insufficiency of the present Confederation to preserve that Union," the "necessity of a government at least equally energetic with the one proposed," the "conformity of the proposed Constitution to the true principles of republican government," the Constitution's "analogy to your own State constitutions," and, finally, the "additional security."[28] It was a daunting list, but they felt that only such a wave of maneuvers could fortify the Constitution against its enemies.

Hamilton then made the fateful decision to ask James Madison to join as well.[29] Madison could not help but be flattered. He also thought the operation was strategically necessary, given the anxiety flooding out of Virginia. He believed that precisely those citizens who could be influenced by essays in newspapers—the nation's leading men, the merchants, planters, and lawyers—could breathe life into the contraption from Philadelphia. Madison agreed to participate. He then urged Hamilton to enlist his friend Rufus King, a New Yorker of whom Madison thought highly. But Hamilton, with characteristic sharpness, dismissed King as not "altogether of the sort required for the task in view."[30] Madison was the only one he wanted.

Madison kept silent about his enlistment in Hamilton's project. After so many years of cipher, his insistence on anonymity for the Memorial and Remonstrance, and the gag order of the Constitutional Convention, he found the shadows familiar terrain. He began writing at 19 Maiden Lane. His boardinghouse became the headquarters of a burgeoning national operation whose tentacles reached throughout the thirteen states, gathering intelligence from the people while inducing them to support the Constitution. Madison was in the very brain of the new body politic.

F OR MADISON, THE THRALL OF THOSE DAYS WAS NOT DISSIMILAR TO A political or even a military campaign. Decades later, his fine hair almost completely gone, his thin fingers still turning out his precise, curved script, he telescoped the experience of writing the Federalist Papers with the dramatic shading only time can afford. He remembered a great rush of activity, as if he and Hamilton and Jay were almost hurtling toward the states' ratifying conventions. Most of the papers, he remembered, were written in "great haste." He and Hamilton put themselves under such tremendous pressure to produce what ended up being eighty-five essays—many of them several pages in length—that they often hurried new ones to the newspaper as "the printer was putting into type the parts of a number." They were always already at work on new papers, constantly aware of the printers' deadlines. They were almost literally cranking the essays out, their own drive to crush every quarter of resistance requiring constant battle.

In the beginning weeks, the demands of their outline and the hungry maw of the New York papers drew the three writers together, and Madison and Hamilton and Jay collegially exchanged drafts of everything. But when Jay dropped out for health reasons after two months, Madison and Hamilton took up the slack by increasing their own shares of the outline. Soon enough, the "shortness of the time allowed" simply made their prior level of coordination impossible. They began sending their essays directly to the papers, the typesetters scrambling madly to get their scrawl into type, so their ideas could reach a hungry public.[31]

Hamilton—who had proven himself a masterful military commander during the Revolutionary War—astutely assigned Madison the topics he had already mastered: constitutional history, separation of powers, the different governmental departments, and the nature of the social and economic ills they were trying to prevent. Madison went on to write twenty-nine of the essays, Hamilton fifty-one, and Jay eight. Ranging through a vast landscape of topics—some sweeping in scope, others more narrow—the two independent men, as the elderly Madison later remembered, discovered it was "most agreeable to each" not to try to "give a positive sanction to all the doctrines and sentiments of the other." They wanted to let breathe the "known difference in the general complexion of their political theories."[32] Through that remarkable freedom, Madison would directly share his most deeply felt convictions with those he felt most desperately needed guidance.

As he prepared to write his first essay, he heard from Joseph Jones that minds in Virginia were not yet "ripe for the great change which the new plan will ultimately effect." It was impossible to tell, Jones said, whether the Constitution was gaining or losing ground in the legislature.[33] With that discomfiting intelligence, Madison began employing, again, his Method.

Find passion in your conscience. Focus on the idea, not the man. Develop multiple and independent lines of attack. Embrace impatience. Establish a competitive advantage through preparation. Conquer bad ideas by dividing them. Master your opponent as you master yourself. Push the state to the highest version of itself. Govern the passions.

H E COMPLETED WHAT WOULD BE KNOWN AS FEDERALIST NUMBER IO ON November 22. It was a cathedral of his philosophy.

He knew that Americans found their state governments far more comfortable and accessible than their federal counterpart. He also believed that the democracies that had developed so well in the thirteen colonies had succeeded *because* they developed in states. Consequently, he felt the new nation could fail precisely *because* it was so large, so remote, and so new. He suspected Henry would attack on that front, preying on the Virginia farmer or merchant who feared the new federal government would destroy their familiar apparatus in Richmond. It was to them he addressed his argument.

The country was afflicted, he declared, by "unsteadiness and injustice." The culprit was faction—a "number of citizens" who are "united and actuated by some common impulse of passion" that sets them against the rights of other citizens and the "permanent and aggregate interests of the community." The Anglicans in Culpeper, the enemies of the forced contribution, the opponents of legal reform, and the supporters of the religious assessment—they were all faces of the same demon.

There were, he explained, only two ways to cure the "mischiefs" of faction: the first, to remove its causes, the second, to control its effects. Removing the causes led to a fork in the road with another two—and only two—options. The first was to destroy the liberty that is "essential to [faction's] existence." He brusquely dismissed that cure as "worse than the disease." The second possibility was to give every citizen of America the "same opinions, the same passions, and the same interests." That, he observed flatly, was as "impracticable, as the first would be unwise."

His point was not to choose between those equally bad options, but to escape the fork entirely. He told his readers to consider one central truth: that the "latent causes" of faction are "sown in the nature of man." We cannot, in other words, *eliminate* the cause of faction, because it is natural to us. The passions are part of being human. He enumerated examples from his readers' own lives—their "zeal for different opinions" about religion or government, their attachment to politicians "ambitiously contending for pre-eminence and power." Those appetites, he said, lead all humans to "mutual animosities," where even the most "frivolous and fanciful distinctions" can "kindle their unfriendly passions" and "excite their most violent conflicts."

So, he concluded, we must accept the passions, and even embrace them, for not even leadership—not even statesmanship—can stop such forces of nature. It is "vain," he wrote, to believe that even the "enlightened statesmen will be able to adjust these clashing interests." And, anyway, even if statesmen *could* solve the problem, that was beside the point, because if history proves anything, he said, it is that "Enlightened statesmen will not always be at the helm."

But there was a solution. The new country, he explained, had been designed to be a republic rather than a "pure democracy" where a common passion would be quickly "felt by a majority of the whole." And in a republic, the goal was to "refine and enlarge the public views, by passing them through a chosen body of citizens, whose wisdom may best discern the true interest of their country, and whose patriotism and love of justice, will be least likely to sacrifice it to temporary or partial considerations." In spite of all of his adverse experiences in Richmond and Philadelphia, his optimism about the public's ability to self-govern was remarkable. Madison had come to believe that a special class of citizens—standing sentinel over the country, almost like stewards—not only *should* be created, but *could* be.

With that, he drove toward the essay's stunning conclusion, which matched his vision for the nation in sweep and scope. A larger rather than a smaller republic, he declared, would make it more difficult for "unworthy candidates" to be successful in the "vicious arts, by which elections are too often carried." He obviously relished making such a counterintuitive case. The country should be *larger* and *more federal* in order to become *more just* and *more stable*. "Extend the sphere" of the republic, he told his readers, and you "take in a greater variety of parties and interests." That would deprive the majority of their "common motive to invade the rights of other citizens."

It was his grandest effort yet to channel the torrent of passions. In the larger republic he envisioned, leaders of factions would still be able to "kindle a flame within their particular states." But they would be rendered unable to cause that conflagration to spread through the other states. That applied as well to Daniel Shays as to Patrick Henry. The very government Henry hated would finally govern him—which was, of course, why he hated it.

MADISON HANDED THE ESSAY TO HAMILTON AND JAY, WHO QUICKLY reviewed it. It was sent to the *New York Packet* on Friday, November 23. One of Western history's most profound statements of constitutional values was about to reach the reading public. Madison again was relying on his anonymous words to seize the public's imagination—and they would.

ONLY A WEEK LATER, HE SAT DOWN TO WRITE HIS SECOND ESSAY. HENRY had attacked the "novelty" of the Constitution. Madison took up his quill to write a near-parody of a Tom Paine–style pamphlet in response. "Hearken not to the voice which petulantly tells you," he urged, that the

Constitution was a "novelty in the political world," and that it belonged to the "theories of the wildest projectors." He implored his "countrymen" to "shut your ears against this unhallowed language," condemning the "poison" of the attacks for polluting the "kindred blood which flows in the blood of American citizens." The Constitution, he countered, was in fact the Revolution's sweetest fruit, the result of a "manly spirit" and "numerous innovations displayed on the American theatre."

In his zeal to defend innovation, he ignored any hesitations he had previously held about the Constitution. The men in Philadelphia, he declared, had achieved something which had "no parallel in the annals of human society." They had "formed the design of a great confederacy," and if it had any imperfections, he wrote, "we wonder at the fewness of them."

So it was that a skeptic, in the heat of defending the vulnerable Constitution from his enemies, fell in love with it.

M ADISON WAS NOT THE ONLY AMERICAN SHIFTING POSITIONS. THE colonies themselves, like an alarmed animal, were at once bucking and stampeding forward. On December 7, a worried Washington sent Madison a note observing that the Constitution seemed to have lost so much ground in Virginia that it no longer had a majority.[34] But that same day, Delaware became the first state to ratify the Constitution, by a unanimous vote. Pennsylvania followed four days later with a large majority, and then New Jersey on December 18, with another unanimous vote.

Madison set to work mining his research on confederacies for three rapidly written new essays. In Federalist Number 18, which he wrote on December 7, he praised the ancient Greek Achaean league for mastering popular government through a central authority and laws.[35] In Number 19, written the same day, he described the "violent and bloody contests" that can result from religious factions.[36]

Three days later, he pressed on with Number 20, where his concern was the current system's *imperium in imperio*—its divided center. He hammered on that vulnerability repeatedly, even obsessively. A "sovereignty over sovereigns, a government over governments, a legislature for communities," he explained, was "subversive of the order and ends of civil policy" by "substituting *violence* in place of *law*." He acknowledged that his blizzard of facts and histories demanded a lot from readers, but he wrote, "I make no apology for having dwelt so long on the contemplation of these federal precedents." Ever Witherspoon's student, he explained that experience was the "oracle of truth," and that where history's lessons were "unequivocal," they should be "conclusive and sacred."[37]

Would that a majority in every state could share his historically informed conviction about the Constitution. But as winter gripped Manhattan, and as he burrowed deeper into Mrs. House's to study the letters arriving every day from Richmond, it seemed Henry and his band of anti-Federalists were growing even more aggressive.

MADISON LEARNED FROM VIRGINIA THAT CITIZENS WHO WERE OTHERwise "equally respectable in every point of character" were still "marshalled in opposition to each other."[38] He thought Richmond was "rapidly degenerating." He sniped to George Washington that the legislature's shameful weakness proved the need for an "anchor against the fluctuations which threaten shipwreck to our liberty."[39] The time for him to fight in the arena was nigh. But he began to have second thoughts.

His friends were pressuring him to return, and soon. On December 16, from Rose Hill, Virginia, Lawrence Taliaferro, a friend from his youth, pled with him to come home to lead the Federalists at the ratification convention. Then fifty-three years old, Taliaferro had a nephew at Princeton, but he himself had never been properly educated and could barely write. He wrote Madison anyway: "I am a vary pore Penman & dont wish to take up two Much of you time in reding a Long Letter." But he plowed ahead. "I am sorry to inform you," he went on, that the "Federal Sistum is rufly Handeled by sum vary Able Men in this State." It was the "sincere Wish & desier of Myself & a Grate Many others," he said, that Madison lead the ratification effort in the spring. Goading Madison, the wily Taliaferro informed him of a rumor that he was "Opos'd to the Sistum" and even that he was "Actually writing a Pece against it."[40]

Henry Lee, too, implored Madison to attend, warning that a conspiracy was gaining ground in Orange to prevent his election. He told Madison he ought to undercut it, regardless of "any delicacy or any other motive."[41] A friend named Andrew Shepherd also sent word from Orange warning that "artfull persons" were "injecting their poison into the unwary." He begged Madison to allow him to "recommend your presence as soon as you conveniently could."[42]

But Madison refused to tell his friends he would be coming back. Even in his own mind, he wasn't sure he wanted the political fight ahead.

21 Several Mad Freaks

A S THE NEW YEAR ARRIVED, MADISON WAS NESTLED INSIDE HIS BOARD-inghouse, protected from freezing New York by fire and woolen coats, and surrounded by his spread of work. A bound volume of Hamilton's first three essays had already appeared. The copies had been snapped up in Virginia, and, from everything he heard, Madison felt the papers were already having "a very valuable effect" in Richmond.[1]

Georgia unanimously ratified the Constitution on January 2, moving the colonies ever closer to the required golden number: nine states. Connecticut followed on January 9 with a massive majority. Five states had ratified the Constitution.

The major anti-Federalist strategists in Virginia included Patrick Henry, George Mason, Richard Henry Lee, and Governor Benjamin Harrison.[2] They were a formidable but heterogeneous group. Henry Lee wrote Madison that Patrick Henry was still the undisputed "leader of this band" that opposed "any system, was it even sent from heaven," that might "strengthen the union of the states."[3] Under Henry's sway, the whole city of Richmond seemed to have gone crazy; the General Assembly, Madison declared in a letter to Jefferson, was "engaged in several mad freaks." They included a bill that Madison said was a "child of Mr. Henry, & said to be his favorite one," which would have prohibited the importation of almost anything not made in America, including rum, brandy, beef, cheese, and candles, while imposing a heavy fine on anyone possessing these foreign goods. Madison darkly noted that the transparently jingoistic bill was garnering, through Henry's "violent opposition," a large majority.[4]

The Federalist Papers were further provoking the "mad freaks." On January 8, Madison learned about a devious new anti-Federalist effort under way in Richmond—a bill George Mason introduced that would refuse any further payments to Congress until Congress gave Virginia the "fullest indemnification" for Virginia's help in conquering the Illinois country. The bill was eventually struck down, but not before alarming Madison afresh about a newly ferocious clash between a sort of Virginia nationalism and the new central government.[5] Randolph wrote Madison that the Constitution was no longer even spoken of in Virginia. The silence stemmed "not from a want of zeal," he assured Madison, but from "downright weariness."[6]

The ratifying convention, once a distant glimmer, now appeared imminent, and the campaign to haul Madison back to Virginia increased in intensity. Randolph pleaded with Madison, "You must come in," to secure his role at the ratifying convention. He warned that many in Orange were "opposed to your politicks." Madison's election was still certain, he said—reassuring himself as much as Madison—but Madison could not risk it any further by his absence.[7]

R ANDOLPH, MEANWHILE, WAS WRESTLING WITH HIS OWN CONSCIENCE. Bruised by his exhausting confessional in Philadelphia and now out of office, he had been licking his wounds by staying "much at home," especially because, he told Madison, the "current sets violently against the new constitution." But he was coming to recognize the repercussions of his iconoclastic opposition for the entire country. "I need not assure you," he wrote, "that it would give me no pleasure to see my conduct in refusing to sign, sanctified, if it was to produce a hazard to the union." He attempted to reassure Madison that the "high-toned friends" of the Constitution were "still very sanguine," and that the bill would "run thro with ease."[8]

That Randolph was so self-soothing was cold comfort for Madison, who responded that while every man wanted to make decisions on the basis of his personal judgment—"no man feels more of it than I do"—all men must also be "governed by those with whom they happen to have acquaintance and confidence." The convention coming up in Richmond was, he wrote, just such a case. He desperately needed Randolph on the Federalist side and told him so.

As for Henry, Madison had much harsher words. "[I] have for some time considered him as driving at a Southern Confederacy," he told Randolph.

Henry was advocating a second amending convention only to "render it subservient to his real designs."[9] In those "real designs" lay Henry's real villainy—to destroy the federal union.

MEANWHILE, FROM PARIS, JEFFERSON REACTED TO THE SUMMARIES Madison send him about the Constitution with a commingled enthusiasm and chagrin. The sensation of being an ocean away from such crucial events was not easily captured. But in December 1787, he unburdened himself to his friend. He began by offering "a few words on the Constitution proposed by our Convention"—and then went on for several pages. He listed six things that he "liked," including the three branches of government and the executive veto. He was also, he said, "captivated" by Wilson's compromise of the Senate to the states and the House to the people.

But he rapidly moved on to add "what I do not like." First was the absence of a bill of rights. To have such a bill was, he said, the natural right of people "against every government on earth, general or particular, & what no just government should refuse or rest on inference." He also disliked that the president could, on paper, serve for life. That, he argued, could create a new American emperor, pope, or king.

Jefferson took his "few words" much further to launch an astonishing aside about Shays' Rebellion, which was then over a year old. "The late rebellion in Massachusetts" had created "more alarm than I think it should have done," he said. He told Madison to do the math. One rebellion in thirteen states in eleven years would equate to "but one for each state in a century & a half." "No country," wrote Jefferson, "should go so long without one." He even praised the Shaysites' "moderation" and their "almost self extinguishment."

And then he really crossed Madison, exposing the fault lines between their two philosophies and their different visions for the nation, by declaring, "After all, it is my principle that the will of the Majority should always prevail."[10] He wrote this to James Madison, whose avowed ambition was to protect *minorities* at all cost. There was a deep canyon between these two poles. But to the immense credit of both men, it was bridged by respect.

In the months to come, Jefferson's opinion about Shays' Rebellion spread, as wisdom from a distant oracle. On May 28, 1788, just before Virginia's

IMAGE 21.1. *THOMAS JEFFERSON*, BY REMBRANDT PEALE.
COURTESY OF THE LIBRARY OF CONGRESS.

ratifying convention began, a friend who had seen a copy of Jefferson's letter asked Madison querulously, that even though it seemed to contain the man's handwriting, "Can this possibly be Jefferson?"[11]

T HE COUNTRY'S SITUATION WAS UNSTABLE, SHIFTING BY THE DAY. IN JANuary, Madison felt the virus of Henry's opposition might infect North Carolina as well. As Virginia's sister state, a rejection of the Constitution there would, he worriedly told Randolph, "endanger the Union more than any other circumstance that could ever happen." He spoke candidly. "My apprehensions of this danger," he confessed, "increase every day."[12]

In the coming weeks, he hurled himself into the task of stopping that event however he could, from his stubborn redoubt in New York. On January 11, Madison composed Federalist Number 37, a majestically twisting essay that swore readers to the creed of stability ("essential to national character," he said) and energy ("essential to that security against external and internal danger" and to the "prompt and salutary execution of laws"). The "real wonder" of Philadelphia, he wrote, was its virtual unanimity. It was "impossible for the man of pious reflection not to perceive in it," he declared, a "finger of that Almighty Hand" that had blessed the country repeatedly in the revolution's critical stages.

But certain men of "sinister nature," he said, had decided to oppose the Constitution—they must "be culpable." With the march to final judgment in Richmond beginning, Madison was essentially sanctifying the Constitution. Anyone standing in his way was also standing in the way of a blessed young nation.[13]

IN NUMBER 38, WHICH MADISON JOTTED OUT SOON AFTER, HE CONDEMNED the anti-Federalists for holding up perfection as their standard while recklessly failing to offer an alternative, let alone to admit the crippling failures of the confederacy. He was angry, and even a little shrill. From the "lifeless mass" of the confederacy, he argued, had grown an "excrescent power," which generated the dangers natural to such a "defective construction of the supreme government of the union." America was like a patient with a "disorder daily growing worse." Skilled doctors had prescribed medicine, but squabbling naysayers were intervening—though they could neither "deny the necessary of a speedy remedy" nor "agree in proposing one." If the quacks' fix was taken, the "dissolution of usurpation" would be the "dreadful dilemma"—a cure even worse than the disease.[14]

THAT PROVOCATIVE ESSAY, ALONG WITH THE DOZENS OF OTHERS BY Hamilton and Jay, was reprinted, bound into books, and sent into an eager public's hands. Archibald Stuart wrote Madison that Publius's "greatness is acknowledged universally."[15] Madison redoubled his work. In response to the specter Henry was conjuring up of an insidious, distant, rapacious power, Madison wrote Number 39. He methodically spelled out how the Constitution would actually work in practice. It was "essential," he said, that the new government be "derived from the great body of society, not from an inconsiderable portion, or a favored class of it." He ripped apart the charge that Philadelphia was an illegitimate conclave, deftly explaining that the convention had effectively required the "assent and ratification of the people" through their "deputies for the special purpose."

His writing was clever, crisp, and reassuring. No new nation was actually being created, he assured his readers; the thirteen states (and the country to come) were becoming *only more like themselves.* The Constitution, like the nation, was neither "wholly *national,* nor wholly *federal.*" The national majority did not control outcomes all of the time; nor did the states. The nation was *already* a "composition of both."[16] The anti-Federalists, he was making clear, could offer nothing whatever to compete with that.

Back in Virginia, under the pounding artillery of the Federalist Papers, Henry was growing increasingly bellicose.

I N JANUARY 1788, MADISON LEARNED HENRY WAS THREATENING THAT because the other states could not "do without" Virginia, that Virginia could "dictate to them what terms we please." The former governor was determined, he said, to kill the Constitution by subjecting its ratification to prior amendments. Henry was further asserting that Virginia could enter into foreign alliances on her own, as if it were a separate nation, as if the United States had no claim on Virginia at all.[17] There was no reconciling his position and Madison's; one would have to win, and one would have to lose.

The election of delegates to the ratifying convention was set for early March. Time was running out for Madison to come home to campaign for a seat. But he also needed to cut Henry's latest assault off at the pass with more essays, which further kept him in New York. In less than two weeks, he wrote five essays at a blistering pace: Numbers 41 (defending the new Constitution's design for the federal military),[18] 42 (defending the new government's sweeping range of powers, from foreign relations to the prohibition of slavery),[19] 43 (plowing through the Constitution's "miscellaneous powers," from copyright to the creation of a federal district for the capitol),[20] 44 (defending as "completely invulnerable" the Constitution's clause giving Congress the power to make all "necessary and proper" laws for executing its powers),[21] 45 (arguing that the states would remain "constituent and essential parts of the federal government"),[22] and 46 (explaining that the federal government's military would never allow for an army of more than twenty-five or thirty thousand men, whereas the states could easily convene a militia of "near half a million of citizens with arms in their hands"[23]).

He was working desperately hard to convince the public that the states they loved had nothing to fear from the new government, and hoped his words might be enough. But then, in early February, a letter in his father's familiar hand arrived in the mail.

H E OPENED THE ENVELOPE. ALTHOUGH MOST OF THE MEN OF ORANGE County had originally supported the Constitution, the senior Madison sternly wrote, after visiting Richmond during the Assembly—and hearing the anti-Federalist attacks—they had "altered their opinions." Even the Baptists—Madison's favored minority—were "now generally opposed to it." "I think you had better come in as early in March as you can," urged his father. Madison's friends wished him to be there; others would "suspend their opinion till they see you," but wanted an explanation for Madison's conspicuous absence. Others, he said more ominously, "wish you not to come" and would even attempt to "shut you out the Convention."[24] In other words, his son needed to be elected a delegate to save the Constitution, and he would now have to fight for the privilege.

But Madison delayed further still, frustrating his family and friends to no end. Their campaign intensified. William Moore lectured Madison about the "disadvantage of being absent at Elections." "[I] must therefore intreat and conjure you nay commd." The entire county was on tenterhooks, "anxiously awaiting for an Explanation from you," he wrote, begging "your Sentiments from your own mouth."[25] With February over half over, James Gordon wrote Madison that it was "incumbent on you with out delay, to repair to this state, as the loss of the constitution in this state may involve consequences most alarming to every citizen of America."[26]

Then George Washington himself took up the charge. He informed Madison that many had "asked me with anxious sollicitude, if you did not mean to get into the Convention; conceiving it of indispensable necessity." He warned that the mighty George Mason would be there, representing three counties. He offered Mount Vernon to his fragile young friend as "a warm room, & a good fire" and a not "uncomfortable antidote" to the chilly, snowy journey he would encounter on his way back to Virginia—which he *must* make.[27]

MADISON DEFIED THE PLEAS. HE REMAINED FOCUSED ON PUBLIUS. IN LATE January, he defended the Constitution's separation of the executive and legislative branches in Numbers 47 and 48. In 47, he said that the anti-Federalists had painted a caricature of powers separated to "destroy all symmetry and beauty of form," which would allow the "essential parts of the edifice" to be "crushed by the disproportionate weight of other parts." He laid waste to their argument with logic. He noted that, among all the constitutions currently at work in the states, there was no example where the branches were "kept absolutely separate and distinct."[28] In Number 48, which he wrote the next day, he declared that the departments needed to be "so far connected and blended, as to give to each a constitutional controul over the others."[29] The different departments of government, he explained, needed a *nexus imperii*, each giving up part of its authority for a share in the larger power. In Number 49, he conceded the "great force" in Jefferson's argument from *Notes on the State of Virginia* that the Constitution should be regularly amended. But such "periodic" conventions, he said, posed a familiar peril: They would result in "disturbing the public tranquility by interesting too strongly the public passions."[30] In Number 50, he relentlessly probed even the most innocuous strands of Jefferson's argument, asserting that not even "periodic" revisions would be acceptable.[31]

So much for Jefferson's reckless portrait of free-flowing evolution. The country, Madison was arguing, needed a canal with locks, not a roaring river. Channeling the torrent through governance remained his object. It was the "reason of the public alone that ought to controul and regulate the government," he declared. "The passions," he said in Number 49—perhaps his most concise summary yet of his political philosophy—"ought to be controuled and regulated by government."[32] Experience, and the hard needs of a country in formation, would not survive Jefferson's feckless experimentation.

From Paris, unaware that Madison had been busy savaging his arguments for periodic conventions, Jefferson wrote to ask his friend to "be so good as to continue to mark to me it's progress"—meaning the Constitution. But Madison would wait until August 10, 1788—nearly a year after he began writing his share of the Federalist Papers—to finally tell Jefferson, still abroad in Paris, about the enterprise. He wrote (in cipher): "I believe I never have yet *mentioned to you that publication*."[33] Jefferson was Madison's closest political friend and ally, but their ideas differed so dramatically on the Constitution— particularly on the necessity for a prior bill of rights—that Madison decided to keep him out of this particularly vital loop. In that decision, in that need for control, his emerging philosophy, character, and politics all united.

U NAWARE OF HIS FRIEND'S DAY-TO-DAY CAMPAIGN, JEFFERSON CONFI- dently advised Madison to support a peculiar plan he had in mind— that nine states should pass the Constitution and the other four reject it. The balking faction, Jefferson thought, would force the other states to include a bill of rights. "We shall thus have all it's good," he said of the new Constitu- tion, "and cure it's principal defect."[34] Those words would come back to haunt Madison, when Jefferson's letter would be publicized. Madison hated the idea. Just as Jefferson had refused to support Madison's measure to provide Con- gress with clear coercive authority years before, so Madison now stymied his friend through diversion and inaction.

Meanwhile, Madison learned that Massachusetts, despite the opposition of the Shaysites, had passed the Constitution, 187 to 168, and the minority had even remained in "good Temper."[35] Six states had ratified the Consti- tution. Pressure increased on Virginia, and on Madison, to ratify. He could not dally with Jefferson's hopelessly idealistic scheme to organize an opposing quarter of the states. He needed to drive the states forward.

B Y EARLY FEBRUARY, HE HAD SCYTHED HIS WAY THROUGH DOZENS OF revanchist arguments against the Constitution. But almost all of his Federalist Papers so far had been reactive, merely repulsing the Constitution's enemies. On February 6, he set out to take the offense instead, with a positive account of the Constitution's brilliance. In doing so, he crafted a bold decla- ration that would live for centuries.

For the first time, Madison-as-Publius departed from any obviously organized plan. He wrote, almost apologetically, "I will hazard a few general observations" on the deceptively simple topic of "maintaining in practice" the separation of powers in government.

That goal was a deceptively modest entryway into a sweeping new vista of constitutional theory. The principle of creating "separate and distinct" departments of government, he said, would require "deviations." Those deviations would consist of giving each department not only separate powers, but the ability to "resist encroachments of the others." Here, Witherspoon's warnings, the endless battles with Rhode Island, the machinations of the factions back in Virginia, and the looming force of Henry, all led to a burning imperative: "Ambition," he wrote, "must be made to counteract ambition." That need was a "reflection on human nature." If "angels were to govern men," neither "external nor internal controls on government would be necessary." Even if statesmen took over the US Senate, they would err. That was why *governance* was so crucial. By creating a government "to be administered by men over men," he explained, the task was to "enable the government to control the governed." Only then could you "oblige it to control itself."

As for him, as for Witherspoon before him, conscience was the heart of the matter. Justice, he wrote, was the "end of government" and the "end of civil society." "It ever has been and ever will be pursued, until it is obtained, or until liberty be lost in the pursuit."

But how to get there? He prodded his readers toward a fork in the road of his own making. There were only two ways to prevent the evil of a majority's injustice: The first was to create an authority separate from the majority—as in countries with a king. But that was "at best a precarious security." And it could not work in the democratic United States.

The other alternative was a society with "so many separate descriptions of citizens" that it would "render an unjust combination of the whole very improbable, if not impracticable." On this scenario, Madison radiated self-confidence. That second method, he promised, would be "exemplified in the federal republic of the United States." The "extended republic" of America would be "broken into so many parts, interest and classes of citizens"—so many roiling, shifting passions—that there would be "little danger from interested combinations of the majority." All were vulnerable; therefore all needed strength. When "even stronger individuals are prompted by the uncertainty of their condition," they would gladly submit to a government pledged to protect all, including the weak and them.

Nexus imperii. That which binds all becomes the bind itself. He praised the Constitution's "judicious modification and mixture of the *federal principle.*" The Constitution's cantilevered states, nation-state, and internal governmental branches, together, would mirror the balanced factions that not only survival, but justice, required.[36] Thus Madison described what he had been seeking since he first returned home to Orange from Princeton—the elusive equilibrium of reason and the passions, of control and governance, of government and the very humans who composed it and were dominated by it, and of those who would lead the state.

The statesmen.

B UT THE NEWS FROM VIRGINIA GREW EVER WORSE. AN AGITATED MONROE wrote from Fredericksburg that while Virginia's northern counties were supporting the Constitution, the southern counties were starting to tear away. It was "impossible to say," he said grimly, "which preponderates." He urgently told Madison, "We expect you in soon" and "shall be happy to see you here."[37]

Madison's cousin the reverend again flatly confronted him, this time about whether the new Constitution was "in reality practicable," querying the checks rather than the balances, especially the executive veto. Despite Madison's claim to have resolved this matter, the reverend called the provision just another *imperium in imperio* that would, he feared, "be the fruitful source of a thousand jarring Principles." It would "make the new Machine, notwithstanding all the Oil you can give it, to go heavily along." As for Virginia, he had news Madison did not want to hear. Ratification was, at best, questionable—especially without amendments. That was the last thing Madison wanted to hear.[38]

After taking a trip through Richmond, Cumberland, Powhatan, Chesterfield, and Petersburg—the towns that comprised the heartland of Virginia—Madison's friend Edward Carrington wrote him that the "demagogues in opposition" were behaving as if their popularity would increase in proportion to their clamors. He depicted the surge in familiar, diluvian terms—as a "Torrent"—with Patrick Henry the roaring fount. Carrington ominously noted the danger from "weak men." There was, he said, "no accounting for the effects" that Henry's "address and Rhetoric" would have among the susceptible masses.[39]

But Madison's work in New York was still not done.

AFTER HIS MAJESTIC NUMBER 51, MADISON, IN JUST TWO WEEKS IN FEBruary, composed six essays, which all defended the House of Representatives as essential to the Constitution. Numbers 52 and 53 mined history to defend the House's biennial elections, 55 and 56 justified the number of members in the House, and 58 forcefully argued that the decennial census would allow the House to evolve over time.

It was in Number 54, in the middle of this barrage, that Madison advanced into the most controversial territory. He had the unsavory task of defending the Constitution's three-fifths compromise to achieve ratification in slaveholding states—particularly Virginia. He conceded that "our southern brethren" believed that "representation relates more immediately to persons, and taxation more immediately to property." He ventured a daring argument for the despicable compromise. The "true state of the case," he declared, was that slaves "partake of both these qualities." Because they were at once commanded and owned under law, they were, he said, "degraded from the human rank"—like animals. But he cannily noted that the slaveholding states' laws also protected slaves against the violence of others—even from their masters. And, he observed, a slave, unlike an animal, could be legally punished for violence.

Those laws were well known in the slaveholding states. He was reminding his readers of the political philosophy they were implicitly supporting by their simple complicity in these regimes. The polity had arrived at an uneasy but definitive recognition, he said, that the slave was "evidently regarded by the law as a member of the society." The slave was therefore, he declared, a moral person—not a "mere article of property." Thus he elevated the "great propriety" of the Constitution's three-fifths compromise. It recognized, he said, the real facts about slaves in the colonies—that they were at once human *and* property.

His logic was as warped as the misanthropic compromise the men in Philadelphia had hammered out of their reality. But from that grotesquery, Madison extracted a nugget of truth: Even the slaveholding states were coming to recognize, at long last, that African Americans were human beings.[40]

W ITH THE JUNE LAUNCH OF ITS RATIFICATION CONVENTION LOOMING larger every day, Virginia was turning restless and dyspeptic. "Never perhaps was a state more divided" than Virginia on the new Constitution, Madison's friend John Dawson wrote him from Fredericksburg on February 18.[41] At first, Madison wrote to Jefferson, Virginia seemed enthusiastically in favor. But then the tide had taken a "sudden and strong turn in the opposite direction." Henry's "influence and exertions," Madison explained, were to blame. His "very bold language" was resonating on "self-sufficiency"—appealing to Virginians to tear away from the fragile social compact and return, Madison feared, to the bloody state of nature.[42]

N EARING THE END OF THE SYMPHONIC OUTLINE, MADISON CHARGED toward the Constitution's summit: the Senate. In Number 62, he proclaimed that the Senate would prevent the country from yielding to the "impulse of sudden and violent passions" and from being "seduced by factious leaders into intemperate and pernicious resolutions."[43] In Number 63, he reached back to Athens and to the horrifying example of Socrates's murder by a mob. When the people were "stimulated by some irregular passion, or some illicit advantage, or misled by the artful misrepresentations of interested men," he explained, they could enact measures which they would later "lament and condemn." The Senate could arrest such collective madness.

He took special care to address the concern that the Senate would become too "independent and aristocratic." The resolution to that problem, he explained, lay in the genius of the institution's design. The popular House, he predicted, would restrain the elite Senate by holding its decisions up in the public arena. And if any senators did become antidemocratic, other elected senators would be forced to provide a "display of enlightened policy" and their commitment to the common good to return to the people's good graces.

Thus, even the country's statesmen would always be beholden to the people.[44] The Senate would be self-correcting.

While on paper, his words contained real emotion. He clearly saw something of himself in the Senate. The higher body inspired him, as he hoped it would inspire the country.

B Y MARCH, THE CAMPAIGN TO HAUL MADISON HOME REACHED A FEVER pitch. Joseph Spencer, a Baptist who had been imprisoned in Orange County in 1773 for lacking a license to preach,[45] wrote a sweetly misspelled plea to the man who had defended his sect: The "weker class of people" were "much predegessed (prejudiced)" against the Constitution. Unless Madison and his friends "do Exerte yr. Selves Very much," Spencer warned, "youl not obtain yr. Election in Orange."[46]

Madison finally made up his mind. He was needed. He must do his part. He would stand for election once again. And he would confront Patrick Henry in Richmond.

He informed his friends that he would return to Virginia. Washington wrote at once to congratulate him. He said with sympathy that he knew that Madison worried, regarding his anti-Federalist friends in Orange, that he would have to cross "the Rubicon of their friendship."[47]

Madison took to the road back to Orange. His first order of business was to stop along the way in Mount Vernon, where he conspired with Washington. The ratification would begin in less than three months. Twelve years of work were about to come to a head. The man he had first worshipped, at whose elbow he sat as councilor, was standing squarely in the way.

He intended to knock him down.

PART III

22 Ratification in Richmond

NINE STATES WERE NEEDED TO RATIFY THE CONSTITUTION. SIX WERE supporting it so far. The states who had not yet concluded their conventions were Rhode Island, New Hampshire, Maryland, North Carolina, South Carolina, New York—and Virginia. Of those, Rhode Island was a lost cause. On February 22, New Hampshire had concluded a first session of its convention without voting at all. If New Hampshire ultimately fell out, Madison knew, the Constitution's survival would depend on the remaining five states. That political reality was ratcheting the stakes to an almost unbearable level in the states. From New York, Cyrus Griffin wrote Madison on March 24 that the discussion of the Constitution "seems to deaden the activity of the human mind as to all other matters."[1]

Madison arrived back in Orange from a horrible trip over rutted, muddy late winter roads. He had just turned thirty-seven. He had an ominous feeling about what lay ahead. His initial conversations did not improve matters. While he experienced great "satisfaction" in seeing all his friends, he discovered that Orange was "filled with the most absurd and groundless prejudices against" the Constitution. And he needed those very people to give him a seat to the convention.

On a very windy day, he walked up to a rostrum that had been set up outside. A crowd restlessly shifted before him, stamping their feet to stay warm. Many obviously opposed the Constitution. He had grown accustomed to campaigning before individuals and small groups, but for "the first time in my life," as he later wrote Eliza Trist, he would now need to deliver a speech before a large crowd in public. As he wryly recalled later, Madison "launch[ed] into a harangue" in favor of the Constitution. His speech was choppy but successful. The people elected him a delegate to the convention by the decisive margin of four to one.[2]

IMAGE 22.1. JAMES MADISON IN 1792, FOUR YEARS AFTER THE
RATIFYING CONVENTION, BY CHARLES WILLSON PEALE.
COURTESY OF GILCREASE MUSEUM, TULSA, OKLAHOMA.

From nearby Charlottesville, George Nicholas informed Madison that
Henry had become "almost avowedly an enemy to the union." He was also
conniving and secretive, his "real sentiments industriously concealed" within
the Trojan horse of his amendment strategy.[3] Madison responded that any
conditional amendments, much less a second general convention, would be
"fatal." From his work ramming through legal reform in Virginia and pushing
the Constitution through Congress, Madison had learned that momentum
was crucial to victory. The delay alone that amendments would entail, he
said, was "too serious to be hazarded."

As April arrived, Rhode Island took the expected but still unsettling
step of rejecting the Constitution outright. However, on April 28 in Maryland and May 3 in South Carolina, large majorities voted for ratification.
Eight states had ratified the Constitution. The fate of the Constitution fell on
Virginia, New York, and New Hampshire. Those three states had called their

conventions for June 2, 17, and 18, respectively. Virginia's would be over two weeks before the others, but because of delays in travel, and the uncertainty of the other two conventions' ending dates, there would be no real way for any of the three to know when the crucial ninth-state threshold had been reached. Every day of the convention in Richmond, therefore, would need to be fought as if the very country depended on it.

Meanwhile, Henry was driving Virginia's north and south further apart. From Richmond, Edward Carrington wrote Madison that the upper and middle parts of Southside—Henry's territory—had "been made in Phrenzy." Under Henry's sway, they were sending to the ratifying convention "weak & bad Men," who had already "bound themselves to vote in the negative." They would "in all cases," Carrington predicted, "be the tools of" Henry.[4]

Speaking of Henry, Madison predicted to Randolph that "desperate measures" would be his "game."[5] To Jefferson, he confessed his concern not only about Henry but about the conscience-driven gadfly George Mason, worrying that the "violence of his passions" against the Bill of Rights–less Constitution might lead him to be "thrown into" Henry's camp. If the pair succeeded in their crusade for amendments or a second convention, he wrote, "I think the Constitution, and the Union will be both be endangered."[6]

As May arrived, hearts raced across Virginia whenever the Constitution rose in conversation. Tench Coxe predicted the Constitution was "now hastening to a crisis." "The decision of Virginia," he said, "ensures its existence." If Virginia rejected the Constitution, he fretted, then New York, New Hampshire, and North Carolina probably would also.[7]

In Orange, Madison feverishly began plotting his battalion's plan for Richmond.

MADISON WORKED THROUGH ISSUES WITH HIS FATHER, HIS FRIENDS, and his political allies. In response to a friend who asked for help with Kentucky's new constitution, he said he would not "have a moment's leisure before I set off for Richmond." And once he was there, he said, he would not have time for "any subject distinct from" the Constitution.[8] Totally immersed in strategy, he was preparing to hurl himself into a critical test of his Method.

Find passion in your conscience. Focus on the idea, not the man.
Develop multiple and independent lines of attack. Embrace impatience.
Establish a competitive advantage through preparation. Conquer bad
ideas by dividing them. Master your opponent as you master yourself.
Push the state to the highest version of itself. Govern the passions.

H E LEFT ORANGE ON SUNDAY, JUNE 1, 1788, AND PULLED INTO RICH-
mond that night. The next day, he walked into the New Academy
on Richmond's Shockoe Hill. The New Academy's cornerstone had been laid
only two years earlier, and the auditorium still smelled of freshly cut wood—
and sweat, wigs, and horses. Everything had a feeling of newness; the auditorium sat only blocks from the new capital building, which was busily under
construction.[9]

One hundred and seventy delegates were roaming the room, but just
twenty would participate in the debates. Of those, only a few would emerge
as key players. In every respect, the scene that would play out in the coming
three weeks was a battle between upstarts and the establishment. Madison's
Federalists were, for the most part, a generation younger than their opponents. On his team was the emotional Edmund Randolph, now thirty-five,
who at long last had buckled under his friend's pressure. As Madison happily told Rufus King, Randolph had decided to throw himself "fully into our
scale."[10] There was young John Marshall, just thirty-three, who would go on
to become chief justice of the US Supreme Court. There was loyal Henry
Lee, thirty-two, who would later become Virginia's ninth governor. Their
elders included George Wythe, the law professor who, at sixty-two, had taught
many of the men in the room, and Edmund Pendleton, also sixty-two, who
was one of Virginia's great judges and who had first helped select Madison as a
delegate from Orange County.

On the other side was a daunting triumvirate. First was Patrick Henry,
a robust fifty-two years old, both father and grandfather of the anti-Federalist
movement. Second was George Mason, an august sixty-three, considered wily
and authoritative. Third was Benjamin Harrison, sixty-two, now governor.
The junior member was Madison's friend James Monroe, just thirty, who had

in recent weeks turned decisively against the Constitution, to Madison's great consternation.

The ratification was still Henry's to lose and Madison's to win—and Madison knew it. In the coming weeks, his anxiety about what would happen if the new country disintegrated would become, at certain points, simply too much for him to bear.

O N WEDNESDAY, JUNE 4, HENRY ROSE BEFORE THE CHAIRMAN, THE delegates, and the hundreds of onlookers to make his opening remarks. He held his leonine head impressively; his craggy brow seemed to foretell ominous things. "I consider myself as the servant of the people of this commonwealth, as a sentinel over their rights, liberty, and happiness" he proclaimed. "I represent their feelings when I saw, that they are exceedingly uneasy, being brought from that state of full security, which they enjoyed, to the present delusive appearance of things."

Henry was laying out his terms, assuming the mantle of protector of the people and of a status quo that was superior to the radical changes advanced by the Federalists. Pompous, florid, and alarmist, he forged ahead, describing the new Constitution as "perilous and uneasy" and the people as "exceedingly uneasy and disquieted" and the new federalist scheme as an "annihilation of the most solemn engagement of the states." He painted a pastoral past imperiled by the young men's adventure in Philadelphia. In a fatherly tone, he told the crowd, "You ought to be extremely cautious, watchful, jealous of your liberty, for instead of securing your rights, you may lose them forever." They had been deceived. "Here, sir, no dangers, no insurrection or tumult, has happened—every thing has been calm and tranquil."

The Federalists were reckless adventurers. "We are wandering on the great ocean of human affairs," he said. "I see no land mark to guide us. We are running we know not whither." The cure would be far worse than the disease. "A wrong step made now will plunge us into misery, and our republic will be lost."[11]

The faces of the men in the arena reflected the force of Henry's emotional beginning. Madison could not have been surprised. Intending to make the most of Randolph's Saul-to-Damascus story, Randolph and Madison had agreed that they would begin with Randolph's story, from his own lips. He rose and admitted that he did not sign the Constitution in Philadelphia—and said he would not do so again. Yes, he conceded, he was often "too candid," but he would nonetheless here "depart from the concealment belonging to the character of a statesman." Politics, said Randolph, was "too often nourished by passion, at the expense of understanding."

He then aimed at Henry. "No man," he asserted, had a right to "impose his opinion on others." His remarks were tinged with melancholy. He knew he had alienated thousands of people with his weak middle road in Philadelphia—to be "moderate in politics," he mused sadly, "forbids an ascent to the summit of political fame."[12] The next day, he headed farther down this somber path, abjectly stating that "ambition and popularity are no objects with me." He said he expected to retire in a year to private life.*[13]

Randolph's stance was that of a martyr for the Constitution. He urged the convention to stand with the men who had fought for them—his friend Madison first among them. The Federalists had the "most enlightened heads in the western hemisphere," he claimed. When he had refused to support the Constitution in Philadelphia, "I had not even the glimpse of the genius of America."[14] The fight to come was his penance.

Two of the four main players had now entered the floor. The next up was George Mason, of the anti-Federalist contingent. He regarded the assembly quietly. He began, "I solemnly declare that no man is a greater friend to a firm union of the American states than I am." But the union could not be reached without "hazarding the rights of the people." The power of taxation, he said, was "calculated to annihilate totally the state governments."[15]

The stark contrast that day between Henry's delusional imaginings and Mason's principled recalcitrance must have put a lift in Madison's step as he left the assembly room. That night, he sat in his room, dipped his quill into his inkwell, and rejoiced to George Washington that Henry and Mason together had "made a lame figure," that they appeared to be separated, putting them on "different and awkward ground." Each had managed to throw an unfavorable light on the other, and Madison said he was "elated" by that development. But he hastened to say, "I dare not however speak with certainty as to the

---

* Perhaps because of confessionals just such as this, Randolph would be pulled back into public service soon enough; he would go on to serve as attorney general and then secretary of state in the new federal government.

IMAGE 22.2. *GEORGE MASON* BY ALBERT ROSENTHAL, PRINT OF
GEORGE MASON OF VIRGINIA BASED ON A PAINTING IN THE POSSESSION
OF THE FAMILY. COURTESY OF THE FIRST AMERICAN WEST,
SPECIAL COLLECTIONS RESEARCH CENTER, UNIVERSITY OF CHICAGO LIBRARY.

decision." His adversaries, after all, were relentlessly stoking "local interests &
prejudices."[16] In another letter to Rufus King, Madison admitted that "several
perplexing circumstances" could mean "the majority will be but small, & may
possibly be defeated."[17]

But he was still careful to hedge his bets—"I dare not however," he told
Washington, "speak with certainty as to the decision."[18]

THE NEXT DAY, HENRY ATTEMPTED TO DESTROY WHAT HE HAD ONLY
damaged the first day. His skill lay in his maddening elusiveness; while
his reputation was of a mighty man, he went to great lengths to seem ordinary, to put himself on the side of those mystified by the need for elaborate

changes issuing from the cosmopolis of Philadelphia. "I wish I was possessed of talents, or possessed of any thing," he wheedled, "that might enable me to elucidate this great subject." He proceeded to excoriate the Constitution. Like a spider, he spun a poisonous web around the Constitution, using the word *radical* again and again to describe its provisions. He disingenuously mourned his inability to support it: "[I] am fearful I have lived long enough to become an old fashioned fellow," he said. "Perhaps an invincible attachment to the dearest rights of man may, in these refined enlightened times, be deemed *old fashioned*: If so, I am contented to be so."

One onlooker later said that he unconsciously touched his wrists as Henry spoke, as if he were wearing chains of bondage.[19] Henry wove into his remarks a constant, cutting sarcasm about the "refinement" and "enlightenment" of Madison and the other Federalists. He brandished his own history, depicting himself as a gnarled patriot, a sort of human touchstone. "Twenty-eight years ago was I supposed a traitor for my country. I was then said to be a bane of sedition, because I supported the rights of country: I may be thought suspicious when I say our privileges and rights are in danger." He attacked and attacked. "Guard with jealous attention the public liberty. Suspect every one who approaches that jewel. Unfortunately, nothing will preserve it, but downright force. Whenever you give up that force, you are inevitably ruined." It was clear he had read the Federalist Papers, and carefully. He granted that the new Constitution would guard against factions and licentiousness—but it would also, he seethed, "oppress and ruin the people." Countering Madison's vision of an energetic government, Henry retorted that the idea was "extremely ridiculous" and "cannot be in earnest." The new federal government, he said, "will trample on your fallen liberty."

He pushed ahead, the Federalists in his crosshairs. "However uncharitable it may appear," he believed that the "most unworthy characters" would get into power and prevent amendments to improve the Constitution. Those were true ad hominem fighting words, and the crowd reacted accordingly. Henry proceeded to bombard every foundation stone of Madison's philosophy. A "contemptible minority," he warned, would be able to prevent policies favoring the majority. The standing army would "execute the execrable commands of tyranny." The unlimited taxation power would be "madness." And the Constitution itself, he charged, was illegitimate: The delegates in

Philadelphia had only been empowered to consolidate the existing government—not craft a new one.

He even embraced the very charge he knew the Federalists would drop over his head like a noose. "When I thus profess myself to be an advocate for the liberty of the people," he admitted to the crowd, "I shall be told that I am to be a demagogue." But he did not mind such "illiberal insinuations," he shrugged. He wanted to own and to embody, to *become*, the role of protector of the people—to be a demagogue. After all, he said, the first thing he had in his heart was "American *liberty*," while only the *second* was "American *union*."

Thus Henry sought to expose a hidden Janus face of Madison's statesmanship ambition. Again and again, he ridiculed Madison's vision in the Federalist Papers (particularly Numbers 10 and 51) of an elegant marvel of political engineering. The entire Madisonian scheme was, he declared, just the opposite: reckless, dangerous claptrap. Instead of checks and balances, Henry told the men, they would get "specious, imaginary balances" and "rope-dancing, chain-rattling, ridiculous ideal checks and contrivances." The Constitution was supposed to have "beautiful features," but they were instead "horribly frightful." Among its "other deformities," he claimed the Constitution had an "awful squinting—it squints toward monarchy." The citizens of the eight states that had already acted to ratify the document had been "egregiously misled."

The debate was supposed to proceed clause by clause, but Henry had just stampeded through the document—ironic for one who had attacked the Constitution itself for "chain-rattling." As he closed, he conceded, guiltlessly, that while his speech had been "out of order," his passion was to blame.[20] He had been going on his gut.

I T WAS ALL RETURNING TO PLATO. THE DARK STEED OF THE PASSIONS WAS running rampant in the New Academy, loosed and goaded by Patrick Henry. Henry's anti-Federalist creed contained real ideas, to be sure—about the sanctity of states, the difference between a confederacy and a nation, and the existence of a bill of rights. But what Henry's beginning made clear was that he intended the debate not to be primarily about ideas, but about fears and self-interest. And thus Madison's great challenge: breaking the dark steed and lashing the chariot of state to reason.

Years later, a mysterious man who claimed to have been one of Madison's "warmest opponents" told a historian that he listened with "more delight" to Madison's "clear and cunning argumentation" than to Henry's "eloquent and startling appeals."[21] Thus Madison, like Henry, would seek to transform his defining weakness into his capital strength.

R ANDOLPH FIRST STOOD TO TAKE ANOTHER RUN AT HENRY, REFRAMING his intransigence not as a brave stand but as a stain on patriotism. Through the "most gallant exploits" and by overcoming the "most astonishing difficulties," America had won the "admiration of the world." "Let no future historian inform posterity," he cautioned, that they had failed now to "concur in any regular efficient government."[22]

Randolph sat down. Madison steeled himself. It was a warm Friday afternoon. For two full days, he had absorbed the proceedings, gaining a handle on the breadth of the anti-Federalists' planned assault. Randolph had fought back—but on many of Henry's same terms. Madison saw a clear need for someone to *change* those terms, to recast the debate and seize the field. As in Philadelphia, he took that burden squarely on his small shoulders.

Much had changed since his earliest days as Henry's councilor. The group of men now beheld before them not an upstart or an effete young intellectual, but an accomplished and formidable (if diminutive) *man*. He had grown out of his fragile and slender physique, becoming "muscular and well-proportioned." No longer as pale as during his youth, he had a "ruddy" complexion. He was well and expensively dressed, in a single-breasted coat and a doubled straight collar. Expensive ruffles decorated his wrists and breast. He had lost even more hair, and he still vainly combed what was left from the back of his head over his forehead, but he had also powdered his hair, creating a dignified, almost British impression.[23]

Although he comported himself more formidably than in the past, he did not begin auspiciously. He began speaking in such a low voice that the official transcriber of the proceedings scribbled in frustration that Madison's "exordium could not be heard distinctly."[24]

Yet Madison pushed forward. In his methodical manner, he began by baring the bankrupt basis of Henry's appeal. "I shall not attempt to make impressions by any ardent professions of zeal for the public welfare," he declared. "Professions of attachment to the public good, and comparisons of parties ought not to govern or influence us now."[25] He was targeting Henry's very passions. He pounded that theme again and again. The convention must not "address our arguments to the feelings and passions," he said, but to "understandings and judgments." He looked at the audience and, in a rare personal note, admitted that it "gives me pain" to hear men like Henry "continually distorting the natural construction of language." After all, he said, it wasn't the *majority* that needed protecting in these troubled times. History showed that "turbulence, violence and abuse of power" in fact followed from the "majority trampling on the rights of the minority," producing only "factions and commotions."[26]

Henry had abandoned the clause-by-clause plan of debate in favor of sweeping assaults. Madison now responded in kind. He mockingly recounted Henry's dumbfoundingly pastoral view of the confederacy. If America was "at perfect repose" and in "perfect tranquility and safety," why, he challenged, had so many states already voted for the new Constitution? Why, he pleaded, had the government been so "shamefully disgraced," and the prior constitution so grossly violated?[27] Henry, he said, was recklessly casting embers around a bone-dry country, sparking "the heart-burnings of a majority."[28] Henry must be held to account.

Openly reinstating rationality in the hall, Madison returned again to his research. He explained why the history of confederations dictated the necessity for direct taxation. There would always be a balance between federal and state government. "Direct taxes," he promised, "will only be recurred to for great purposes." That power was "necessary for the preservation of the union."[29]

In that manner, Madison proceeded to bat down every arrow Henry had slung at the Constitution—from its separation of powers to its apportionment scheme. Madison's defense concluded with an emotional peroration: "I hope the patriotism of the people will continue and be a sufficient guard to their liberties."[30] He was saying that the people would require *patriotic faith* to transform his scheme from a blueprint into a living and breathing government. His "rope-dancing, chain-rattling, ridiculous" scheme depended *precisely* on the conviction that men could at last transcend the violent spiral of history. By contrast, Henry's attacks masked a cynical disbelief that men could ever truly govern themselves.

He finally sat down. The people beheld the keeper of the flame of the Constitution from Philadelphia. That night, Madison, exhausted, tried to recover as best as he could. But he suspected he would face another equally draining assault the next day.

R ISING THE NEXT MORNING, MADISON LIKELY ALREADY FELT APPREHEN-sive and jittery. He arrived at the New Academy. Henry, as ever undaunted and assured, rose. He coyly invited Randolph to "continue his observations" from the prior day. Randolph immediately lashed into Henry and the anti-Federalists, lambasting the current system as rife with "imbecility" and but a "ship-wrecked vessel."[31] If the government could not rely on regular taxation, it would have to go begging for donations from the states. Randolph scorned the "absurdity and sophistry" of any argument supporting such voluntary contributions. "You would be laughed at for your folly," for thinking "human nature could be thus operated upon."[32] By holding back such a "necessary power," he warned, the men in the New Academy would "unwarily lay the foundation of usurpation itself."[33]

With this dire warning, Randolph returned to his seat. The fervor of the man, previously so wobbly, must have astounded the crowd. Now it was Madison's turn; precision would follow rage. He dispensed with any pretense of humility or deference. Instead, he drove directly at the heart of the matter. Taxation, he tersely said, was "indispensible and necessary" to a "well-organized government."[34] He attacked Henry's absurd pastoral vision of the status quo. The present system was "pernicious and fatal." History was riddled with similar failures. In ancient Greece, the Amphictyonic confederation had ended in "sanguinary coercion," and the Achean League had been "continually agitated." An early German federal system had collapsed into a "nerveless body." A confederate government in Holland had displayed "characteristic imbecility."[35] "Governments destitute of energy," he concluded tightly, would "ever produce anarchy."[36]

In a fell swoop, Henry's former subaltern had confounded and upended every one of Henry's assertions, capsizing, along with them, the former governor's entire narrative and his self-assumed savior role. Fuming, Madison's former mentor rose in rebuttal. This time, he appealed to the now-hoary authority of the American Revolution itself. The "great principles of a free government," he complained, were being "reversed." The states were being "harassed," while individuals were being "oppressed and subjected to repeated distresses." Like the British empire before it, the federal government was now overseeing the "wanton deprivation of property."[37]

In high dudgeon, Madison rose in response. He summoned, in absentia, George Washington, the greatest authority of all. He referred to the general, mock-obliquely, as "that man who had the most extensive acquaintance with the nature of the country." "I did not introduce that man," he said disingenuously, to "bias any gentleman here." But even Washington, Madison asserted, had himself declared, "Some great change was necessary."[38]

As strong as these words were, the fight with Henry was clearly draining. Madison visibly sagged and told the crowd, "I shall no longer fatigue the committee at this time."[39] He fell back into his chair, his stomach churning, yearning to flee the room—but he could not.

M ADISON'S TRUMP CARD OF GEORGE WASHINGTON INFURIATED HENRY, who responded by scorching everything his former aide had said. If the Constitution was a "little or a trifling evil," it should be adopted. But if it would "entail misery on the free people of this country, I insist rejection ought to follow."[40] In this political hothouse, his rhetoric flowered even more lushly than usual. The Constitution, he fumed, was "impiously irritating the avenging hand of heaven." People "in the full enjoyment of freedom" were launching "out into the wide ocean of human affairs." The Federalists, those wild-eyed radicals, were fecklessly discarding "Poor little humble republican maxims" that had "stood the shock of ages."[41] As for Randolph, he ominously insinuated that "something extraordinary" must have occurred to cause "so great a change in his opinion."[42]

But within the violent bluster, the defiant provincialism, and the obvious hatred of the upstarts, the delegates listening closely also heard an idea worth taking seriously: self-reliance. Henry told the assembly, "We have the animating fortitude and persevering alacrity of republican men." The collective conviction among the men in the room about their mission for freedom against tyranny, he thought, could be a potent source for his own crusade against the Constitution. "Sir," he addressed the crowd, with his endearing habit of addressing an entire audience as a single man, "it is the fortune of a free people, not to be intimidated by imaginary dangers."

He proclaimed, "Fear is the passion of slaves."[43]

This must have hit Madison with the force of a cannon blast. Of all of the former governor's many faces—the flatterer and the agitator, the executive and the military man—this was the most dangerous: muse of men's dreams and their nightmares. This was the Henry who could effortlessly weave optimism, pessimism, and action. This was the Henry who could connect more explosively with men's hearts than anyone in the country, let alone a guarded man like Madison who resisted public oratory like a disease. This was the Henry who had proclaimed so loudly and infectiously, "Give me liberty or give me death!" in St. John's Church in 1775.

And this was the Henry who squarely stood between Madison and the nation he so desperately wanted to achieve.

Having found this electric current, Henry slashed away at Madison and his allies with barely hidden contempt, cannily allying himself with the men in the room. The "middle and lower ranks of people," he slyly admitted to the assembly, lacked the "illumined ideas" that the "well-born"—an absurd attack on Madison and his brethren, given Henry's own "well-born" family—were "so happily possessed of." He mocked the "microscopic eyes of modern statesmen"—completely flipping Madison's proud lifelong pursuit—for obsessing about an "abundance of defects in old systems." In contrast, "My fears are not the force of imagination—they are too well founded." He thundered: "I tremble for my country!"[44]

He then wheeled on Randolph, who had earlier innocently used the word *herd* to describe the people. Henry seized that mistake and battered the lawyer with it. Randolph, he declared, had transformed Virginians from "respectable independent citizens" into "abject, dependent subjects, or slaves." Randolph was "degradingly assimilating our citizens to a herd"—likening the proud men in the assembly to chattel.[45]

Randolph sprang to his feet, at once angry and flummoxed. He protested that he had not used the word to "excite any odium," but simply to "convey the idea of a multitude."[46]

Henry lightly deflected Randolph's umbrage. With an air of self-satisfaction, he countered that Randolph's choice of words had "made a deep impression in my mind." The Federalists believed the federal government "must have our souls." He employed the strongest condemnation available in genteel Virginia: "This is dishonorable and disgraceful," he trumpeted. "I tell you, they shall not have the soul of Virginia!"⁴⁷ He sat down only after declaring that a bill of rights was "indispensibly necessary"—meaning that the Constitution must be destroyed without it.

Absorbing all of this, Madison felt ill.

H E ROSE AND EXCUSED HIMSELF. HIS BOWELS FELT LOOSE, HIS STOMACH churning. He returned to his boardinghouse and fell into his bed. But his condition did not improve. He felt fragile, as if he might break, as if his very mind could shatter and he would go mad. He remained in bed. After two days, his symptoms were unabated, and he wrote to Rufus King, "Writing is scarcely practicable & very injurious to me." The last sentence of his painfully short letter was telling: "I think we have a majority as yet," Madison said, "but the other party are ingenious & indefatigable."⁴⁸

James Madison, the man, was in revolt against James Madison, the *statesman*. He was painfully aware that he had abandoned his Federalist allies, deep in combat on the field of battle in the New Academy. He knew they desperately needed his quiet intellectual force to combat the wrathful anti-Federalists. It was as if he was back in militia exercises in Orange County sixteen years ago. There, he had choked and retreated into himself in the face of adversity. Now, like then, he was conspicuously absent from the battlefield. In his absence, tensions grew between the foes. By Monday, Henry and Randolph's verbal animosity threatened to turn into physical violence.

B ACK IN THE HALL, IT BEGAN WHEN HENRY ROSE AND SNEERED THAT THE Federalists were "illumined genii,"⁴⁹ who viewed ordinary Virginians as a "mobbish suspected herd." Virginia's 180 state legislators lacked "virtue enough to manage its own interests. These must be referred to [as] the chosen ten"—meaning Virginia's federal congressmen.[50] He cast suspicion on the vaunted conclave in Philadelphia, lambasting the "most wicked and pernicious schemes" that had occurred there "under the dark veil of secrecy."[51] He ridiculed the proposal to pass the Constitution with only the possibility of amending it later as an "insult" to himself and the modest folk he mirrored. "I am at a loss what to say," he claimed. "You agree to bind yourselves hand and foot—for the sake of what?—Of being unbound!"[52]

The scholar who later wrote a thorough analysis of the ratifying convention, Hugh Blair Grigsby, reported that Henry's speech was "delivered with transcendent effect." Grigsby also wrote that one witness specifically recalled an instance—conspicuously absent from the official transcript—where Henry "painted in the most vivid colors the dangers likely to result to the black population from the most unlimited power of the general government" and then "suddenly broke out with the homely exclamation: *They'll free your niggers!*" Henry evidently made that proclamation in a sort of outrageous humor, ingratiating himself with the slaveholders in the audience in a spirit that was both satirical and serious. The audience "passed instantly from fear to wayward laughter." Grigsby's source recalled, "It was most ludicrous to see men who a moment before were half frightened to death now with a 'broad grin on their faces.'"[53] Such was Henry's quicksilver ability to manipulate an audience like a marionette on a string.

"Tell me not of checks on paper," he lectured the crowd—a shot at the absent Madison—but of "checks founded on self-love." Henry clearly intended to conceptually destroy Madison's hoped-for "energetic" new center of federal gravity. Henry was arguing that the spokes should govern instead of the hub. The "real rock of political salvation" was "*self-love* perpetuated from age to age in every human breast, and maintained in every action."[54]

Thus encouraged to love themselves, many in the room began to feel the Federalists were standing in their way, and Henry seized the momentum. With Madison gone, he blasted away at Randolph, who he said had "withheld his signature" in Philadelphia precisely because he was "not led by the illumined—the illustrious few."[55] Henry damned Randolph with vanishing praise, acerbically observing the clash between his prior "noble and disinterested conduct" and his now-ardent support, while insinuating that there had been a dastardly quid pro quo for Randolph's conversion. "Such is my situation that as a poor individual, I look for information every where." Perhaps Randolph, notorious for his family's financial troubles, had traded his surprise political support for a financial reward.

Infuriated, Randolph rose. "I find myself attacked in the most illiberal manner," he cried. "I disdain his aspersions and his insinuations," he sputtered, pointing at Henry. Randolph protested Henry's charge of inconsistency and said he had always been "invariably governed by an invincible attachment to the happiness of the people of America." If he did not "stand on the bottom of integrity, and pure love for Virginia," he threatened, "I wish to resign my existence." The "imbecility of the confederation" was obvious. In Philadelphia, he had been "impressed" with the arguments, then swayed by the need for an "intimate and firm union."

Randolph then charged at Henry anew. "I understand not," he said, why Henry would give such "full scope to licentiousness and dissipation," who would, by rejecting the Constitution, "plunge us into anarchy."[56]

Randolph, clearly rattled, was accusing Henry of intentionally trying to destroy the new country, and Henry again jumped up to respond. He "had no intention of offending anyone," he shot back, with crocodile tears. Randolph hurled back an equally insincere thanks—were it not for Henry's concession, he claimed, he would have disclosed "certain facts" that "would have made some men's hair stand on end."[57] Angrily, Randolph then defended himself against the assertion of being "one of the *illumined*" with a tirade, ominously saying that in Henry's reckless attacks, "I see a storm growling over Virginia." By the end, Randolph was still unsated, still attacking Henry for having "perverted my meaning."[58]

The session broke, the hall nervously buzzing. The vitriol between the two men was palpable. Word quickly spread that the two men would duel that evening. That night, in the muggy Richmond air, Colonel William Cabell— Henry's ally and friend—strode out as Henry's second, pistol in hand, ready to duel Randolph's second. A reconciliation was evidently negotiated, as no shots were fired by the men.[59] But the unresolved anger festered like a raw wound.

The proceedings tested all the parties. James Monroe and James Madison had previously been so close they had traveled and invested together. Yet the following Tuesday—with Madison still inert and miserable in his sweltering boarding room—Monroe rose to share his "great anxiety" and "gloomy apprehensions" about Madison's beloved Constitution.[60] He boldly went where no anti-Federalist had dared go before—to confront Madison's supposedly impervious historical proof that confederacies require a strong central government. Monroe picked his way through the same ancient confederacies Madison had studied for a shockingly different conclusion. "Nothing," he declared, "can be adduced from any of them." In fact, he said, foreign interference and foreign aid mattered far more in a confederacy's success or failure than federalism (or the lack of it).[61]

T HE SIGNIFICANCE OF MONROE'S VOLLEY CANNOT BE OVERSTATED, FOR IT shows just why young Madison—here, at the peak of his powers—was so much more than the sum of his parts. His reputation as a research-driven logician by this point was mighty indeed. What Monroe did was present a perfectly respectable replica of Madison's own Method. Monroe marshaled reams of historical studies to assert that the Constitution in fact would create a "dangerous government," founded on "haste" and "wild precipitation."[62] He did so with preparation and conviction, and with the benefit of Madison's absence.

Yet the sine qua non of Madison's Method was not any of the elements individually. It was the chemistry among them, the unique forcefulness of the man as realized in his unique brand of pugilism. And so Monroe's worthy effort still paled next to Madison's.

M EANWHILE, BACK IN HIS BOARDINGHOUSE, MADISON LEARNED OF Monroe's onslaught—and steeled himself to return to the arena.

23 Extremely Feeble

———————◆———————

THE NEXT DAY, MADISON RETURNED TO THE NEW ACADEMY. HE FELT "extremely feeble," and it was obvious to everyone. He had been apprised, of course, of all that happened in his absence. He knew he needed to reassert control and put a spine back into the formless proceedings.

That morning, he rose and named as his enemy "vague discourses" and "mere sports of fancy." He quickly enumerated five exact grounds by which the delegates could determine whether the Constitution's new government was, in fact, needed.

They must first ask themselves, "how far it may be necessary," second, "how far it may be practicable," third, "how far it may be safe," fourth, "with respect to economy," and fifth, "is it necessary."[1]

Madison closed by conceding that experience would probably suggest that the "powerful and prevailing" influence of the states would undermine the union. But he chose to "indulge my hopes [rather] than fears," he told the men around him, "because I flatter myself" that the amendment process would allow for a fix.[2] In other words, the Constitution *could* remedy itself, just as the nation could. But they would have to ratify the new system first.

He closed by demanding a return to the clause-by-clause debate that had been originally agreed upon. No longer would Henry's rambling, roundhouse arguments be allowed. The delegates would have to work through the issues, one by one.[3] It was as if an adult was trying to quiet a room of squabbling children.

Henry stood and sputtered that his "at large mode," where he could attack any issue at any time, was in fact superior to Madison's limited mode. Madison retorted that only a "regular and progressive" discussion could function. Mason quickly rose to plead that with "so important a subject as this," it was "impossible in the nature of things" to avoid disorganized debate. He then attacked Randolph's use of "phantoms" to "terrify and compel us,"

condemning the attorney's "singular skill in exorcisms."[4] Madison—still feeble—stood again to demand that the assembly return to "going through the
business regularly."[5]

The following day, he tried to practice what he had preached. With a
numbing point-by-point refutation of virtually every argument that had been
advanced against the Constitution—from attacks against tax collectors to the
dangers from a divided Europe—he exposed the vacuity of the anti-Federalist
creed. "When we are preparing a government for posterity," he declared, "we
ought to found it on permanent principles and not on those of a temporary
nature."[6] In a fell swoop, he had successfully painted Henry as both short-
sighted and unpatriotic.

Sulfurous, Henry stood. Madison's "catalogue of dangers," he angrily
charged, was "absolutely imaginary." Henry then made an especially nasty
attempt to turn the delegates against one another and all against Madison.
Pointing at the Princeton-educated young man, he snapped that the "dangers
of this system are real," when "those who have no similar interests with the
people of this country, are to legislate for us." Madison, he meant, was not one
of "us."[7]

Henry then invoked the absent Jefferson, citing his notorious letter to
Madison in which Jefferson said he hoped enough states would reject the
Constitution to force the states to pass a bill of rights.[8] If Jefferson wanted at
least *some* states to reject the Constitution, Henry meant, shouldn't Virginia
follow suit? He professed sympathy with Madison's predicament. When "men
of such talents and learning," he oozed, are "compelled to use their utmost
abilities to convince themselves that there is no danger," is it "not sufficient to
make us tremble?"[9]

Henry then turned on Madison's Method itself: his unerring belief in
logic, the calm, cool process of his argumentation. The "sacred and lovely
thing" of such rights as religion, Henry asserted, "ought not to rest on the
ingenuity of logical deduction"; likewise a trial by a jury of one's peers, "ought
not to depend on constructive logical reasoning."[10]

Instead of Madison's extended republic where factions were happily balanced, Henry asked the assembly to picture the humiliated common man
forced to "ask a man of influence how he is to proceed" and "for whom he
must vote."[11] He painted a nation of "rich, fat federal emoluments—your rich,

snug, fine, fat federal offices" demanding taxes and excises from individuals and states alike.[12]

And he ridiculed Madison's notion that statesmen would inevitably surface in the new utopia, pledging that he would "never depend" on "so slender a protection as the possibility of being represented by virtuous men."[13]

Madison, rising to respond, returned to the topic of his close friend Jefferson with obvious distaste. "I wish his name had never been mentioned," he snapped, because the "delicacy of his feelings will be wounded." With that caveat, Madison declared that Jefferson had in fact *approved* of the taxation clause—because it would enable the government to "carry on its operations," because he "admire[d]" the Constitution's many other parts, and because he was "captivated" by the two-senator solution in the Senate, which—pointing to Henry—Madison cuttingly observed, "the honorable gentleman calls the rotten part of this constitution."[14] Madison won this particular exchange—but the crowd knew the fight was far from over.

O N FRIDAY THE THIRTEENTH, THE DEBATE COLLAPSED INTO A BRUTISH back and forth between Henry and Madison over the Mississippi River, with a particular bloc of voting delegates on the anvil: the men of Virginia's Kentucky region. Many of them owned property along the river; others needed it for commercial navigation. The Kentuckians cared more deeply about the river than did anyone else and were therefore far more susceptible to his fearmongering. Even Henry admitted that most people suspected he was "scuffling for Kentucky votes"[15]—and proceeded to do so with gusto. He charged that a current treaty with France allowing navigation rights on the river would be abrogated by the new Constitutional Congress, stormed against the "abominable policy" and its "fatal and pernicious tendency," and threatened that the "people of Kentucky, though weak now, will not let the president and senate take away this right."[16]

For the first time, Madison openly lost his temper at Henry's brazen manipulation of the assembly's emotions. He rose and protested, "It is extremely disagreeable to me to enter into this discussion," arguing that the debate would "sully the reputation of our public councils."[17] He promised flatly that Kentucky would "expect support and succor alone from a strong efficient government."[18] Randolph then stepped in. The actual politics of any cession of the river, he said, exposed Henry's attack as a canard. A treaty to "alienate any part of the United States" would effectively declare war against the "inhabitants of the alienated part."[19] But, he continued, the nation would henceforth be bound together by its grand *nexus imperii*—the "consanguinity between the western people and the inhabitants of the other states."[20] The factions would not pull it apart. American sovereignty over the river was *not* in danger.

The clashing tempers had summoned an oppressive mood in the room. Suddenly, the rising conflict seemed to take on physical form, as a massive thunderstorm descended outside. Lightning bolts flashed hotly through the windows. Enormous sheets of rain began raking the building. Thunder crashed so loudly that nobody could hear anyone speak. The session was quickly called to a close; the delegates left to huddle and plot in small groups.[21]

In his room that night, Madison was deeply disturbed by the events of that day. Despite their best efforts to beat back Henry, the Kentucky bloc was in clear danger of turning against the Constitution. To Washington, he wrote that the situation "at present is less favorable" than before, the progress was "slow," and the anti-Federalists were using the delay to "work on the local prejudices of particular sets of members." Everything might depend on the Kentuckians, he wrote, who he thought were leaning against the Constitution. In sum, he concluded that matters were in the "most ticklish state that can be imagined," and of the ultimate vote, "I dare not encourage much expectation that it will be on the favorable side."[22]

T HE NEXT DAY, AS IF THE STORM HAD BEEN A PREFACE OF HENRY'S OWN fury, he rose and lambasted Congress's ability, under the Constitution, to raise its own pay, promising that they would "indulge themselves to the fullest extent."[23] Madison wearily rose to respond. The "universal indignation of the people," he said, would prevent Congress from exploiting its power. In any event, there was no practical alternative. To fix their compensation at one salary—despite inflation—or to allow state governments to pay them, would be ridiculous.[24] Pivoting and pivoting again, Madison relentlessly recast Henry's attacks as politically motivated, alarmist, false—and absurd. But he could not tell with any certainty what success he was having.

The debate was steadily approaching Madison's great topic of coercion. A large, charismatic, courteous man, Charles Clay had rarely spoken at the ratifying convention. Clay was one of three clergymen at the convention. In 1777, with the Revolutionary War reaching its heights, he had famously preached, "Cursed be he who keepeth back his sword from blood in this war."[25] But he now rose to ask why Congress should have the power of calling forth the militia (made up of citizen soldiers commanded in the states) rather than the federal standing army of professional soldiers for domestic disturbances—such as Shays' Rebellion.

His question was ominous, perhaps the symptom of a broader underlying revolt, and Madison answered with distinct impatience. The "reasons of this power," he retorted, were "so obvious that they would occur to most gentlemen." If there were resistance to the execution of the laws, it "ought to be overcome." There were two—and only two—ways to overcome such resistance: by regular military force or by the people. The military was the superior option to civil war. And the civilian militia was a superior option to a standing army.[26] The militia would not be abused because—here he again drew on his practical knowledge of public opinion—it would excite the "universal indignation of the people" and focus on Congress the "general hatred and detestation of their country."[27]

But Henry was not about to let Madison escape with establishing another new federal power. He rose to say he was "too jealous and suspicious to confide" in the "remote possibility" of Congress keeping the militia armed as a hedge against a standing army.[28] On the question of whether "rulers *might* tyrannize," he charged Madison had only responded that "they *will not*." "In saying they *would not*," Henry maintained, Madison had "admitted they *might*."[29]

I N HIS ATTEMPT TO PARSE MADISON'S WORDS USING LOGIC, HENRY WAS stepping into treacherous territory. Woe to anyone who underestimates the trickster power of logic in politics. While deductive reasoning is a treasured element of classical rhetoric, crowds respond more readily to a politician's character. They vibrate to emotions, such as anger and hope, and resonate with nationalism and hope and fear. Above all, they draw to the passions like a moth to flame. Unsurprisingly, many naturally fear that a fondness for logic will translate into weakness and even ridicule. It's the rare leader who makes logic the foundation stone of his identity, the transparent spine of his arguments.

But logic's power in politics stems precisely from its elegance. Logic can create its own potency, proceeding from premise to conclusion and conquering obstacles in stride. Thus the forcefulness of Madison's Method. As Madison infused not only his arguments but his very character with logic, the assembly began to find itself drawn to his new center of gravity.

MADISON HAD SPIED AN AMBIGUITY IN HENRY'S POSITION. HE ROSE. HE declared that while Henry had laid "much stress" on the maxim that the "purse and sword ought not to be put in the same hands," his position was "totally inapplicable." "What is the meaning of this maxim?" he asked, plainly beleaguered. There "never was, and I say there never will be, an efficient government, in which both are not vested." He offered that Henry could only have meant that the *same member* of government should not have the purse and sword.[30] The real question, he told the crowd, was not whether, but in *what part*, of the government military power should rest.

Amid this onslaught of logic, something strange then happened: Madison took a sudden confessional turn, and he began talking about his own hopes and fears. "I profess myself," he said, "to have had an uniform zeal for a republican government." As if Henry's torrent had finally breached his own rigid canals, Madison began gushing with sentiment and nostalgia. "From the first moment that my mind was capable of contemplating political subjects," he remembered, "I never, till this moment, ceased wishing success to a well regulated republican government." That goal, he confessed to the men—listening intently—had been "my most ardent desire." If the "bands of the government be relaxed," he continued fervently, "confusion will ensue. Anarchy had, and I fear ever will, produce despotism," as well as "dissipation and licentiousness."[31]

He then trailed off into a soft, contemplative tone, as if counseling himself. According to the transcriber, he "spoke so very low that he could not be distinctly heard."[32] For a moment, Madison perhaps imagined that he and the audience—perhaps even Henry—could share in the same sense of conscience that had spurred his passion for the Constitution all along. But in that, he was sorely mistaken.

ENRY, WHO HAD SPIED A NEW WEAKNESS WHEN MADISON SPOKE SO nakedly about his ambitions for the nation, shot up with an air of triumph. "Mr. Chairman," Henry loudly announced, "It is now confessed that this is a national government! There is not a single federal feature in it." He drove at the distinction between *federal*—the design of government with interlocking federal and state parts—and *national*—the scheme under which the states would purportedly be dissolved into a new whole. Under the Constitution, Henry said, Virginia's government would become "but a name." "Where are your checks?" he asked theatrically. Putting both purse and sword into the same hands, he went on—transparently relishing the opportunity to compete with Madison as a logician—was "by logical and mathematical conclusions, the description of despotism."[33]

Madison burst out, "Mr. Chairman, the honorable gentleman expresses surprise that I wished to see an experiment made of a republican government, or that I would risk the happiness of my country on an experiment." He appeared plainly incredulous. "What is the situation of this country at this moment?" he cried. "Is it not rapidly approaching anarchy?"[34]

Perhaps sensing that his friend was reaching the end of his rope, Randolph took over. Calling for "common sense," he tried to refocus everyone on what the actual militia provision said.[35] The militia, he explained, could only be called forth when the federal government's civil power had failed. Moreover, the *states* would appoint the militia's officers. Dispensing with those essential facts, he then went on the attack. Henry, he asserted, had "mistaken facts," and he angrily catalogued Henry's long list of errata.[36]

After George Mason rose to describe the "ignominious punishments" that Congress might deliver, Henry Lee stood to announce a damning conclusion—that Henry had raised suspicions "against possibility and not against probability." He caustically recast Henry's "great triumph and exultation" that the government was national, and his laughable attempt to transform himself into a logician. "The honorable gentleman is so little used to triumph on the grounds of reasoning," he announced, "that he suffers himself to be quite captivated by the least appearance of victory."[37] Madison then rose and tried to steer the debate to its natural end, recurring to Lee's elegant paradigm calling for probability rather than possibility. "If a possibility be the cause of objection," he said, "we must object to every government in America."[38] Debate finally closed, with the Sunday break ahead, but with so much tension, it was hardly a respite at all.

O N MONDAY, HENRY ENTERED THE CHAMBER FULL OF FIRE. HE STOOD and assailed the federal militia power all over again. Madison stood to kill off that line of attack once and for all. He divided Henry's argument, as per his Method, in two; the militia power, he urgently explained, could only be vested in Congress or the state government—"or there must be a division or concurrence." Madison then marched Henry down the path of his own logic: "He is against division—It is a political monster. He will not give it to congress for fear of oppression. Is it to be vested in the state governments? If so," he challenged, "where is the provision for general defense?" Ineluctably, he proved that Henry's position would lead to a nightmare for the country. If America ever was attacked, he concluded, the states would "fall successfully."[39]

By seizing the high ground so definitively, Madison at once sustained and quickened the Federalists' momentum. When the fight turned toward the new district for the nation's capital—where Congress would exercise total authority—George Mason attacked the power as too plenary. Madison tartly responded that it was "one of those parts" of the Constitution that could "speak its own praise."[40]

Henry rose to predict that only the "most tyrannical and oppressive deeds" could result from the "sweeping clause."[41] "Mr. Chairman," Madison theatrically cried, "I am astonished that the honorable member should launch out into such strong descriptions!" Every nation in the world, he declared, gave its legislature jurisdiction over its home. He expressed amazement that Henry could find "new terrors" in such a "superfluity." In the process, he was making it seem as though it was Henry and the anti-Federalists who were the grasping, radical party in the hall.[42]

Henry stood defensively to state that his real concern was vesting Congress with a "supreme power of legislation" that would be "paramount to the constitution and laws of the states."[43] Melodramatically, he moved that the eighth to thirteenth articles of Virginia's Declaration of Rights be read out loud. This was done, but it was a crucial miscalculation by Henry. Under

Madison's sway, the crowd's appetite for the passions was waning. The Federalists—and others now becoming more sympathetic to the earnestness and factuality of their cause—must have rolled their eyes as they heard the rights for a trial, against excessive bail, for freedom of the press, against standing armies, and so on, redundantly read out.[44]

When it was done, George Nicholas—a well-regarded army colonel, lawyer, and legislator with a famously powerful voice and deep knowledge of legislative process[45]—castigated Henry for his antics: "Let him prove them to be violated" in the new Constitution.[46] Henry retorted that a bill of rights could be "summed up in a few words." Did the Constitution not include one, he sneered, because it would "consume too much paper?"[47]

Despite Henry's missteps, the day was raw and uneasy, and anxiety overpowered Madison yet again. He again escaped the clashing noise and smell of the New Academy for his quiet, dark bed. That night, Madison wrote Hamilton a disarmingly candid letter. With his remove from the hall, he could think a bit more clearly, and told Hamilton he thought he had at last discerned Henry's real strategy beneath all the bluster and bluffing and feints. It was to "spin out the Session" to delay a Virginia victory so as to force New York to vote against the Constitution. Even if they didn't succeed in New York, Madison thought the anti-Federalists saw another alternative still: to "weary the members into an adjournment without taking any decision." If they then succeeded in Virginia in requiring prior amendments to the Constitution, the other states would then need to reratify the Constitution—a process almost certain to fail.

He was not confident about the state of affairs in Richmond. Even if the Federalists won, he said, their majority would "not exceed three or four." And if they lost, Kentucky—the sole target of so many of Henry's withering assaults—"will be the cause."

He confessed that he had relapsed that day. "My health is not good," he pitiably complained, "and the business is wearisome beyond expression."[48]

MADISON WAS ALREADY WORRIED ABOUT PATRICK HENRY; BUT WHEN HE returned to the chamber, he knew he would also have George Mason to contend with. The next week, Mason stood and ripped open what he called the Constitution's "fatal section"—the continuation of slavery for at least another twenty years. Madison listened warily as Mason ruthlessly probed the Constitution's ungainly compromise, its allowance of what he called a "disgraceful trade" and "infamous traffic."[49] Reassuringly motivated by conscience rather than popularity or special interests, the planter was a counterpoint to Henry—and more alarming for that very reason.

Unsteadily rising to defend the measure, Madison explained, simply, that the southern states would not have supported the Constitution if slavery had not been allowed at least for some period of time. If they had been excluded, he said, the consequences would have been "dreadful to them and to us." But Madison did not stop at the border of political expediency. To assure his Virginian slaveholding brethren, he recounted the difficulties of recapturing slaves, and boasted that the Constitution included a clause "expressly inserted to allow owners of slaves to reclaim them."[50] He was adverting to the simple but ungainly defense of politics. Madison made these points without pride. He was not attempting to elevate Virginia on this fraught moral point. He simply wanted to drive the Constitution through the narrow gate of ratification without tearing the whole thing apart. He was aware that his defense, while compelling on political grounds, was bankrupt on the Constitution's own aspirational moral principles, which was exactly Mason's point. Fortunately for the Federalists, the mostly conservative men surrounding Madison were not profoundly concerned about the glaring absence of rights for enslaved men and women and children in the Constitution.

Spying an opportunity in this agita, Henry now rose and nimbly focused the delegates on a different face of the issue: the profound if liminal power the new Constitution gave Congress, as seen on the slavery issue.[51] At some point, he threatened, the Constitution's new federal government could actually "compel the southern states to liberate their negroes." But that "property" would be "guarded," he said, hinting at violence ahead.[52]

D ESPITE HENRY'S PROTESTS AND RHETORICAL FLOURISHES, MADISON HAD succeeded in swaying the delegates to support a clause-by-clause debate, which they began to follow, significantly constraining the anti-Federalists' theatrics. Like a large animal trapped in a small cage, Henry began to thrash about. Again and again, he grasped for his most provocative theme—that Congress, under the new Constitution, would become tyrannical. In a discussion of the Constitution's Section 9, which included the right of the people to habeas corpus and against ex post facto laws, Henry charged that without a complete new bill of rights, Congress could "do every thing they are not forbidden to do."[53] He complained that Section 9 was the Constitution's sole guarantor of any rights, and that it "alone" could never "sufficiently secure" liberties. In that case, he cried, "Every word of mine is lost."[54]

Madison perhaps too exhausted, Randolph quickly stood instead. He attacked the "rhetoric of the gentleman" for having "highly coloured" the notion of empowering the new Congress with the "indefinite power of providing for the general welfare." But the Constitution did no such thing. *Every power was circumscribed. Every authority was controlling, but also controlled.*[55] Trying to bring the debate to a close, Randolph employed the peculiar authority of a former fence-sitter. "I would take the Constitution were it more objectionable than it is," he asserted. He painted the nightmare of an "enterprizing man" who could "enter into the American throne"—a professed demagogue like Patrick Henry who—without the Constitution—could become a tyrant as well.[56]

The debate now turned to the tortuous topic of existing paper money, which would be eliminated by the new government's rights to create new currency. On swiftly changing ground, Henry asserted that the existing paper money in circulation "must be discharged, shilling for shilling," and complained that speculators would get it at "one for a thousand."[57] Mason then raised the fear that Congress might simply decide not to redeem certain paper money at all.[58]

Madison was flabbergasted by the gall of men who had enabled so much paper money to be recklessly printed in the first place. Exasperated, he rose to berate Henry's "ingenuity." He promised the crowd that Congress would make regulations regarding the money supply "as will be just." *Because* Congress would have coercive authority over the states, he said, the states would not interfere—because they *could not.*[59]

Madison's puissant logic again overpowered practical politics. As it turned out, the states would not always comply with his confident prediction. In the "nullification" crisis of the early nineteenth century (more on this to come in Chapter 27), states, led by South Carolina, would openly defy federal laws on the grounds of their own continued independence. But, for the moment, Madison seemed to win the argument. He convinced the crowd so decisively that Mason was left pleading plaintively that he was "still convinced of the rectitude of his former opinion."[60]

As the day's discussion plodded through remaining clauses—such as the creation of the office of vice president—it seemed that Madison had finally gained the upper hand.

But not for long.

PERHAPS AIMED AT THE BROADER GOAL MADISON SUSPECTED OF DELAYING the proceedings, Henry, Mason, and Monroe—increasingly desperate—began trying to snarl the debate in minutiae.

From the floor, Madison openly confronted them on these tactics, in point-for-point declarations of dismay expressed from the vantage point of the high ground he had indisputably earned. He was "astonished," he said, by their dilatory tactics. He was "astonished" by Mason's expressed concern that the Electoral College's voting process might allow only "the five highest on the list" to elect the president, with the election therefore "entirely taken from the people."[61] He was "astonished" by Mason's worry that the president might make treaties with the support of only a few states. If such an "atrocious" thing were to happen, he explained, the president would be impeached and convicted.[62] Moreover, if a president were somehow to seduce the Senate into supporting his crimes, the faction who was *not* so seduced "would pronounce sentence against him." And so the factions would balance and check each other—even within government itself—and certainly without the anti-Federalists' antics.[63]

In the middle of an agonizing speech by Mason on state courts, Madison again lost his temper, snapping that Mason's suggestion that federal courts might seize power was ludicrous and entirely unfounded within the Constitution. Undaunted, the older man clung to his theme, asserting, "I think it will destroy the state governments, whatever may have been the intention." Madison brusquely interrupted to demand that Mason substantiate his "insinuation" that every member of the Constitutional Convention wanted to destroy the state governments. Mason retorted, "I shall never refuse to explain myself," defensively insisting that his was "at least the opinion of many gentlemen" at the convention in Philadelphia.

But then Madison forced Mason to admit that Madison himself, in private conversations in Philadelphia (back when the men were allies), had definitely stated that he would stand by state governments. Under the younger man's withering pressure, Mason admitted it was so. Madison, victorious, announced he was "satisfied." He had won, yet again.[64]

N EVERTHELESS, THAT EVENING, THE DAY'S STRESS AND STRAIN LINGERED with Madison. Henry had not made an effort on the floor this day, but Madison felt sure he was lying in wait for renewed assaults the next day. He wrote George Washington that he was "not yet restored & extremely feeble."[65] He grumbled in a letter to Rufus King that Richmond had become "extremely disagreeable for sundry reasons," complaining that the anti-Federalists' strategy was calculated to "weary out the patience of the House."[66]

His allies began panicking at reports of his anxiety and illness. Hamilton wrote, "[I] own I fear something from your indisposition."[67] Cyrus Griffin, also in New York, wrote, "We are all extremely uneasy at your Indisposition," particularly when "such important matters are under deliberation." And, he added—increasing the pressure on Madison—"We are not very sanguine" about ratification in Virginia.[68]

Writing a letter to his friend Tench Coxe that evening, Madison held the page with his left hand as he furiously scribbled with his right hand, his quill almost running off on the page's right side at the end of each line, while he hurriedly hyphenated almost every word. His words were messy, his penmanship garbled and blotchy, and he mistakenly crossed the t out of the word *not*. He was manifesting his distraction and misery in his very handwriting. He wrote Coxe that while each party hoped for victory, the division was agonizingly close, possibly "half a dozen for a majority on either side." "When the balance is so extremely nice, it is improper not to mingle doubts with our expectations. A few days will probably decide the matter." He signed the letter "in haste," and it must have been obvious to Coxe it was written that way.[69]

In the fog of battle, Madison had no choice but to push ahead.

RIDAY THE TWENTIETH OPENED WITH MADISON ON THE FLOOR LOOKING watchfully out at the friends and foes arrayed around him. On the day's topic—the congressional power to appoint federal judges—he saw a window to deliver a rousing new vision of republicanism that might, at long last, decisively capture a majority in the room.

He began by conceding that many gentlemen supposed the new Congress would do "every mischief they possibly can." While he admitted that he did not expect the "most exalted integrity and sublime virtue" from the men in the new federal government, he proudly declared his faith notwithstanding in "this great republican principle": that the people would have "virtue and intelligence to select men of virtue and wisdom." He then pulled back the veil on the hidden cynicism in Henry's "self-love" doctrine. "Is there no virtue among us?" he demanded. Without virtue, he said, "We are in a wretched situation." No "theoretical checks" could save the country. Without "virtue in the people," even liberty itself was a "chimerical idea."[70]

With the furnace of his conscience thus roaring, Madison called the assembly's attention to a summit rising above the Constitution. He believed that the anti-Federalists were not only weakening the new nation's politics and economics; they were embracing the nation's defeat. He reminded them that the Constitution required "confidence" from Americans—and proceeded to use that word four times in four sentences. Recurring to the theme of his long-ago essay on inflation, he said that the "circulation of confidence" was "better than the circulation of money." Confidence, he repeated, "produces the best effects in" justice. And it would even "raise the value of property."[71] Confidence *in the federal government and in its statesmen*, in other words, *was* the Constitution.

Henry—who had been silent for some time—jumped to his feet, clearly angered by Madison's soliloquy. He ponderously began recollecting the "painful sensations" and "mournful recollection" of his quest against the Constitution. Madison's faith in statesmen, he said, was the very problem. Of the notion that federal representatives would "mend every deed,"[72] and that the nation could "rely on the wisdom and virtue of our rulers,"[73] he snapped, "I can find no consolation in it."[74] On the prospect of trusting the legislature to appoint wise federal judges, he claimed that the Constitution recklessly left the judiciary as the sole bulwark against the "tyrannical execution of laws," predicting if the nation were to "lose our judiciary, we must sit down, and be oppressed,"[75] and adding, "If this will satisfy republican minds, there is an end of everything."[76]

It was coming down to Henry's fustian skepticism versus Madison's logical optimism. That evening, Madison appraised the situation. He thought he had defeated Henry that day. He wrote to Hamilton that the Federalists still probably had a majority of three or four votes. If "we can weather the storm," he wrote, "the danger" would be "pretty well over." Even so, he refused to indulge in sanguine thoughts. There was still "a very disagreeable uncertainty in the case," as well as a very real chance that he had miscalculated the numbers.[77] But he allowed himself—like a sweet, like an indulgence—a bit more latitude writing to his father that night. The Federalists, he wrote, had become "most confident of superiority."[78]

STRATEGIZING THAT SAME EVENING, THE ANTI-FEDERALISTS EVIDENTLY concluded that Madison's optimism represented a great vulnerability for the Federalists. The next day was a Saturday. After the customary ten a.m. start time, Madison's old friend Grayson (who had so cheerfully chided his friend from Philadelphia about his single status) rose. He declared that a conviction in the "excellency of human nature" was "invariably the argument" when the "concession of power has been in agitation."[79] In other words, you only rely on optimism when you want power yourself; the Federalists were duping the people, their politics as cynical as that which they claimed to abhor.

Madison allowed Randolph to lead the rebuttal. His friend stood and admitted that he would be the last man to hold that human nature was "just and absolutely honest." On the contrary, he said, just the *potential* that man was, in pure fact, capable of virtue, was enough to validate the new Constitution.[80] While formally about the judicial appointment power and about judges, the debate was ascending to the highest questions—whether, given the structural role the Constitution gave to good leaders and a just people, rights not explicitly assured would still be retained, and therefore whether the freedom of religion and other rights would be secure.[81] The security of the nation, the Federalists were saying, would stem from Americans collectively rising, in the generations ahead, to realize their ideals. The anti-Federalists were left to offer a pragmatic pessimism—thin gruel for the hungry majority in the room.

Among the many ideas for which Madison is most well known, none probably ranks higher than his assertion in Federalist Number 51, "If men were angels, no government would be necessary." Some have equated that argument with a wholesale political philosophy of pessimism, aligning Madison with the theologian and philosopher John Calvin, who sermonized, "If we were like angels, blameless and freely able to exercise perfect self-control, we would not need rules or regulations. Why, then, do we have so many laws and statutes? Because of man's wickedness, for he is constantly overflowing with evil; this is why a remedy is required."[82]

However, the events at the ratifying convention reveal a more powerful strand of teleological optimism in Madison's thinking—and in the country he helped design. If the government could not trust Americans to strengthen and improve the country through their own voluntary conduct, then the country's only solution for dangerous ideas would be jail cells—as Culpeper's had been for the Baptists in 1774. In other words, democratic freedom was not just a proposition involving the application of governmental power. It required a commitment—a faith—in the people to better themselves.

But Madison's optimism was neither self-executing nor secret. On the contrary, it was a primary political ground on which he sought support for ratifying the Constitution. Thus, this singular application of his Method for the roiling crowd in Richmond: He had to convince them to believe in themselves, and to trust one another, to advance the country's future.

When the short Saturday session closed, all things considered, Madison felt content. He must have contemplated with pleasure the much-needed day of rest ahead. But when Sunday came, he found he could not rest.

He confessed his remnant fears to Hamilton. Although their attacks on the judiciary "have apparently made less of an impression that was feared," the anti-Federalists would still try to kill the Constitution with their Trojan horse—a bill of rights as a prior condition of ratification. Counting votes as always, he still thought he might win by "3 or 4" or "possibly 5 or 6 votes." But "ordinary casualties," he said, could still kill the ratification.

In fact, the Virginia legislature was meeting in Richmond the next day, and it had a "considerable majority" of anti-Federalists. He warned that it was another event that "ought to check our confidence."[83]

24 Bugbears and Hobgoblins

THE NEXT DAY, MONDAY, HUNDREDS OF POLITICIANS AND HANGERS-ON flooded the city for the beginning of the legislative session. Many crowded into the New Academy to watch the debate that day. They knew the ratifying convention was close to concluding. Although many believed the Federalists had the upper hand, suspense still swirled around last-minute anti-Federalist stratagems. Henry, of course, had no intention to disappoint.

As the session got under way, the burly man rose to attack Madison's faith in men. Approaching the nerve center of Madison's Constitution—the country's reliance on statesmen like James Madison himself—he was more cutting than ever. The new country, Henry declared, would be an "empire of men and not of laws." "Their wisdom and integrity may preserve you," but "should they prove ambitious, and designing, may they not flourish and triumph upon the ruins of their country?" he darkly predicted.[1]

But the attack did not seem to be resonating with the audience, many of whom skeptically stared back at Henry with open disinterest in this line of reasoning—perhaps because Madison himself did not appear to be "ambitious, and designing" in the slightest.

Henry seemed to notice he was losing his grip on the assembly. But trapped on a path of his own making, he plunged ahead. In a last-gasp attempt to recapture the crowd, he inflated his rhetoric to the bursting point. The "whole history of human nature," Henry shouted, could not produce a government like the one envisioned in the new Constitution. "A constitution, sir, ought to be like a beacon held up to the public eye so as to be understood by every man." But the product of Philadelphia, he said, was as obfuscatory as the minds of the elitists who had contrived it. It "cannot be understood," he protested. It was "calculated to lay prostrate the states." He stormed that the Constitution took away the right to a trial by one's peers and that British debtors would even be "ruined by being dragged to the federal court!"[2]

General Adam Stephen, who had courageously commanded Virginia's Fourth battalion in battle at Portsmouth,[3] rose to try to stop Henry's stampede. Henry, he said angrily, was trying to "frighten us" by "his bugbears and hobgoblins."[4] Scandalized, the crowd whispered.

George Nicholas then stood to attack Henry's obstructionism. Henry had "objected to the whole" of the Constitution, he observed derisively. If he had his way, not a single part of the Constitution would pass. And then Nicholas moved in for the Federalists' kill.

His clear voice echoing around the whole hall, Nicholas boldly suggested that Henry himself had gotten rich off the confederacy—that his "large possessions" were "not easily to account for."[5] Those who live by the sword die by it. Just as Henry seemed to have wanted, the debate had crossed from a heated exchange about ideas to the raw ad hominem terrain that Madison had always so studiously avoided. But the move now was to Henry's decided disadvantage.

Henry quickly and loudly barked that he "hoped the honorable gentleman meant nothing personal."[6] He protested that such "personal insinuations" and attempts to "wound my private reputation" were "improper." On the particular charge of his personal wealth, he sputtered that he could "tell how I came by what I have" but that Nicholas had "no right to make that enquiry of me."

Despite his windy front, the brutal offensive seemed to puncture Henry's usually buoyant self-confidence. He seemed confused, on his heels, and pled, "If I have offended in private life, or wounded the feelings of any man, I did not intend it."

Nicholas smoothly accepted Henry's defense and his apology, stating that he "did not mean any resentment."[7] But the damage to Henry, it seemed, had been done.

MASON BURST OUT WITH A SHRILL LITANY AGAINST THE "DANGERS" that "must arise" from the "insecurity of our rights and privileges" in "several parts" of the Constitution. He ominously invoked "alarming consequences," adding that he had "dreaded popular resistance to its operation."[8] That was the equivalent of threatening a rebellion, and Henry Lee stood, infuriated, to assail opinions "so injurious to our country." He accused Mason, through the "dreadful picture" he had drawn, of having pursued the "very means to bring into action, the horrors which he deprecates." Mason—a "character so venerable and estimable," he said, was risking the "dreadful curse" of "impious scenes." The assembly, Lee announced, must collectively condemn fearmongering, through the firmness and fortitude that the country demanded.[9]

The eve of the epochal vote was nigh. Nerves were fraying, tempers boiling, pulses racing, and even Madison could not guess with any real certainty what would happen.

T HE FINAL ACT OF THE CONVENTION WAS NOW AT HAND. THE FORCES were arrayed, the personalities opposed, the decision imminent, and all the cards more or less played. But that did not stop the anti-Federalists from attempting to halt the Federalists' momentum through sheer muscle. Henry—who clearly now recognized his side was losing—stood. "I exhort gentlemen to think seriously, before they ratify this constitution," he said with a pleading note in his voice, to make a "feeble effort to get amendments after adoption."[10]

Alluding to Madison's proposal for amendments after ratification, Henry castigated Madison's attempt to "amuse the committee." "I know his candor," he said, gesturing at his adversary. Madison's idea, he declared with spite, was "dreadful." "Do you enter into a compact of government first, and afterwards settle the terms of the government?" That idea, he sneered, was "most abhorrent." It would "stab" the country's "repose."[11]

Henry then brusquely dismissed the idea that he would advocate for secession. He instead hurled that suspicion back onto his adversary's narrow shoulders. It was, Henry declared, *Madison* who threatened the union. "If gentlemen fear disunion," he charged, the "very thing they advocate will inevitably produce it."[12]

Randolph, looking hard at Henry, rose to defend his friend. The previous day, he said angrily, Henry had promised to "submit, and that there should be peace." Randolph exclaimed, "What a sad reverse today!" He then threw down the greatest gauntlet of the convention, demanding that Henry pledge, once and for all, not to lead a movement to secede from the union.

The room waited with unbearable tension. Would Henry submit to the government, or would he not?

Pushing himself to his feet, Henry at last gave Madison the answer he had been striving for during all the draining months before. He would not, he said, have anything to do with secession. He would, he said, remain in the New Academy and vote. And afterward, he sighed, "I will have no business here."[13]

The gathered men must have expelled a collective gasp of relief. But Henry still had not yielded on his amendment strategy, and Randolph pressed his advantage. Even prior amendments, he asserted, would "bid a long farewell to the union."[14] A majority of the assembly seemed to agree. But Madison knew the Federalists could not savor victory until he himself hauled the necessary votes into his quarter. He rose.

"MR. CHAIRMAN," HE BEGAN, "NOTHING HAS EXCITED MORE ADMIRATION in the world, than the manner in which free governments have been established in America." America was the "first instance from the creation of the world" where the world had observed free citizens "deliberating on a form of government." He again came back to statesmen. The young nation had elected leaders who "possessed their confidence, to determine union, and give effect to it."

He explained that the new Constitution had bottled the lightning of the Revolution, proving that Americans could "peaceably, freely and satisfactorily" create a general government. The accomplishment was extraordinary, considering the country's "diversity of opinions, and interests," and that the union was not "cemented or stimulated by any common danger."[15] Virginia, said Madison, could not rebuff the eight other states that had already ratified the Constitution. Such a rejection would be a "mortification." It would force the other states to think they had "done wrong."[16] Chaos would result if the "contrariety" in Virginia convention were to contaminate the nation as a whole.[17]

He pleaded with the audience to defer to the divine. He viewed the Constitution, he declared emotionally, as "one of the most fortunate events that ever happened in human nature." Nearing the end of his exhausting, enervating campaign, he was becoming intimately, intensely personal on the floor. "I cannot, without the most excruciating apprehensions, see a possibility of losing its blessings." He admitted that it gave him "infinite pain to reflect" that the Constitution could be "blasted by a rejection."[18] Henry's proposal for prior amendments was simply "pregnant with dreadful dangers," and he could "never consent" to it.[19]

Spent, he sat down. It was now left to Henry—revolutionary hero, first governor, Madison's former chief—to take one final stab at Madison's quiet and urgent eloquence.

Henry would not disappoint.

P ATRICK HENRY STOOD. ALL OF THE PROCEEDINGS HAD BEEN A PROLOGUE to this moment, and he seemed to savor the drama. He gestured at young Madison with distaste: "*He* tells you of important blessings which he imagines will result to us and mankind in general from the adoption of this system." He tremulously announced, "I see the awful immensity of the dangers with which it is pregnant." Looking skyward, he added, "I see it—I feel it—I see *beings* of a higher order anxious concerning our decision." Those "intelligent beings which inhabit the aetherial mansions" who determine the "final consummation of all human things," would determine the "consequence happiness or misery of mankind." Henry had evidently decided to spend the residue of his political capital all at once, relying exclusively on *his* authority.

Glaring at the collected men around him, he reminded them that this great question depended on "what we now decide." The men in the room were not only determining their own happiness. They were performing on the world stage, he informed them, with "all nations" eagerly watching. "We have it in our power," he shouted, "to secure the happiness of one half of the human race!"

At that moment, an enormous thunderstorm again descended with fury on the New Academy. Gusts of wind swirled around the building and, with the alarming sound of muskets firing, the doors slammed shut. Blinding lightning bolts flashed through the windows, revealing the anxiety on the delegates' faces in white flashes. Vast glassy sheets of rain raked the building. Thunder crashed so loudly that nobody could hear anyone speak, and the wooden structure actually rocked.[20] Years later, a Federalist recalled the scene describing "those terrific pictures which the imaginations of Dante and Milton have drawn of those angelic spirits that, shown of their celestial brightness, had met in council to war with the hosts of heaven." Henry stood before the men as if he was "rising on the wings of the tempest" and "seizing on the artillery of Heaven."[21] Eventually, the storm put the assembly in such a state of disorder that Henry could not even continue speaking.[22]

The session was quickly called to a close. When the sun reappeared and the house returned to order, the force of Henry's provocation seemed to have dissipated like the storm itself. It was as if the tempest was a purging of Henry's passions, not an apotheosis of them. In the squall's wake, Madison seemed to have taken control. He stood to respond to attacks on the practicability of amendments after ratification, and calmly explained that the Constitution would be able to resolve any amendment problems through its own mechanisms. He said that he himself would support amendments that were not dangerous. He was at once anticipating the campaign he would shortly lead for the Bill of Rights, while removing the sting of the most venomous remaining suspicions about their absence in the Constitution.[23] The assembly then adjourned.

25 The Revelations of Zachariah Johnson

WEDNESDAY, JUNE 25, WAS THE DAY OF THE FINAL VOTE. THE MEN filed edgily into the New Academy. Madison, wanting to kill off any lingering resistance, rose and declared that any prior amendments would produce "such unnecessary delays" and would be "so pregnant with such infinite dangers" that he could not "contemplate it without horror." He wanted the men to recognize and make a stark choice, and told them so: There was, he said, only "uncertainty and confusion" on the one hand, and "tranquility and certainty" on the other.[1]

The convention had strained the members, and it showed. The dignified and polite General Adam Stephen rose with obvious distress. Mournfully, he asked, "What has become of that genius" in Philadelphia? A military man groping for eloquence, he said, "Yonder she is in mournful attire, her hair dishevelled, distressed with grief and sorrow—supplicating our assistance, against gorgons, fiends and hydras, which are ready to devour her, and carry desolation throughout her country."[2]

After this mawkish soliloquy, the assembly was in a mood for simplicity, and in one of the great unheralded moments of American constitutional history, a man named Zachariah Johnson now chose to stand and speak his mind. He had rarely spoken before. Very little is known about Johnson, but his remarks would reveal both a personality and a philosophy that mirrored the hopeful, uncertain, and ultimately conscientious common citizen far better than Henry's forced attempt. "Mr. Chairman," Johnson began, "I am now called upon to decide the greatest of all questions—a question which may involve the felicity or misery of myself and posterity." He gathered himself. In an obvious reference to Patrick Henry, he condemned "the strained construction which has been put, by the gentlemen on the other side, on every word and syllable, in endeavouring to prove oppressions which can never possibly happen." Channeling the collective turn against Henry's florid rhetoric and torrid passions, Johnson announced, "My judgment is convinced of the safety and propriety of this system."[3]

He concluded, "It is my lot to be among the poor people. The most that I can claim, or flatter myself with, is to be of the middle rank. I wish no more, for I am contented. But I shall give my opinion unbiassed, and uninfluenced—without erudition or eloquence, but with firmness and candor. And in so doing, I will satisfy my conscience."

There could have been no clearer validation of Madison's Method. Johnson's plain reliance on his own reason and his conviction connected the delegates, as if by invisible heartstrings, to their undisputed guide. Johnson ended with an emotional reflection. "If this constitution be bad," he said, "it will bear equally as hard on me, as on any member of the society. It will bear hard on my children, who are as dear to me, as any man's children can be to him. Having their felicity and happiness at heart, the vote I shall give in its favor, can only be imputed to a conviction of its utility and propriety."[4]

Zachariah Johnson was an avatar for all those men Madison had actually persuaded through his Method, starting with the Constitutional Convention, going through the Federalist Papers campaign, and now ending with the ratification.

And with that heartfelt statement, by a plain man speaking plainly from his conscience, it was clear to the entire assembly that young James Madison would defeat the great Patrick Henry.

THAT DEVELOPMENT HAD BECOME CLEAR TO HENRY AS WELL. IN THE convention's closing minutes, he spoke with the equanimity of the peaceably vanquished. He begged the "pardon of this house" for having "taken up more time than came to my share." If he lost the vote, he said, "I shall have those painful sensations, which arise from a conviction of being overpowered in a good cause." And here everyone waited to see what would come next. Unequivocally, overflowing with emotion, he told them what they needed to hear: "Yet I will be a peaceable citizen!"

But he allowed an ominous note to linger. "I wish not to go to violence," but he would "wait," he promised, with "hopes that the spirit which predominated in the revolution, is not yet gone," and with the expectation of seeing the government "changed so as to be compatible with the safety, liberty and happiness of the people."[5]

Henry, it was clear, might lose the day. But he would not give up. On the contrary.

A VOTE ON PRIOR AMENDMENTS—ON THE CONDITIONAL RATIFICATION of the Constitution—was approved. The vote was called for "aye," and eighty hands rose, including Harrison, Mason, and Henry. The "no" vote was then called. Eighty-eight hands went up.

The effort to kill the Constitution through amendments was dead. Mason asked for the names to be recorded. They included Edmund Randolph, Edmund Pendleton, John Marshall, Zachariah Johnson—and James Madison.[6]

Now, at last, the real question: whether or not to ratify the Constitution. The vote was again called. For "aye," eighty-nine men raised their hands. Mason, defeated, again moved for the names to be recorded. They again included Randolph, Pendleton, Marshall, Johnson—and Madison. The Federalists had prevailed by a margin of eighty-nine to seventy-nine. Their margin was five votes—precisely one less than Madison, scarred and expert veteran of political warfare, had ever allowed himself to hope for.[7]

A FTER HIS GREAT VICTORY, MADISON OPTIMISTICALLY WROTE TO WASH-ington that there was "no doubt that acquiescence if not cordiality will be manifested by the unsuccessful party." But he noted that "*Two*" of the anti-Federalists had visibly betrayed their disappointment, "marked in their countenances."[8] One was almost certainly Patrick Henry.

Two days later, his suspicion growing, Madison wrote Hamilton that Henry's hatred of the Constitution would "produce every peaceable effort to disgrace & destroy it."[9] Henry was already "shaking off the yoke."[10] Yes, Henry would only oppose the Constitution in a "Constitutional" way, he predicted—he would not lead a violent secession to rip the nation apart. But he had already begun angling for a second convention that could replace and undermine the first. That, Madison growled, would be a "pestilent tendency."[11]

Still, he began to relax, at least a little. About a month later, resting in New York, where the Constitution was ratified by a majority of five states, he wrote to his father that he had been "perfectly free from my bilious symptoms."[12]

And no wonder. The nation was beginning to applaud him, as the people digested the majesty of what young Madison had accomplished. In August, a letter from Williamsburg arrived, praising his "immortal Honor." The sender wrote, "I confess I have always attributed to you the Glory of laying the Foundation of this great Fabric of government."[13] Word traveled back to Witherspoon as well. Madison soon found in his mail a large envelope. He opened it carefully to unfold a diploma from Princeton with an honorary degree of doctor of laws and a letter from Witherspoon praising Madison's "honour by his publick Conduct." His teacher proudly wrote, "It has been my peculiar Happiness to know perhaps more than any, your Usefullness in an important Station." Witherspoon concluded, "There was none to whom it gave more Satisfaction than to, Sir, your most obedient humble Servant."[14]

But while Madison was finally receiving some garlands for his labors from those who loved him, his enemies were feeling the insult of his triumph more keenly than ever. Back at Leatherwood, Patrick Henry was fulminating about the young upstart to anyone who would listen.

BY SEPTEMBER, RANDOLPH WROTE MADISON THAT HENRY "GROWS IN violence against the constitution," and that he had only accelerated his plot for another constitutional convention.[15] The outrageous prospect tormented the Federalists. George Washington wrote Madison that to be "shipwrecked in sight of the Port would be the severest of all possible aggravations to our misery."[16] But the worst part of Henry's vengeance, for Madison, would be personal.

26 Retaliation

THROUGH THE AUTUMN OF 1788, HENRY FULMINATED AGAINST THE Constitution on the floor of the General Assembly. One friend wrote Madison from Richmond that "the Cloven hoof begins to appear."[1] In October, Madison traveled to New York for a wistful event—the final quorum of the now-defunct Continental Congress. As Henry plotted for a second convention, the forces were again arraying themselves into young versus old. In Richard Bland Lee's words, the Federalists, all "young & inexperienced," formed "but a feeble band against" Henry.[2] Trying to recover his power after the Richmond debacle, Henry sought to become even more of a colossus, and for his Virginia to become a redoubt of anti-Federalist might. He specifically intended to hand pick a new General Assembly and congressional delegation that would serve as his personal political machine. By November, Washington wrote Madison of Henry, "He has only to say let this be Law—and it is Law."[3]

A crucial question facing Virginia was the election of two new senators to the new federal government. Were it not for Patrick Henry, James Madison was the natural choice. But Henry wanted to destroy him as a political force in Virginia. In November, he asserted on the floor of the General Assembly that Madison could not be trusted with the people's confidence "in the station of Senator." His election, insisted Henry, would lead to civil war between north and south, to "rivulets of blood throughout the land."[4]

Washington wanted Madison in the Senate, where he told his young friend his services would "be of more importance than in the other House."[5] Another friend wrote Madison from Richmond to argue that he must pursue a Senate seat, in part because it would prevent the dreadful scenario of two anti-Federalist Virginia senators.[6] Although some have suggested Madison did not want to be in the Senate,[7] this is unpersuasive. True, he wrote Randolph that of the Senate and House "I prefer the latter chiefly because if I can render any service there, it can only be to the public, and not even in imputation, to myself."[8] But by the point he wrote this letter, he knew Henry had decided to kill his chances for the Senate; and his words to Randolph suggest self-protective reassurance, rather than his actual preference. After all, his vision of statesmanship in America had dictated not only his own course toward the common good but also his contributions to the design of the US Senate itself.

His friends, sensing the danger of Henry's machinations, urgently demanded that Madison return home and actively campaign for the Senate. A surprise then came in the mail. "Your friends have resolved to nominate you," Randolph wrote, "being well assured, that their labours will not be in vain."[9] Now an official candidate, Madison would have to defeat either Richard Henry Lee or Grayson. But his aversion to political campaigns had only increased. In an eerie echo of the ratifying convention, he delayed and delayed his return home. He confessed to Randolph that he might prefer the House to the Senate because a House victory could be easily arranged by his Orange County friends, which would avoid the "spirit of electioneering which I despise."[10] But he viewed even a campaign for the House with distaste and avoided the inevitable for over a month. He wrote Randolph that even though his friends were pressing him to return to fight the "machinations agst. my election" to the House, "I am extremely disinclined."[11]

At last, he decided to return to Virginia to campaign for the Senate, and, if he lost there, for the House. But in a cruel blast from fortune, he was waylaid by horrendously painful hemorrhoids. In a candid letter to Eliza Trist, he blamed the attack on "my sedentary life." The piles were so painful that he could not even ride in a carriage. He was stuck in New York for over a week before leaving for Philadelphia.[12]

In the meantime, he knew he was losing valuable political ground in absentia. He fruitlessly complained to Washington that Virginia was the only state that had ratified the Constitution where the politics of the legislature—controlled by Henry—were "at variance with the sense of the people expressed by their representatives in Convention."[13]

Madison, who was then in Philadelphia, stopped en route by another bout of hemorrhoids, never made it back to Virginia in time to campaign for the Senate. The day after the vote, a shaken Edward Carrington wrote to tell Madison that he had lost; the vote was 98 for Lee, 86 for Grayson, and 77 for Madison. It was Madison's first electoral loss since April of 1777, when he was twenty-six years old and lost his reelection as a Virginia delegate. Carrington tried to reassure his friend. Because two-thirds of the assembly had opposed the new Constitution, he said, Madison's relatively large total must have meant they voted "from personal regard against their own principles."[14] That Carrington took such pains to solace his friend further suggests Madison deeply wanted to serve in the nation's highest body.

Henry Lee tried to reassure Madison, advising him to lose in the House, as well, so that he could go into George Washington's administration—"the place proper for you." But he also inadvertently admitted that the Senate loss was a "dreadful blow."[15]

But Henry wasn't finished yet.

H ENRY WANTED TO ANNIHILATE MADISON IN VIRGINIA'S POLITICS AS definitively as Madison had conquered him in Virginia's ratification. Madison's backup plan was to return to Orange to run for, and win, a seat in the House of Representatives, but Henry and his allies began machinating against him on this front as well. The anti-Federalists inserted a clause in a new elections bill requiring any candidate to have maintained residence in their district for twelve straight months prior to the election—which, Carrington informed Madison, was "inserted with a veiw to you."[16]

Madison's supporters were appalled at Virginia's "base ingratitude" toward him and the passions against him that Henry was shamelessly stoking. "They are all become abominable," Francis Corbin railed, "and gone astray."[17] Madison's countrymen urged him not to make the same mistake as with the Senate seat. "Come onwards to yr. Native Country," wrote George Lee Turberville, declaring that there was "not a man upon Earth so adequate as you are to her salvation."[18]

The second phase of Henry's plot against Madison then appeared. With a wide-ranging speech on the General Assembly floor, Henry convinced a large majority to support a scheme that created a new congressional district that reached into deeply conservative areas of the Shenandoah Valley and Southside, shoving Madison's own Orange County into a district of counties "most tainted with antifederalism."[19] Even worse, Henry had put Orange in the same House district with James Monroe's home county of Spotsylvania.[20] Monroe had already decided to run for the House, and so Henry's maneuver was especially cruel, for Madison still was tremendously fond of Monroe despite their spirited opposition at the ratifying convention. Now, one would win and the other lose. Madison's friend Turberville demanded that Madison "wing your way towards Virginia with all possible expedition."[21]

A third phase of the strategy then surfaced: to ruin Madison's venerated image. Henry and his allies began painting him as an arrogant enemy of any and all new rights for the average Virginian. It was being "busily circulated," Carrington warned Madison, that he had "declared in Convention that the Constitution required no alteration whatever."[22]

Madison had a hard time accepting the collision that loomed ahead, especially because it would require a new level of intensity in the campaigning he detested. As December arrived, he further put off his return to Virginia. The agonizing hemorrhoids made everything worse. He admitted to Washington that they had "not yet entirely gone off" and might detain him in Philadelphia "for some days longer."[23]

When he finally started off for Virginia, he must have winced with every bounce on the rutted road. Along the way, he wrote Jefferson that the trip was "very disagreeable" and grumbled that going to Virginia would serve no purpose other than to "satisfy the Opinions and intreaties of my friends."[24] But he was going. He had decided to fight, and he meant to win.

H E SUSPECTED THE ELECTION WOULD BE RAZOR THIN. A FRIEND reported that while both sides were sanguine of victory, "great exertions" were being made for Monroe—though the "assiduity & importunity" of his friends were stirring controversy.[25] Henry risked overshooting his mark, his brazen political intrigues tarnishing the image of the anti-Federalists. The "violence of the Antifederals," Madison heard from Turberville, had "begun to arrouse suspicion." Once the "Conduct of the *great high preist*" was known—Patrick Henry—his friend assured him the voters would side with Madison.[26] Another friend warned Madison not to trust anyone; his most "fervent open friends" could yet "prove the most Secret Enemys."[27]

IMAGE 26.1. JAMES MONROE. COURTESY OF THE LIBRARY OF CONGRESS.

Along the way home, Madison stopped at Mount Vernon for seven days around Christmas. Henry Lee and several others joined to celebrate a festive if nervy Christmas Eve with Washington, the conversation revolving around Washington's soon-to-come inaugural address as the nation's first president, as well as Madison's hopeful election to the House.[28] On December 27, Madison finally arrived back in Orange, with plans to begin campaigning in earnest after the New Year, for an election scheduled for February 2.

He had returned just in time. Monroe was already campaigning hard, writing "Myriads of Letters" to all the district's counties,[29] and delivering speeches to "explain the *Constitution* to the *People*," and to "erase any false impressions from their minds." David Jameson, Madison's dear old friend from their earliest days working as councilors to Patrick Henry as governor, urged Madison to immediately address the "anxiety to remove some false prejudices."[30] Alarmed, Madison began to campaign in earnest.

Travel over the wintry roads could take over a day—Louisa alone was twenty-five miles away from Orange—and it was challenging to talk with voters in large groups. Madison thus visited with freeholders at county court days in Louisa and Culpeper to strenuously confront the "erroneous reports propagated agst. me."[31] He wrote detailed letters to local leaders and ministers that were then published in the local newspapers.

In these forums, in keeping with his Method, he ignored his opponent and concentrated on his ideas instead. In a letter to a resident of Monroe's Spotsylvania County, quickly reprinted in the local paper, Madison expressed his "serious apprehensions" about a new constitutional convention. He proposed that with the Constitution safely embedded in the law, the better option was a bill of rights, which should include the popular rights of conscience, the press, and trial by jury.[32] In another letter to a constituent, he defended his old system of forced contributions and swiped at the anti-Federalists' alternative of periodic, and ad hoc, requisitions. "Reason tells us," he wrote fervently, that such a plan "can never succeed."[33]

One day in January, he found himself alongside his old friend Monroe in the cold open air of the flat hills of Culpeper. Under the portico of a Lutheran meeting-house, after services had concluded, the two men stood next to each other on the steps, trying to stay warm. They spoke to the crowd in turn, so urgently and at such length that one of Madison's ears became severely frostbitten. Years later, he would wryly describe the damaged ear as one of the "honorable scars he had borne from the battle-field."[34]

On February 2, 1789, on a day when ten inches of snow drifted onto the frozen grass, men across the rambling district trudged to their county offices to vote for Madison or Monroe. The ballots were slowly gathered and counted, in a process that took days to complete. The results were finally printed in the Fredericksburg *Virginia Herald* on February 12.

Madison won, by 1,308 to 972 votes—57 to 43 percent. Monroe naturally beat Madison soundly in three conservative counties—Amherst, Fluvanna, and his home of Spotsylvania. Madison, however, won a remarkably close total of 115 votes to Monroe's 189 in Monroe's own home county of Spotsylvania, where he had boldly ventured and campaigned hard. He earned a striking victory in Culpeper, where he beat Monroe 256 to 103, which was perhaps partly attributable to the friends he had made years earlier there when he courageously challenged the imprisonment of the Baptists. And he secured a stunningly large margin in his loyal home county of Orange, which gave him 216 votes to Monroe's paltry 9. His friends in Orange had come together in a great surge to reward their beloved hometown hero.

In the end, hundreds of Zachariah Johnsons had decided to entrust the young statesman with the government he had helped to create.

After their battle, Madison took great pride in sustaining his friendship with Monroe. A few weeks later, he wrote to Washington that the "distinction" he maintained between "political and personal views" had "saved our friendship from the smallest diminution."[35] Things were not going so well for Patrick Henry, however. In 1789, the same year that Madison defeated Monroe, Henry flirted with moving to North Carolina. The state had refused to sign the Constitution and he thought could provide fertile ground for his anti-Federalism. But a series of attacks then appeared against Henry in the *Virginia Independent Chronicle* by a writer using the pseudonym Decius, savaging Henry's "AMBITION, AVARICE, ENVY, HATRED, AND REVENGE," and he dropped the scheme.[36]

The next year, Henry declined a US Senate seat that opened up when William Grayson died. He explained bathetically that he had become "too old to fall into those awkward imitations which are now become fashionable" in Philadelphia.[37] By late 1791, with the Bill of Rights (which Madison helped pass and ratify in 1789) in place, Henry seemed at last to recognize that the country might not only survive, but thrive. Mellowed, he had a striking change of heart about his sworn foe.

Henry contacted Madison's brother Willey to ask whether he might be able to broker a reconciliation with Madison. Willey in turn wrote Madison, "I wish to suggest to you the renewal of a correspondence with Col Henry." He suggested that "such an intercourse" would "not only be extreemly acceptable"—but that "its decline" had been a "subject of regret" to Patrick Henry and his wife.[38]

At this, Madison rose and went to his files. He easily confirmed his suspicion—he had, in fact, received no letters from Henry in recent years. The notion that he had ever "declined" any correspondence was another of Henry's manipulations. Madison took out paper and quill to respond to his brother. "I do not well understand," he wrote, "what is meant by the words in your letter—'but *its decline* (that is of intercourse) is a subject of regret to Col. Henry and his lady.'" Employing the at times insular logic that could so frustrate his enemies, Madison elaborated that if a letter *had* been written "to which it is supposed an answer was *declined* (a construction extremely improbable)," he wanted Willey—and Henry—to know that "no such letter has been recd. and for that reason only, not answered."[39]

Whether there had been letters was, of course, not the point. Madison was cutting Henry off. Henry not only had opposed him, he had tried to destroy him, and not through argument, but through ad hominem attacks. Henry was not only an enemy of the nation or its people, he had become an enemy of reason itself. And for that, Madison would never forgive him.

27 Sedition

ADECADE AFTER THE RATIFICATION BATTLE IN RICHMOND, MADISON AND Henry clashed again. It was the summer of 1798, and the nation was again in domestic turmoil. In the wake of the French Revolution, the upheaval sweeping across Europe seemed likely to spread to the United States. In America, the federal government was suppressing a wave of new secessionist sentiment. Meanwhile, a "quasi war" was afoot between the American and French navies. Scuffles were breaking out on the streets over whether America should support the French. The *Aurora* began viciously attacking John Adams, now president. Adams responded with what Madison described as an "abominable and degrading" speech, proposing legislation that would become known as the Alien and Sedition Acts. The legislation allowed the president to imprison and deport aliens deemed "dangerous to the peace and safety" of the United States, and to suppress speech critical of the federal government with criminal sanctions. Adams's allies in Congress passed those bills into law in June and July of 1798.

For Madison's part, the Alien and Sedition Acts created an enduring puzzle. Madison, who had returned to Montpelier from eight years in the House of Representatives, publicly denounced Adams's "violent passions and heretical politics" and castigated him as a "perfect Quixote as a statesman."[1] He and Thomas Jefferson, Adams's vice president, collaborated on a rebuttal. In what became known as the Virginia Resolutions, Madison argued that the Alien and Sedition Acts violated the "general principles of free government, as well as the particular organization and positive provisions of the Federal Constitution." He asked other states to join Virginia in declaring that the acts aforesaid were unconstitutional.[2]

He had come a long way in the eighteen years since 1781, when a younger and more fiery man had proposed the amendment stating that if any state "shall refuse or neglect to abide by the determinations of the United States in

Congress assembled," Congress would be "fully authorized to employ the force of the United States as well by sea as by land to compel such State or States to fulfill their federal engagements." The new resolution plainly asserted that the states should resist an abusive federal government that had run off its constitutional rails.

P UBLIC LIFE IS A JOURNEY THROUGH PEAKS AND VALLEYS. ALL PUBLIC leaders find their apotheosis at one time or another; very few can sustain the same achievement, or image, or theme, from one month to the next, save year to year or over the course of decades. They are buffeted by history itself, becoming a hero one year, an antagonist the next. So it went with Patrick Henry, who exhausted his political philosophy with the revolution he was born to lead. Once the revolution was finished and the business of building a country was at hand, Henry found himself poorly suited to the new climate.

And so it also went for James Madison. His support in 1781 for an unqualified coercive power matched the level of control he thought necessary for the nascent country's existential crisis. Madison gradually moved beyond that radical proposal to embrace the contraption of sophisticated compromises that emerged from Philadelphia in the summer of 1788. In the decade after, the country further evolved. By 1798, the existential challenge became not the country's structure—its spine—but freedom itself—its heart.

Madison's Virginia Resolution was as intricately brocaded with compromises as the Constitution itself. In the case of a "deliberate, palpable, and dangerous exercise" of powers not granted by the compact of the Constitution, the Resolution declared, states who were "parties thereto" had the right, and were "duty bound," to "interpose for arresting the progress of the evil, and for maintaining within their respective limits, the authorities, rights and liberties appertaining to them."

The resolution expressed Virginia's "deep regret" (but not her rebellious or violent intent) about the federal government's "spirit" to enlarge its powers by "forced constructions of the constitutional charter which defines them." These actions could transform the republican system, Madison wrote, into an "absolute, or at best a mixed monarchy." The resolution declared that the Alien and Sedition Acts were unconstitutional and pledged Virginia's support for "the necessary and proper measures" in maintaining the "Authorities, Rights, and Liberties, referred to the States respectively, or to the people"—those given, of course, by the 10th Amendment of the very Constitution itself.

The tone of the Virginia Resolution was sadness rather than anger. It was a characteristically intricate expression of the precise authority by which Virginia could defy the Constitution and the Congress that had, save for the 10th Amendment, plainly superior authority over Virginia. Madison had carefully marshaled the Constitution to sanction a state's conditional rebellion against the federal government to which it belonged.

Meanwhile, Thomas Jefferson privately had drafted what became known as the Kentucky Resolution. The differences between the two friends' temperaments and political philosophies could not have been expressed more dramatically than in the two documents' very different declarations of defiance. The first sentence of the Kentucky Resolution was: "*Resolved,* That the several States composing, the United States of America, are not united on the principle of unlimited submission to their general government." The document moved on to declare that the Alien and Sedition Acts were "so palpably against the Constitution" that the Acts meant the federal government could now "proceed in the exercise over these States, of all powers whatsoever." And for that reason, Jefferson explained, the states, "recurring to their natural right in cases not made federal," were declaring the acts "void, and of no force," and promising that each state would each take "measures of its own" to prevent the Acts from taking force.

Madison's version was more nuanced—threatening rather than declaring rebellion. Appearing before the Virginia House of Delegates to present the resolution in December 1798, Madison employed his Method. One by one, he presented a volley of well-founded arguments, marshalling principle, history, and practice. On December 24, 1798, the Virginia General Assembly, again following the master of the Constitution, passed Madison's bill.

The next spring, Patrick Henry, exploring a return to Virginia's legislature, attacked the opponents of the Alien and Sedition Acts as unpatriotic. Jefferson, meanwhile, had begun running for president. As hot toward Henry as Madison was cold, he excoriated Henry, declaring that his "apostacy must be unaccountable to those who do not know all the recesses of his heart."[3]

Henry, fighting hard against Jefferson and Madison, had stomach cancer the whole time. He never actually stood for the legislative seat. On June 6,

1799, he died. He was sixty-three years old. In December of 1800, Thomas Jefferson defeated John Adams for president. He named James Madison his secretary of state. Once in office, they allowed the Alien and Sedition Acts to expire, the insidious attacks on their most treasured freedoms dying an appropriate death—withering on the legislative vine.

The fight not only with Patrick Henry, but with the forces he represented in American politics, seemed, for a time, to have concluded. But it was only an interregnum. Those fundamental tensions in America's constitutional system and in America herself would continue to bedevil Madison into his old age—as they do the country today.

Epilogue

AFTER HE HAD SERVED ONE TERM AS SECRETARY OF STATE, THEN TWO terms as president, and then retired to Montpelier, the top of Madison's head was almost completely bald. But instead of growing his hair long and combing it forward, as he had in his youth, he now allowed his hair to grow long in the back, to his collar. The effect, while startling at first, was not unpleasant. During a visit by Lafayette to Montpelier, one of the French general's entourage described Madison in old age as having a "well preserved frame" and a "youthful soul full of sensibility." Although decades of "reflection and application" had etched his spare face with a certain "aspect of severity," he now seemed much less high-strung than in his youth. The "impressions of his heart" were now "rapidly depicted in his features," the visitor recalled, and his conversation lightly leaped, animated by a "gentle gaiety."[1] Another visitor to Montpelier in those years described Madison as "very hale and hearty," and remarked that his face was "full of good humour."[2]

All this probably had much to do with his wife. In a joke of history, when Madison at long last married, it was to a woman who had spent her childhood living in Patrick Henry's former home; Dolley Payne's father, John Payne, bought the large clapboard house, called Scotchtown, in the 1760s. Payne, a Quaker, emancipated his slaves in 1783, after the end of the Revolutionary War. He moved his family to Philadelphia, where he opened up a starch business. When his daughter Dolley turned twenty-one, she married a kind, promising young man named John Todd, soon became pregnant, and had a son. The infant quickly and tragically died. Recovering, Dolley and John had two more children. Yellow fever then attacked the city. John spent two months caring for the ill in a plague center, hundreds perishing each day. John's father died; ten days later, his mother. And then, three days later, it was him, but only after he cried about Dolley, "I must see her once more." Dolley

IMAGE E.1. *DOLLEY MADISON*. COURTESY OF THE
MONTPELIER FOUNDATION, JAMES MADISON'S MONTPELIER.

herself came close to death. One of her infant sons then died, leaving her with just her son, Payne.

She overcame all this grief through the natural buoyancy of her spirit. By the time James Madison met her, she was a congenitally cheerful, bustling Southern belle, with natural wit and the gravity of the bereaved. She was twenty-six years old and a widow, a single mother in the capital city.

Madison, serving in Congress, lived one block north of the State House, she two blocks east of it, and he frequently saw her on the street and at social functions—and she him. At forty-three, he was ready for real love, for a true partner.

His friend Aaron Burr knew Dolley well. In a feat of directness he could not have mustered in his youth, Madison asked Burr to make an introduction. Burr—who would later go on to kill Alexander Hamilton in a duel—told Dolley about the request. She quickly accepted and excitedly wrote a friend that "the great little Madison has asked to be brought to see me this evening."[3]

Madison was enchanted by her. He resolved to pursue her. That summer, they both returned to Virginia. He proposed to her by letter. She wrote back to accept. He responded, rejoicing in her "precious favor," admitting, "I cannot express, but hope you will conceive the joy it gave me." Madison married Dolley on September 15, 1794. He did not tell his parents until three weeks had passed—a remarkable and long-delayed act of independence.[4]

His years with Dolley were generally deeply contented. The couple never had children. Madison, of course, never expressed his feelings about this matter. We can only speculate about whether impotence or deeper intimate problems might have been to blame. They also had great difficulty managing Dolley's wayward, temperamental son, Payne. But, as life partners, they achieved a wonderful balance. Her warmth played off his restraint, her gaiety meshed with his discipline, well into old age. And they seemed, quite simply, to get a kick out of each other.

Dolley never grew to love Orange County, however. She adored, as her husband had in his youth, the cosmopolitan energy of the cities. When Madison was appointed secretary of state by Jefferson, the couple moved to Washington, and Dolley effervescently transformed the town into a city of light and drama. After Madison was elected president in 1808, Dolley invented the role of First Lady, cheerfully convening weekly parties. She dressed in colorful fabrics and exotic accessories, such as turbans, serving delicacies and generally spicing up a dry town, just as she did her husband.

During the War of 1812, as the brutal British soldiers methodically approached the White House, Dolley instructed her servants to salvage valuable documents and silver. She rolled up herself Gilbert Stuart's full-length portrait of George Washington to save it from their torches. She then fled with it—a quick-minded decision that endeared her to generations of Americans.

The couple spent the years after his presidency living in Orange County. The sitting room where they received guests was draped in red silk, with lush curtains framing the windows in the French style. A portrait of Thomas Jefferson—sternly facing left—hung on the wall. That portrait was to the left of another painting of Mary Magdalene, the Bible's iconic prostitute. The orientation permanently put the famously carnal Jefferson in the inauthentic position of turning away from lust, probably amusing Madison and Dolley daily. Near the fireplace hung a large painting, *Pan, Youths, and Nymphs*, featuring a grinning satyr, a bare-breasted woman, and flirting young people. Brought back by Payne Todd after attending the Treaty of Ghent, it dominated the room.[5]

Contrasted with the tightly wound, emotionally brittle character of Madison's youth, the room reflected the arc of his personal life. He had softened and warmed, with Dolley at his side. Yet the aging man never forgot the heartbreak of Kitty Floyd. When Jefferson passed away in 1826, the letters Madison wrote to him were returned to Madison. When the long-married man read the letters about Kitty from almost five decades before, he took out a quill and scratched through the ciphered sections with heavy dark lines. He then wrote, along the side of the page, one word: "undecipherable."

This was a lie to himself, and to history. It was as if he was trying to obliterate the painful memories just as he had vanquished obnoxious ideas with his Method. But he of course could not vanquish his own passions by pretending they did not exist.

IN RETIREMENT AT MONTPELIER, MADISON DELIGHTED IN SITTING WITH DOLley and regaling visitors with stories about the men now known as America's "Founding Fathers," whether Washington, Jefferson, or Patrick Henry. Especially with visitors he and Dolley trusted, his droll sense of humor could break up a room, his guests laughing "very heartily." In the words of another visitor, he was "an entertaining, interesting, and communicative personage." But when strangers entered the room, Madison's shyness and reserve returned, and he would become "mute, cold, and repulsive." Dolley, on the other hand, would remain as outgoing as ever.[6]

In 1821, when he was seventy, Madison had the luxury of overseeing a political system that seemed to have fulfilled his designs as a much younger man. He wrote his old friend Lafayette that the United States was, "on the whole, doing well, and giving an example of a free system." He proudly described the "safety-valves" that gave "vent to overheated passions," as part of the broader scheme that "carries within itself a relief against the infirmities from which the best of human Institutions can not be exempt."[7]

But his contented enjoyment about his accomplishments would not last.

IMAGE E.2. MONTPELIER, BY PRUD'HOMME AFTER J. G. CHAPMAN. COURTESY OF
THE MONTPELIER FOUNDATION, JAMES MADISON'S MONTPELIER.

THE COUNTRY WAS HEAVING AROUND MADISON, AS IF THROUGH PLATE
tectonic shifts. When Andrew Jackson was elected president, the
event sent tremors all the way to Richmond. The masses loved him for his
wild-haired, Indian-fighting persona. But Jackson—a practicing lawyer,
student of history, and accomplished military tactician—was not the ple-
beian his gruff demeanor suggested. On March 4, 1829, after his inauguration, Jackson looked out with amazement on the crowd entering the White
House. Drunken commoners were flooding in, carousing inside the building.
Rough-looking men broke windows and stamped their boots on the polished
wood tabletops. Jackson escaped by a side window.

A hundred miles south in Richmond, the election unleashed more unpredictable events. The prior year, Virginians had voted for a constitutional convention to decide whether citizens other than property-holders should be able
to vote—a new Jackson-era notion that was catching on in states around the
country. One hundred delegates planned to traveled to Richmond to develop

a new constitution for the Old Dominion. At the time, Madison was suffering from yet another bout of likely anxiety-driven illness. But after much pleading from the organizers, the fourth president of the United States, seventy-eight years old, agreed to serve as the 101st delegate from Orange County.

In October, he took to the jostling road from Orange County to Richmond. He must have watched the dusty red Virginia clay pass under the carriage's wheels with a mixture of anticipation and dread. Nobody knew what would happen next in the age of Andrew Jackson: whether the country would rampage into chaos (as at the now-infamous inauguration), or whether it would settle into a gentler groove, tamed by its own constitutional culture. For his part, Madison was holding fast to the principle that had guided him for a half-century: Democracy should constantly expand, events and public opinion left to arrange themselves around that unbending pillar. But he was powerfully aware that many not only did not share his opinion, but they violently opposed it.

As Madison pulled into Richmond, few suspected that the convention's principal agitator in favor of progressive notions of national justice would be, yet again, the little old man from Orange County.

T HE FORMER PRESIDENT ENTERED THE CHAMBER IN SMALL STEPS, HOLDing his body carefully. He was dressed in a formal and refined black, with silk dress socks pulled up over his thin legs. His skin had a dried yet warm appearance, and he looked younger than his age. He warmly greeted his friends, with a quiet smile and a direct glance from his gray eyes.

As the convention began, the delegates witnessed a touching scene as Madison helped walk the ailing James Monroe to his seat. After introducing Monroe, Madison suggested to the assembled men that they select Monroe president of the convention. They of course instantly agreed.

The convention proceeded for several weeks, with Madison generally listening quietly and speaking only on procedural matters. The cold descended on Richmond, his aged joints registering the familiar chill of winter. On December 1, when discussion turned to the question of how to count populations for the House of Delegates and the State Senate, Madison suddenly made it be known that he wanted to speak.

The delegates knew they were in the presence of history, and they responded accordingly.

The members "rushed from their seats," according to the stenographer, and "crowded around him." Madison spoke softly and precisely. Dozens of other members nearby strained to hear him, craning over the shoulders and heads of others.

He was about to try to convince Virginia to transcend, again, the lowest common denominator, to persuade the men around him to become a new generation of Zachariah Johnsons.

"Having been, for a very long period, withdrawn from any participation in proceedings of deliberative bodies," Madison began, he would only offer a few observations on the topic of property. He instantly had their attention, for the vast majority of the men in the room, like Madison, enjoyed the life of Virginia's elite. The "essence of Government is power," he said, and "power, lodged as it must be in human hands," would always "be liable to abuse." He said that he knew many of them were well intentioned. In their voting and their legislation on matters of social policy, they would consult the "purity and generosity" of their own mind and recur to the "dictates of the monitor within"—their own consciences.

But Madison told them that this faith was nonsense. Their own good intentions would offer only the flimsiest restraints against their own self-interest. The ugly fact, he declared, was that man was a "selfish, as well as a social being." The "favorable attributes of the human character" were valuable as "auxiliaries," but could not substitute for the "coercive provisions belonging to Government and Law." In other words, the hundred men in the auditorium *could not trust themselves* to avoid oppressing their lesser. Like Ulysses, they must lash themselves to the mast to avoid the sirens of injustice.

Madison's evolution on the fundamental question of whether to trust humanity or not to self-improve the human condition was striking. The optimism of his youth had become the pessimism of his old age; what was once a butterfly was now a moth. In this, he was naturally responding to the country itself, which was preparing to tear apart on precisely the issues surfacing in Richmond—race, class, and the rights of states vis-à-vis the federal government.

He had worked up to the great topic of slavery and the question of whether Virginia should count slaves when determining the population basis for legislative districts. The question mattered most for western and eastern Virginia, the state's harshly divided regions. They already had profound cultural differences. The east, home to the College of William and Mary, was frequented by visitors from the north and considered itself sophisticated. The west was proudly conservative, stubbornly fastened to its cultural and religious traditions. They differed in population, as well. The east included the cities of Tidewater Virginia, which, due to their greater concentration of merchants and shipping interests, had more dense populations and greater concentrations of slaves. The west, on the other hand, was agrarian, dominated by planters and their plantations, and much more sparsely populated—and would receive fewer delegates under a population scheme that counted African Americans.

The question of whether to include blacks in the districting scheme could tip the balance of power between the two regions. The west would have fifty-three delegates if the "white basis"—which ignored slaves—was used, but it would lose thirteen of its representatives—a quarter of its political power— if slaves were counted. It was expected that the west would use its existing dominance to maintain its political control.

And so Madison urged the western delegates, who were his own people, to include blacks at least in their count for the House of Delegates. He pressed them to take this path because conscience dictated it. In his fine voice, he employed again his Method. "It is due to justice; due to humanity; due to truth; to the sympathies of our nature," he declared, and "to our character as a people, that they should be considered, as much as possible, in the light of human beings, and not as mere property." Virginia's enslaved people, he argued, *must* be recognized as at least *partly* human. For that reason, he said, they were "acted upon by our laws," and therefore "have an interest in our laws."

The men from the west looked at each other with open skepticism, some flashing with anger, but the old man was undaunted. He accused the advocates of the white basis of plain racism. If the slaves were *white*, he argued— like the serfs of Europe or the Vikings in England—his brethren would have no problem counting them. He marshaled every possible argument. The slaves were not "equally diffused through the state," and for that reason, the difference around the state "resembles that between the slave-holding and non-slave-holding States." In that way, he said, the east and the west of Virginia resembled the North and the South of the nation itself, which had overcome their differences in Philadelphia in 1787. If Virginia could not similarly rise above self-interest, how could the nation? Even *Georgia* was counting slaves. Virginia, he pleaded, must rise to the moment; Virginia must lead.

He ventured a final argument. When Virginians had ratified the Constitution in 1788, it was "in the eyes of the world, a wonder," the "harmonious establishment of a common Government," and a "miracle." "I have now," he proclaimed emotionally, "more than a hope—a consoling confidence" that the men around him could "at last find, that our labours have not been in vain."[8]

To HIS ALLIES, MADISON'S CONFIDENT, URGENT SPEECH SOUNDED LIKE scripture. One ally told the crowd that his speech "*must* and *will* carry conviction to the mind of every *cool-reflecting* man."[9] But there was still the plainly political fact that his supporters comprised only a minority of the assembly. And instead of a happy coalescence of opinion, the old man's stubborn challenge sparked a conflagration.

Temperatures quickly rose to an almost violent level as the abject political reality of his proposal—the loss of political power by the west—sank in. One western delegate rose to attack an easterner. Pointing at his foe, the westerner declared that "if he brings us to Bannockburn," alluding to the famously bloody Scottish battle for independence, he would find that "Old Virginia" was "as little disposed to submit to injustice as New Virginia." The battle between east and west Virginia had somehow transformed into one between "Old" and "New" Virginia. Could the "gentleman suppose," the westerner taunted, that they were "prepared to submit to any yoke, that they propose to fasten upon us?"[10]

Delegates lobbed more bombs at Madison's proposal. One westerner attacked his compromise—to apply the federal basis only in the House of Delegates—for hypocrisy, even though the principle of equality "applied equally to both" houses of the legislature.[11]

His proposal was ultimately defeated. While that may not have been a surprise to anyone taking the temperature of the assembly, the outcome bitterly disappointed the old man. But he could take grim satisfaction from the obvious fact that his turn to pessimism had been justified. In the months to come, as he reckoned with his great state's unwillingness—or inability—to rise above its self-interest for the sake of the common good, he grew only more upset. After he returned home, he took to bed. He remained there for almost a year, racked by wave upon wave of his old fits of anxiety.[12] Not only Richmond was to blame; he despaired about the nation itself.

Not only Virginia was in upheaval. America herself was undergoing its greatest test yet of the federalist compromise he had helped to design. That would, in turn, throw open the breach for secession, the Civil War, and the nation's violent reconsolidation.

It had begun the prior year, with the "nullification" creed Vice President John Calhoun had introduced in 1828 to enable South Carolina to challenge new federal tariff legislation. Calhoun argued that each state, though part of a voluntary compact, had always retained its fundamental sovereignty. South Carolina could therefore void, at will, any federal law she decided violated that compact.

Although Madison had supported Virginia's right to repudiate the Alien and Sedition Acts, he saw Calhoun's action in a far different light and with real alarm. The Virginia Resolution was about John Adams's unconstitutional abrogation of the freedom of speech; nullification laid bare the fundamentally unresolved tension in the Constitution about coercion itself regarding the whole range of self-interested pursuits and passions of the states.[13]

The nullification crisis became a crisis for Madison himself. As debate on nullification raged in Congress, he remonstrated with friends that the Constitution was *not* just a compact between separately acting states. In 1833— four years after the Virginia constitutional convention—he argued that the Constitution was a "mixed form" that forged together "one people, nation, or sovereignty for certain purposes."[14] Anyone who thought the sovereign federal power should be divided—that the *nexus imperii* should be unraveled— did not grasp the divine magic of what had happened at the Constitutional Convention.

Madison was sending a blizzard of letters to friends, trying to repudiate the nullification doctrine while rationalizing the Virginia Resolution. In

1834, he wrote Edward Coles that there was nothing "more dangerous" to the country than nullification, "either in its original shape, or in the disguises it assumes." Nullification, he declared, would put "powder under the Constitution and Union, and a match in the hand of every party to blow them up at pleasure." Nullification was a shape-shifting beast, a "figure which the anarchical principle now makes." The southern states were particularly susceptible to the "contagion."[15]

He raged, striving to employ his Method in a final gasp for country. In a 9,500-word essay he wrote in December 1834—he was then eighty-three years old—Madison grappled with the question of whether there was any valid constitutional basis at all for states to nullify federal acts. When could a state defy the very qualified coercion young Madison had fought so strenuously to build into the Constitution? *His* support of nullification, he said, had been valid because the Alien and Sedition Acts were plainly unconstitutional, and because Virginia, in opposing them, had explained precisely that basis, in good faith and with specifics. In attempting to nullify federal tariffs, South Carolina, on the other hand, was just as plainly arguing from self-interest.

What had been clear to him from the beginning was even more crucial now. There *was* such a thing as statesmanship. It *was* possible to decide and differentiate between the general and the special interest. Both "de jure & de facto," he explained, the nation's "true character" would be sustained by an "appeal to the Law & the testimony of the fundamental charter." The nation must again choose between a "government purely consolidated" and an "association of governments purely federal."[16] He railed against South Carolina for the consequences of its rash position. In some states, there would be war with a foreign power, while in others, there would be "peace and commerce."

Chaos would result. He pleaded for faith in his original design. A *single* state's "remedial right" to protect the Constitution might be "deficient," he conceded, but there would always be an "ultimate and adequate remedy" in the "rights of the *parties* to the Constitution." That is, any complaining state could always gather together others for a new compact, forging a new majority faction. In the hands of such a powerful group, he declared, the Constitution would be "at all times but clay in the hands of the potter." The Constitution could always—and must always—seek to remedy itself, rather than fall prey to dissenting factions.

Through all this turmoil, the elderly man returned to his own private lode-star—the conscience that had guided him, and the country, during his youth.

I N THE SPRING OF 1831, WHEN HE WAS EIGHTY YEARS OLD AND AILING, MAD-ison discovered a letter in his mail from James Kirke Paulding. Paulding was an author and popular satirist who had earned a loyal following. He later served as secretary of the navy under President Martin Van Buren. He informed Madison that he was writing a series of biographies of America's Founding Fathers.[17] He asked the former president whether he would consider writing a "sketch of the principal incidents of [his] life."

Madison thought it over. As a younger man, he would never have enter-tained Paulding's request. But Madison respected Paulding. And for years, he *had* been taking sporadic autobiographical notes, picking them up and put-ting them down again, never confident of his project. Now that he was eighty, perhaps the time had come for a final stab at the project.

He picked up a quill to write back to Paulding. He admitted that he was "flattered" by the proposal. Yet, he confided, he felt some "awkwardness" from the enterprise. He admitted that years ago he had begun an "abortive biography," but said "whether I shall be able to give it any amplification, is too uncertain to admit of a promise."[18]

N INE MONTHS LATER, PAULDING OPENED HIS MAIL TO FIND A FIFTEEN-page manuscript from the former president, accompanied by a letter from Madison apologizing that while his intention was to have "enlarged some parts" of the essay, and to have "revised and probably blotted out others," he simply had been too ill to do so. Indeed, Madison complained, the "crippled state of my health" had made him "shun the task." Madison had feared he would die too soon even to send the essay off to Paulding; the "uncertainty of the future," he wrote, had led him to "commit the paper, crude as it is, to your friendly discretion."[19]

When Paulding read the document, he must have found it surpassingly strange. Madison wrote the "autobiography" in the third person. He took obvious pains to remove any emotional drama from the events he recorded, as if an anonymous writer were dispassionately describing a minor historical figure. He also systematically avoided the natural highlights of his public life to concentrate on personal minutiae instead. Whenever the narrative got most interesting—when he approached, for instance, the as ever controversial War of 1812—Madison just referred the reader to his letters.

There was one major exception.

When he described his life as a young man—especially the years and events leading up to 1788, when, at thirty-seven years old, he had confronted and defeated the mighty Patrick Henry in Richmond—the old man's writing came alive, as he narrated his passions, pains, hopes, failures, and fears with disarming candor.

He recalled studying with Donald Robertson ("a man of extensive learning, and a distinguished Teacher"), and causing himself "infirm health" by compressing two years of study into one, with his long-dead friend Joseph Ross by his side.

He fondly remembered his mentor and ally John Witherspoon, including an anecdote about being summoned to speak French to a visitor to Princeton in Witherspoon's absence (a scene "as awkward as possible").

He proudly evoked his early fights for the liberties, whether for the Baptists in Culpeper ("being under very early and strong impressions in favour of Liberty both Civil and Religious") and about the Virginia Convention of 1776, where he proudly described successfully arguing that the freedom of conscience should be a *natural and absolute* right."

He remembered collapsing on the battlefield during the Orange County militia exercises, blaming "the unsettled state of his health" and the "discourageing feebleness of his constitution."

He told the story of losing his only election by challenging the custom of providing liquor to voters and being blamed for "pride or parsimony."

He recalled his struggle of studying the law in the forenoon after returning home from Congress.

He recollected his "attention and researches to the sources ancient & modern" before the Constitutional Convention—but he almost totally ignored the convention itself.

He explained the story of the Federalist Papers, which he said were "meant for the important and doubtful state of new York."

He remembered the ratifying convention in Richmond, which he said he attended when he was not "absent from confinement from bilious fever."

He barely mentioned passing the Bill of Rights into law, or serving for eight years in the new Congress between 1789 and 1797.

Even more strangely, out of the document's fifteen pages, Madison gave only two sentences to his presidency. After passing quickly through the highlights of his time as secretary of state, he raced through his "career in the Executive Magistracy"—not even mentioning the word *president*—largely referring his reader to his letters and speeches.

But he did describe returning to Montpelier, because he "had become wearied with public life, and longed for a return to a state in which he could indulge his relish for the intellectual pleasures of the closet, and the pursuits of rural life."

He described having "entered the married state, with a partner who favoured these views, and added every happiness to his life which female merit could impart."

He recounted how, after "the close of his public life," he had "devoted himself to his farm & his books."

Reading through all of this, Paulding must have found it even more odd that, toward the end, Madison decided to spend about 10 percent of his autobiography's total words on the Richmond Convention of 1829. He told the story of how he was "prevailed upon, notwithstanding his age & very feeble health, being but convalescent from a spell of sickness," to serve there. He recalled with evident pain his failure to win his battles against using the white basis for the House of Delegates, as well as a separate effort to allow the people rather than the legislature to elect the governor. Ever cautious about giving free rein to the passions, he confessed that he was concerned about universal suffrage, but said he favored extending political rights nevertheless "so far as to secure" the "majority of people on the side of people: a "Government resting on a minority is an aristocracy not a Republic."[20]

That political philosophy began in his youth. In the twilight of his life, he still saw his sunrise as his signal era—as, indeed, it was.

O N JUNE 28, 1836, THE EIGHTY-FIVE-YEAR-OLD WAS HAVING BREAKFAST with his favorite niece, Nelly, who was named after his mother. He seemed at ease and comfortable, but pain suddenly twisted his face. Nelly asked him whether anything was wrong. Seeming to recover quickly, he

IMAGE E.3. JAMES MADISON BEFORE HIS DEATH IN 1836.
COURTESY OF THE MONTPELIER FOUNDATION, JAMES MADISON'S MONTPELIER.

responded with a customary joke: "Nothing more than a change of mind, my dear." But his head fell to his chest, he stopped breathing, and he died.[21]

Just the day before, he had composed a letter to an old friend authoring a book on Jefferson dedicated to Madison. Madison said that his "ardent zeal" had always been in "promoting such a reconstruction of our political system as would provide for the permanent liberty and happiness of the United States." He recalled the "efforts and anxieties" his effort had demanded, but thought they had been "well rewarded" by their "many good fruits"—and that "no one has been a more rejoicing witness than myself."[22] Even though he was still fighting and wrestling with the nation's current trauma and tensions, Madison was at peace with his own role within it.

Madison died on the sixtieth anniversary of the adoption of the Virginia Constitution. The news of his death raced across the country, triggering a collective exhalation of grief, of affection, of national memory of the country's earliest days. He had been the last of the Founding Fathers still alive. Around the country, bells tolled, artilleries fired, and funeral processions marched. In the words of a contemporary biographer, it was at once a celebration and a mourning "such as in the Old World only commemorate the obsequies of kings."[23]

Conclusion

T HIS BOOK HAS MOSTLY BEEN ABOUT JAMES MADISON'S YOUNGER YEARS, the period of his life that ended soon after the Constitution was ratified in Virginia, and the meaning of those years for a more vital understanding of statesmanship and the role for leaders in a healthy and vibrant democracy.

The *young* James Madison had a singular impact on the country's future and—this is not overstating matters—human history. Madison's narrow but irrefutable defeat of Patrick Henry at the convention was the result of the near-genetic force of two entwined strands: his political philosophy and his personal character. As Stanford's Jack Rakove has observed, "In the end, among a generation of leaders well steeped in the literature of political theory, [Madison's] greatest contributions to the founding of the republic flowed from the force of his intellect."[1]

His ideas included intricate checks and balances; enmeshed factions; the collective embrace of a great but uncertain future; bending the states to the federal government's will; granting the federal government only enumerated powers; and grounding the entire enterprise on both optimism about humanity's potential and skepticism about our innate moral goodness. Together, it was a seductive, and all-encompassing, philosophy of political life.

His character was forceful without declaring it; controlling in subtle (and often infuriating) ways; dauntingly logical and precise against his opponents; sweepingly well-prepared with facts, history, and seriatim arguments; good-humored and self-deprecating; bold; endearing to those he trusted and his allies; and, overall, surprisingly charismatic.

Those two strands—his philosophy and his character—married in his quest for *governance*. He believed the passions possessed tremendous destructive force. His political mission became mastering them by channeling them—not denying their existence or cutting them off.

And so young Madison helped transform raw democracy into something subtle and exquisitely cantilevered, giving human form to philosophical ideas. Bernard Bailyn, the celebrated Harvard colonial historian, has observed that the hundreds of American revolutionary pamphlets, with their heavy emphasis on new ideas, were the "distinctive literature of the Revolution."[2] The historian Gordon Wood notes that Bailyn illuminates the sheer "importance of ideas in bringing on the Revolution." The "idealist" explanation helps explain Americans' profound concern—then and now—with tyranny and freedom and government itself.[3] Ideas, in the founding period, could not be translated into action—could not change political reality so profoundly—without a human being like Madison to research, reflect on, improve, innovate, and proselytize for them.

In young Madison's case especially, this was the essence of his statesmanship. His statesmanship inhered in his restless, impatient drive to push a nation to achieve the highest version of itself. Statesmanship was young Madison's lodestar. It lit his path through the darkest of nights and over the rockiest of roads. And it gave him the inspiration to defeat the most formidable of obstacles, including the rebellion of his own body against the mission his mind had foisted on him, as well as Virginia's most formidable political figure, Patrick Henry.

This is the story of young James Madison, statesman. He not only changed his country, but his example can change us today. The United States and all modern democracies face profound internal tensions not dissimilar to those of young Madison's young country. His enemies were at once ruthless and unashamed about their pursuit of the lowest common denominator. They brazenly pursued self-interest rather than the common good. And they reacted with hostility to the attempts to create a vigorous, effective, and united nation-state.

On all of these frontiers, young Madison employed his Method. He hurled himself into the gears of power. He did so not without fear (because he was human), but he *overcame* that fear. What was weakest in him became the fuel for his fight. He exhausted his whole being for the sake of the republic he loved.

Perhaps most remarkably, he accomplished all these things without seeking to become the story. Young Madison almost always sought to elide himself as the protagonist. This was in the days before Freud had invented the ego;

yet had the ego been invented, he would have ignored the topic. While all of his founding brethren were busy polishing their legacies for history, Madison simply seemed uninterested. The ideas were the thing, and the accomplishments were, for him, the end of the story.

That he has been punished for his active disinterest in his fame seems at once unfair to America's history and damaging to any prospect for resuscitating statesmanship. Madison's presidency is unpopular not only because of the controversial War of 1812 and his role in it, which will probably continue to be debated for centuries. It is hard to celebrate his presidency because it is hard to celebrate James Madison. The way in which he conducted himself in his ending years—the pleasant smallness of it all, the defiance he showed when falling on the sword of his principles—only compounds the problem.

Just as the people of Madison's day were seduced by Henry—until Madison taught them not to be—so today we are seduced by celebrity's hall of mirrors. In the age of Pericles, ancient Athens routinely celebrated statesmen. After the demagogue Cleon ruthlessly engineered Pericles's downfall, he unleashed a spate of ruinous demagogues on the city. The city responded by instituting harsh punishments for whoever catered to their own benefit at the expense of the state. Today, we should elevate those, like Madison, who do not particularly seek to elevate themselves.[4]

The great idea in Madison's young life was that a constitutional democracy like America's could only function properly if it cultivated statesmanship within society itself. Democracy was not just checks and balances, which, taken alone, are the machine without the ghost. To survive, constitutional democracy also requires both statesmen who will lead and the "certain classes of men" (of course, including women) that John Witherspoon said in 1775 must support them. The two are symbiotic, these statesmen and these stewards. Together, they compose a self-sustaining culture that gives life and energy to democracy itself, where leaders are supported in tackling the most intractable of problems and realizing the greatest of visions.

Most significantly, young Madison was not merely envisioning these ideas on paper—they were the practical guide to what he *did*. The logic of his young life *was* the kind of democracy he wanted to build. He could only build it if *he built it*.

These are costly battles, as young Madison's life showed—but the victory of helping a nation achieve greatness is worth fighting for. Young Madison was such a statesman with such a cause. His story means the democracy he loved can still be refreshed and invigorated today by the sorts of leaders—by the statesmen—essential to our flourishing.

Acknowledgments

BECOMING MADISON IS A SEQUEL OF SORTS TO MY BOOK *DEMAGOGUE:* *The Fight to Save Democracy from Its Worst Enemies.* That book was about a bottom-up problem of democracies. Left to their own devices, democracies will often fall prey to the seductions of predatory mass leaders, demagogues, who will then become tyrannical. That "cycle of regimes," as the ancient political philosophers deemed it, was replayed most horrendously in the last century in Weimar Germany, the hopeful but naive democracy that gave rise to the Nazi Party and Adolf Hitler. But it has also occurred recently in Egypt and Iraq. The cycle can be arrested through a countervailing bottom-up force—through constitutionalism, a culture of civic values concentrated on controlling authority and strengthening self-governance.

Becoming Madison explores what makes a democracy healthy from a different angle—the top. To that end, my conversations with several long-time students of political leadership in America today were essential to this book, including Tom Perriello, Tim Kaine, Chuck Robb, Ron Klain, Dave McCurdy, Bob Dallek, A. E. Dick Howard, and Mike Klarman. Conversations with friends, including Tyson Belanger, Matt Dallek, Rachel Kleinfeld, Ganesh Sitaraman, Christopher Hamner, David Greenberg, and Marc Grinberg, were also especially helpful, as were my biweekly breakfasts with Andy Kaufman. The great Madison scholar Ralph Ketcham provided invaluable assistance on multiple drafts.

The Center for the Constitution at Montpelier hosted me on two long research stays. My thanks to the tremendous leadership and staff there for their very helpful guidance—Michael Quinn, Kat Imhoff, Doug Smith, Meg Kennedy, Sean O'Brien, Sterling Howell, Matt Reeves, and Tom Watson. Virginia Tech's School of Public and International Affairs provided extensive research support. At the University of St. Andrews, Professor Barbara Crawford generously lent me a desk at the Strathmartine Center, where I learned more about John Witherspoon and the Scottish Enlightenment. At Virginia Tech, my colleagues, including Anne Khademian, Gerard Toal, and Patrick Roberts, were unfailingly supportive and also hosted a workshop for me in the spring of 2013. Professors Jim Ceaser and Paul Freedman were kind enough to invite me to teach a class called "Leadership, Statesmanship, and Democracy" at the University of Virginia's Woodrow Wilson School of Politics. Gabriel Swift and his skilled staff at Princeton's Rare Books Collection were incredibly helpful in unearthing several documents. Professors Jim Coan of the University of Virginia and Joseph Cooper of Marymount University provided very helpful analysis of Madison's psychological condition. The Truman National Security Project provided not only many willing and enthusiastic readers, but a warm and encouraging community of like-minded friends.

Many friends and colleagues read part or all of various manuscripts and gave invaluable advice. They include Bob Signer, Marj Signer, Mike Gubser, Ric Mayer, Matt Spence, Dallas Dickinson, Micah Schwartzman, Steve Glickman, Justin Oberman, Jonathan Morgenstein, Amanda Mattingly, Jim Morin, Grant Neely, Meredith Wilson, J. J. Saulino, Tyson Barker, Denver Brunsman, Joe Costa, Zaid Zaid, Alex Rossmiller, Stacy Hope, Jon Davey, Alex Toma, Doug Campbell, Dave Solimini, Erik Woodhouse, Marc Sorel, Matt Seidman, and Daniel Moore.

As an undergraduate and graduate student, I was fortunate to learn at the elbow of several great thinkers about constitutionalism: Professors George Kateb and Stan Katz at Princeton, Mike Rogin at Berkeley, and Dick Howard at UVA. This book reflects all of their various approaches to political theory, applied.

My agent, Larry Weissman, and his partner and wife, Sascha Alper, had faith in this project and helped me make the tough calls necessary to bring it to fruition. My editor at PublicAffairs, John Mahaney, embraced the book from the beginning and was a stalwart friend throughout.

My love and gratitude to my family for their love, honesty, and support: Marj Signer, Bob Signer, Rebecca Signer Roche, Mira Signer, and Rachel Signer.

My greatest thanks go to my wife, Emily, who provided keen and thoughtful edits, endless encouragement, and bottomless love during the four years it took to complete this manuscript, as well as the greatest gift of all—the title.

Notes

Introduction

1. In late 2014, Montpelier announced a $10 million gift from the philanthropist David Rubenstein, part of which would support more furnishings and interpretations at the mansion—a promising development.

2. Charles Thomas Chapman, *Who Was Buried in James Madison's Grave: A Study in Contextual Analysis*, MA thesis, Department of Anthropology, College of William and Mary, 2005, 23.

3. *Fredericksburg News*, October 6, 1857, cited in Chapman, 2.

4. Chapman, 22.

5. Henry Wiencek, *Master of the Mountain: Thomas Jefferson and His Slaves* (New York: Farrar, Straus and Giroux, 2012), 3.

6. Thomas Jefferson, n.d., Epitaph, *The Thomas Jefferson Papers*, Series 1. General Correspondence. 1651–1827, Library of Congress, Washington, DC.

7. Vi-An Nguyen, "What's the Most Visited Presidential Memorial?" *Parade Magazine*, July 31, 2013, available at http://www.parade.com/59283/viannguyen/whats-the-most-visited-presidential-memorial-in-america/.

8. Library of Congress, "The James Madison Memorial Building," available at http://www.loc.gov/loc/walls/madison.html.

9. James Thomas Flexner, *The Young Hamilton: A Biography* (Boston: Little, Brown, 1978), 35.

10. Richard B. Morris, *Witnesses at the Creation: Hamilton, Madison, Jay, and the Constitution* (New York: Holt Rinehart and Winston, 1985), 37.

11. John Corbin, *The Unknown Washington: Biographic Origins of the Republic* (New York: Charles Scribner's Sons, 193), 32.

12. Ibid., 43.

13. Ibid., 47–48.

14. Ibid., 49.

15. Ibid., 121.

16. "To Thomas Jefferson," February 11, 1783, Robert A. Rutland et al., eds., Papers of James Madison [PJM], vol. 6 (Chicago: University of Chicago Press and Charlottesville: University of Virginia Press, 1962–), 221.

17. "From Thomas Jefferson," January 30, 1787, PJM, vol. 9, 249.

18. "From John Francis Mercer," November 12, 1784, PJM, vol. 8, 135.

19. Norine Dickson Campbell, *Patrick Henry: Patriot and Statesman* (New York: Devin-Adair, 1969), 306.

20. "Beverly Randolph to James Monroe," November 26, 1784, cited in PJM, vol. 8, 196n.

21. Elizabeth Fleet, "Madison's 'Detatched Memoranda,'" *William and Mary Quarterly*, 3rd ser., vol. 3, 1946, 555.

22. "To Thomas Jefferson," January 9, 1785, PJM, vol. 8, 229; "Beverly Randolph to James Monroe," November 26, 1784, cited in PJM, vol. 8, 196n.

23. "To James Monroe," December 4, 1784, PJM, vol. 8, 175.

24. Ibid., 175–76.

25. "To Thomas Jefferson," January 9, 1785, PJM, vol. 8, 229.

26. "To James Monroe," April 12, 1785, PJM, vol. 8, 261.

27. "Memorial and Remonstrance Against Religious Assessments," ca. June 20, 1785, PJM, vol. 8, 298–304.

28. Ibid., 296n.

29. "To Edmund Randolph," July 26, 1785, PJM, vol. 8, 328.

30. "From George Nicholas," July 7, 1785, PJM, vol. 8, 316.

31. "Memorial and Remonstrance Against Religious Assessments," ca. June 20, 1785, PJM, vol. 8, 297–98n.

32. "Eliza House Trist to Thomas Jefferson," April 13, 1784, Papers of Thomas Jefferson, VII, 97–8, cited in Irving Brant, *James Madison: The Virginia Revolutionist, 1750–1780*, vol. 1 (New York: Bobbs-Merrill, 1941), 17.

33. Ralph Ketcham, *James Madison: A Biography* (New York: Macmillan, 1971), 630.

34. Robert Merry, *Where They Stand: The American Presidents in the Eyes of Voters and Historians* (New York: Simon & Schuster, 2012).

35. Brant, ii.

36. "113th Congress on Track to Be Least Productive Ever," National Public Radio *NewsHour*, December 4, 2013, available at http://www.pbs.org/newshour/rundown/113th-congress-on-track-to-be-least-productive-ever/. Andrew Dugan, "Congressional Approval Rating Languishes at Low Level," *Gallup Politics*, July 15, 2014, available at http://www.gallup.com/poll/172859/congressional-approval-rating-languishes-low-level.aspx.

37. Thomas Mann and Norman Ornstein, *It's Even Worse Than It Looks: How the American Constitutional System Collided with the New Politics of Extremism* (New York: Basic Books, 2012).

38. Ibid., 39.

39. Robert M. Gates, "The Quiet Fury of Robert Gates," *Wall Street Journal*, January 7, 2014, available at http://online.wsj.com/news/articles/SB10001424052702304617404579306851526222552.

40. See also David Singh Grewel, *Network Power: The Social Dynamics of Globalization* (New Haven, CT: Yale University Press, 2009).

41. David Robertson, *Debates and Other Proceedings of the Convention of Virginia* (Richmond: Enquirer-Press, 1805), 108.

42. Drew R. McCoy, *The Last of the Fathers: James Madison and the Republican Legacy* (Cambridge: Cambridge University Press, 1989), 34.

43. Dylan Thomas, *The Selected Poems of Dylan Thomas* (New York: New Directions Publishing, 2003), 9.

44. Plato, "Phaedrus," in *The Dialogues of Plato*, trans. Benjamin Jowett, vol. 1 (New York: Random House, 1937), 257–58.

45. Ibid., 243.

1. "Our Passions Are Like Torrents"

1. For more on Indians in central and western Virginia, see John M. Boback, *Indian Warfare, Household Competency, and the Settlement of the Western Virginia Frontier, 1749–1794*, dissertation, College of Arts and Sciences, West Virginia University, 2007; and Matthew L. Rhoades, *Long Knives and the Longhouse: Anglo-Iroquois Politics and the Expansion of Colonial Virginia* (Madison, NJ: Fairleigh Dickinson University Press, 2011).

2. "James Madison, Sr. to Joseph Chew," February 19, 1793, James Madison Collection, box 1, folder 8, Manuscripts Division, Department of Rare Books and Special Collections, Princeton University Library.

3. Douglas B. Chambers, *Murder at Montpelier: Igbo Africans in Virginia* (Jackson: University Press of Mississippi, 2005), 15.

4. Paul Jennings, *A Colored Man's Reminiscences of James Madison* (Brooklyn, NY: George C. Beadle, 1865), 15.

5. Matthew G. Hyland, *Montpelier and the Madisons: House, Home and American Heritage* (Charleston, SC: History Press, 2007), 14.

6. Ann Miller, *The Short Life and Strange Death of Ambrose Madison* (Orange, VA: Orange County Historical Society, 2001), 17–18.

7. Ibid., 27–28.

8. "John C. Payne to J. Q. Adams," August 1836, Adams mss., Massachusetts Historical Society, cited in *James Madison: A Biography* by Ralph Ketcham (New York: Macmillan, 1971), 21.

9. Ibid.

10. Dorothy Boyd-Rush, "Gray Matters: Molding a Founding Father," *Montpelier Magazine*, December 9, 2003.

11. "James Madison, Autobiographical Notes, AMs, 4 pp. 1800 (though Ralph Ketcham writes on the folder itself "too early"), James Madison Collection, box 1, folder 1, Manuscripts Division, Department of Rare Books and Special Collections, Princeton Library.

12. Editorial note, "Commonplace Book," PJM, vol. 1, 5.

13. Ibid.

14. Original preface, *Memoirs of Jean Francois Paul de Gondi, Cardinal de Retz, written by himself* (Boston: L. C. Page & Company, 1899).

15. "Abstracts from the Memoirs of the Cardinal de Retz," PJM, vol. 1, 7–16.

16. "From Mont. chiefly," PJM, vol. 1, 16–18.

2. The Good Doctor

1. Willis Rudy, *The Campus and a Nation in Crisis: From the American Revolution to Vietnam* (Cranbury, NJ: Associated University Presses, 1996), 31–33.

2. Ralph Ketcham, *James Madison: A Biography* (New York: Macmillan, 1971), 25–27.

3. Ibid.

4. "A Brief History of Nassau Hall," Princeton University, available at http://www.princeton.edu/mudd/news/faq/topics/nassau.shtml (last accessed on December 19, 2012).

5. Jeffry H. Morrison, *John Witherspoon and the Founding of the American Republic* (Notre Dame, IN: University of Notre Dame Press, 2005), 10.

6. L. Gordon Tait, *The Piety of John Witherspoon: Pew, Pulpit, and Public Forum* (Louisville, KY: Geneva Press, 2001), 2.

7. Varnum Lansing Collins, Introduction to *Lectures on Moral Philosophy*, by John Witherspoon (Princeton, NJ: Princeton University Press, 1912), viii.

8. Tait, 3.

9. Ibid., 5.

10. Ibid., 6.

11. Collins, Introduction to *Lectures on Moral Philosophy*, viii.

12. "The Battle of Falkirk 1746," British Battles, available at: http://www.britishbattles.com/battle_of_falkirk.htm (last accessed on October 10, 2014).

13. James McCosh, *Witherspoon and His Times* (Philadelphia: Presbyterian Board of Publication and Sabbath-School Work, 1890), 19.

14. Frank Moore, *American Eloquence: A Collection of Speeches and Addresses by the Most Eminent Orators of America* (New York: D. Appleton and Company, 1857), 290–91.

15. Varnum Lansing Collins, *President Witherspoon: A Biography*, vol. 1 (Princeton, NJ: Princeton University Press, 1925), 19, 23–24, cited in J. Walter McGinty, *An Animated Son of Liberty: A Life of John Witherspoon* (St. Edmunds: Arena Books, 2012), 270.

16. Anand C. Chitnis, *The Scottish Enlightenment: A Social History* (Totowa, NJ: Rowman & Littlefield, 1976), 5.

17. Morrison, 58.

18. Tait, 7.

19. Ibid., 9.

20. Ibid., 7–8.

21. Ibid., 10.

22. Jane Rendall, *The Origins of the Scottish Enlightenment: 1707–1776* (London: Macmillan, 1978), 219.

23. Ibid.

24. Tait, 75–76.

25. John Witherspoon, *The Works of the Rev. Dr. John Witherspoon* (Philadelphia: John Woodward, 1803), i.

26. Matthew F. Rose, *John Witherspoon: An American Leader* (Washington, DC: Family Research Council, 1999), 17–20.

27. Ibid.

28. Ibid., 21.

29. Morrison, 9, 63–64.

30. Ibid., 48.

31. Ketcham, 31.

32. Douglas Adair, "James Madison's Autobiography," *William and Mary Quarterly*, 3rd series, 2, no. 2 (April 1945), 197.

33. Ibid., 197–98.

34. Ketcham, 31.

35. Ibid., 33.

36. Ibid., 33.

37. Paul Jennings, *A Colored Man's Reminiscences of James Madison* (Brooklyn: George C. Beadle, 1865), 17.

38. Ward W. Briggs, Jr., *Soldier and Scholar: Basil Laneau Silversleeve and the Civil War* (Charlottesville: University Press of Virginia, 1998), 55n25.

39. James Madison, "Clio's Proclamation," Robert A. Rutland et al., eds., *Papers of James Madison* [PJM], vol. 1 (Chicago: University of Chicago Press and Charlottesville: University of Virginia Press, 1962–), 64–65.

3. A *Nexus Imperii*

1. L. Gordon Tait, *The Piety of John Witherspoon: Pew, Pulpit, and Public Forum* (Louisville, KY: Geneva Press, 2001), xviii.

2. Thaddeus Dod, "Lectures on Moral Philosophy," C0199, No. 333, Department of Rare Books and Special Collections, Princeton University Library.

3. "A Brief System of Logick," PJM, vol. 1, 37.

4. Ibid.

5. John Witherspoon, *Lectures on Moral Philosophy* (Princeton, NJ: Princeton University Press, 1912), 58.

6. Jeffry H. Morrison, *John Witherspoon and the Founding of the American Republic* (Notre Dame, IN: University of Notre Dame Press, 2005), 72–73.

7. Ibid., 73.

8. J. Walter McGinty, *An Animated Son of Liberty: A Life of John Witherspoon* (St. Edmunds: Arena Books, 2012), 199.

9. "A Brief System of Logick," PJM, vol. 1, 39.

10. Ibid., 41.

11. Dod, 91.

12. Ibid., 92.

13. Ibid.

14. Ibid.

15. Ibid., 92–93.

16. Ibid., 98.

17. Ibid., 94.

18. E-mail to author from Daniel Moore, September 12, 2014.

19. Dod, 94.

20. Ibid., 99.

21. Morrison, 25.

22. Ibid., 27.

23. "To James Madison, Sr.," July 23, 1770, Robert A. Rutland et al., eds., *Papers of James Madison* [PJM], vol. 1 (Chicago: University of Chicago Press and Charlottesville: University of Virginia Press, 1962–), 50.

24. "To James Madison, Sr.," October 9, 1771, PJM, vol. 1, 69.

25. James Madison, "Autobiographical Sketch," 1, n.d., box 1, folder 1, James Madison Collection, MS CO207, Department of Rare Books and Special Collections, Princeton University Library.

26. Irving Brant, *James Madison: The Virginia Revolutionist*, 1751–1780, vol. 1 (New York: Bobbs-Merrill, 1941), 97–99.

4. The High Tract of Public Life

1. "To William Bradford," November 9, 1772, Robert A. Rutland et al., eds., *Papers of James Madison* [PJM], vol. 1 (Chicago: University of Chicago Press and Charlottesville: University of Virginia Press, 1962–), 76.

2. Author interview with Jayne Blair, Orange County Historical Society, Orange, Virginia, April 4, 2013.

3. William C. Rives, *History of the Life and Times of James Madison*, vol. 1 (Freeport, NY: Books for Libraries Press, 1970), 8.

4. Irving Brant, *James Madison: The Virginia Revolutionist*, 1751–1780, vol. 1 (New York: Bobbs-Merrill, 1941), 31.

5. James Madison, "Autobiographical Notes," AMs, 4 pp, 1800. James Madison Collection, box 1, folder 1, Manuscripts Division, Department of Rare Books and Special Collections, Princeton Library.

6. Baron de Montlezun, *Voyage fait dans les années 1816–1817, de New-Yorck à la Nouvelle-Orléans, et de l'Orénoque au Mississippi* (Paris: Gide Fils, 1818), 63–64.

7. Rives, vol. 1, 8.

8. Against the stereotype of eldest brothers as autocratic, power-driven personalities, modern psychology has found that strength is only part of the story. The typical eldest brother develops a complex, emotionally interdependent life with his younger siblings. For the eldest brother competing with younger siblings for his parents' attention and affection, "dark and savage fantasies of outright mayhem can sometimes put in an appearance," two modern psychologists write. Eldest brothers sometimes decide to "befriend the newcomer, to be a third parent," even "serving as guardian, mentor, and guide," in order to make them dependent, while creating an "aura of solicitous and benevolent know-how." [Bradford Wilson and George Edington, *First Child, Second Child . . . Your Birth Order Profile* (New York: McGraw-Hill, 1981), 62.] Instead of being a tyrant within the house, most eldest brothers are actually grounded by others. The eldest brother becomes "holistic" rather than "atomistic," meaning he grasps facts as an integrated whole, accustomed to negotiating boundaries between squabbling siblings. He "internalizes" rather than "externalizes," meaning he takes emotional experiences in, rather than projects them onto others. He is conceptual rather than perceptual, given to broad schemes of control—a natural attribute in a family of underlings—rather than immediate emotional reactions. Where the younger sibling is "concrete," focusing on the facts at hand, the eldest becomes "abstract," tending toward dreams and metaphysical schemes. And while the younger sibling is "activistic," working on action itself, the eldest brother becomes drawn into the dreamy side of life, to the interior space in which he plots and designs the management of his siblings, while retreating from their management. Brian Sutton-Smith and Benjamin George Rosenberg, *The Sibling* (New York: Holt, Rinehart, and Winston, 1970), 9.

9. "To James Madison, Sr.," December 8, 1779, PJM, vol. 1, 316.

10. "To Ambrose Madison," October 11, 1787, PJM, vol. 10, 192.

11. "From William Bradford," October [13, 1772], PJM, vol. 1, 73.

5. "The Annals of Heaven"

1. "James Madison, Sr. to Joseph Chew," February 19, 1793, James Madison Collection, box 1, folder 8, Manuscripts Division, Department of Rare Books and Special Collections, Princeton University Library.

2. On October 13, 1772, Bradford sent a letter to Madison. The friends had seen each other last in Philadelphia in April, as Madison forlornly headed back down the hot dusty road to Virginia. Bradford apologized for not writing earlier, but he had a reason: "I should have given myself that pleasure sooner," he wrote, "had I not heard you were at the springs." Robert A. Rutland et al., eds., *Papers of James Madison* [PJM], vol. 1 (Chicago: University of Chicago Press and Charlottesville: University of Virginia Press, 1962–), 72.

3. "To William Bradford," October 30–November 5, 1779, PJM, vol. 1, 311.

4. "To William Bradford," November 9, 1772, PJM, vol. 1, 75.

5. Ibid.

6. Ibid., 76.

7. "To William Bradford," April 28, 1773, PJM, vol. 1, 83.

8. "To William Bradford," January 24, 1774, PJM, vol. 1, 106.

9. "To William Bradford," April 1, 1774, PJM, vol. 1, 112–13.

10. Ibid., 114n7.

11. William Parks, "Religion and the Revolution in Virginia," in *Virginia in the American Revolution,* by Richard A. Rutyna and Peter C. Stewart (Norfolk, VA: Old Dominion University Press, 1977), 42–43.

12. Ibid., 43.

13. "To William Bradford," April 1, 1774, PJM, vol. 1, 112.

14. Richard Brookhiser, *James Madison* (New York: Basic Books, 2011), 20.

15. Douglas Adair, "James Madison's Autobiography," *William and Mary Quarterly,* 3rd series, 2, no. 2 (April 1945), 198.

16. "To William Bradford," January 24, 1774, PJM, vol. 1, 106.

17. Adair, 198.

18. "To William Bradford," January 24, 1774, PJM, vol. 1, 106.

19. "From William Bradford," March 4, 1774, PJM, vol. 1, 109.

20. Ibid.

21. "To William Bradford," April 1, 1774, PJM, vol. 1, 111.

22. "To William Bradford," July 28, 1775, PJM, vol. 1, 161.

23. "To William Bradford," April 1, 1774, PJM, vol. 1, 112.

24. "From William Bradford," December 25, 1773, PJM, vol. 1, 103.

25. "To William Bradford," January 24, 1774, PJM, vol. 1, 105.

26. *New State v. Liebmann,* 285 U.S. 262 (1932).

27. "To William Bradford," January 24, 1774, PJM, vol. 1, 105.

28. "To William Bradford," August 23, 1774, PJM, vol. 1, 121.

29. "From William Bradford," August 1, 1774, PJM, vol. 1, 118–19.

30. Ibid., 118.

31. "To William Bradford," August 23, 1774, PJM, vol. 1, 121.

32. Ibid.

33. Kara Pierce, "A Revolutionary Masquerade: The Chronicles of James Rivington," Department of History, SUNY–Binghamton, available at http://www2 .binghamton.edu/history/resources/journal-of-history/chronicles-of-james-rivington .html.

34. "To William Bradford," [early March 1775], PJM, vol. 1, 141.

35. "To William Bradford," June 19, 1775, PJM, vol. 1, 152.

36. "From William Bradford," July 10, 1775, PJM, vol. 1, 156.

37. "To William Bradford," July 28, 1775, PJM, vol. 1, 161.

38. "To William Bradford," December 1, 1773, PJM, vol. 1, 100–101.

39. "To William Bradford," September 25, 1773, PJM, vol. 1, 96.

40. Mary Sarah Bilder, "James Madison, Law Student and Demi-Lawyer," *Law & History Review* 28 (2010), 389, 400. Bilder speculates that Madison probably took the notes on Salkeld in the 1780s because the handwriting in them is small and upright, a style he used more frequently in other writing in the 1780s; Bilder, 410. However, because Madison began his law studies in the 1770s, I think it is safe to assume that he began the Salkeld notes in this period.

41. Ibid., 426.

42. Ibid., 429.

43. "To William Bradford," January 24, 1774, PJM, vol. 1, 105.

44. Ibid.

45. "Indenture," September 22, 1774, PJM, vol. 1, 123.

46. "From William Bradford," March 4, 1774, PJM, vol. 1, 109.

47. "To William Bradford," April 1, 1774, PJM, vol. 1, 112.

48. John Witherspoon, *The Dominion of Providence over the Passions of Man* (London: Fielding and Walker, 1778), 2.

49. Ibid., 4.

50. Ibid., 26

51. Ibid., 26–27.

52. Ibid., 28.

53. Ibid., 34.

54. Ibid., 36.

55. Ibid., 39–40.

56. Adair, 199.

6. "If This Be Treason, Make the Most of It!"

1. George Morgan, *The True Patrick Henry* (Philadelphia and London: J. B. Lippincott, 1907), 119.

2. Richard R. Beeman, *Patrick Henry: A Biography* (New York: McGraw-Hill, 1974), 65–67.

3. Ibid., 9.

4. Jacob Axelrad, *Patrick Henry: The Voice of Freedom* (New York: Random House, 1947), 45.

5. Beeman, 35–39.

6. Morgan, 109.

7. Kevin J. Hayes, *The Mind of a Patriot: Patrick Henry and the World of Ideas* (Charlottesville: University of Virginia Press, 2008), 13.

8. Norine Dickson Campbell, *Patrick Henry: Patriot and Statesman* (New York: Devin-Adair, 1969), 10.

9. Ibid., 5.

10. Ibid., 5.

11. Ibid.

12. Ibid., 11, 13.

13. Ibid., 19.

14. Ibid., 20.

15. Ibid., 22.

16. Ibid., 65–66.

17. Ibid.

18. Morgan, 447.

19. Ibid., 442.

20. Campbell, 64.

21. Robert Douthat Meade, *Patrick Henry: Practical Revolutionary* (Philadelphia: J. B. Lippincott, 1969), 15–16n3.

22. "To William Bradford," May 9, 1775, Robert A. Rutland et al., eds., *Papers of James Madison* [PJM], vol. 1 (Chicago: University of Chicago Press and Charlottesville: University of Virginia Press, 1962–), 145.

23. Irving Brant, *James Madison: The Virginia Revolutionist*, 1751–1780, vol. 1 (New York: Bobbs-Merrill, 1941), 179.

24. "To William Bradford," May 9, 1775, 145.

25. "Address to Captain Patrick Henry and the Gentlemen Independents of Hanover," May 9, 1775, PJM, vol. 1, 146–47.

26. "Letter from Patrick Henry, Jr. to James Madison Esqr.," May 11, 1775, PJM, vol. 1, 147n.

7. Suspending His Intellectual Functions

1. "To William Bradford," July 28, 1775, Robert A. Rutland et al., eds., *Papers of James Madison* [PJM], vol. 1 (Chicago: University of Chicago Press and Charlottesville: University of Virginia Press, 1962–), 160.

2. "To William Bradford," June 19, 1775, PJM, vol. 1, 153.

3. Douglas Adair, "James Madison's Autobiography," *William and Mary Quarterly*, 3rd series, 2, no. 2 (April 1945), 199.

4. Ralph Ketcham, *James Madison: A Biography* (New York: Macmillan, 1971), 51–52.

5. Lynne Cheney, *James Madison: A Life Reconsidered* (New York: Viking, 2014), 18.

6. Ibid., 51–52.

7. Ketcham, 51–52.

8. Irving Brant, *James Madison: The Virginia Revolutionist*, 1751–1780, vol. 1 (New York: Bobbs-Merrill, 1941), 106.

9. James Madison, [Autobiographical] Memorandum sent to Mr. Delaplaine at his request, September 1816, Andre De Coppet Collection, MS C0063, box 23, Princeton University Library.

10. Edward Coles, "Notes on the Life and Ancestry of James Madison," n.d., box 1, folder 4, Edward Coles Papers, MSC0037, Princeton University Library.

11. James Madison, "Biographical Sketch," Andre De Coppet Collection, box 23, folder 17, Princeton University Library. (Emphasis added.)

12. "Commission as Colonel of Orange County Militia," October 2, 1775, PJM, vol. 1, 164n1.

13. Adair, 199.

14. Michael B. First and Allan Tasman, *Clinical Guide to the Diagnosis and Treatment of Mental Disorders* (New York: Wiley & Sons, 2006), 292–93. These criteria were repeated in the DSM-V, which was published in 2013.

15. Psychodynamic theory, which focuses on the physical expression of emotion, the existence of "triggers" in a patient, and recurring themes and patterns of symptoms, is among the most successful schools of therapy in helping patients with psychological disorders. The framework is especially helpful in analyzing such patterns as Madison's seizures. In a wide-ranging series of controlled studies, psychodynamic therapy has been substantially more effective on average than other schools of therapy, such as general psychotherapy, cognitive-behavioral therapy, and antidepressant medication. Jonathan Shedler, "The Efficacy of Psychodynamic Psychotherapy," *American Psychologist* 65, no. 2(20), 98–109. Four studies have found psychodynamic therapy is effective in reducing "somatic symptoms with psychogenic movement disorder." Three studies comparing short-term intensive psychodynamic therapy with pharmaceuticals as a treatment for panic disorders found that 80 percent of patients remained symptom-free after eighteen months, compared with a high relapse rate with patients taking drugs or not provided with psychodynamic therapy. Although Madison of course could not have seen a therapist, these findings suggest that the framework is at least helpful in analyzing his symptoms. Allan Abbass, Joel M. Town, and Ellen Driessen, "Intensive Short-Term Dynamic Psychotherapy: A Review of the Treatment Method and Empirical Basis," *Research in Psychotherapy: Psychopathology, Process and Outcome* 16, no. 1 (2013), 6–15.

16. Author interview with Dr. Joseph Cooper, August 4, 2014.

17. Ibid.

18. Marcia J. Kaplan, Alok K. Dwivedi, Michael D. Privitera, Kelly Isaacs, Cynthia Hughes, and Michelle Bowman, "Comparisons of Childhood Trauma, Alexithymia, and Defensive Styles in Patients with Psychogenic Non-epileptic Seizures vs. Epilepsy: Implications for the Etiology of Conversion Disorder," *Journal of Psychosomatic Research*, 75 (2013), 145.

19. Ibid., 143.

20. N. M. G. Bodde, J. L. Brooks, G. A. Baker, P. A. J. M. Boon, J. G. M. Hendriksen, O. G. Mulder, A. P. Aldenkamp, "Psychogenic Non-epileptic Seizures—Definition, Etiology, Treatment and Progonistic Issues: A Critical Review," *Seizure* 18 (2009), 543–53.

21. Author interview with Jim Coan, August 22, 2014.

22. Ketcham, 66.

8. All Men Are Equally Entitled

1. "To William Bradford," May 9, 1775, Robert A. Rutland et al., eds., *Papers of James Madison* [PJM], vol. 1 (Chicago: University of Chicago Press and Charlottesville: University of Virginia Press, 1962–), 145.

2. "To William Bradford," July 28, 1775, PJM, vol. 1, 160.

3. William Gordon, *The History of the Rise, Progress, and Establishment of the Independence of the United States of America, Including an Account of the Late War, and the Thirteen Colonies, from Their Origin to That Period* (London: Charles Dilly, 1788), 152.

4. Jacob Axelrad, *Patrick Henry: The Voice of Freedom* (New York: Random House, 1947), 143.

5. *The Political Works of Thomas Paine: Secretary for Foreign Affairs to the Congress of the United States of America During the Revolutionary War* (Springfield, MA: Tannatt & Co., Printers, 1826), 201.

6. William C. Rives, *History of the Life and Times of James Madison*, vol. 1 (Freeport, NY: Books for Libraries Press, 1970), 167.

7. "The Druid, No. 1," *The Pennsylvania Magazine: Or, American Monthly Magazine*, May 1776, 204, 208.

8. Jeffry H. Morrison, *John Witherspoon and the Founding of the American Republic* (Notre Dame, IN: University of Notre Dame Press, 2005), 13.

9. J. David Hoeveler, *Creating the American Mind: Intellect and Politics in the Colonial Colleges* (Lanham, MD: Rowman & Littlefield, 2002), 312.

10. Morrison, 13.

11. Ibid.

9. Councilor to Governor Henry

1. William C. Rives, *History of the Life and Times of James Madison*, vol. 1 (Freeport, NY: Books for Libraries Press, 1970), 170.

2. Ibid., 172.

3. "Case of Unsettled Claims from Dunmore's War," Robert A. Rutland et al., eds., *Papers of James Madison* [PJM], vol. 1 (Chicago: University of Chicago Press and Charlottesville: University of Virginia Press, 1962–), 186, ed. note.

4. Ralph Ketcham, *James Madison: A Biography* (New York: Macmillan, 1971), 77.

5. Douglas Adair, "James Madison's Autobiography," *William and Mary Quarterly*, 3rd series, 2, no. 2 (April 1945), 199.

6. Rives, vol. 1, 180–81.

7. "Editorial Note," PJM, vol. 1, 214.

8. Ketcham, 79.

9. Lyon Gardiner Tyler, ed., *Encyclopedia of Virginia Biography*, vol. 2 (New York: Lewis Historical Publishing Company, 1915), 329.

10. "From David Jameson," May 21, 1780, PJM, vol. 2, 30.

11. "Session of the Virginia Council of State," January 14, 1778, PJM, vol. 1, 216–17n3.

12. John Buchanan, *The Road to Valley Forge: How Washington Built the Army That Won the Revolution* (New York: John Wiley & Sons, 2004), 287.

13. Ibid., 289.

14. "Session of the Virginia Council of State," January 14, 1778, PJM, vol. 1, 216.

15. "Patrick Henry in Council to Virginia Delegates in Congress," January 20, 1778, PJM, vol. 1, 221, 219.

16. Ibid., 221n2.

17. Ibid., 219.

18. Ibid., 220.

19. "Session of Virginia Council of State," April 7, 1778, PJM, vol. 1, 236–37.

20. "Session of Virginia Council of State," January 23, 1778, PJM, vol. 1, 224n2.

21. "To James Madison, Sr.," January 23, 1778, PJM, vol. 1, 223.

22. "Election to Virginia House of Delegates Voided," May 27, 1778, PJM, vol. 1, 242–43.

23. Howard Payson Arnold, *Historic Side-Lights* (New York: Harper & Brothers, 1877), 272.

24. "To Benjamin Harrison, Speaker of the Virginia House of Delegates," December 17, 1788, in Worthington Chauncey Ford, *The Writings of George Washington* (New York: G. P. Putnam's Sons, 1890), 301–2.

25. Ibid.

26. "To Benjamin Harrison," December 16, 1779, PJM, vol. 1, 319.

27. "To Marquis de Lafayette," March 18, 1780, in *The Writings of George Washington*, ed. Jared Sparks, vol. 6 (New York: Harper & Brothers, 1847), 487.

10. "Distrust of the Public Ability"

1. "To Benjamin Harrison, Speaker of the Virginia House of Delegates," December 17, 1788, in Worthington Chauncey Ford, *The Writings of George Washington*, (New York: G. P. Putnam's Sons, 1890), 301–2.

2. "Money," September 1779–March 1780, Robert A. Rutland et al., eds., *Papers of James Madison* [PJM], vol. 1 (Chicago: University of Chicago Press and Charlottesville: University of Virginia Press, 1962–), 302–9.

3. Thomas Paine, *The Crisis* (London: R. Carille, 1819), 120.

4. William C. Rives, *History of the Life and Times of James Madison*, vol. 1 (Freeport, NY: Books for Libraries Press, 1970), 217.

5. Irving Brant, *James Madison: The Nationalist, 1780–1787*, vol. 2 (New York: Bobbs-Merrill, 1941), 17–18.

6. Ibid., 27.

7. Rives, vol. 1, 218.

8. "To James Madison, Sr.," March 20, 1780, PJM, vol. 2, 3.

9. "To Thomas Jefferson," March 27, 1780, PJM, vol. 2, 5–7.

10. Julian Boyd, ed., *The Papers of Thomas Jefferson*, vol. 3 (Princeton, NJ: Princeton University Press, 1950), 337n1.

11. A Defect of Adequate Statesmen

1. "To Thomas Jefferson," June 23, 1780, Robert A. Rutland et al., eds., *Papers of James Madison* [PJM], vol. 2 (Chicago: University of Chicago Press and Charlottesville: University of Virginia Press, 1962–), 41.

2. William C. Rives, *History of the Life and Times of James Madison*, vol. 1 (Freeport, NY: Books for Libraries Press), 219.

3. "To Thomas Jefferson," June 2, 1780, PJM, vol. 2, 38.

4. Ralph Ketcham, *James Madison: A Biography* (New York: Macmillan, 1971), 91.

5. "From Reverend James Madison," August 3, 1780, PJM, vol. 2, 55.

6. "To Joseph Jones," October 24, 1780, PJM, vol. 2, 145.

7. "To Joseph Jones," October 24, 1780, PJM, vol. 2, 146.

8. "To Edmund Pendleton," January 2, 1781, PJM, vol. 2, 272.

9. Ketcham, 107.

10. "To Joseph Jones," November 14, 1780, PJM, vol. 2, 173.

11. "From Joseph Jones," November 18, 1780, PJM, vol. 2, 183.

12. "To Joseph Jones," November 28, 1780, PJM, vol. 2, 209.

13. "From Joseph Jones," December 8, 1780, PJM, vol. 2, 233.

14. "From Edmund Pendleton," March 19, 1781, PJM, vol. 3, 26.

15. "From the Reverend James Madison," March 9, 1781, PJM, vol. 3, 10.

16. "From Edmund Pendleton," March 19, 1781, PJM, vol. 3, 26.

17. Jacob Axelrad, *Patrick Henry: The Voice of Freedom* (New York: Random House, 1947), 208–9.

18. Eric Foner, *Tom Paine and Revolutionary America* (New York: Oxford University Press, 1976), 23.

19. "From Edmund Randolph," March 29, 1783, PJM, vol. 6, 415.

20. "To Edmund Randolph," April 23, 1782, PJM, vol. 4, 180.

21. "To Edmund Randoph," July 16, 1782, PJM, vol. 4, 417.

22. "From Edmund Randolph," August 16, 1782, PJM, vol. 5, 59.

23. "To Edmund Randolph," September 30, 1782, PJM, vol. 5, 170.

24. "From Edmund Randolph," November 22, 1782, PJM, vol. 5, 308.

25. Irving Brant, *James Madison: The Nationalist,* 1780–1787, vol. 2 (New York: Bobbs-Merrill,1941), 211.

26. "To James Madison, Sr.," February 1782 (ca. 12), PJM, vol. 4, 64.

27. "To James Madison, Sr.," March 30, 1782, PJM, vol. 4, 127.

28. Ibid.

29. "To James Madison, Sr.," May 20, 1782, PJM, vol. 4, 256.

30. "Motion on Impost," PJM, vol. 3, 78n.

12. The Coercive Power

1. "Proposed Amendment of Articles of Confederation," March 12, 1781, Robert A. Rutland et al., eds., *Papers of James Madison* [PJM], vol. 3 (Chicago: University of Chicago Press and Charlottesville: University of Virginia Press, 1962–), 18.

2. "To Thomas Jefferson," April 3, 1781, PJM, vol. 3, 45.

3. "To Thomas Jefferson," April 16, 1781, PJM, vol. 3, 71.

4. "To Thomas Jefferson," May 1, 1781, PJM, vol. 3, 97–98.

5. "From Thomas Jefferson," September 30, 1781, PJM, vol. 3, 269–70.

6. "To Thomas Jefferson," January 15, 1782, PJM, vol. 4, 34.

7. "Report on Instructions on Peace Negotiations," PJM, vol. 4, 4.

8. "To Edmund Randolph," July 2, 1782, PJM, vol. 4, 387.

9. Ibid.

10. "Instructions to Virginia Delegates," May 24, 1782, PJM, vol. 4, 271–72.

11. "Notes on Debates," January 25, 1783, PJM, vol. 6, 134–35.

12. Ibid., 137n.

13. "Notes on Debates," January 28, 1783, PJM, vol. 6, 142.

14. Ibid., 143–47.

15. Ibid., 148–49.

16. "Notes on Debates," January 29, 1783, PJM, vol. 6, 162.

17. Ibid., 164.

18. "To Edmund Randolph," January 28, 1783, PJM, vol. 6, 155–56.

19. William C. Rives, *History of the Life and Times of James Madison,* vol. 1 (Freeport, NY: Books for Libraries Press), 612.

20. "Report on Address to the States by Congress," PJM, vol. 6, 488–94.

21. Irving Brant, *James Madison: The Nationalist,* 1780–1787, vol. 2 (New York: Bobbs-Merrill, 1941), 247.

22. "From the Reverend James Madison," August 27, 1783, PJM, vol. 7, 291.

23. "Notes on Debates," April 4, 1783, PJM, vol. 6, 432.

24. See also Brant, vol. 2, 248–52.

25. "From Thomas Jefferson," May 7, 1783, PJM, vol. 7, 24.

26. "From Edmund Randolph," May 9, 1783, PJM, vol. 7, 32.

27. Ibid.

28. "From Edmund Randolph," May 15, 1783, PJM, vol. 7, 44–45.

29. "To Edmund Randolph," May 20, 1783, PJM, vol. 7, 59.

30. "From Edmund Randolph," May 24, 1783, PJM, vol. 7, 73.

31. "From Joseph Jones," June 8, 1783, PJM, vol. 7, 118–19.

32. "From Joseph Jones," June 14, 1783, PJM, vol. 7, 144.

33. "From Edmund Randolph," June 14, 1783, PJM, vol. 7, 147–48.

34. "From Edmund Randolph," June 21, 1783, PJM, vol. 7, 186.

35. Ralph Edward Weber, *United States Diplomatic Codes & Ciphers, 1775–1938* (Piscataway, NJ: Rutgers University Press, 1979), 22.

36. "To Joseph Jones," May 28, 1782, PJM, vol. 4, 288.

37. "From Edmund Randolph," June 20, 1782, PJM, vol, 4, 355.

38. "From Edmund Randolph," July 5, 1782, PJM, vol. 4, 396.

39. "To Edmund Randolph," July 16, 1782, PJM, vol. 4, 417.

40. "To Edmund Randolph," December 3, 1782, PJM, vol. 5, 357.

13. A Sad Reunion

1. "From Edmund Randolph," September 20, 1782, Robert A. Rutland et al., eds., *Papers of James Madison* [PJM], vol. 5 (Chicago: University of Chicago Press and Charlottesville: University of Virginia Press, 1962–), 150–51.

2. "To Edmund Randolph," September 30, 1782, PJM, vol. 5, 170.

3. "Notes on Debates," November 12, 1782, PJM, vol. 5, 268–69.

4. "From Edmund Randolph," December 13, 1782, PJM, vol. 5, 401.

5. "From Benjamin Harrison," January 4, 1783, PJM, vol. 6, 11–12.

6. "Notes on Debates," December 31, 1782, PJM, vol. 5, 476.

7. Ibid.

8. "Report on Books for Congress," PJM, vol. 6, 63n.

9. Ibid., 62–117.

10. Alden T. Vaughan and Virginia Mason Vaughan, *Shakespeare in America* (Oxford: Oxford University Press, 2012), 31.

11. Ibid., 7.

14. Kitty

1. "To James Madison, Sr.," February 12, 1783, Robert A. Rutland et al., eds., *Papers of James Madison* [PJM], vol. 6 (Chicago: University of Chicago Press and Charlottesville: University of Virginia Press, 1962–), 228–29.

2. "From Thomas Jefferson," January 31, 1783, PJM, vol. 6, 179–80.

3. "To Edmund Randolph," March 25, 1783, PJM, vol. 6, 392.

4. "From Thomas Jefferson," April, 14, 1783, PJM, vol. 6, 459.

5. "To Thomas Jefferson," April 22, 1783, PJM, vol. 6, 481.

6. "To Thomas Jefferson," May 6, 1783, PJM, vol. 7, 18–19. See also Irving Brant, *James Madison: The Nationalist*, 1780–1787, vol. 2 (New York: Bobbs-Merrill, 1941), 285.

7. "From David Jameson," May 24, 1783, PJM, vol. 7, 71.

8. "To James Madison, Sr.," May 27, 1783, PJM, vol. 7, 88.

9. "To James Madison, Sr.," June 5, 1783, PJM, vol. 7, 116.

10. "Benjamin Harrison to Virginia Delegates," January 31, 1783, PJM, vol. 6, 176–77.

11. "Notes on Debates," June 21, 1783, PJM, vol. 71, 177.

12. "A Proclamation," Elias Boudinot, June 24, 1783, PJM, vol. 7, 197.

13. "Tellingly, after Congress . . ." and "With nothing to do . . .": "To Thomas Jefferson," September 20, 1783, PJM, vol. 7, 354.

14. "From Alexander Hamilton," July 6, 1783, PJM, vol. 7, 214–15n.

15. "To Edmund Randolph," June 30, 1783, PJM, vol. 7, 205–7

16. "To Edmund Randolph," July 8, 1783, PJM, vol. 7, 217n.

17. "To Thomas Jefferson," September 20, 1783, PJM, vol. 7, 354.

18. "From Edmund Pendleton," June 16, 1783, PJM, vol. 7, 151.

19. Brant, vol. 2, 287.

20. "To Thomas Jefferson," August 11, 1783, PJM, vol. 7, 268

21. Ibid.

22. "From Thomas Jefferson," August 31, 1783, PJM, vol. 7, 298–99.

23. Brant, vol. 2, 287.

24. "Madison Paid Court to 'Sweet Dulcinea' Outside Old Nassau's Sequestered Walls," *Daily Princetonian*, vol. 62, no. 35, March 23, 1937.

25. "To James Madison, Sr.," September 8, 1783, PJM, vol. 7, 304–5.

26. Jacob Axelrad, *Patrick Henry: The Voice of Freedom* (New York: Random House, 1947), 216.

15. A Remonstrance

1. "To Thomas Jefferson," September 20, 1783, Robert A. Rutland et al., eds., *Papers of James Madison* [PJM], vol. 7 (Chicago: University of Chicago Press and Charlottesville: University of Virginia Press, 1962–), 353.

2. Ralph Ketcham, *James Madison: A Biography* (New York: Macmillan, 1971), 145.

3. Ibid., 150.

4. "To Thomas Jefferson," February 11, 1784, PJM, vol. 7, 418.

5. "To Thomas Jefferson," March 16, 1784, PJM, vol. 8, 11.

6. "From Thomas Jefferson," March 16, 1784, PJM, vol. 8, 16.

7. "From Patrick Henry," April 17, 1784, PJM, vol. 8, 18.

8. Robert Douthat Meade, *Patrick Henry: Practical Revolutionary* (Philadelphia: J. B. Lippincott, 1969), 273.

9. "To Thomas Jefferson," May 15, 1784, PJM, vol. 8, 34.

10. George Morgan, *The True Patrick Henry* (Philadelphia and London: J. B. Lippincott, 1907), 332.

11. Irving Brant, *James Madison: The Nationalist, 1780–1787*, vol. 2 (New York: Bobbs-Merrill, 1941), 324–25.

12. "To Thomas Jefferson" September 7, 1784, PJM, vol. 8, 113.

13. Brant, 324–37.

14. "From Thomas Jefferson," December 8, 1784, PJM, vol. 8, 178.

15. "Meteorological Journal for Orange County, Virginia, in Madison's Hand," PJM, vol. 8, 528.

16. "To James Monroe," March 21, 1785, PJM, vol. 8, 256.

17. "To James Monroe," January 8, 1785, PJM, vol. 8, 220.

18. "From Thomas Jefferson," March 18, 1785, PJM, vol. 8, 250n.

19. "From Lafayette," March 16, 1785, PJM, vol. 8, 245.

20. "From Thomas Jefferson," December 8, 1784, PJM, vol. 8, 179.

21. "To Thomas Jefferson," April 27, 1785, PJM, vol. 8, 270.

22. "Meteorological Journal for Orange County, Virginia, in Madison's Hand," PJM, vol. 8, 528.

23. "To Lafayette," March 20, 1785, PJM, vol. 8, 254.

24. "To Edmund Randolph," July 26, 1785, PJM, vol. 8, 328.

25. "To George Wythe," April 15, 1785, PJM, vol. 8, 262–63.

26. "To Edmund Randolph," July 26, 1785, PJM, vol. 8, 328.

27. "Meteorological Journal for Orange County, Virginia, in Madison's Hand," PJM, vol. 8, 532.

28. "To Thomas Jefferson," April 27, 1785, PJM, vol. 8, 266.

29. "From James Monroe," July 12, 1785, PJM, vol. 8, 319.

30. "To James Monroe," July 28, 1785, PJM, vol. 8, 332.

31. "To James Monroe," August 7, 1785, PJM, vol. 8, 333n2.

32. "From Caleb Wallace," July 12, 1785, PJM, vol. 8, 321.

33. "To Caleb Wallace," August 23, 1785, PJM, vol. 8, 350.

34. "Meteorological Journal for Orange County, Virginia, in Madison's Hand," PJM, vol. 8, 542; "To James Monroe," March 19, 1786, PJM, vol. 8, 504–5.

35. "From William Grayson," March 22, 1786, PJM, vol. 8, 510.

16. Solitude and Reform

1. "Act for Establishing Religious Freedom," October 31, 1785, Robert A. Rutland et al., eds., *Papers of James Madison* [PJM], vol. 8 (Chicago: University of Chicago Press and Charlottesville: University of Virginia Press, 1962–), 401n.

2. "Act for Establishing Religious Freedom," October 31, 1785, PJM, vol. 8, 399–401.

3. "To Thomas Jefferson," January 22, 1786, PJM, vol. 8, 474.

4. "Archibald Stuart to John Breckinridge," December 7, 1785 (DLC: Breckinridge Family Papers).

5. "To James Monroe," December 9, 1785, PJM, vol. 8, 436–37.

6. "From James Monroe," December 19, 1785, PJM, vol. 8, 446n.

7. "Bills for a Revised State Code of Laws," PJM, vol. 8, 394–99.

8. "To James Monroe," January 22, 1786, PJM, vol. 8, 483–84.

9. "To Edmund Pendleton," November 30, 1786, PJM, vol. 9, 186.

10. Ibid.

11. "From James Monroe," February 9, 1786, PJM, vol. 8, 490.

12. "To James Monroe," April 9, 1786, PJM, vol. 9, 25.

13. "Notes on Ancient and Modern Confederacies," PJM, vol. 9, 6–7.

14. "To Thomas Jefferson," August 12, 1786, PJM, vol. 9, 97.

15. Ibid., 98.

16. "From Thomas Jefferson," December 16, 1786, PJM, vol. 9, 212–13.

17. "To James Monroe," November 30, 1786, PJM, vol. 9, 185.

18. "Meteorological Journal for Orange County, Virginia," PJM, vol. 9, 424.

19. "To Ambrose Madison," August 7, 1786, PJM, vol. 9, 89.

20. "To James Monroe," August 12, 1786, PJM, vol. 9, 90–91.

21. "To Thomas Jefferson," August 12, 1786, PJM, vol. 9, 96.

22. Ibid., 97–98.

23. "The Annapolis Convention September 1786," PJM, vol. 9, 118n.

24. "Lodging Account from George Mann," September 4–15, 1786, PJM, vol. 9, 119.

25. Paul Jennings, *A Colored Man's Reminiscences of James Madison* (Brooklyn, NY: George C. Beadle, 1865), 15.

26. "To Thomas Jefferson," August 20, 1785, PJM, vol. 8, 345.

27. "Bill Providing for Delegates to the Convention of 1787," November 6, 1787, PJM, vol. 9, 163.

17. "A Little Rebellion"

1. Michael Signer, *Demagogue: The Fight to Save Democracy from Its Worst Enemies* (New York: Palgrave Macmillan 2009), 79.

2. Leonard L. Richards, *Shays's Rebellion: The American Revolution's Final Battle* (Philadelphia: University of Pennsylvania Press, 2003), 16–32.

3. William C. Rives, *History of the Life and Times of James Madison*, vol. 1 (Freeport, NY: Books for Libraries Press), 172.

4. Ibid.

5. "From Henry Lee," October 19, 1786, Robert A. Rutland et al., eds., *Papers of James Madison* [PJM], vol. 9 (Chicago: University of Chicago Press and Charlottesville: University of Virginia Press, 1962–), 144.

6. "From Henry Lee," October 25, 1786, PJM, vol. 9, 145.

7. "To James Madison, Sr.," November 1, 1786, PJM, vol. 9, 154.

8. "Virginia Delegates to Edmund Randolph," February 12, 1787, PJM, vol. 9, 266.

9. "To Edmund Randolph," February 15, 1787, PJM, vol. 9, 270.

10. "Notes on Debates," February 19, 1787, PJM, vol. 9, 278. Madison suspected that Great Britain had been supporting the rebels, and this provided yet more reason to bring the federal government in for a "meditated interference." Ibid.

11. "To Edmund Randolph," March 11, 1787, PJM, vol. 9, 307.

12. "To George Washington," February 21, 1787, PJM, vol. 9, 286.

13. "To Thomas Jefferson," March 19, 1787, PJM, vol. 9, 321.

14. "To George Muter," January 7, 1787, PJM, vol. 9, 231.

15. "Notes for Speech Opposing Paper Money," ca. November 1, 1786, PJM, vol. 9, 159.

16. "From George Washington," November 5, 1786, PJM, vol. 9, 162.

17. "Bill Providing for Delegates to the Convention of 1787," November 6, 1786, PJM, vol. 9, 163.

18. "To Thomas Jefferson," December 4, 1786, PJM, vol. 9, 191.

19. "To George Washington," December 7, 1786, PJM, vol. 9, 200.

20. "From John Blair Smith," ca. December 10, 1786, PJM, vol. 9, 204.

21. "From George Washington," November 18, 1786, PJM, vol. 9, 170.

22. "To Thomas Jefferson," March 19, 1787, PJM, vol. 9, 318.

23. "From George Washington," March 31, 1787, PJM, vol. 9, 343.

24. "To Eliza House Trist," February 10, 1787, PJM, vol. 9, 259.

25. "To George Washington," February 21, 1787, PJM, vol. 9, 285.

26. "Notes on Debates," February 21, 1787, PJM, vol. 9, 290–91.

27. "To Edmund Pendleton," February 24, 1787, PJM, vol. 9, 294.

28. "To Edmund Randolph," February 25, 1787, PJM, vol. 9, 299.

29. John Edward Oster, *The Political and Economic Doctrines of John Marshall* (New York: Neale Publishing, 1914), 40.

30. "From Edmund Randolph," March 1, 1787, PJM, vol. 9, 301.

31. "To Thomas Jefferson," March 19, 1787, PJM, vol. 9, 319.

32. "To George Washington," March 18, 1787, PJM, vol. 9, 316.

33. "To Edmund Randolph," March 25, 1787, 352n1.

34. "To Thomas Jefferson," March 19, 1787, PJM, vol. 9, 318.

18. The Vices

1. "To Eliza House Trist," March 19, 1787, Robert A. Rutland et al., eds., *Papers of James Madison* [PJM], vol. 9 (Chicago: University of Chicago Press and Charlottesville: University of Virginia Press, 1962–), 323.

2. "To James Madison, Sr.," April 1, 1787, PJM, vol. 9, 359.

3. "To Edmund Randolph," April 8, 1787, PJM, vol. 9, 369.

4. Ralph Ketcham, *James Madison: A Biography* (New York: Macmillan, 1971), 184.

5. "Vices of the Political System of the United States," PJM, vol. 9, 345–58.

6. "To Edmund Pendleton," PJM, April 22, 1787, vol. 9, 395.

7. "To George Washington," PJM, April 16, 1787, vol. 9, 382–87.

8. "To Edmund Pendleton," PJM, April 22, 1787, vol. 9, 395.

19. "On My Right & Left Hand"

1. Catherine Drinker Brown, *Miracle at Philadelphia* (Boston: Little, Brown 1966), 17.

2. "To Thomas Jefferson," May 15, 1787, Robert A. Rutland et al., eds., *Papers of James Madison* [PJM], vol. 9 (Chicago: University of Chicago Press and Charlottesville: University of Virginia Press, 1962–), 415.

3. "To James Madison, Sr.," May 27, 1787, PJM, vol. 10, 10.

4. Drinker Brown, 16.

5. "To Thomas Jefferson," May 15, 1787, PJM, vol. 9, 415.

6. "From James Monroe," May 23, 1787, PJM, vol. 9, 416.

7. Drinker Brown, 49–50, 3.

8. "The Federal Convention," PJM, vol. 10, 7, citing Farrand, Records, vol. 3, 550.

9. "Edmund Randolph's Essay on the Revolutionary History of Virginia," *Virginia Magazine of History and Biography*, vol. 43, no. 4 (October 1935), 307–8.

10. "Resolutions Proposed by Mr. Randolph in Convention," May 29, 1787, PJM, vol. 10, 15–18.

11. "Powers of the National Legislature," May 31, 1787, PJM, vol. 10, 20–21.

12. For Madison's habit of seesawing back and forth when giving speeches, see Gaillard Hunt, *Life of James Madison* (New York: Doubleday, Page & Co., 1902), 151.

13. "Popular Election of the First Branch of the Legislature," June 6, 1787, PJM, vol. 10, 34, ed. note. 2, citing Harold C. Syrett and Jacob E. Cooke, eds. *The Papers of Alexander Hamilton*, vol. 4 (New York: Columbia University Press, 1961–87), 165–66.

14. Ibid., 32–34.

15. "To Thomas Jefferson," October 24, 1787, PJM, vol. 10, 213–14.

16. "Election of the Senate," June 7, 1787, PJM, vol. 10, 39–40.

17. "Term of the Senate," June 26, 1787, PJM, vol. 10, 76–77.

18. "Power of the Legislature to Negative State Laws," June 8, 1787, PJM, vol. 10, 41.

19. "From Thomas Jefferson," June 20, 1787, PJM, vol. 10, 64.

20. "Power of the Legislature to Negative State Laws," July 17, 1787, PJM, vol. 10, 102.

21. "To Thomas Jefferson," June 6, 1787, PJM, vol. 10, 29–31.

22. "From John Dawson," June 12, 1787, PJM, vol. 10, 47.

23. "To William Short," June 6, 1787, PJM, vol. 10, 31–32.

24. "To James Monroe," June 10, 1787, PJM, vol. 10, 43.

25. "To Ambrose Madison," June 13, 1787, PJM, vol. 10, 51.

26. "To Thomas Jefferson," July 18, 1787, PJM, vol. 10, 105.

27. "From the Reverend James Madison," August 1, 1787, PJM, vol. 10, 120–21.

28. "Rule of Representation in the First Branch," June 28, 1787, PJM, vol. 10, 79–82n1.

29. "Rule of Representation in the First Branch of the Legislature," June 29, 1787, PJM, vol. 10, 86.

30. "Reply to New Jersey Plan," PJM, vol. 10, 55–61.

31. "To Thomas Jefferson," July 18, 1787, PJM, vol. 10, 105.

32. "From James McClurg," August 5, 1787, vol. 10, 134–35.

33. "Method of Appointing the Executive," July 19, 1787, PJM, vol. 10, 107–8.

34. "Method of Appointing the Executive," July 25, 1787, PJM, vol. 10, 115–17.

35. Aristotle, *Politics*. Benjamin Jowett, trans. (Oxford: Oxford University Press, 1941), 1190.

36. Ibid.

37. "To James Madison, Sr.," August 12, 1787, PJM, vol. 10, 146.

38. "To James Madison, Sr.," September 4, 1787, PJM, vol. 10, 161.

39. "Power of Congress to Prohibit the Slave Trade," August 25, 1787, PJM, vol. 10, 157.

40. "James Madison to Edward Coles," September 3, 1819, box 1, folder 19, Edward Coles Papers, MS C0037, Princeton University Library.

41. "Edward Coles to James Madison," January 8, 1832, James Madison Collection, Department of Rare Books and Special Collections, Princeton University Library.

42. "Mr. Madison to Mr. Coles," October 3, 1834, James Madison Collection, Department of Rare Books and Special Collections, Princeton University Library.

43. David Hacker, "Recounting the Dead," *New York Times*, September 20, 2011, available at http://opinionator.blogs.nytimes.com/2011/09/20/recounting -the-dead/#more-105317.

44. He cites, for example, a two-thirds requirement for navigation acts.

45. Now that the Constitution has been passed as an integrated document by the Constitutional Convention (if not ratified yet), from this point forward, the term will be capitalized as a proper noun.

46. Clinton Rossiter, *1787: The Grand Convention* (New York: Macmillan Company, 1966), 230–38.

47. "To Thomas Jefferson," September 6, 1787, PJM, vol. 10, 164.

48. "To Edmund Pendleton," September 20, 1787, PJM, vol. 10, 171.

49. "To Thomas Jefferson, October 24, 1787, PJM, vol. 10, 209–10.

50. "From the Reverend James Madison," October 1, 1787, PJM, vol. 10, 184.

51. "From Lafayette," August 5, 1787, PJM, vol. 10, 133–34.

52. "To Thomas Jefferson," September 6, 1787, PJM, vol. 10, 164.

53. Ketcham, 231.

54. "To Thomas Jefferson," September 6, 1787, PJM, vol. 10, 164.

20. The Campaign Begins

1. "From John Dawson," September 25, 1787, Robert A. Rutland et al., eds., *Papers of James Madison* [PJM], vol. 10 (Chicago: University of Chicago Press and Charlottesville: University of Virginia Press, 1962–), 173.

2. "From James Monroe," October 13, 1787, PJM, vol. 10, 193.

3. "To James Madison, Sr.," September 30, 1787, PJM, vol. 10, 178.

4. "To George Washington," September 30, 1787, PJM, vol. 10, 181.

5. "To William Short," October 24, 1787, PJM, vol. 10, 221.

6. "To Edmund Pendleton," October 28, 1787, PJM, vol. 10, 224.

7. "To George Washington," October 18, 1787, PJM, vol. 10, 197.

8. "From Archibald Stuart," October 21, 1787, PJM, vol. 10, 202.

9. "From George Washington," October 22, 1787, PJM, vol. 10, 204.

10. "From Edmund Randolph," October 29, 1787, PJM, vol. 10, 230.

11. "From George Washington," November 5, 1787, PJM, vol. 10, 242.

12. "From Archibald Stuart," November 9, 1787, PJM, vol. 10, 246.

13. "To George Washington," November 18, 1787, PJM, vol. 10, 252.

14. "From Henry Lee," December 7, 1787, PJM, vol. 10, 295.

15. "From Archibald Stuart," December 2, 1787, PJM, vol. 10, 290.

16. "To Ambrose Madison," November 8, 1787, PJM, vol. 10, 244.

17. "To Thomas Jefferson," December 9, 1787, PJM, vol. 10, 312.

18. Ibid., 313.

19. Willard Sterne Randall, *Alexander Hamilton: A Life* (New York: HarperCollins, 2003), 29.

20. Ibid., 61–63.

21. Noemie Emery, *Alexander Hamilton: An Intimate Portrait* (New York: G. P. Putnam's Sons, 1982), 87.

22. "To Thomas Jefferson," April 22, 1783, PJM, vol. 6, 481.

23. Lance Banning, *The Sacred Fire of Liberty: James Madison and the Founding of the Federal Republic* (Ithaca, NY: Cornell University Press, 1995), 150.

24. *Notes of Debates in the Federal Convention of 1787, Reported by James Madison* (New York: W. W. Norton, 1966), 656.

25. Ron Chernow, *Alexander Hamilton* (New York: Penguin Press, 2004), 247.

26. Alexander Hamilton, "Federalist Paper Number One," in *The Federalist Papers*, ed. Clinton Rossiter (New York: Penguin Books, 1961), 35.

27. "From Archibald Stuart," November 9, 1787, PJM, vol. 10, 245.

28. Hamilton, "Federalist Paper Number One," 36.

29. "Madison's Authorship of The Federalist, 22 November 1787–1 March 1788," ed. note, PJM, vol. 10, 259.

30. Ibid., 260.

31. Elizabeth Fleet, "Madison's 'Detatched Memoranda,'" *William and Mary Quarterly*, 3rd. ser., vol. 3 (1946), 564–65.

32. Ibid., 565.

33. "From Joseph Jones," November 22, 1787, PJM, vol. 10, 256.

34. "From George Washington," December 7, 1787, PJM, vol. 10, 298.

35. "The Federalist Number 18," December 8, 1787, PJM, vol. 10, 299–305.

36. "The Federalist Number 19," December 8, 1787, PJM, vol. 10, 305–9.

37. "The Federalist Number 20," December 11, 1787, PJM, vol. 10, 320–24.

38. "To Archibald Stuart," December 14, 1787, PJM, vol. 10, 326.

39. "To George Washington," December 14, 1787, PJM, vol. 10, 327.

40. "From Lawrence Taliaferro," December 16, 1787, PJM, vol. 10, 328–29.

41. "From Henry Lee," ca. December 20, 1787, PJM, vol. 10, 339–40.

42. "From Andrew Shepherd," December 22, 1787, PJM, vol. 10, 344.

21. Several Mad Freaks

1. "To Tench Coxe," January 3, 1788, Robert A. Rutland et al., eds., *Papers of James Madison* [PJM], vol. 10 (Chicago: University of Chicago Press and Charlottesville: University of Virginia Press, 1962–), 349.

2. "To Thomas Jefferson," December 20, 1787, PJM, vol. 10, 331–33.

3. "From Henry Lee," ca. December 20, 1787, PJM, vol. 10, 339.

4. "To Thomas Jefferson," December 20, 1787, PJM, vol. 10, 331.

5. "From George Lee Turberville," January 8, 1788, PJM, vol. 10, 352.

6. "From Edmund Randolph," January 3, 1788, PJM, vol. 10, 350.

7. Ibid.

8. "From Edmund Randolph," December 27, 1787, PJM, vol. 10, 346–47.

9. "To Edmund Randolph," January 10, 1788, PJM, vol. 10, 355.

10. "From Thomas Jefferson," December 20, 1787, PJM, vol. 10, 335–39.

11. "From Daniel Carroll," May 28, 1788, PJM, vol. 11, 62–66, 65.

12. "To Edmund Randolph," January 10, 1788, PJM, vol. 10, 356.

13. "The Federalist Number 37," January 11, 1788, PJM, vol. 10, 359–65.

14. "The Federalist Number 38," January 12, 1788, PJM, vol. 10, 365–71.

15. "From Archibald Stuart," January 14, 1788, PJM, vol. 10, 374.

16. "The Federalist Number 39," January 16, 1788, PJM, vol. 10, 377–82.

17. "From Edward Carrington," January 18, 1788, PJM, vol. 10, 383.

18. "The Federalist Number 41," January 19, 1788, PJM, vol. 10, 390–98.

19. "The Federalist Number 42," January 23, 1788, PJM, vol. 10, 403–9.

20. "The Federalist Number 43," January 23, 1788, PJM, vol. 10, 411–18.

21. "The Federalist Number 44," January 25, 1788, PJM, vol. 10, 420–26.

22. "The Federalist Number 45," January 26, 1788, PJM, vol. 10, 428–32.

23. "The Federalist Number 46," January 29, 1788, PJM, vol. 10, 443.

24. "From James Madison, Sr.," January 30, 1788, PJM, vol. 10, 446.

25. "From William Moore," January 31, 1788, PJM, vol. 10, 454–55.

26. "From James Gordon, Jr.," February 17, 1788, PJM, vol. 10, 516.

27. "From George Washington," February 5, 1788, PJM, vol. 10, 469.

28. "The Federalist Number 47," January 30, 1788, PJM, vol. 10, 448–54.

29. "The Federalist Number 48," February 1, 1788, PJM, vol. 10, 456–60.

30. "The Federalist Number 49," February 2, 1788, PJM, vol. 10, 460–64.

31. "The Federalist Number 50," February 5, 1788, PJM, vol. 10, 470–73.

32. "The Federalist Number 49," February 2, 1788, PJM, vol. 10, 463.

33. "To Thomas Jefferson," August 10, 1788, PJM, vol. 11, 227.

34. "From Thomas Jefferson," February 6, 1788, PJM, vol. 10, 474.

35. "From Rufus King," February 6, 1788, PJM, vol. 10, 475.

36. "The Federalist Number 51," February 6, 1788, PJM, vol. 10, 476–80.

37. "From James Monroe," February 7, 1788, PJM, vol. 10, 480–81.

38. "From the Reverend James Madison," February 9, 1788, PJM, vol. 10, 488.

39. "From Edward Carrington," February 10, 1788, PJM, vol. 10, 493–94.

40. "The Federalist Number 54," February 12, 1788, PJM, vol. 10, 499–503.

41. "From John Dawson," February 18, 1788, PJM, vol. 10, 516–18.

42. "To Thomas Jefferson," February 19, 1788, PJM, 518–21, 520.

43. "The Federalist Number 62," February 27, 1788, PJM, vol. 10, 524–40, 538.

44. "The Federalist Number 63," March 1, 1788, PJM, vol. 10, 544–50, 546, 550.

45. Roger C. Richards, A History of Southern Baptists (Bloomington, IN: Crossbooks Publishing, 2012), 41.

46. "From Joseph Spencer," February 28, 1788, PJM, vol. 10, 540–41.

47. "From George Washington," March 2, 1788, PJM, vol. 10, 553.

22. Ratification in Richmond

1. "From Cyrus Griffin," March 24, 1788, Robert A. Rutland et al., eds., *Papers of James Madison* [PJM], vol. 11 (Chicago: University of Chicago Press and Charlottesville: University of Virginia Press, 1962–), 4.

2. "To Eliza House Trist," March 25, 1788, PJM, vol. 11, 5.

3. "From George Nicholas," April 5, 1788, PJM, vol. 11, 9.

4. "From Edward Carrington," April 8, 1788, PJM, vol. 11, 15.

5. "To Edmund Randolph," April 10, 1788, PJM, vol. 11, 19.

6. "To Thomas Jefferson, April 22, 1788, PJM, vol. 11, 28.

7. "From Tench Coxe," May 19, 1788, PJM, vol. 11, 51.

8. "To John Brown," May 27, 1788, PJM, vol. 11, 60.

9. Hugh Blair Grigsby, *The History of the Virginia Federal Convention of 1788* (New York: Da Capo Press, 1969), 67n81.

10. "To Rufus King," June 4, 1788, PJM, vol. 11, 76.

11. David Robertson, *Debates and Other Proceedings of the Convention of Virginia* (Richmond: Enquirer-Press, 1805), 27.

12. Ibid., 29.

13. Ibid., 57.

14. Ibid., 29.

15. Ibid., 32–34.

16. "To George Washington," June 4, 1788, PJM, vol. 11, 77.

17. "To Rufus King," June 4, 1788, PJM, vol. 11, 76.

18. "To George Washington," June 4, 1788, PJM, vol. 11, 77.

19. Morgan, 352.

20. Robertson, 42–55.

21. Grigsby, 97.

22. Robertson, 70.

23. Grigsby, 95.

24. Robertson, 70.

25. Ibid., 71.

26. Ibid.

27. Ibid., 72.

28. Ibid., 74.

29. Ibid., 77.

30. Ibid., 78.

31. Ibid., 90.

32. Ibid., 91.

33. Ibid., 94.

34. Ibid., 100.

35. Ibid., 100–101.

36. Ibid., 102.

37. Ibid., 103–4.

38. Ibid., 104.

39. Ibid., 105.

40. Ibid.

41. Ibid., 106.

42. Ibid.

43. Ibid., 107.

44. Ibid., 108.

45. Ibid., 113.

46. Ibid.

47. Ibid.

48. "To Rufus King," June 9, 1788, PJM, vol. 11, 102.

49. Robertson, 131.

50. Ibid., 119.

51. Ibid., 128.

52. Ibid., 131.

53. Grigsby, 157n.

54. Robertson, 124.

55. Ibid., 121.

56. Ibid., 140.

57. Ibid.

58. Ibid., 144.

59. Grigsby, 165.

60. Robertson, 153–54.

61. Ibid., 156.

62. Ibid., 163.

23. Extremely Feeble

1. David Robertson, *Debates and Other Proceedings of the Convention of Virginia* (Richmond: Enquirer-Press, 1805), 181.

2. Ibid., 188.

3. Ibid., 189–90.

4. Ibid., 196.

5. Ibid., 204.

6. Ibid., 222.

7. Ibid., 224.

8. Ibid., 225.

9. Ibid., 227.

10. Ibid., 228.

11. Ibid., 230.

12. Ibid., 231.

13. Ibid., 234.

14. Ibid., 235.

15. Ibid., 251.

16. Ibid., 252.

17. Ibid., 246.

18. Ibid., 257.

19. Ibid., 258.

20. Ibid., 259.

21. Ibid., 260.

22. "To George Washington," June 13, 1788, Robert A. Rutland et al., eds., *Papers of James Madison* [PJM], vol. 11 (Chicago: University of Chicago Press and Charlottesville: University of Virginia Press, 1962–), 134.

23. Robertson, 262.

24. Ibid., 265.

25. Hugh Blair Grigsby, *The History of the Virginia Federal Convention of 1788* (New York: Da Capo Press, 1969), 255.

26. Robertson, 269.

27. Ibid., 271.

28. Ibid., 274.

29. Ibid., 275.

30. Ibid., 279.

31. Ibid., 280.

32. Ibid.

33. Ibid., 281.

34. Ibid., 283.

35. Ibid., 284.

36. Ibid., 285.

37. Ibid., 288.

38. Ibid., 290.

39. Ibid., 301.

40. Ibid., 307.

41. Ibid., 310.

42. Ibid., 311.

43. Ibid., 312.

44. Ibid., 314.

45. Grigsby, 286–87.

46. Robertson, 315.

47. Ibid., 318.

48. "To Alexander Hamilton," June 16, 1788, PJM, vol. 11, 144.

49. Robertson, 321.

50. Ibid., 322.

51. Ibid., 323.

52. Ibid.

53. Ibid., 327.

54. Ibid., 328.

55. Ibid., 331.

56. Ibid., 334.

57. Ibid., 332.

58. Ibid., 340.

59. Ibid., 341.

60. Ibid.

61. Ibid., 352.

62. Ibid., 354–55.

63. Ibid., 367.

64. Ibid., 371.

65. "To George Washington," June 18, 1788, PJM, vol. 11, 153.

66. "To Rufus King," June 18, 1788, PJM, vol. 11, 152.

67. "From Alexander Hamilton," June 21, 1788, PJM, vol. 11, 165.

68. "From Cyrus Griffin," June 18, 1788, PJM, vol. 11, 153.

69. James Madison, "Letter to Tench Coxe," June 18, 1788, Crane Collection, box 2, folder 16, Princeton Library.

70. Robertson, 381.

71. Ibid., 382.

72. Ibid., 384.

73. Ibid., 386.

74. Ibid., 384.

75. Ibid., 383.

76. Ibid., 387.

77. "To Alexander Hamilton," June 20, 1788, PJM, vol. 11, 157.

78. "To James Madison, Sr.," June 20, 1788, PJM, vol. 11, 157.

79. Robertson, 402–3.

80. Ibid., 411.

81. Ibid., 412.

82. John Calvin, "Sermon on Galatians 3:19–20," *Sermons on Galatians* (Edinburgh: Banner of Truth, 1997), 313. See, for instance, Thomas S. Kidd, *God of Liberty: A Religious History of the American Revolution* (New York: Basic Books, 2010), 8: "The confluence of republican and Calvinist doubts about human nature took full force in the framing of the Constitution. Madison, having attended Calvinist-leaning Princeton, knew well the doctrines of original sin and human depravity."

83. "To Alexander Hamilton," June 22, 1788, PJM, vol. 11, 166.

24. Bugbears and Hobgoblins

1. David Robertson, *Debates and Other Proceedings of the Convention of Virginia* (Richmond: Enquirer-Press, 1805), 413.

2. Ibid., 414.

3. Hugh Blair Grigsby, *The History of the Virginia Federal Convention of 1788* (New York: Da Capo Press, 1969), 300–301.

4. Robertson, 414.

5. Ibid., 415.

6. Ibid.

7. Ibid., 416.

8. Ibid., 418.

9. Ibid., 419.

10. Ibid., 421.

11. Ibid., 423.

12. Ibid., 426.

13. Ibid., 427.

14. Ibid., 431.

15. Ibid., 440.

16. Ibid., 441.

17. Ibid., 442.

18. Ibid.

19. Ibid., 444.

20. Ibid., 260.

21. Grigsby, 317–18.

22. Robertson, 446.

23. Grigsby, 318.

25. The Revelations of Zachariah Johnson

1. David Robertson, *Debates and Other Proceedings of the Convention of Virginia* (Richmond: Enquirer-Press, 1805), 450.

2. Ibid., 459.

3. Ibid., 460.

4. Ibid., 462.

5. Ibid., 465.

6. Ibid., 466–67.

7. Ibid., 468.

8. "To George Washington," June 25, 1788, Robert A. Rutland et al., eds., *Papers of James Madison* [PJM], vol. 11 (Chicago: University of Chicago Press and Charlottesville: University of Virginia Press, 1962–), 178.

9. "To Alexander Hamilton," June 27, 1788, PJM, vol. 11, 182.

10. "To George Washington," June 27, 1788, PJM, vol. 11, 183.

11. "To John Witherspoon," August 11, 1788, PJM, vol. 11, 230.

12. "To James Madison, Sr.," July 27, 1788, PJM, vol. 11, 208.

13. "From John Page," August 6, 1788, PJM, vol. 11, 225.

14. "From John Witherspoon," August 11, 1788, PJM, vol. 11, 231.

15. "From Edmund Randolph," September 12, 1788, PJM, vol. 11, 251.

16. "From George Washington," September 23, 1788, PJM, vol. 11, 262.

26. Retaliation

1. "From George Lee Turberville," October 27, 1788, Robert A. Rutland et al., eds., *Papers of James Madison* [PJM], vol. 11 (Chicago: University of Chicago Press and Charlottesville: University of Virginia Press, 1962–), 319.

2. "From Richard Bland Lee," October 29, 1788, PJM, vol. 11, 323.

3. "From Edward Carrington," November 18, 1788, PJM, vol. 11, 351.

4. "From Henry Lee," November 19, 1788, PJM, vol. 11, 356.

5. "From Edward Carrington," October 19, 1788, PJM, vol. 11, 306.

6. "From Edward Carrington," October 22, 1788, PJM, vol. 11, 311.

7. Ketcham, for instance, writes that Madison "actually preferred the House of Representatives to the Senate." Ralph Ketcham, *James Madison: A Biography* (New York: Macmillan, 1971), 275. See also Jeff Broadwater, *James Madison: A Son of Virginia and a Founder of the Nation* (Chapel Hill: University of North Carolina Press, 2012), 76.

8. "To Edmund Randolph," October 17, 1788, PJM, vol. 11, 305.

9. "From Edmund Randolph," November 5, 1788, PJM, vol. 11, 335.

10. "To Edmund Randolph," October 17, 1788, PJM, vol. 11, 305.

11. "To Edmund Randolph," November 23, 1788, PJM, vol. 11, 363.

12. "To Eliza House Trist," October 29, 1788, PJM, vol. 11, 321.

13. "To George Washington," November 5, 1788, PJM, vol. 11, 334.

14. "From Edward Carrington," November 9, 1788, PJM, vol. 11, 336.

15. "From Henry Lee," November 19, 1788, PJM, vol. 11, 357.

16. "From Edward Carrington," November 9, 1788, PJM, vol. 11, 337.

17. "From Francis Corbin," November 12, 1788, PJM, vol. 11, 342.

18. "From George Lee Turberville," November 10, 1788, PJM, vol. 11, 341.

19. "Madison's Election to the First Federal Congress, October 1788–February 1789," ed. note, PJM, vol. 11, 301–2.

20. "From George Lee Turberville," November 13, 1788, PJM, vol. 11, 344.

21. Ibid.

22. "From Edward Carrington," November 15, 1788, PJM, vol. 11, 346.

23. "To George Washington," December 2, 1788, PJM, vol. 11, 378.

24. "To Thomas Jefferson," December 8, 1788, PJM, vol. 11, 384.

25. "From George Lee Turberville," December 12, 1788, PJM, vol. 11, 393.

26. "From George Lee Turberville," December 14, 1788, PJM, vol. 11, 397.

27. "From Andrew Shepherd," December 14, 1788, PJM, vol. 11, 395.

28. Ketcham, 276.

29. "From George Lee Turberville," December 14, 1788, PJM, vol. 11, 396.

30. "From David Jameson, Jr.," January 14, 1789, PJM, vol. 11, 419.

31. "To George Washington," January 14, 1789, PJM, vol. 11, 418.

32. "To a Resident of Spotsylvania County," January 27, 1789, PJM, vol. 11, 428.

33. "To George Thompson," January 29, 1789, PJM, vol. 11, 433.

34. William C. Rives, *History of the Life and Times of James Madison*, vol. 2 (Freeport, NY: Books for Libraries Press), 41–42n.

35. "To Thomas Jefferson," March 29, 1789, PJM, vol. 11, 37.

36. Richard R. Beeman, *Patrick Henry: A Biography* (New York: McGraw-Hill, 1974), 169.

37. Robert Douthat Meade, *Patrick Henry: Practical Revolutionary* (Philadelphia: J. B. Lippincott, 1969), 394.

38. "From William Madison," December 3, 1791, PJM, vol. 14, 136.

39. "To William Madison," December 13, 1791, PJM, vol. 14, 149.

27. Sedition

1. "To Thomas Jefferson," May 20, 1798, *PJM*.

2. Ralph Ketcham, *James Madison: A Biography* (New York: Macmillan, 1971), 392.

3. Ibid., 393–97.

4. Jacob Axelrad, *Patrick Henry: The Voice of Freedom* (New York: Random House, 1947), 189–90.

Epilogue

1. Auguste Levausseur, *Lafayette in America in 1824 and 1825* (Philadelphia: Carey and Lea, 1829), 221.

2. Ralph Ketcham, *James Madison: A Biography* (New York: Macmillan, 1971), 620.

3. Ibid., 376.

4. Irving Brant, *James Madison: Father of the Constitution, 1787–1800*, vol. 3 (New York: Bobbs-Merrill, 1950), 402–10.

5. Interview with Meg Kennedy, March 2013.

6. Ketcham, 620.

7. David B. Mattern, ed., *James Madison's "Advice to My Country"* (Charlottesville: University Press of Virginia, 1997), 14.

8. David Robertson, *Debates and Other Proceedings of the Convention of Virginia* (Richmond: Enquirer-Press, 1805), 537–39.

9. Ibid., 558.

10. Ibid., 543.

11. Ibid., 559.

12. Drew McCoy writes, "For the better part of a year in 1831 and 1832 he was bedridden, if not silenced, by a joint attack of severe rheumatism and chronic bilious fevers. Literally sick with anxiety, he began to despair of his ability to make himself understood by his fellow citizens." Drew R. McCoy, *The Last of the Fathers: James Madison and the Republican Legacy* (Cambridge: Cambridge University Press, 1989), 151.

13. Ibid., 130–51.

14. Ibid., 149.

15. "James Madison to Edward Coles, 29 August 1834," Founders Online, National Archives, available at http://founders.archives.gov/documents/Madison/99-02-02-3022, ver. 2013–09–28.

16. McCoy, 150.

17. Adair, 192n2.

18. Ibid., 192.

19. Ibid.

20. Ibid., 196–209

21. Jack N. Rakove, *James Madison and the Creation of the American Republic* (New York: Longman, 2002), 218.

22. "James Madison to George Tucker," June 22, 1836, National Archives, available at http://founders.archives.gov/documents/Madison/99-02-02-3290.

23. Hugh Blair Grigsby, *The History of the Virginia Federal Convention of 1788* (New York: Da Capo Press, 1969), 87.

Conclusion

1. Jack N. Rakove, *James Madison and the Creation of the American Republic* (New York: Longman, 2002), 48.

2. Bernard Bailyn, *The Ideological Origins of the American Revolution* (Cambridge: Harvard University Press, 1992), 8.

3. Gordon Wood, *The Idea of America: Reflections on the Birth of the United States* (New York: Penguin Press, 2011), 36.

4. Josiah Ober, *Mass and Elite in Democratic Athens* (Princeton: Princeton University Press, 1989), 95, 169.

Index

Adams, John, 99, 149
   Alien and Sedition Acts proposal of,
      295–297
   Treaty of Paris signed by, 160
   vanity of, 6
Albemarle County militia, 87
the Alien and Sedition Acts, 295–297,
   309
Allen, Moses, 46
Ambassador to France, 162
Amendments effort, 285
American colonies
   free citizens deliberating government
      of, 280–281
   paying for debt of, 136
   Robertson leaving for, 30
   self-governing problems of, 8
   should take offensive, 73
   Stamp Act infuriating, 32
   statesman needed to save, 116–117
   united national purpose lacking in,
      114
   See also United States
American Colonization Society, 207
the Anglicans, 33, 68–70, 220
Annapolis, Maryland, 175, 216
Anti-Federalists, 16
   constitutional convention delay
      tactics of, 270–271
   Federalist Paper condemning, 229
   Henry, P., and aggression of, 223,
      244–245
   Madison, J., battling, 18–19
   pragmatic pessimism of, 274

Randolph lambasting, 252
   vacuity exposed of, 260
   Virginia strategy of, 225–226
Anti-Semitism, 127
Anxiety attacks, 19, 57, 90–96, 124, 257
"An Apology for the Church of England
      as by Law Established" (Tucker), 97
Aristocracy, 53
Aristotle, 149, 203–204
Armed revolt, 100
Army, 122–123, 155
Articles of Confederation, 131, 188–189
Ashby v. White, 76
Attachment figures, 95
Attack, lines of, 139
Autobiography, 310–312

Bailyn, Bernard, 316
Baptists, 69–70
Barbour, Thomas, 97
Bennis, Warren, 17
Berkeley, Edward, 42
Bicameral legislature, 195
the Bill of Rights, 312
   Constitution destroyed without, 255
   Jefferson, T., seeking, 227–228, 233,
      243, 260, 275
   passed and in place, 293
Billey (slave), 159
Biography, 61
Blair, John, 106–107
Bland, Martha, 121–122
Bland, Theodorick, 122, 133–135, 148
Board of Admiralty, 120

CAT THRASHER

MICHAEL SIGNER IS AN AUTHOR, ADVOCATE, POLITICAL THEORIST, AND ATTORNEY. He holds a PhD in political science from U.C., Berkeley, where he was a National Science Foundation Graduate Research Fellow; a JD from the University of Virginia School of Law; and a BA in politics, *magna cum laude*, from Princeton University. He has taught political theory, leadership, and governance at the University of Virginia, Virginia Tech, and the University of California. He was counsel to Governor Mark Warner in Richmond, senior policy advisor at the Center for American Progress, and a candidate for lieutenant governor of Virginia in 2009. Dr. Signer is the author of *Demagogue: The Fight to Save Democracy from Its Worst Enemies* (2009). His writing has appeared in *The Washington Post, The New Republic,* and *USA Today,* and he reviews books for the *Daily Beast.* He has appeared on MSNBC, Fox News, the BBC, and NPR. He lives with his wife and twin boys in Virginia.

PublicAffairs is a publishing house founded in 1997. It is a tribute to the standards, values, and flair of three persons who have served as mentors to countless reporters, writers, editors, and book people of all kinds, including me.

I. F. STONE, proprietor of *I. F. Stone's Weekly*, combined a commitment to the First Amendment with entrepreneurial zeal and reporting skill and became one of the great independent journalists in American history. At the age of eighty, Izzy published *The Trial of Socrates*, which was a national bestseller. He wrote the book after he taught himself ancient Greek.

BENJAMIN C. BRADLEE was for nearly thirty years the charismatic editorial leader of *The Washington Post*. It was Ben who gave the *Post* the range and courage to pursue such historic issues as Watergate. He supported his reporters with a tenacity that made them fearless and it is no accident that so many became authors of influential, best-selling books.

ROBERT L. BERNSTEIN, the chief executive of Random House for more than a quarter century, guided one of the nation's premier publishing houses. Bob was personally responsible for many books of political dissent and argument that challenged tyranny around the globe. He is also the founder and longtime chair of Human Rights Watch, one of the most respected human rights organizations in the world.

. . .

For fifty years, the banner of Public Affairs Press was carried by its owner Morris B. Schnapper, who published Gandhi, Nasser, Toynbee, Truman, and about 1,500 other authors. In 1983, Schnapper was described by *The Washington Post* as "a redoubtable gadfly." His legacy will endure in the books to come.

Peter Osnos, *Founder and Editor-at-Large*